Two Kingdoms and one world

edited by Karl H. Hertz

AUGSBURG PUBLISHING HOUSE
Minneapolis, Minnesota

Manufactured in the United State of America

Two Kingdoms and one world

edited by Karl H. Hertz

AUGSBURG PUBLISHING HOUSE
Minneapolis, Minnesota

CONTENTS

C O N T E N T S

INTRODUCTION

For more than a generation Lutheran ethicists, theologians, and church leaders in many parts of the world have been asking serious questions about the original meaning and contemporary validity of Luther's teaching about the two kingdoms or God's two forms of governance.[1] While the debate has probably been sharpest in Germany, where the issues of the *Kirchenkampf* of the 1930s accentuated the crucial importance of the Christian response to political events, Christians elsewhere have also found these issues of central importance. Very recently the issue has also been sharply joined between black and white Lutherans in Namibia.

The twentieth century has seen a new and critical step forward within the churches in their reflections on the proper stance to be taken over against governments and on the scope of the individual Christian's obligation to obey. After the great missionary expansion of the 19th century, in which Christian churches almost everywhere seemed free to proclaim the gospel to all, a century during which the churches, particularly of the Protestant parts of Europe and the United States, seemed free to grow and to provide the moral support for an expanding civilization, the climate has suddenly turned colder. Repression of organized religion as well as rejection of its claims have called into question many of the propositions once taken for granted. Political theologies, theologies of liberation and of revolution, have presented their claims.

In this connection one may well ask whether a teaching which came out of the struggles of the sixteenth century has any meaning for the twentieth. Since many theologians have appealed to its authority, we may also ask how they came to use the doctrine in its contemporary statement and whether that statement reflects faithful adherence to the spirit and content of the original.

The contemporary discussion manifests several remarkable qualities. First, a quick transition is generally made from an exposition of what Luther is believed to have taught to a twentieth century application; what may lie in between is not examined. It is assumed that the heritage of the sixteenth century has been handed over for our use unspoiled. Second, much of the discussion both for and against the use of two kingdoms occurs in the midst of significant controversies about the role Lutheran churches or people should be playing in a concrete historical situation. Yet the specific references to the historical contexts are often left implicit. For example, references to Luther's tract *On Secular Government* may be cited rather copiously without any recognition that the intent of that particular writing was to instruct evangelical believers about the limits of their obedience, about the circumstances under which they must disobey; similarly, a contemporary treatment may never mention the situation out of which it comes. Third, the sources in Luther's writings which are taken into account are often very meager; the full riches of Luther's utterances on Christian responses to political and social issues are left largely untouched.

There is another facet to the contemporary discussion. Although it is public doctrine among Lutherans that only the Scriptures and the Confessions have normative status in defining what Lutherans believe, one frequently encounters both in the popular mind and in more learned circles the assumption that the correct exposition of what is properly Lutheran must be found in the theological and ethical writings of that line of German theologians which somewhat self-consciously identifies itself as confessional. Thus one assumes that certain theologians stood closer to Luther, but this assumption is left unexamined.

Nothing said here intends to derogate the academic credentials of German theologians. Far from it. The issue is not, however, an academic one. Lutherans in a variety of settings have been called upon to respond to very concrete demands. They have had to give an account of themselves; they have had to take responsibility for themselves for their understanding of the Word of God. Thus in Scandinavia and in the United States, where for different reasons and under different historical conditions, Lutherans developed independent traditions of theological and ethical reflection, we also hear independent voices speaking to the issues of their day. In the twentieth century we hear these voices in

10

South Africa, in Namibia, Ethiopia, and Tanzania, in India and
Indonesia, and in other places as well. That is as it should be.
For our loyalty is not to one another's traditions, not even to
our missionary mentors, but solely to the Lord of the Church, to
his Word, and to our common confessions.

During the centuries from Luther's day to ours, Lutheran
understandings of political obligations and the nature of political
order did not remain static. In the turmoil of change that ushered
in the modern period of history, Lutherans sometimes used Luther
in ways more ideological than theological. They called upon him
at times to give legitimacy to a particular ordering of public
affairs; they sometimes used him to inculcate political obedience
rather than the obedience of faith.

More seriously perhaps, among American Lutherans, to whom this
volume is particularly addressed, Luther's teachings on the two
kingdoms were apparently largely forgotten during the nineteenth
century. If explicit adherence to the format of the two kingdoms
doctrine is essential for defining a particular ethic as Lutheran,
then in any explicit sense American Lutherans had no Lutheran ethic
in the nineteenth century.

The limited development of themes explicitly drawn from Luther
no doubt reflects the inadequate access to Luther's writings from
which most American Lutherans suffered. Yet this cannot be the
whole story, for the majority of the theologians could read German.
However inadequate, the Erlangen edition of Luther's works did
contain certain basic writings. Furthermore, scholars like Henry
E. Jacobs went to great lengths to get traditional materials
translated and to make the heritage of the Reformation available.
For most Lutherans in the United States political questions were
simply not salient.

The only nineteenth-century exception must be found in circles
whose Lutheranism has generally been regarded as suspect, that is,
among the "American Lutherans" under the leadership of S.S. Schmucker.
Here the question of political responsibility under the conditions
of American democracy received an answer which called upon positive
elements in the traditions of the Reformation. This tradition
received its most positive formulation in the work of J.H.W.
Stuckenberg.

The increasing domination of "confessional Lutheranism," even
in the General Synod, pushed the contributions of "American Lutherans"
into the background, and Stuckenberg became a forgotten figure.
For the Lutheran churches in the United States political ethics fell
increasingly under the influence of German models. Social concerns
expressed themselves almost exclusively through inner-mission
activities.

It took the tragedy of Nazi tyranny to bring back on to the agenda of American Lutherans both an examination of Luther's teachings and a critical and constructive elaboration of a political ethic on the basis of a rediscovery of salient emphases in the reformer's work. Even then the American development has been uneven, involving a limited segment of the fragmented American Lutheran community, while old stereotypes and truncated versions continue to prevail in other parts.

The American situation is not unique. An examination of the sources shows that in Europe, particularly in Germany, Lutheran theologians drew on limited elements in Luther's writings, picked up bits and pieces which they put together in their own way, in order to provide instruction on political matters.

Not until recently has it become clear that at least two major and in many respects opposed interpretations of what Luther taught are possible. In the United States a number of ethicists and theologians through both popular and scholarly publications and by the membership on official commissions of their church bodies have articulated an understanding of Lutheran political ethics that clearly stresses participation and service to neighbor, rather than obedience, as the dominant theme. In Germany likewise a critical reexamination has gone on. Here too the emphasis has fallen on looking at a larger range of materials from Luther than earlier ethicists did. The most significant work defining this alternative interpretation is Ulrich Duchrow, *Christenheit und Weltverantwortung* (Stuttgart: Klett Verlag, 1970).

This volume clearly stands in the participatory tradition. At the same time it has tried to provide materials that illustrate the other, essentially dualistic, approach. This volume of readings runs parallel to three companion volumes in German, of which Ulrich Duchrow is the primary editor.

The volume of materials in German is overwhelming. Because the scholarly debate has found adequate documentation in Heinz-Horst Schrey, *Reich Gottes und Welt* (Darmstadt: Wissenschaftliche Buchgesellschaft, 1969), we have emphasized selections dealing with specific political situations or official statements on policy questions.

For a variety of reasons, therefore, the primary historical contrast in this volume will be between German developments and developments in the United States. We offer, in addition, materials from one East European community (Hungary), documents illustrating the struggle for human rights in Southern Africa, and a brief over-view of the response of Lutherans in Brazil. For the most part, these documents will illustrate the influence of German theology, but they will also illuminate the rediscovery of political responsibility among Lutheran Christians.

The Commission on Studies of the Lutheran World Federation is the sponsor of these efforts to document the development and use of Luther's doctrine of the two kingdoms. I am particularly indebted to Dr. Ulrich Duchrow, director of the Department of Studies, not only for his administrative initiative in getting this project underway but also for the expert knowledge and scholarship he has brought to the project, especially for his work on the history of the two kingdoms tradition, *Christenheit und Weltverantwortung*. It should be clear, however, that as editor I accept the responsibility both for the choice of the selections and for the opinions expressed in the introductions and the conclusion.

A number of persons contributed in important ways in helping with the selection of the materials and providing introductory materials for some of the sections. Particular thanks must be expressed to Dr. Wolfgang Huber, co-editor with Dr. Duchrow of two of the German volumes. Tibor Fabing, Gjula Nagy, Klaus Eichholz, W. Kistner, F. Heidler, and H.J. Prien provided the materials from which certain selections were made. Specific credits are noted at the appropriate place.

Mr. Louis Reith, an American historian working at Tübingen, translated a number of items from Luther for which no English text is as yet available. He also provided translations of most of the nineteenth- and twentieth-century German documents. Unless some English text is indicated in the notes, the reader may assume that Mr. Reith made the translation.

Gerald Anderson helped research the American periodical literature; Judith Ann Hertz and Betty Webb typed the manuscript.

The final responsibility for what is in this volume rests with me. In particular, I am responsible for the interpretive framework within which the materials are set.

KARL H. HERTZ
Springfield, Ohio

PART I:

THE FORMING OF THE TWO KINGDOMS TRADITION:

FROM THE BIBLICAL SOURCES TO LUTHER

INTRODUCTION

All the selections in Part I come from Duchrow and Hoffmann, *Die Vorstellung von Zwei Reichen und Regimenten bis Luther*, the first in the three-volume German series of sourcebooks on the doctrine of the two kingdoms. While some omissions have been made, we have tried to preserve the full range of Luther's political thought.

In order to provide readers with a chart of the various elements in the argument, we have also reproduced the detailed tabular presentation of Luther's understanding in Duchrow and Hoffman, p. 13.

We wish to draw attention to several characteristics of Luther's doctrine:

1. There are two major dualisms, two pairs of kingdoms, distinguished in the doctrine: We have kingdom of God--kingdom of the devil, and God's spiritual government--God's secular government of the world.

2. We must deal with three major institutional complexes: *ecclesia*, the church; *politia*, political institutions; and *economia*, the domestic economy. God's governance of the world, both spiritual and secular, expresses itself through these institutional complexes.

3. Within these kingdoms and institutional complexes we find both law and gospel at work; we discover the use of both reason and coercion.

4. There is a central ethical accent in the distinction, for self--for others; this distinction leads to a positive accent on the Christian's activity in the world.

16

5. We must take particular note of the role of voluntary cooperation; the Christian as an ethical actor is a free person.

6. Finally, we must note the distinction between the kingdoms (of God, of the devil) and governance. Quite properly we should speak of God's two ways of ruling the world. These ways of governing the world are central to understanding Luther's ethics, but these ways must always be seen against the background of the larger struggle against the evil powers seeking to dominate God's creation.

The tabular presentation along with the outline of Part I enables readers to get a fuller grasp of the complex nature of both the traditions before Luther and of Luther's own exposition of the doctrine. To limit the discussion to questions of obedience to constituted authority, as has so often been done, is to distort; service of the neighbor is an indispensible element in Luther's understanding of the role of the Christian in public office. Similarly to limit the discussion to political questions is to overlook Luther's concern for the full range of human needs (e.g. his admonition on keeping children in school); finally to fail to see God's twofold governance in the context of the spiritual warfare against evil (the kingdom of the devil) is to reduce the comprehensiveness of Luther's thinking and to open the doors to the kind of severance of the two realms from one another by which the nineteenth century so consistently distorted Luther's teachings.

This tabular presentation also helps readers recognize which elements various theologians employed or ignored in their expositions, and helps them to see both how American theologians often employed the tradition unconsciously (the use of the three institutional complexes), not recognizing the changed setting in which they were working, and how key elements of the total complex were not used at all. The fuller presentation of both the traditions up to Luther and Luther's own writings helps us to a better understanding of the full complex of the doctrine of God's two kingdoms and twofold rule.

TABLE I: LUTHER'S UNDERSTANDING SEEN AGAINST
THE BACKGROUND OF TRADITION*

1. The Cosmic Conflict: the Power of God versus the Power of
Evil in the Struggle for Humankind

As seen in Augustine
City (kingdom) of God   City (kingdom) of Evil
Humankind divided into
New Christians   and   Old Children of Adam

God rules through Spirit
a) corporatively: true church vs. false church
b) individually: saved vs. sinners
c) eschatologically: eternal life vs. eternal torment

The distinguishing element in the relation to God
Belief   Unbelief

2. God's Twofold Rule of the World

As seen in the Middle Ages
God's governance of the world through
the two swords (*gladii*)
a) the spiritual sword (which is above)
b) the secular sword

As seen in Luther
God's governance employs spiritual power

--the preaching office (Theological use of *law*
and *gospel* in the first institutional complex
ecclesia (the church)

God's governance employs worldly power

--the civil use of the law in the second institutional
complex using reason and the sword
voluntary and coerced cooperation *politia* (government)
for self: suffering injustice; witnessing to justice
for others: protection of rights; political love of neighbor

God's governance employs domestic power

--in the third institutional complex the use of
reason and common sense *economia* (household
economy)

_____
*Adopted with simplifications from Ulrich Duchrow and Heiner
Hoffmann, *Die Vorstellung von Zwei Reichen und Regimenten bis
Luther*, p. 13.

CHAPTER 1

THE TWO DIVISIONS OF HUMANKIND:

UNDER THE DOMINION OF GOD OR UNDER THE DOMINION OF SATAN[3]

A. APOCALYPTIC

1. *Daniel 2:31-35*

"You saw, O king, and behold, a great image. This image,
mighty and of exceeding brightness, stood before you, and its
appearance was frightening. The head of this image was of fine
gold, its breast and arms of silver, its belly and thighs of bronze,
its legs of iron, its feet partly of iron and partly of clay. As
you looked, a stone was cut out by no human hand, and it smote the
image on its feet of iron and clay, and broke them in pieces; then
the iron, the clay, the bronze, the silver, and the gold, all
together were broken in pieces, and became like the chaff of the
summer threshing floors; and the wind carried them away, so that
not a trace of them could be found. But the stone that struck the
image became a great mountain and filled the whole earth."

2. *Luke 20:34-36*

And Jesus said to them, "The sons of this age marry and are
given in marriage; but those who are accounted worthy to attain to
that age and to the resurrection from the dead neither marry nor
are given in marriage, for they cannot die any more, because they
are equal to angels and are sons of God, being sons of the
resurrection."

B. THE HELLENISTIC TRADITION

Cf. Plato, *The Republic*, 588b-589d, and Philo, *On Flight and
Finding*, 71-72[4]

C. THE ESCHATOLOGICAL RESTATEMENT OF PLATONIC, STOIC
AND JEWISH ANTHROPOLOGY IN PAUL AND HIS DISCIPLES

3. Romans 7:7-8; 7:13-8:6

What then shall we say? That the law is sin? By no means!
Yet, if it had not been for the law, I should not have known sin.
I should not have known what it is to covet if the law had not
said, "You shall not covet." But sin, finding opportunity in the
commandment, wrought in me all kinds of covetousness. Apart from
the law sin lies dead....

Did that which is good, then, bring death to me? By no means!
It was sin, working death in me through what is good, in order
that sin might be shown to be sin, and through the commandment might
become sinful beyond measure. We know that the law is spiritual;
but I am carnal, sold under sin. I do not understand my own actions.
For I do not do what I want, but I do the very thing I hate. Now
if I do what I do not want, I agree that the law is good. So then
it is no longer I that do it, but sin which dwells within me.
For I know that nothing good dwells within me, that is, in my flesh.
I can will what is right, but I cannot do it. For I do not do the
good I want, but the evil I do not want is what I do. Now if I do
what I do not want, it is no longer I that do it, but sin which
dwells within me.

So I find it to be a law that when I want to do right, evil
lies close at hand. For I delight in the law of God, in my inmost
self, but I see in my members another law at war with the law of
my mind and making me captive to the law of sin which dwells in
my members. Wretched man that I am! Who will deliver me from this
body of death? Thanks be to God through Jesus Christ our Lord!
So then, I of myself serve the law of God with my mind, but with
my flesh I serve the law of sin.

There is therefore now no condemnation for those who are in
Christ Jesus. For the law of the Spirit of life in Christ Jesus
has set me free from the law of sin and death. For God has done
what the law, weakened by the flesh, could not do: sending his
own Son in the likeness of sinful flesh and for sin, he condemned
sin in the flesh, in order that the just requirement of the law
might be fulfilled in us, who walk not according to the flesh but
according to the Spirit. For those who live according to the
flesh set their minds on the things of the flesh, but those who
live according to the Spirit set their minds on the things of the
Spirit. To set the mind on the flesh is death, but to set the
mind on the Spirit is life and peace.

4. Colossians 3:9-10

Do not lie to one another, seeing that you have put off the old nature with its practices and have put on the new nature, which is being renewed in knowledge after the image of its creator.

D. THE ESCHATOLOGICAL CONFLICT BETWEEN THE CITY OF GOD AND THE CITY OF THE DEVIL IN AUGUSTINE

5. Free Choice of the Will*

AUGUSTINE: It is, therefore, manifest that some men are lovers of eternal things, others of temporal things, and we have agreed that there are two laws, one eternal and the other temporal. Now assuming that you have a sense of justice, which of these two classes of men would you hold was obedient to the eternal law, and which to the temporal law? EVODIUS: The answer is obvious, I think. Those who are happy on account of their love of eternal things I hold act under obedience to the eternal law, while on unhappy men the temporal law is imposed. AUG.: You are perfectly right, so long as you hold firmly what reason has clearly demonstrated, that those who serve the temporal law cannot be set free from subjection to the eternal law. For from the eternal law are derived all just laws even when they are variable according to circumstances, as we have said. But those who with a good will cleave to the eternal law do not need the temporal law, as apparently you well understand. EV.: I see your point.

AUG.: The eternal law bids us turn our love away from temporal things, to cleanse it and turn it towards eternal things. EV.: It does. AUG.: What, then, does the temporal law bid us do? Is it not that men may possess the things which may be called "ours" for a season and which they eagerly covet, on condition that peace and human society be preserved so far as they can be preserved in earthly things? These are, first, the body and bodily goods, such as good health, keenness of the senses, strength, beauty, and anything else that may be necessary for the good arts of life, which are to be more highly valued than those which are of less value and importance. Next comes liberty. Of course there is no true liberty except the liberty of the happy who cleave to the eternal law. But for the moment I mean the liberty which people think they enjoy when they have no human masters, and which slaves desire who wish to be manumitted by their human masters. Then, parents, brothers, wife, children, kinsfolk near and remote, friends, and

---

*The text is from John H.S. Burleigh, tr., *Augustine: Earlier Writings*, "The Library of Christian Classics," Vol. VI (Philadelphia: The Westminster Press, 1953), pp. 131-132, 133.

21

any others who may be attached to us by any bond. Then our citizenship, which is usually reckoned from the home of our parents,
together with honours and praise and popular glory, as it is called.
Finally there is money, which in one word covers all that we
lawfully possess and which we have the right to dispose of by sale
of gift. To explain how in all these matters the law distributes
to each his due would be difficult and would take a long time, but
clearly it is not necessary to our purpose. It is sufficient to
see that the authority of this law in punishing does not go beyond
depriving him who is punished of these things or of some of them.
It employs fear as an instrument of coercion, and bends to its own
ends the minds of the unhappy people to rule whom it is adapted.
So long as they fear to lose these earthly goods they observe in
using them a certain moderation suited to maintain in being a city
such as can be composed of such men. The sin of loving these things
is not punished; what is punished is the wrong done to others when
their rights are infringed. Have we not accomplished a task which
you thought would be infinite? For we set out to inquire how far
the law which governs earthly peoples and cities may rightly punish.
EV.: I see we have accomplished our task....

     EV.: Very true. The things are not to be blamed, but the men
who make a bad use of them. AUG.: Quite right. We begin to see
now, I think, the force of the eternal law; and how far the temporal
law can go in punishing we have also discovered. We have made a
sufficiently clear distinction between two classes of things, the
eternal and the temporal, and between two classes of men, those
who love and pursue eternal things and those who pursue temporal
things. What each one chooses to pursue and embrace is within the
power of his will to determine.

6. *Of True Religion**

     This is the tradition concerning God's temporal dispensation
and his providential care for those who by sin had deservedly
become mortal. First, consider the nature and education of any
individual man who is born. His first age, infancy, is spent in
receiving bodily nourishment, and it is to be entirely forgotten
when he grows up. Then follows childhood when we begin to have
some memories. To this, adolescence succeeds, when nature allows
propagation of offspring and fatherhood. After adolescence comes
young manhood, which must take part in public duties and be brought
under the laws. Now sins are more strictly forbidden, and sinners
have to undergo the servile coercion of penalty. In carnal souls
this of itself causes more dreadful onsets of lust, and wrong-doing

---

Ibid., pp. 248-250

is redoubled. For sin has a double aspect. It is not merely wrong-doing. It is disobedience. After the labours of young manhood, a little peace is given to old age. But it is an inferior age, lacking in lustre, weak and more subject to disease, and it leads to death. This is the life of man so far as he lives in the body and is bound by desires for temporal things. This is called "the old man" and "the exterior or earthly man," even if he obtain what the vulgar call felicity in a well-ordered earthly city, whether ruled by kings or princes or laws or all of them together. For without these things no people can be well-ordered, not even a people that pursues earthly goods. Even such a people has a measure of beauty of its own.

I have described "the old or exterior or earthly man." He may be a moderate man after his kind, or he may transgress the measure of servile justice. Some live thus from the beginning to the end of their days. But some begin in that way, as they necessarily must, but they are reborn inwardly, and with their spiritual strength and increase of wisdom they overcome "the old man" and put him to death, and bring him into subjection to the celestial laws, until after visible death the whole is restored. This is called "the new man," "the inward and heavenly man," whose spiritual ages are marked, not according to years, but according to his spiritual advance. In the first stage he is taught by the rich stores of history which nourish by examples. In the second stage he forgets human affairs and tends towards divine things. He is no longer kept in the bosom of human authority, but step by step by the use of reason he strives to reach the highest unchangeable law. In the third stage he confidently marries carnal appetite to strong reason, and inwardly rejoices in the sweetness of the union. Soul and mind are joined together in chaste union. There is as yet no compulsion to do right, but, even though no one forbids sin, he has no pleasure in sinning. The fourth stage is similar, only now he acts much more firmly, and springs forth as the perfect man, ready to endure and overcome all the persecutions, tempests and billows of this world. In the fifth stage he has peace and tranquility on all sides. He lives among the abundant resources of the unchange-able realm of supreme ineffable wisdom. The sixth stage is complete transformation into life eternal, a total forgetfulness of temporal life passing into the perfect form which is made according to the image and likeness of God. The seventh is eternal rest and perpetual beautitude with no distinguishable ages. As the end of "the old man" is death, so the end of "the new man" is eternal life. The "old man" is the man of sin, but the "new man" is the man of righteousness.

No one doubts that these two lives are related as follows: A
man can live the whole of this life as "the old and earthly man."
But no one in this life can live as "the new and heavenly man,"
but must associate with the "old man." For he must begin these,
and must so continue till death, though the old grows weaker and
the new progresses. Similarly, the entire human race, whose life,
like the life of an individual from Adam to the end of the world,
is so arranged by the laws of divine providence that it appears
divided among two classes. In one of these is the multitude of
the impious who bear the image of the earthly man from the beginning
to the end of the world. In the other is the succession of the
people devoted to the one God. But from Adam to John the Baptist
they live the life of the earthly man under a certain form of
righteousness. Their history is called the Old Testament having
the promise of a kind of earthly kingdom, which is nothing but the
image of the new people and the New Testament, with the promise of
the kingdom of heaven. Meantime the life of this people begins
with the coming of the Lord in humility and goes on till the day of
judgment, when he will come in all clearness. After the judgment
the "old man" will come to an end, and there will take place the
change that betokens the angelic life. For we shall all be raised,
but we shall not all be changed (1 Cor. 15:51). The pious people
will be raised as they transform the remnants of the "old man" that
cling to them into the "new man." The impious people who have
kept the "old man" from the beginning to the end, will be raised in
order to be precipitated into the second death. Those who read
diligently can make out the divisions of the ages. They have no
horror of tares or chaff. For the impious lives with the pious,
and the sinner with the righteous, so that, by comparing the two,
men may more eagerly rise to seek perfection.

7. *On Catechizing the Uninstructed**
        Neither ought we to be moved by the consideration that many
consent unto the devil, and few follow God; for the grain, too,
in comparison with the chaff, has greatly the defect in number.
But even as the husbandman knows what to do with the mightly heap
of chaff, so the multitude of sinners is nothing to God, who knows
what to do with them, so as not to let the administration of His
kingdom be disordered and dishonoured in any part. Nor is the
devil to be supposed to have proved victorious for the mere reason
of his drawing away with him more than the few by whom he may be
overcome. In this way there are two communities--one of the ungodly,

---

*Tr. by S.D.F. Salmond, in Marcus Dods ed., *The Works of St.
Augustine*, Vol IX (Edinburgh: T. and T. Clark, 1873), p. 310.

and another of the holy--which are carried down from the beginning of the human race even to the end of the world, which are at present commingled in respect of bodies, but separated in respect of wills, and which, moreover, are destined to be separated also in respect of bodily presence in the day of judgment. For all men who love pride and temporal power with vain elation and pomp of arrogance, and all spirits who set their affections on such things and seek their own glory in the subjection of men, are bound fast together in one association; nay, even although they frequently fight against each other on account of these things, they are nevertheless precipitated by the like weight of lust into the same abyss, and are united with each other by similarity of manners and merits. And, again, all men and all spirits who humbly seek the glory of God and not their own, and who follow Him in piety, belong to one fellowship. And, notwithstanding this, God is most merciful and patient with ungodly men, and offers them a place for penitence and amendment.

E.   THE TWO SOVEREIGN ASSOCIATIONS IN AUGUSTINE'S
MAJOR WORK, *THE CITY OF GOD**

8. *City of God, XIV, 1*

The kingdom of death so reigned over men, that the deserved penality of sin would have hurled all headlong even into the second death, of which there is no end, had not the undeserved grace of God saved some therefrom. And thus it has come to pass, that though there are very many and great nations all over the earth, whose rites and customs, speech, arms, and dress, are distinguished by marked differences, yet there are no more than two kinds of human society, which we may justly call two cities, according to the language of our Scriptures. The one consists of those who wish to live after the flesh, the other of those who wish to live after the spirit; and when they severally achieve what they wish, they live in peace, each after their kind.

9. *City of God, XIV, 4, 1*

When, therefore, man lives according to man, not according to God, he is like the devil....When, then, a man lives according to the truth, he lives not according to himself, but according to God; for He was God who said, "I am the truth." When, therefore, man lives according to himself--that is, according to man, not according to God--assuredly he lives according to a lie; not that man himself is a lie, for God is his author and creator, who is certainly not

---

*The text used is Marcus Dods, tr., *The City of God* (New York: The Modern Library, 1950). References are to book and chapter.

the author and creator of a lie, but because man was made upright, that he might not live according to himself, but according to Him that made him--in other words, that he might do His will and not his own; and not to live as he was made to live, that is a lie.

10. *City of God, XIV, 28*

Accordingly, two cities have been formed by two loves: the earthly by the love of self, even to the contempt of God; the heavenly by the love of God, even to the contempt of self. The former, in a word, glories in itself, the latter in the Lord. For the one seeks glory from men; but the greatest glory of the other is God, the witness of conscience. The one lifts up its head in its own glory; the other says to its God, "Thou art my glory, and the lifter up of mine head."

11. *City of God, XV, 1*

Yet I trust we have already done justice to these great and difficult questions regarding the beginning of the world, or of the soul, or of the human race itself. This race we have distributed into two parts, the one consisting of those who live according to man, the other of those who live according to God. And these we also mystically call the two cities, or the two communities of men, of which the one is predestined to reign eternally with God, and the other to suffer eternal punishment with the devil. This, however, is their end, and of it we are to speak afterwards. At present, as we have said enough about their origin, whether among the angels, whose numbers we know not, or in the two first human beings, it seems suitable to attempt an account of their career, from the time when our two first parents began to propagate the race until all human generation shall cease. For this whole time or world-age, in which the dying give place and those who are born succeed, is the career of these two cities concerning which we treat.

Of these two first parents of the human race, then, Cain was the first-born, and he belonged to the city of men; after him was born Abel, who belonged to the city of God. For as in the individual the truth of the apostle's statement is discerned, "that is not first which is spiritual but that which is natural, and afterward that which is spiritual," whence it comes to pass that each man, being derived from a condemned stock, is first of all born of Adam evil and carnal, and becomes good and spiritual only afterwards, when he is grafted into Christ by regeneration: so it was in the human race as a whole. When these two cities began to run their course by a series of deaths and births, the citizen of this world was the first-born, and after him the stranger in this world, the citizen of the city of God, predestined by grace, elected by grace, by grace a stranger below, and by grace a citizen above.

Accordingly, it is recorded of Cain that he built a city, but Abel, being a sojourner, built none. For the city of the saints is above, although here below it begets citizens, in whom it sojourns till the time of its reign arrives, when it shall gather together all in the day of the resurrection; and then shall the promised kingdom be given to them, in which they shall reign with their Prince, the King of the ages, time without end.

12. *City of God, XV, 4*

But the earthly city, which shall not be everlasting (for it will no longer be a city when it has been committed to the extreme penalty), has its good in this world, and rejoices in it with such joy as such things can afford. But as this is not a good which can discharge its devotees of all distresses, this city is often divided against itself by litigations, wars, quarrels, and such victories as are either life-destroying or short-lived. For each part of it that arms against another part of it seeks to triumph over the nations though itself in bondage to vice. If, when it has conquered, it is inflated with pride, its victory is life-destroying; but if it turns its thought upon the common casualties of our mortal condition, and is rather anxious concerning the disasters that may befall it than elated with the successes already achieved, this victory, though of a higher kind, is still only short-lived; for it cannot abidingly rule over those whom it has victoriously subjugated. But the things which this city desires cannot justly be said to be evil, for it is itself, in its own kind, better than all other human good. For it desires earthly peace for the sake of enjoying earthly goods, and it makes war in order to attain to this peace; since, if it has conquered, and there remains no one to resist it, it enjoys a peace which it had not while there were opposing parties who contested for the enjoyment of those things which were too small to satisfy both. This peace is purchased by toilsome wars; it is obtained by what they style a glorious victory. Now, when victory remains with the party which had the juster cause, who hesitates to congratulate the victor, and style it a desirable peace? These things, then, are good things, and without doubt the gifts of God. But if they neglect the better things of the heavenly city, which are secured by eternal victory and peace never-ending, and so inordinately covet these present good things that they believe them to be the only desirable things, or love them better than those things which are believed to be better--if this be so, then it is necessary that misery follow and ever increase.

13. *City of God, XIX, 4, 1*

If, then, we be asked what the city of God has to say upon
these points, and, in the first place, what its opinion regarding
the supreme good and evil is, it will reply that life eternal is
the supreme good, death eternal the supreme evil, and that to
obtain the one and escape the other we must live rightly.

14. *City of God, XIX, 27-28*

Whence it is said, "God resisteth the proud, but giveth grace
to the humble." In this, then, consists the righteousness of a man,
that he submit himself to God, his body to his soul, and his vices,
even when they rebel, to his reason, which either defeats or at
least resists them; and also that he beg from God grace to do his
duty, and the pardon of his sins, and that he render to God thanks
for all the blessings he receives. But, in that final peace to
which all our righteousness has reference, and for the sake of
which it is maintained, as our nature, shall enjoy a sound immortality
and incorruption, and shall have no more vices, and as we shall
experience no resistance either from ourselves or from others, it
will not be necessary that reason should rule vices which no longer
exist, but God shall rule the man, and the soul shall rule the body,
with a sweetness and facility suitable to the felicity of a life
which is done with bondage. And this condition shall there be
eternal, and we shall be assured of its eternity; and thus the
peace of this blessedness and the blessedness of this peace shall be
the supreme good.

But, on the other hand, they who do not belong to this city
of God shall inherit eternal misery, which is also called the second
death, because the soul shall then be separated from God its life,
and therefore cannot be said to live, and the body shall be subjected
to eternal pains.

15. *City of God, XXII, 30, 5*

This Sabbath shall appear still more clearly if we count the
ages as days, in accordance with the periods of time defined in
Scripture, for that period will be found to be the seventh. The
first age, as the first day, extends from Adam to the deluge; the
second from the deluge to Abraham, equalling the first, not in
length of time, but in the number of generations, there being ten
in each. From Abraham to the advent of Christ there are, as the
evangelist Matthew calculates, three periods, in each of which are
fourteen generations--one period from Abraham to David, a second
from David to the captivity, a third from the captivity to the birth
of Christ in the flesh. There are thus five ages in all. The sixth
is now passing, and cannot be measured by any number of generations,

as it has been said, "It is not for you to know the times, which the Father hath put in His own power." After this period God shall rest as on the seventh day, when He shall give us (who shall be the seventh day) rest in Himself. But there is not now space to treat of these ages; suffice it to say that the seventh shall be our Sabbath, which shall be brought to a close, not by an evening, but by the Lord's day, as an eighth and eternal day, consecrated by the resurrection of Christ, and prefiguring the eternal repose not only of the spirit, but also of the body. There we shall rest and see, see and love, love and praise. This is what shall be in the end without end. For what other end do we propose to ourselves than to attain to the kingdom of which there is no end?

F. THE YOUNG LUTHER'S USE OF THE AUGUSTINIAN TRADITION

16. The First Lectures on the Psalms (1513/1514) *

"I will sing praises with the spirit and I will sing praises with the mind." (A) "To sing praises with the spirit" means to sing psalms with spiritual devotion and with passion. This is said in opposition to those who sing psalms only according to the flesh. Such criticism applies to two kinds of people. First, it applies to those who sing with a wavering and weary heart, who move only their tongue and their lips. Secondly, it applies to those who, to be sure, sing with joyful and devout heart, but whose rejoicing is more carnal, as with little children who pay more attention to the voice, the sound, the instrument, or the music than to the sense or the fruit of lifting up the spirit to God.

(B) Similarly, "to sing praises with the mind" means to sing praises with spiritual understanding. Here there are again two kinds of opponents: First, those who do not understand what they are singing--as the nuns are said to read the psalter--and secondly, those who have a carnal understanding of the psalms, like the Jews, who always apply them to the ancient histories apart from Christ. But Christ "opens their mind that they might understand the Scriptures." It is more often the case the the spirit enlightens the mind and passion the intellect than vice versa, for the spirit elevates the mind to the place where the "illuminating light" is to be found, while the mind shows this place to passion. Both are therefore necessary, but more important is the uplifting spirit, etc.

*The Latin original is in *Luther's Works*, Weimar Ansgabe (WA), vol. 55, first part, first section, pages 2-4. Normally references will be to volume, page, and the line at which the original text starts.

Section B - The Mind:	Allegorical	Tropological	Anagogical
Jerusalem	good	virtues	rewards
Babylon	evil	vices	punishments

Section A - Passion:	the letter that kills	the spirit that makes alive
	the Babylonian body	the ecclesiastical body

Mount Zion:	1) historical:	land of Canaan	dwellers in Zion
	2) allegorical:	the synagogue or one of its eminent persons	the church or one of its eminent teachers, bishops, or leaders
	3) tropological:	justification according to the Pharisees and the Law	justification by faith or other worthwhile matters
	4) anagogical:	the glory to come according to the flesh	the eternal glory in heaven

Opposed to this is the valley of Kidron.

Section B: In the Scriptures, neither the analogical nor the tropological nor the anagogical sense apply unless they are expressly indicated elsewhere by the historical sense. Otherwise Scripture would become a laughing-stock. The allegorical interpretation can only be used where it is verbally expressed, such as when "mountain" is used in place of "justification" in Psalm 57: "Your justification is like the mountain of God."

Section A: Similarly, it is best to distinguish in the Holy Scriptures between the letter and the spirit. This is what ultimately makes one a true theologian. The church has this ability to distinguish only from the Holy Spirit and not from human under-standing. As Psalm 7 states: "He shall reign from sea to sea." "To reign" here signifies spiritual rule, something which no one would be able to discover on the basis of the literal sense alone unless the Spirit had revealed it, especially since it continues, "from sea to sea."

Hence all who understand this rule to be a rule in carnal and temporal majesty possess "the letter that kills," while the others have "the spirit that makes alive."

The reason for this is that "we know that what the Law asserts is spoken to those who stand under the Law, "and here I often take the Psalms to be speaking of the Jews.

30

17. Explanation of the Second Petition of the Lord's Prayer
(1519) (LW 42:38-40)*

The first kingdom is a kingdom of the devil. In the Gospel
the Lord calls the devil a prince or king of this world (John 16:11),
that is, of a kingdom of sin and disobedience....

Now, all of us dwell in the devil's kingdom until the coming
of the kingdom of God. However, there is a difference. To be sure,
the godly are also in the devil's kingdom, but they daily and
steadfastly contend against sins and resist the lusts of the flesh,
the allurements of the world, the whisperings of the devil. After
all, no matter how godly we may be, the evil lust always wants to
share the reign in us and would like to rule us completely and
overcome us. In that way God's kingdom unceasingly engages in
combat with the devil's kingdom. And the members of the former are
preserved and saved because they, within themselves, fight against
the devil's kingdom in order to enlarge the kingdom of God. It is
they who pray this petition with words, hearts, and deeds. Thus the
holy apostle Paul says that "we must not let sin reign in our mortal
bodies, to make us obey its passions" (Rom. 6:12). He says as it
were: You will indeed have and feel evil lusts, a love of and
inclination to anger, greed, unchastity, and the like, all of which
would lure you into the devil's kingdom, that is, into sin. These
emotions issue out of that same kingdom and are sins in themselves.
However, you must not give way to them, but fight against them
and forcibly subdue these traitors left behind from the old kingdom
of the devil, just as the children of Israel did with the Jebusites
and Amorites (II Sam. 5:6-7). In that way you increase the kingdom
of God--that is, the true promised land--in you.

The others dwell in this kingdom, enjoy it, and freely do the
bidding of the flesh, the world, and the devil. If they could, they
would always stay there. They yield to the devil; they impair, yes,
devastate God's kingdom. To that end they amass goods, build
magnificent houses, and covet all that the world can bestow, just
as though they wanted to remain here forever. They do not pause to
consider that as St. Paul says "here we have no lasting city" (Heb.
13:14). These people utter this prayer with their lips, but
contradict it with their hearts....

The other kingdom is that of God, namely, a kingdom of truth
and righteousness, of which Christ says, "Seek first the kingdom of
God and his righteousness" (Matt. 6:33). What is God's or his

---

*The English texts for Luther are from the American edition of
Luther's Works (St. Louis and Philadelphia) unless otherwise
indicated. The standard abbreviation will be LW, volume number, and
page.

kingdom's righteousness? It is the state when we are free from sin, when all our members, talents, and powers are subject to God and are employed in his service, enabling us to say with Paul, "I live, but it is no longer I but Christ who lives in me" (Gal. 2:20). To the Corinthians he said, "You are not your own; you were bought with a price. So glorify and bear God in your body" (I Cor. 6: 19-20). He says as it were: Christ bought you with his very self. Therefore you must be his and let him live and reign in you. That comes to pass when we are ruled not by sin, but only by Christ and his grace. Thus God's kingdom consists only of peace, discipline, humility, chastity, love, and every other virtue, and is devoid of wrath, hatred, bitterness, unchastity, and every other vice.

Now let everyone test himself to see whether he is inclined in this or that direction, and he will know to which kingdom he belongs. There is, of course, no one who will not find some trace of the devil's kingdom in himself. Therefore he must pray, "Thy kingdom come." For God's kingdom does indeed begin and grow here, but it will be perfected in yonder life.

18. *Commentary on Psalms (1519-1521)* *

Just as the Word of God has never been absent from the world, so it is with the worship of God. For in the worship of God either hypocrisy or false teaching has the upper hand (they always seem to stimulate and contaminate even the best!). Just as genuine piety and false hypocrisy struggled with one another in the two primal brothers, Cain and Abel, so this psalm (which we will consider tomorrow) struggles mightily against the piety of the godless and their false teaching concerning the worship of God. For whatever is genuine among human beings in their works of lesser significance becomes pernicious and injurious in the most sublime and significant of all works, namely the worship of God. For where is pretense more damaging than where it resembles a splendid and excellent work? In summary: Nothing is more dangerous in the world than false religion or idolatry.

19. *The Bondage of the Will (LW 33:287-288)*

For Christians know there are two kingdoms in the world, which are bitterly opposed to each other. In one of them Satan reigns, who is therefore called by Christ "the ruler of this world" (John 12:31) and by Paul "the god of this world" (II Cor. 4:4). He holds captive to his will all who are not snatched away from him by the Spirit of Christ, as the same Paul testifies, nor does he allow them to be snatched away by any powers other than the Spirit of God, as Christ testifies in the parable of the strong man guarding his palace

*WA 5, 142, 16ff.

in peace (Luke 11:21). In the other Kingdom, Christ reigns, and his Kingdom ceaselessly resists and makes war on the kingdom of Satan. Into this Kingdom we are transferred, not by our own power but by the grace of God, by which we are set free from the present evil age and delivered from the dominion of darkness.

The knowledge and confession of these two kingdoms perpetually warring against each other with such might and main would alone be sufficient to confute the dogma of free choice, seeing that we are bound to serve in the kingdom of Satan unless we are delivered by the power of God.

CHAPTER 2

THE DIRECT RELATION OF GOD TO HUMANKIND:

SPIRITUAL GOVERNANCE AND SERVICE THROUGH THE CHURCH

A. JESUS: SOVEREIGNTY COMES FROM GOD

20. *Mark 4:26-28*

And he said, "The kingdom of God is as if a man should scatter seed upon the ground, and should sleep and rise night and day, and the seed should sprout and grow, he knows not how. The earth produces of itself, first the blade, then the ear, then the full grain in the ear.

B. PAUL: GOD GIVES THE GROWTH

21. *1 Corinthians 3:5-7*

What then is Apollos? What is Paul? Servants through whom you believed, as the Lord assigned to each. I planted, Apollos watered, but God gave the growth. So neither he who plants nor he who waters is anything, but only God who gives the growth.

C. AUGUSTINE: THE KINGDOM OF GOD AND THE CHURCH

22. *City of God, XX, 9, 1, 2*

We must understand in one sense the kingdom of heaven in which exist together both he who breaks what he teaches and he who does it, the one being least, the other great, and in another sense the kingdom of heaven into which only he who does what he teaches shall enter. Consequently, where both classes exist, it is the Church as it now is, but where only the one shall exist, it is the Church as it is destined to be when no wicked person shall be in her. Therefore the Church even now is the kingdom of Christ, and the kingdom of heaven. Accordingly, even now His saints reign with

34

Him, though otherwise than as they shall reign hereafter; and yet, though the tares grow in the Church along with the wheat, they do not reign with Him. For they reign with Him who do what the apostle says, "If ye be risen with Christ, mind the things which are above, where Christ sitteth at the right hand of God. Seek those things which are above, not the things which are on the earth." Of such persons he also says that their conversation is in heaven. In fine, they reign with Him who are so in His kingdom that they themselves are His kingdom.

It is then of this kingdom militant, in which conflict with the enemy is still maintained, and war carried on with warring lusts, or government laid upon them as they yield, until we come to that most peaceful kingdom in which we shall reign without an enemy, and it is of this first resurrection in the present life, that the Apocalypse speaks in the words just quoted.

D. THE MIDDLE AGES: THE "SPIRITUAL POWER" OF THE ECCLESIASTICAL HIERARCHY

In the medieval texts the discussion of "spiritual power" normally occurs together with the discussion of "worldly power." Rather than tear some quotations out of context, the relevant texts are gathered in one place in Chapter 5, E below. Cf. Duchrow and Hoffmann, *Die Vorstellung von zwei Reichen und Regimenten bis Luther*, p. 54, note 65.

E. LUTHER: GOD'S LIBERATING POWER COMES THROUGH THE HOLY SPIRIT

23. *Sermon in the Castle Church at Weimar (1522)* *

It is impossible for spiritual governance to prosper, no matter that it consists of the Law and the Kingdom of God, no matter whether it be spiritual or secular. It is not enough that this Law and the Kingdom of God be written down on paper or stored in a filing cabinet. No, it must be written in the heart by the Lord God Himself. The spiritual kingdom must be ruled by God alone and by no one else. The kingdom of the sophists is nothing in comparison with this kingdom. For the kingdom of the sophists (as a means to piety through the performance of good works) is a temptation to the Christian and a blasphemy to God.

Hence one ought to preach only the Kingdom of God to men, that it may come into being and that the Law, rather than holding us prisoner, should stand under our power so that we believe in Christ. Since Christ wishes that his kingdom be great, living, good, and

_____

*WA 10, part III, pp. 371, 372, 378.

just, according to these criteria, the kingdom of the pope is most certainly no true kingdom. Now it is important that we be able to identify the Law by which we are governed and led; this Law is none other than the Holy Spirit, who must rule in us and fulfill the Law within us, and the Spirit must be given to us by God.

This should be our prayer, that God may rule within us through his Holy Spirit; then we shall prosper.

Therefore you preachers should preach the Kingdom of God and nothing else--and not in a longwinded manner! For the spiritual governance and office are to be nothing more than a message by which you preach Christ's kingdom and not about some powerful ruler riding along with many horses and many followers. No, God does not want that. The rulers should go on foot and let God ride as is proper; least of all should they tinker with the pope's kingdom and governance. For the pope teaches nothing but how to control everything by means of the Law or how to smear and consecrate the stones in the churches. But that has nothing to do with the kingdom of Christ! Whoever does not preach the kingdom of Christ, be he monk, bishop, or priest, that person is a devil, and nothing good will come out of him. You should not preach for money, as has been done in the past, but we should seek after the wealth of Christ, that God may rule within us through his Spirit. That is what you should preach! For that is what you have received from Christ's spiritual kingdom and not from the pope! They, to be sure, wish to be spiritual but only become that much more secular. They are but bloated bellies and remain bloated bellies! May God therefore grant us his grace and his kingdom, that this kingdom may exercise dominion over us. Amen.

24. *The Babylonian Captivity of the Church, 1520 (LW 36:113)*

Therefore we are all priests, as many of us as are Christians. But the priests, as we call them, are ministers chosen from among us. All that they do is done in our name; the priesthood is nothing but a ministry. This we learn from I Cor. 4(:1): "This is how one should regard us, as servants of Christ and stewards of the mysteries of God."

CHAPTER 3

THE INDIRECT RELATION OF GOD TO HUMANKIND:
SECULAR GOVERNANCE AND SERVICE THROUGH SOCIO-POLITICAL INSTITUTIONS

A. THE CREATION ACCOUNT IN GENESIS 1: GOD'S MANDATE
OF WORLD DOMINION GIVEN TO HUMANKIND

25. *Genesis 1:26-28*

Then God said, "Let us make man in our image, after our likeness;
and let them have dominion over the fish of the sea, and over the
birds of the air, and over the cattle, and over all the earth, and
over every creeping thing that creeps upon the earth." So God
created man in his own image, in the image of God he created him;
male and female he created them. And God blessed them, and God
said to them, "Be fruitful and multiply, and fill the earth and
subdue it; and have dominion over the fish of the sea and over the
birds of the air and over every living thing that moves upon the
earth."

B. JESUS: LOVE TO NEIGHBOR AS WELL AS LOVE TO GOD

26. *Matthew 22:37-40*

And he said to him, "You shall love the Lord your God with all
your heart and with all your soul, and with all your mind. This
is the great and first commandment. And a second is like it, You
shall love your neighbor as yourself. On these two commandments
depend all the law and the prophets."

C. PAUL: THE RELATIONSHIP OF THE COMMUNITY AS THE NEW HUMANITY IN THE
PUBLIC POLITICAL SPHERE IN THE LIGHT OF GOD'S ACTION IN THE OLD EON

27. *Romans 12:1-2*

I appeal to you therefore, brethren, by the mercies of God, to

present your bodies as a living sacrifice, holy and acceptable to
God, which is your spiritual worship. Do not be conformed to this
world but be transformed by the renewal of your mind, that you may
prove what is the will of God, what is good and acceptable and
perfect.

28. *Romans 13:1-7*

Let every person be subject to the governing authorities. For
there is no authority except from God, and those that exist have
been instituted by God. Therefore he who resists the authorities
resists what God has appointed, and those who resist will incur
judgment. For rulers are not a terror to good conduct, but to bad.
Would you have no fear of him who is in authority? Then do what is
good, and you will receive his approval, for he is God's servant for
your good. But if you do wrong, be afraid, for he does not bear
the sword in vain; he is the servant of God to execute his wrath on
the wrongdoer. Therefore one must be subject, not only to avoid
God's wrath but also for the sake of conscience. For the same
reason you also pay taxes, for the authorities are ministers of
God, attending to this very thing. Pay all of them their dues,
taxes to whom taxes are due, revenue to whom revenue is due, respect
to whom respect is due, honor to whom honor is due.

D. AUGUSTINE: GOD'S SOVEREIGN ASSOCIATION COOPERATES WITH
      ALL HUMANKIND TO UNDERGIRD SECULAR PEACE

29. *City of God, XIX, 13, 1*

The peace of the body then consists in the duly proportioned
arrangement of its parts. The peace of the irrational soul is the
harmonious repose of the appetites, and that of the rational soul
the harmony of knowledge and action. The peace of body and soul
is the well-ordered and harmonious life and health of the living
creature. Peace between man and God is the well-ordered obedience
of faith to eternal law. Peace between man and man is well-ordered
concord. Domestic peace is the well-ordered concord between those
of the family who rule and those who obey. Civil peace is a similar
concord among the citizens. The peace of the celestial city is
the perfectly ordered and harmonious enjoyment of God, and of one
another in God. The peace of all things is the tranquillity of
order. Order is the distribution which allots things equal and
unequal, each to its own place.

30. *City of God, XIX, 13, 2*

God, then, the most wise Creator and most just Ordainer of all
natures, who placed the human race upon earth as its greatest ornament, imparted to men some good things adapted to this life, to wit,

38

temporal peace, such as we can enjoy in this life from health and
safety and human fellowship, and all things needful for the preservation and recovery of this peace, such as the objects which are
accommodated to our outward senses, light, night, the air, and
waters suitable for us, and everything the body requires to sustain,
shelter, heal, or beautify it: and all under this most equitable
condition, that every man who made a good use of these advantages
suited to the peace of his mortal condition, should receive ampler
and better blessings, namely, the peace of immortality, accompanied
by glory and honour in an endless life made fit for the enjoyment
of God and of one another in God; but he who used the present
blessings badly should both lose them and should not receive the
others.

31. *City of God, XIX, 21-26*
     This, then, is the place where I should fulfil the promise I
gave in the second book of this work, and explain, as briefly and
clearly as possible, that if we are to accept the definitions laid
down by Scipio in Cicero's *De Republica*, there never was a Roman
republic; for he briefly defines a republic as the weal of the
people. And if this definition be true, there never was a Roman
republic, for the people's weal was never attained among the Romans.
For the people, according to his definition, is an assemblage
associated by a common acknowledgment of right and by a community
of interests. And what he means by a common acknowledgment of
right he explains at large, showing that a republic cannot be
administered without justice. Where, therefore, there is no true
justice there can be no right. For that which is done by right is
justly done, and what is unjustly done cannot be done by right....
Thus, where there is not true justice there can be no assemblage of
men associated by a common acknowledgment of right, and therefore
there can be no people, as defined by Scipio or Cicero; and if no
people, then no weal of the people, but only of some promiscuous
multitude unworthy of the name of people. Consequently, if the
republic is the weal of the people, and there is no people if it
be not associated by a common acknowledgment of right, and if there
is no right where there is no justice, then most certainly it follows
that there is no republic where there is no justice. Further,
justice is that virtue which gives every one his due. Where, then,
is the justice of man, when he deserts the true God and yields
himself to impure demons? Is this to give every one his due? Or
is he who keeps back a piece of ground from the purchaser, and gives
it to a man who has no right to it, unjust, while he who keeps back
himself from the God who made him, and serves wicked spirits, is
just?

This same book, *De Republica*, advocated the cause of justice
against injustice with great force and keenness. The pleading for
injustice against justice was first heard, and it was asserted that
without injustice a republic could neither increase nor even subsist,
for it was laid down as an absolutely unassailable position that
it is unjust for some men to rule and some to serve; and yet the
imperial city to which the republic belongs cannot rule her provinces
without having recourse to this injustice. It was replied in behalf
of justice, that this ruling of the provinces is just, because
servitude may be advantageous to the provincials, and is so when
rightly administered--that is to say, when lawless men are prevented
from doing harm. And further, as they became worse and worse so
long as they were free, they will improve by subjection. To confirm
this reasoning, there is added an eminent example drawn from nature:
for "why," it is asked, "does God rule man, the soul the body, the
reason the passions and other vicious parts of the soul?" This
example leaves no doubt that, to some, servitude is useful; and,
indeed, to serve God is useful to all. And it is when the soul
serves God that it exercises a right control over the body; and in
the soul itself the reason must be subject to God if it is to govern
as it ought the passions and other vices. Hence, when a man does
not serve God, what justice can we ascribe to him, since in this
case his soul cannot exercise a just control over the body, nor his
reason over his vices? And if there is no justice in such an
individual, certainly there can be none in a community composed of
such persons. Here, therefore, there is not that common acknowledgment of right which makes an assemblage of men a people whose
affairs we call a republic.

And therefore, where there is not this righteousness whereby
the one supreme God rules the obedient city according to His grace,
so that it sacrifices to none but Him, and whereby, in all the
citizens of this obedient city, the soul consequently rules the
body and reason the vices in the rightful order, so that, as the
individual just man, so also the community and people of the just,
live by faith, which works by love, that love whereby man loves God
as He ought to be loved, and his neighbour as himself--there, I say,
there is not an assemblage associated by a common acknowledgment of
right, and by a community of interests. But if there is not this,
there is not a people, if our definition be true, and therefore
there is no republic; for where there is no people there can be no
republic.

But if we discard this definition of a people, and, assuming
another, say that a people is an assemblage of reasonable beings
bound together by a common agreement as to the objects of their

love, then, in order to discover the character of any people, we
have only to observe what they love. Yet whatever it loves, if
only it is an assemblage of reasonable beings and not of beasts,
and is bound together by an agreement as to the objects of love,
it is reasonably called a people; and it will be a superior people
in proportion as it is bound together by higher interests, inferior
in proportion as it is bound together by lower. According to this
definition of ours, the Roman people is a people, and its weal is
without doubt a commonwealth or republic. But what its tastes
were in its early and subsequent days, and how it declined into
sanguinary seditions and then to social and civil wars, and so
burst asunder or rotted off the bond of concord in which the health
of a people consists, history shows, and in the preceding books I
have related at large. And yet I would not on this account say
either that it was not a people, or that its administration was
not a republic, so long as there remains an assemblage of reasonable
beings bound together by a common agreement as to the objects of
love. But what I say of this people and of this republic I must be
understood to think and say of the Athenians or any Greek state,
of the Egyptians, of the early Assyrian Babylon, and of every other
nation, great or small, which had a public government. For, in
general, the city of the ungodly...is void of true justice.

Wherefore, as the life of the flesh is the soul, so the blessed
life of man is God, of whom the sacred writings of the Hebrews say,
"Blessed is the people whose God is the Lord." Miserable, therefore, is the people which is alienated from God. Yet even this
people has a peace of its own which is not to be lightly esteemed,
though, indeed, it shall not in the end enjoy it, because it makes
no good use of it before the end. But it is our interest that it
enjoy this peace meanwhile in this life; for as long as the two
cities are commingled, we also enjoy the peace of Babylon. For
from Babylon the people of God is so freed that it meanwhile sojourns
in its company. And therefore the apostle also admonished the
Church to pray for kings and those in authority, assigning as the
reason, "that we may live a quiet and tranquil life in all godliness
and love." And the prophet Jeremiah, when predicting the captivity
that was to befall the ancient people of God, and giving them the
divine command to go obediently to Babylonia, and thus serve their
God, counselled them also to pray for Babylonia, saying, "In the
peace thereof shall ye have peace"--the temporal peace which the
good and the wicked together enjoy.

But, what is the meaning of not returning evil for evil, if it is not abhorrence of the passion of revenge; and what is the meaning of preferring to pardon wrongs suffered rather than avenge them, if it is not forgetfulness of wrongs?

When men read of these traits in their authors, they publish and applaud them; such conduct as is described and praised seems to them worthy of the beginning of a state which was to rule over so many nations, as when they say that "they preferred to pardon wrongs suffered rather than avenge them." But, when they read the command of divine authority that evil is not to be returned for evil, when this advice is preached from the pulpit to congregations of people, in these universal schools of both sexes and of every age and rank, religion is charged with being an enemy of the state. If this teaching had been heard as it deserved to be, it would have founded, sanctified, strengthened, and enlarged the state very much more sucessfully than Romulus, Numa, Brutus and those other famous men of Roman birth did. For, what is the commonwealth if not the common property? Therefore, the common property is the property of the state. And what is the state but the generality of men united by the bond of common agreement? In their authors we read: "In a short time a scattered and wandering mob became a state by mutual agreement." But, indeed, what precept of agreement did they ever decree to be read in their temples, when they were unhappily obliged to find out how they could worship gods without offense to any of them, when these disagreed among themselves? For, if they chose to imitate them in their discord, their state was likely to fall apart, by the breaking of the bond of agreement, so that, as their morals declined and lost their purity, they began to be involved in civil war.

But, who is so ill-versed in our religion, or so deaf, as not to know the great precepts of agreement, not worked out by human arguments but written by divine authority, which are read in the Churches of Christ? To this teaching those precepts belong which look rather to action than to learning: to turn the other cheek to the striker; to give the coat to him who tries to take away the cloak; to make a double journey when forced to go with anyone. Thus it happens that the evil man is overcome by the good one, or, rather, evil is overcome by good in the evil man, and the man is set free, not from an exterior foreign evil, but from an interior, personal

*Sister Wilfrid Parsons, tr. *Saint Augustine Letters*, "The Fathers of the Church" (New York: Fathers of the Church, Inc. 1953) III, 42-44.

one, by which he is more grievously and ruinously laid waste than
he would be by the inhumanity of any enemy from without. Therefore, he overcomes evil by good who suffers the loss of temporal
goods with patience, in order to show how far these goods are to
be despised for the sake of faith and justice. And the one who
becomes evil by loving these goods to excess, and who does the
wrong, is to learn from the very one to whom he did the wrong what
kinds of goods these are that made him do the wrong, and so he is
to be brought to repentance and to agreement--than which nothing
is more useful to the state--overcome by the goodness of his victim
rather than by the strength of an avenger. The right time for this
to be done is when it seems likely to benefit the one for whose
sake it is done, in order to bring about correction and a return
to agreement. And this certainly is the intention one must have
when this remedy is applied to correct and win over the offender,
and, in a sense, to cure and restore him to sanity, and it must be
done even if the outcome is otherwise and he refuses to accept
either correction or peace-making.

E. THE MIDDLE AGES--SECULAR POWER IN A CHRISTIAN WORLD

The Roman-Byzantine Imperial Church--Gelasius I

*33. Gelasius I. Letters From Your Grace's Servant to Emperor
Anastasius (494)* *

I beg that your grace will not regard as presumptuous the
fulfilling of one's duty in the affairs of God, just as I beg that
the prince of Rome may not consider it unjust for him to be made
aware of a profound truth. Two are the authorities, most noble
emperor, which actually govern the world: the sacred authority
of the bishops and the power of the crown. Of these authorities,
the most important is the priestly office, since the priests must
also render account for these rulers of men before the judgment
throne of God.

You know, of course, most gentle son, that even though you
enjoy foremost dignity among the sons of men, yet you still do
obeisance before the chief spiritual leaders, and you strive to
obtain from them the basis of your salvation. And you realize
that it is better for you to submit yourself as is proper to the
regulation of religion that is concerned with the reception of the
heavenly sacrament and the proper administration of the same than
to issue commands, just as you realize that you should accept their
judgment in these matters and not wish to bind them to your will.

---

*Cf. Duchrow and Hoffmann, pp. 74-76.

For if the religious leaders themselves obey your laws and do not see fit to oppose a decree that has been issued in secular affairs-- thus acknowledging that the dominion in the area of public affairs has been transferred to you by divine ordinance--with how much greater zeal should you not obey those who are entrusted with the most important and venerable mysteries?

No less serious than the danger which confronts those priests who have kept silent in matters pertaining to the worship of God is that danger which threatens those who despise these priests when they must obey. And if it is regarded as proper for the hearts of the believers to submit themselves to all priests who administer the divine office properly, how much sooner should not agreement be established with the bishop of each see, him who the highest divinity desired to take a pre-eminent position over the entire priesthood and whom the piety of the entire church has always praised?

As your grace has clearly observed, one is never able to raise himself as high through human counsel as by the privilege and praise of that person whom the voice of Christ has placed above everything else in the whole world, whom the church has always revered, praised, and held in respect as her primate. That which is established by divine ordinance cannot be attacked by human presumption. It cannot be conquered by any kind of power. Let not those who are opposed display such dangerous audacity, for whatever is firmly established by the founder of religion himself cannot be rendered ineffective by any kind of power: "For the firm foundation of God remains."

34. Tome on the Binding Nature of the Curse: The Unity of the Spiritual and Secular Authority*

If they fear to put this to the test and remain unaware of the true dimension of the power which allows them to make decisions in human affairs, not however to exercise control over divine matters, how can they presume to pass judgment upon those who manage such affairs of God?

It came to pass before the coming of Christ that a few persons appeared symbolically as kings and priests simultaneously, and these were employed only in secular activities until that time. Sacred history relates that the holy Melchizedek was one of that number.

The devil also imitated this example among his own followers, since, tyrant that he is, he has never hesitated to claim for himself whatever is appropriate to the worship of God. That is why the Roman emperor was also called the *pontifex maximus* (high priest).

*Cf. Duchrow and Hoffmann, pp. 77-78.

But after that moment in time when the true king and true priest had arrived, the emperor no longer called himself a priest, and the priest no longer laid claim to imperial dignity.

Despite this, it is still asserted that Christ's members, as members of the true king and the true priest, have received both titles in a splendid gesture of holy magnanimity by virture of their participation in his nature, thus giving rise to a race which is simultaneously royal and priestly. Because Christ took human frailty into account and regulated by means of a splendid dispensation whatever is necessary for the salvation of his followers, He distinguished between the offices of both powers according to their respective activities and their various dignities. His desire was that his followers be healed by the beneficial medicine of humility, not that they be disqualified once more because of human pride.

Hence even the Christian emperor needs the priest for eternal life, just as the priest makes use of the imperial regulations to dispose of secular affairs. In this way, spiritual activity is able to be distinguished from secular pursuits; the person who is struggling on behalf of God is never involved in secular matters, just as the person who is involved in secular matters does not appear to have any say in religious affairs. A measure of order is thus maintained, not that the one power be exalted with the support of the other, but that each estate be specially trained in keeping with the nature of its activity.

The Church in France

35. *The Constantinian Donation**

And so, on the first day after receiving the mystery of the holy baptism, and after the cure of my body from the squalor of the leprosy, I recognized that there was no other God save the Father and the Son and the Holy Spirit; whom the most blessed Sylvester the pope doth preach; a trinity in one, a unity in three. For all the gods of the nations, whom I have worshipped up to this time, are proved to be demons; works made by the hand of men; inasmuch as that same venerable father told to us most clearly how much power in Heaven and on earth He, our Saviour, conferred on his apostle St. Peter, when finding him faithful after questioning him He said: "Thou art Peter, and upon this rock (petram) shall I build My Church, and the gates of hell shall not prevail against it." Give heed ye powerful, and incline the ear of your hearts to that which the good Lord and Master added to His disciple, saying: "and I will

---

*Ernest F. Henderson, *Select Historical Documents of the Middle Ages* (London: Geo. Bell and Sons, 1907), pp. 324-325.

45

give thee the keys of the kingdom of Heaven; and whatever thou
shalt bind on earth shall be bound in Heaven also, and whatever
thou shalt loose on earth shall be loosed also in Heaven." This
is very wonderful and glorious, to bind and loose on earth and to
have it bound and loosed in Heaven.

And when, the blessed Sylvester preaching them, I perceived
these things, and learned that by the kindness of St. Peter himself I had been entirely restored to health: I--together with all
our satraps and the whole senate and the nobles and all the Roman
people, who are subject to the glory of our rule--considered it
advisable that, as on earth he (Peter) is seen to have been
constituted vicar of the Son of God, so the pontiffs, who are the
representatives of that same chief of the apostles, should obtain
from us and our empire the power of a supremacy greater than the
earthly clemency of our imperial serenity is seen to have had
conceded to it,--we choosing that same prince of the apostles, or
his vicars, to be our constant intercessors with God. And, to the
extent of our earthly imperial power, we decree that his holy Roman
church shall be honoured with veneration; and that, more than our
empire and earthly throne, the most sacred seat of St. Peter shall
be gloriously exalted; we giving to it the imperial power, and
dignity of glory, and vigour and honour.

*36. Aethelhard of Canterbury. Letter of 802**
Sovereign authority is subdivided into a priestly and into a
royal sphere. The priests carry the key to the heavenly kingdom
in their word, while the kings carry the sword for the purpose of
punishing the guilty. But the sovereign authority which makes alive
is superior to that which kills, just as life is superior to death
and eternal blessedness superior to temporal joys.

*37. Wala of Corbia (d. 836)***
Meanwhile, you know which orders make up the church of Christ.
What is certain, in view of each order's respective obligations,
is that the one order is required for teaching, the other to manage
the affairs of state. Hence religious affairs must be considered
as belonging to the inner order above all, then human affairs to
the external order. There can be no doubt that the organization of
the entire church is determined by these two orders.

*38. Peter of Damian (d. 1072)****
1. Christ alone founded the Church of Rome, establishing her
upon the rock of faith to which she would eventually give birth. At

---
*Cf. Duchrow and Hoffmann, pp. 80-81.
**Cf. Duchrow and Hoffmann, p. 81.
***Cf. Duchrow and Hoffmann, pp. 82-83.

the same time, it is He Who entrusted to the blessed doorkeeper
of eternal life (i.e. Peter) laws governing both the earthly and the
heavenly kingdoms.

Thus it is not just any kind of earthly saying that has
established the Church of Rome but that Word which formed heaven
and earth and which is ultimately responsible for all the elements.

2. It is fortunate when the royal sword allies itself with
the priestly sword, so that the sword of the priest may soften the
sword of the king, while the sword of the king may sharpen the
sword of the priest. These are the two swords of which it is said
in the passion history of our Lord: "They are enough!" For where-
ever the royal authority is promoted, there the priesthood also
prospers, with both enjoying equal honor as long as they are united
in the happy union referred to previously by our Lord.

3. The kingship, like the priesthood, is recognized as a
divine institution, and hence the office--which in and of itself
is good--is accompanied by an appropriate grace even in cases where
the officeholder turns out to be thoroughly undeserving of it....
For kings and priests are also called kings and priests of God and
of Christ, even though some of them are depraved as a result of their
conspicuous life-style--because they have received the sacrament
of service.

The Conflict between Emperor and Pope for Universal Sovereignty

The temporary victory of the papacy: the investiture controversy

39. *Gregory VII (1072-1085)**

Who does not know that kings and leaders are sprung from those
who--ignorant of God--by pride, plunder, perfidy, murders--in a
word by almost every crime, the devil, who is the prince of this
world, urging them on as it were--have striven with blind cupidity
and intolerable presumption to dominate over their equals; namely
over men? To whom, indeed, can we better compare them, when they
seek to make the priests of God bend to their footprints, than to
him who is head over all sons of pride....

40. *Hugo of St. Victor (1096-1141): Concerning the Sacraments of
the Christian Faith***

1. This totality, however (i.e. the church), is made up of two
orders: laity and clergy, as alike as two sides of a single body.
To some extent, the laity, who serve the necessities of this present
life, are similar to the left side of the body...The clergy, who

---

**"Letter of Gregory VII to Bishop Hermann of Metz, March 15,
1081" in Henderson, *Select Documents*, pp. 397-398.
**Duchrow and Hoffmann, pp. 84-85.

administer what applies to the spiritual life, form in a certain
sense the right side of the body of Christ.

2. There are two kinds of life: one earthly, the other
heavenly; one material, the other spiritual. In the one, the body
derives its life from the soul; in the other, the soul derives its
life from God. Just as the spiritual life is of higher value than
the earthly life and the spirit of higher value than the body, so
spiritual authority is likewise superior to earthly or secular
authority in honor and dignity. For spiritual authority has
established earthly authority, that is, it has to pass judgment
when earthly authority has acted unwisely. Spiritual authority for
its part has been established in the beginning by God, and when
it goes astray, it can be judged by God alone, as it is written:
"Whatever is spiritual orders all things and is judged by no one"
...That is the reason why to this very day the priestly dignity
consecrates the royal authority in the church, sanctifying as well
as forming it by blessing and installing it in office.

41. *Henry IV (1050-1106) and the Voice of the Imperial Past*[*]

For, to mention a few cases out of many, he usurped for himself
the kingdom and the priesthood without God's sanction, despising
God's holy ordination which willed essentially that they--namely
the kingdom and the priesthood--should remain not in the hands of
one, but, as two, in the hands of two. For the Saviour Himself,
during His Passion, intimated that this was the meaning of the typical
sufficiency of the two swords. For when it was said to Him:
"Behold, Lord, here are two swords"--He answered: "It is enough,"
signifying by this sufficing duality that a spiritual and a carnal
sword were to be wielded in the church, and that by them every
thing evil was about to be cut off--by the sacerdotal sword, namely,
to the end that the king, for God's sake, should be obeyed; but by
the royal one to the end that the enemies of Christ without should
be expelled, and that the priesthood within should be obeyed.

42. *Bernard of Clairvaux (1090-1153)*[**]

1. The fulness of power over the entire church throughout the
entire world is a unique prerogative which is granted by the
apostolic see. Whoever resists this power resists the ordinance
of God (Romans 13:2).

2. Now as Christ suffers anew where He already has suffered
once before, it is necessary that both of the swords mentioned in
our Lord's passion be drawn. And who should do this if not you

---

[*]"Summons of Henry IV to the Council of Worms," in Henderson,
Select Documents, pp. 378-379.
[**]Cf. Duchrow and Hoffmann, p. 86.

yourselves! Both swords belong to Peter, the one standing at his command, the other to be drawn forth by his hand as often as is necessary. And concerning this sword, which appears to be of lesser value, it is said to Peter: "Put your sword back into the sheath!" (John 18:11). Hence the sword beongs to him, but he dare not draw it forth with his own hand.

The renewal of the sacred empire on the basis of Roman law

43. *John of Salisbury (1115-1180). Policratus**

1. For this reason, it is only proper that authority over all subjects be transferred to the ruler, so that he himself may be strong enough to be of service in all of the individual and collective matters which he must inquire into and perform. The affairs of a human state are best disposed of where all of its members relate together harmoniously. Here we can follow nature as our best guide in life, since nature has put all the intelligence of the microcosm, that is, the world in miniature (i.e. the world of human beings) into the head, thus subjecting every member of the body to it, so that all the members move properly as long as they follow the judgment of the sound head. But as soon as the individual members of the state turn their attention instead toward one another, then all kinds of difficulties descend upon the ruler....

The privileges with which the crown of the ruler is exalted and gleaming may be as great and as numerous as he considers necessary. There is nothing wrong with this, for nothing is more useful for the people than to have their ruler's needs satisfied just as no one can discover a will that is in opposition to his justice. The ruler, just as most people imagine him to be, is thus a public authority and an image of God's power upon earth.

2. The ruler's official capacity, moreover, requires that he investigate what each one must do in the sphere of custom or morality. Of course, the individual acts of the individual person harmonize with this. What has to be done affects the situation of every individual, partly in a public and partly in a private sense.

3. What is the proper function of the knightly order? It is to protect the church, to combat disloyalty, to honor the priesthood, to hold injustice away from the poor, to bring peace to the province, to shed one's blood for the brother (as the reception of the sacrament instructs), and, if necessary, to sacrifice one's own life--but to what end? That they might serve the passion, vanity, and avarice of their own will? Not at all! They act in these matters on the basis of the written law, according to which each

---

*Cf. Duchrow and Hoffmann, pp. 87-88.

person seeks not so much his own advantage as rather the approval
of God, the angels, and other human beings, out of a concern for
justice and for the common welfare.

The age of Aristotelian reception

44. *Giles of Rome. On Ecclesiastical Power**

Let us therefore conclude by asserting that since there is no
lordship--neither one that is useful, fruitful, or powerful enough
to administer justice--in which one can participate without being
subject to God, and since no one can be subject to God except by
means of the church's sacraments, as we have already noted, you
are therefore the lord of your possessions and of all that you have
in a higher sense as a son of the church according to the Spirit
than as a son of your father according to the flesh...At the same
time, it should be noted that although we designate the church as
the mother and ruler of all possessions and temporal gifts, nevertheless we do not deprive the believers of their property and
possessions just because--as we shall explain--the church and the
believers as well possess some kind of lordship. The church's
lordship is universal and superior, that of the believers, however,
limited and inferior. Thus we give to Caesar what is Caesar's and
to God what is God's, assigning to the church a lordship over
temporal matters that is universal and superior while granting to
the believers a lordship that is limited and inferior.

45. *Thomas Aquinas (1225-1274). On the Government of Princes***

It must therefore be necessary that the same criterion serve
as the goal of both society and the individual. Were the purpose
of a human being some good existing within himself, then it would
resemble the ultimate purpose of the governing society, which is
to obtain what is good and to continue in it. Should this ultimate
purpose of either the individual or the society be something
physical, such as life or bodily health, this would lie within the
professional competence of the physician. Should the ultimate
purpose be to acquire great wealth, then the economist would be
king of society. Should what is good consist in the ability to
recognize some kind of truth to which the society should strive,
then the king would fill the function of a teacher. But it appears
that the purpose of the entire society is to lead a virtuous life.
For this purpose, human beings join together in order to enjoy the
good life together, something which they could not pursue if
everyone lived by himself. A good life, therefore, is a life that

*Cf. Duchrow and Hoffmann, pp. 89-90.
**Cf. Duchrow and Hoffmann, pp. 91-96.

is virtuous. Hence a life of virtue is the ultimate purpose of human society.

The evidence for this is that only those individuals are part of the collective society who have come to a mutual understanding about what it means to live well. For if human beings joined together only in order to keep alive, then animals and slaves would also be members of the civil community. But if they joined together in order to acquire wealth, then all those who are engaged in business would likewise form their own political society. Thus we see that these individuals are all gathered together in a society of people directed by the same laws and by the same government for the purpose of living well.

Since man, by his virtuous life, is destined for a higher purpose, namely the enjoyment of God, as we have noted above, the goal for the society as a whole must be similar to that for a solitary individual. In effect, the ultimate purpose of society as a whole consists not in living virtuously but in attaining the enjoyment of God by means of a virtuous life.

Now if one were able to attain this purpose through some virtue residing within human nature, then the king would of necessity have to direct men toward this purpose. Here we assume that some person will be chosen to whom the entire government of human affairs will be entrusted. But the more such a government is directed toward the ultimate purpose, the more distinguished it is. For it is always the case that someone who is concerned about the ultimate purpose issues commands to those who then perform what is necessary for its attainment. In the same way, it is the duty of the helmsman to arrange for the voyage and to order the shipbuilder to construct a seaworthy vessel, just as the citizen who bears arms commands the smith to provide him with the proper weapons.

Since man, however, attains the enjoyment of God not by means of human virtue but by means of divine virtue--in keeping with the apostolic word, "The grace of God is eternal life" (Romans 6:23)-- it is the task of divine and not of human government to lead the way to that goal. Such a government is exercised by the king who is both man and God, namely our Lord Jesus Christ, who turns men into children of God and admits them into the heavenly splendor. This is the incorruptible government which is entrusted to him and for whose sake he is named priest as well as king in the Holy Scriptures, as Jeremiah 23:5 says: "A king shall rule, and he will be wise." Therefore the royal priesthood is derived from him. And, what is more, all who believe in Christ, no matter how numerous they may be, are also called to be kings and priests.

In order that spiritual matters may be differentiated from

earthly matters, the administration of this kingdom is entrusted
not to earthly kings but to priests, especially to the highest
priest, the successor to Peter and the representative of Christ,
or the Bishop of Rome, to whom all kings of the Christian nations
must be subject as to the Lord Jesus Christ himself. Thus everyone must be subject to him whose task is to provide for the ultimate
purpose and whose duties include a concern for the antecedent
purposes, and they must be directed by his command.

Since the priesthood among the heathen and the entire worship
of the gods served the purpose of procuring temporal blessings,
the priests were quite properly subordinated to the kings, for all
that is disposed to serve the common welfare of the society is the
king's concern. The Old Testament promises earthly blessings,
provided not by demons but by God himself, for a people that truly
fears him. Thus the Old Testament priesthood enjoys a higher
position, since it directs man to the heavenly blessings. Hence
it is the Law of Christ that kings be subject to priests.

Divine Providence has miraculously seen to it that in the
city of Rome--which God already in earlier times had chosen to
become the future capital of his Christian people--the custom
gradually developed by which the leaders of the political community
were placed under the priesthood. As Valerius Maximus says: "Our
community life always considered it proper for everything to be
subordinated to religion; it wished to see in religion something
worthy of the highest dignity as an ornament of the state. It was
always the practice that heads of state officiate at sacrifices,
because they believed that they could maintain their role in the
managing of human affairs only as long as they served the divine
power consistently and well." Since it would come to pass in the
future that the Christian priesthood would be especially honored in
Gaul, divine providence allowed that even among the pagan Gauls
it was the priests--under the name of Druids--who established the
law for all of Gaul, as recorded by Julius Caesar in his book on
the Gallic Wars.

46. *William of Ockham (1300-1349). Short Treatise on the Rule
of Tyrants**

On the other hand, the high priest of the New Testament is
farther removed from temporal and secular activities than was the
high priest of the Old Testament, just as the new Law in general
is more spiritual than the old. Not only did the old Law lack
such complete power in temporal affairs, but in these same affairs
it was subordinated to the king. This is why the pope does not

*Cf. Duchrow and Hoffmann, pp. 96-97.

enjoy similar full power in temporal affairs.

F. LUTHER'S RECEPTION AND MODIFICATION OF THE MEDIEVAL
        TEACHINGS CONCERNING POWER AND ESTATES

The traditional task of secular authority as peaceful protection
against the consequences of evil in the civil communities of
humankind

47. *Secular Authority (LW 45:88-91)*

Here we must divide the children of Adam and all mankind into
two classes, the first belonging to the kingdom of God, the second
to the kingdom of the world. Those who belong to the kingdom of
God are all the true believers who are in Christ and under Christ,
for Christ is King and Lord in the kingdom of God, as Psalm 2 (:6)
and all of Scripture says. For this reason he came into the world,
that he might begin God's kingdom and establish it in the world....

He also calls the gospel a gospel of the kingdom of God; because
it teaches, governs, and upholds God's kingdom....

Now observe, these people need no temporal law or sword. If
all the world were composed of real Christians, that is, true
believers, there would be no need for or benefits from prince, king,
lord, sword, or law. They would serve no purpose, since Christians
have in their heart the Holy Spirit, who both teaches and makes
them to do injustice to no one, to love everyone, and to suffer
injustice and even death willingly and cheerfully at the hands of
anyone. Where there is nothing but the unadultereated doing of right
and bearing of wrong, there is no need for any suit, litigation,
court, judge, penalty, law, or sword....

A good tree needs no instruction or law to bear good fruit;
its nature causes it to bear according to its kind....

Just so, by the Spirit and by faith all Christians are so
thoroughly disposed and conditioned in their very nature that they
do right and keep the law better than one can teach them with all
manner of statutes....

Why, then, did God give so many commandments to all mankind,
and why does Christ prescribe in the gospel so many things for us
to do? Of this I have written at length in the Postils and elsewhere.
To put it here as briefly as possible, Paul says that the law has
been laid down for the sake of the lawless (I Tim. 1:9), that is,
so that those who are not Christians may through the law be
restrained outwardly from evil deeds, as we shall hear later. Now
since no one is by nature Christian or righteous, but altogether
sinful and wicked, God through the law puts them all under restraint
so they dare not willfully implement their wickedness in actual deeds.

In addition, Paul ascribes to the law another function in Romans 7 and Galatians 2, that of teaching men to recognize sin in order that it may make them humble unto grace and unto faith in Christ....

All who are not Christian belong to the kingdom of the world and are under the law. There are few true believers, and still fewer who live a Christian life, who do not resist evil and indeed themselves do no evil. For this reason God has provided for them a different government beyond the Christian estate and kingdom of God. He has subjected them to the sword so that, even though they would like to, they are unable to practice their wickedness, and if they do practice it they cannot do so without fear or with success and impunity. In the same way a savage wild beast is bound with chains and ropes so that it cannot bite and tear as it would normally do, even though it would like to; whereas a tame and gentle animal needs no restraint, but is harmless despite the lack of chains and ropes.

If this were not so, men would devour one another, seeing that the whole world is evil and that among thousands there is scarcely a single true Christian. No one could support wife and child, feed himself, and serve God. The world would be reduced to chaos. For this reason God has ordained two governments: the spiritual, by which the Holy Spirit produces Christians and righteous people under Christ; and the temporal, which restrains the un-Christian and wicked so that--no thanks to them--they are obliged to keep still and to maintain an outward peace.

A new horizon for secular governance; human appointment to responsibility for the world

Secular governance in the framework of a view of vocation based on reason and love, not force

48. *Secular Authority (LW 45:99-100)*

In short, since Paul says here that the governing authority is God's servant, we must allow it to be exercised not only by the heathen but by all men. What can be the meaning of the phrase, "It is God's servant," except that governing authority is by its very nature such that through it one may serve God? Now it would be quite un-Christian to say that there is any service of God in which a Christian should not or must not take part, when service of God is actually more characteristic of Christians than of anyone else. It would even be fine and fitting if all princes were good, true Christians. For the sword and authority, as a particular service of God, belong more appropriately to Christians than to any other men on earth. Therefore, you should esteem the sword or

54

governmental authority as highly as the estate of marriage, or
husbandry, or any other calling which God has instituted. Just
as one can serve God in the estate of marriage, or in farming or
a trade, for the benefit of others--and must so serve if his neighbor
needs it--so one can serve God in government, and should there
serve if the needs of his neighbor demand it. For those who punish
evil and protect the good are God's servants and workmen. Only,
one should also be free not to do it if there is no need for it,
just as we are free not to marry or farm where there is no need
for them.

49. *Sermon on Matthew 5-7 (1532)* *(LW 21:237)*

If you are a manual laborer, you find that the Bible has been
put into your workshop, into your hand, into your heart. It teaches
and preaches how you should treat your neighbor. Just look at your
tools--at your needle or thimble, your beer barrel, your goods,
your scales or yardstick or measure--and you will read this statement inscribed on them. Everywhere you look, it stares at you.
Nothing that you handle every day is so tiny that it does not
continually tell you this, if you will only listen. Indeed, there
is no shortage of preaching. You have as many preachers as you
have transactions, goods, tools, and other equipment in your house
and home. All this is continually crying out to you: "Friend,
use me in your relations with your neighbor just as you would want
your neighbor to use his property in his relations with you."

50. *Keeping Children in School (1530)* *(LW 46:237-239)*

For all the works of this estate belong only to this temporal,
transient life. They protect body, wife, child, house, property,
and honor, and whatever else pertains to the needs of this life.
As far, then, as eternal life surpasses this temporal life, so far
does the preaching office exceed the temporal office--even as the
substance surpasses the shadow. For worldly lordship is an image,
shadow, or figure of the lordship of Christ. The office of preaching--
where it exists as God ordained it--brings and bestows eternal
righteousness, eternal peace, and eternal life; thus does St. Paul
extol it in II Corinthians 4. Worldly government, on the other
hand, preserves peace, justice, and life, which is temporal and
transient....

For if men were to rule solely by the fist, the end result
would surely be a bestial kind of existence: whoever could get
the better of another would simply toss him into the discard pile.
We have enough examples before our eyes to see what the fist can
accomplish apart from wisdom or reason....

All experience proves this and in all the histories we find
that force, without reason or wisdom, has never once accomplished
anything. Indeed, even murderers and tyrants, if they are not
clever enough to adopt for themselves and among themselves some
kind of laws and regulations to control and limit the power of the
fist (even though these be equally wicked), will not be able to
continue; they will fall out among themselves and perish by each
other's hand. Briefly, then, it is not the law of the fist but
the law of the head that must rule--not force but wisdom or reason--
among the wicked as well as among the good.

51. *"A Proposal on the Existing Order..." (1526)**
    This recent turmoil has taught us a good lesson, since we see
well enough what kind of rubbish appears before our eyes when we
do not see to it that the feelings of the common man are satisfied
and harmonized to the extent that this is possible. Thus it is
necessary that he be handled not only with force--as is now the
case--but also with reason. For force alone without reason cannot
last and only serves to keep the subjects in a state of eternal
hatred over against their governing authorities, as all the histories
point out to us.

52. *To the Councilmen of all Cities in Germany (1524) (LW 45:357, 372)*
    Are we then to permit none but louts and boors to rule, when
we can do better than that? That would certainly be a crude and
senseless policy. We might as well make lords out of swine and
wolves, and set them to rule over those who refuse to give any
thought to how they are ruled by men....
    We have been German beasts all too long. Let us for once make
use of our reason, that God may perceive our thankfulness for his
benefits, and other nations see that we too are human beings, able
either to learn something useful from others or to teach them in
order that even through us the world may be made better.

    Humans as Co-Workers with God in the Creation

53. *Bondage of the Will (LW 33:242-243; 70)*
    For the answer we give is this: (1) Before man is created and
is a man, he neither does nor attempts to do anything toward becoming
a creature, and after he is created he neither does nor attempts
to do anything toward remaining a creature, but both of these things
are done by the sole will of the omnipotent power and goodness of
God, who creates and preserves us without our help; but he does not
work in us without us, because it is for this he has created and

_____
    *WA 15, 35ff, and 48, 27, ff.

preserved us, that he might work in us and we might cooperate with
him, whether outside his Kingdom through his general omnipotence,
or inside his Kingdom by the special virtue of his Spirit. (2) In
just the same way (our answer continues), before man is changed
into a new creature of the Kingdom of the Spirit, he does nothing
and attempts nothing toward remaining in this Kingdom, but the
Spirit alone does both of these things in us, recreating us without
us and preserving us without our help in our recreated state, as
also James says: "Of his own will he brought us forth by the word
of his power, that we might be a beginning of his creature" (James
1:18)--speaking of the renewed creature. But he does not work
without us, because it is for this very thing he has recreated and
preserves us, that he might work in us and we might cooperate with
him. Thus it is through us he preaches, shows mercy to the poor,
comforts the afflicted....

So that free choice is allowed to man only with respect to what
is beneath him and not what is above him. That is to say, a man
should know that with regard to his faculties and possessions he
has the right to use, to do, or to leave undone, according to his
own free choice, though even this is controlled by the free choice
of God alone, who acts in whatever way he pleases. On the other
hand in relation to God, or in matters pertaining to salvation or
damnation, a man has no free choice, but is a captive subject and
slave either of the will of God or the will of Satan.

Institutional Mediation of human responsibility for the world

54. *Whether Soldiers, Too, Can Be Saved (1526) (LW 46:94-95)*

In the first place, we must distinguish between an occupation
and the man who holds it, between a work and the man who does it.
An occupation or a work can be good and right in itself and yet be
bad and wrong if the man who does the work is evil or wrong or does
not do his work properly. The occupation of a judge is a valuable
divine office. This is true both of the office of the trial judge
who declares the verdict and the executioner who carries out the
sentence. But when the office is assumed by one to whom it has not
been committed or when one who holds it rightly uses it to gain
riches or popularity, then it is no longer right or good. The
married state is also precious and godly, but there are many rascals
and scoundrels in it. It is the same way with the profession or
work of the soldier; in itself it is right and godly, but we must
see to it that the persons who are in this profession and who do the
work are the right kind of persons, that is, godly and upright, as
we shall hear.

57

In the second place, I want you to understand that here I am not speaking about the righteousness that makes men good in the sight of God. Only faith in Jesus Christ can do that; and it is granted and given us by the grace of God alone, without any works or merits of our own, as I have written and taught so often and so much in other places. Rather, I am speaking here about eternal righteousness which is to be sought in offices and works.

55. *Sermons on Exodus (1525)**

God gives us rational ability so that we can master physical affairs, educate our children, administer the household, etc. Scripture is here unnecessary, for God has distributed this rational ability among all the nations. It is, therefore, not necessary that he send down a word from heaven. "You are to exercise dominion," He tells mankind....

Even though God did not directly institute secular power in Israel, he nevertheless confirms it and wishes to have it. For this reason, he accepts the heathen who may institute it and desires that his people obey such a person.

How Christians Respond to Injury to Themselves or the Neighbor

56. *Scholia to Romans (1515-1516)* *(LW 25:443-444)*

Yet all of these things have been said concerning those people who have the power to do this and who are on their own responsibility. But it is different in the case of those who have been placed over other people, for they do not act for themselves but for God. Hence it is their duty to rule with justice over those who are subject to them and not permit them to do harm to one another. For now they do not have the right to tolerate, and patience has no place here. For humility, patience, and endurance are not proper for God, but rather judgment, glory, and vengeance. And these people function as His representatives. But where any of them can do it without becoming guilty himself, even though he may sustain harm and injury, he ought to make concessions, as we have said.

57. *Two Forms of Righteousness (1519)* *(LW 31:304-305)*

The things which have been said do not pertain at all to public individuals, that is, to those who have been placed in a responsible office by God. It is their necessary function to punish and judge evil men, to vindicate and defend the oppressed, because it is not they but God who does this. They are his servants in this very matter, as the Apostle shows at some length in Romans 13:4: "He does not bear the sword in vain, etc." But this must be understood

---

*WA 16, 353, 5ff.

as pertaining to the cases of other men, not to one's own. For no
man acts in God's place for the sake of himself and his own things,
but for the sake of others. If, however, a public official has a
case of his own, let him ask for someone other than himself to be
God's representative, for in that case he is not a judge, but one
of the parties.

58. *The Magnificat (1521)* *(LW 21:334-338)*

But someone might say: "How is that? Are we not bound to
defend the right? Should we let the truth go? Are we not commanded
to die for the sake of the right and the truth? Did not the holy
martyrs suffer for the sake of the Gospel? And Christ himself, did
not He desire to be in the right? It happens indeed that such men
are now and then in the right publicly (and as they prate, before
God) and that they do wisely and well." I reply: Here it is high
time and most necessary that we open our eyes, for here lies the
crux of the whole matter. Everything depends on our proper understanding of "being in the right." It is true, we are to suffer all
things for the sake of the truth and the right, and not to deny it,
however unimportant the matter may be. It may also be that those
men are now and then in the right; but they spoil all by not rightly
asserting their right, by not going about it in fear or setting
God before their eye. They suppose it is sufficient that it is
right, and then they desire to continue and carry it out by their
own power. Thus they turn their right into a wrong, even if it was
in itself right. But it is much more dangerous when they only think
they are in the right, yet are not certain, as they do in the
important matters that pertain to God and His right. Let us, however,
deal first with the more tangible human right and use a simple
illustration that all may grasp.

Is it not true that money, property, body, wife, child, friends,
and the like are good things created and given by God Himself?
Since, then, they are God's gifts and not your own, suppose that He
were to try you, to learn whether you were willing to let them go
for His sake and to cleave to Him rather than to such gifts of His.
Suppose He raised up an enemy, who deprived you of them in whole or
in part, or you lost them by death or some other mischance. Do you
think you would have just cause to rage and storm and to take them
again by force or to sulk impatiently until they were restored to
you? And if you said that they were good things and God's creatures,
made with His own hands, and that, since all the Scriptures called
such things good, you were resolved to fulfill God's Word and defend
or get back such good at cost of life and limb, not suffering their
loss voluntarily or surrendering them patiently--what a farce that

59

would be! To do right in this case, you should not rush in headlong,
but fear God and say: "Dear Lord, they are good things and gifts
of Thine, as Thine own Word and Scripture; nevertheless I do not
know whether Thou wilt permit me to keep them. If I knew that I
was not to have them, I would not move a finger to get them back.
If I knew that Thou wouldst rather have them remain in my possession
than in that of others, I would serve Thy will be taking them back
at risk of life and property. But now, since I know neither and
see that for the present Thou permittest them to be taken from me,
I commit the case to Thee. I will await what I am to do, and be
ready to have them or to do without them."

That, mark you, is a right soul, and one that fears God. There
is God's mercy, as the Mother of God sings. Hence we can see why
in times past Abraham, David, and the people of Israel waged war
and slew many. They went into battle by the will of God, they
stood in fear, and fought not for the sake of the goods but because
God commanded them to fight, as the narratives show, in which this
command of God is usually set forth at the beginning. In this way
the truth is not denied, for the truth declares they are good things
and God's creatures. But the same truth declares also and teaches
that you should let such good things go, be ready at all times to
do without them, if God so wills it, and cleave to God alone. The
truth, by saing they are good, does not compel you to take the good
things back again, nor to say they are not good; but it does compel
you to regard them with equanimity and to confess that they are
good and not evil.

In the same manner we must treat the right and the manifold
good things of reason or wisdom. Who can doubt that right is a
good thing and a gift of God? God's Word itself says that right
is good, and no one should admit that his good and righteous cause
is unrighteous or evil, but should sooner die for it and let go
everything that is not God. To do otherwise would be to deny God
and His Word, for He says right is good and not evil. But if such
right is snatched from you or suppressed, would you cry out, storm
and rage, and slay the whole world? Some do this; they cry to
heaven, work all manner of mischief, ruin land and people, and fill
the world with war and bloodshed. How do you know whether or not
it is God's will that you keep such a gift and right? It belongs
to Him, and He can take it from you today or tomorrow, outwardly
or inwardly, by friend or foe, just as He wills. He tries you to
see whether you will dispense with your right for His will's sake,
be in the wrong and suffer wrong, endure shame for Him, and cleave
to Him alone. If you fear God and think: "Lord, it is Thine; I
will not keep it unless I know Thou willest me to have it. Let go

what will: only be Thou my God."--then this verse is fulfilled:
"His mercy is on those who fear Him," who refuse to do anything
apart from His will. Then both sides of God's Word are observed.
In the first place, you confess that the right, your reason,
knowledge, wisdom, and all your thoughts are right and good, as
God's Word teaches. In the second place, you are willing to dispense
with such good things for God's sake, to be wrongfully despoiled
and put to shame before the world, as God's Word also teaches. To
confess the right and good is one thing, to obtain it is another.
It is enough for you to confess that you are in the right; if you
cannot obtain it, commit that to God. To you is committed the
confession, the obtaining God has reserved to Himself. If He desires
you also to obtain, He will perform it Himself or put it in your
way, without any thought of yours, so that you must come into possession of it and win the victory, above all that you asked or thought
(Eph. 3:20). If He does not desire you to obtain it, let His mercy
be sufficient for you (2 Cor. 12:9). Though they deprive you of the
victory of the right, they cannot deprive you of the confession. Thus
we must refrain, not from the good things of God but from wickedly
and falsely cleaving to them; so that we may use them or suffer the
lack of them with equanimity, and cling, whatever befalls, to God
alone. Oh, this is a thing that ought to be known to all princes
and rulers who, not content with confessing the right, immediately
want to obtain it and win the victory, without the fear of God; they
fill the world with bloodshed and misery, and think what they do
is right and well done because they have, or think they have, a just
cause. What else is that but proud and haughty Moab, which calls
and makes itself worthy to possess the right, that fine and noble
good and gift of God; while if it regards itself right in the sight
of God, it is not worthy to live on earth or eat a crust of bread,
because of its sins. Oh, blindness, blindness! Who is worthy of
the least creature of God? Yet we desire not only to possess the
highest creatures, right, wisdom, and honor, but to keep them or
regain possession of them with furious shedding of blood and every
disaster. Thereupon we go and pray, fast, hear Mass, and found
churches, with such bloody, furious, raving hearts, it is a wonder
the stones do not burst asunder in our face.

Here a question arises. If a ruler did not defend his land
and subjects against injustice, but followed my advice, made no
resistance, and let all be taken from him, what would the world
come to? I will briefly set down my view of the matter. Temporal
power is in duty bound to defend its subjects, as I have frequently
said; for it bears the sword in order to keep in fear those who do
not heed such divine teaching, and to compel them to leave others

in peace. And in this the temporal power seeks not its own but its
neighbor's profit and God's honor; it would gladly remain quiet
and let its sword rust, if God had not ordained it to be a hindrance
to evildoers. Yet this defense of its subjects should not be
accompanied by still greater harm; that would be but to leap from
the frying pan into the fire. It is a poor defense to expose a
whole city to danger for the sake of one person, or to risk the
entire country for a single village or castle, unless God enjoined
this by a special command, as He did in former times. If a robber
knight robs a citizen of his property and you, my lord, lead your
army against him to punish this injustice, and in so doing lay waste
the whole land, who will have wrought the greater harm, the knight
or the lord? David overlooked many things when he was unable to
punish without bringing harm upon others. All rulers must do the
same. On the other hand, a citizen must endure a certain measure
of suffering for the sake of the community, and not demand that all
other men undergo the greater injury for his sake. Christ did not
want the weeds to be gathered up, lest the wheat also be rooted up
with them (Matt. 13:29). If men went to war on every provocation
and passed by no insult, we should never be at peace and have nothing
but destruction. Therefore, right or wrong is never a sufficient
cause indiscriminately to punish or make war. It is a sufficient
cause to punish within bounds and without destroying another. The
lord or ruler must always look to what will profit the whole mass
of his subjects rather than any one portion. That householder will
never grow rich who, because someone has plucked a feather from
his goose, flings the whole goose after him. There is no time now
to go into the subject of war.

We must do the same in things divine, such as faith and the
Gospel, which are the highest goods and which no one should let go.
But the right, favor, honor, and acceptance of them we must cast
in the balance and commit them to God. We should be concerned not
to obtain but to confess, and willingly endure being reviled before
all the world, being persecuted, banished, burned at the stake, or
otherwise slain, as unrighteous, deceivers, heretics, apostates,
blasphemers, and what not; for then God's mercy is upon us.

59. *Major Sermon on Usury (1520)**

This is the command which Christ has given us, that he establishes
within us a life that is peaceable, pure, and heavenly. Now it is
not the way that leads to peace for each person to demand justice
for himself while being unwilling to suffer injustice, as it is said
concerning the blind in Psalm 13: "They do not know the way that

*WA 6, 40, ff.

62

leads to peace"--a way which leads only through suffering, as also
the heathen with their reason and we with our daily experience come
to realize as true. One part of the human race must keep silent,
suffer, and hold their peace over against the other part. Although
they may quarrel and feud incessantly, it must one day come to an
end. This will not happen, however, until they have suffered much
harm and evil; this would not have occurred if they had kept this
commandment of Christ from the very beginning and if they had overcome the temptation by which God tests them. Instead, they allowed
themselves to be driven away from the commandment. Thus God ordains
that whoever is not willing to give up something small for the sake
of his commandments must risk losing a great deal or all that he
has through strife and warfare. For this reason, it is only fair
that the person who does not forgive his neighbor a paltry six or
ten florins for the sake of God and eternal blessings must pay off
the judge, procurator, or secretary with twenty, thirty, or forty
florins in the service of the devil. Thus he who would be obedient
to God and still retain sufficient temporal and eternal blessings
will in the long run lose both. It will be the same with respect
to the powerful lords who occasionally devastate an entire land with
war, slaughtering large numbers of people with their soldiers merely
for the sake of some paltry advantage of freedom. That is in keeping
with the perverted wisdom of this world, which fishes with golden
nets despite the fact that expenses outweigh profits and those who
gain a little ultimately end up losing a great deal.

60. *Secular Authority (LW 45:91)*

If anyone attempted to rule the world by the gospel and to
abolish all temporal law and sword on the plea that all are baptized
and Christian, and that, according to the gospel, there shall be
among them no law or sword--or need for either--pray tell me, friend,
what would he be doing? He would be loosing the ropes and chains
of the savage wild beasts and letting them bite and mangle everyone,
meanwhile insisting that they were harmless, tame, and gentle
creatures; but I would have the proof in my wounds. Just so would
the wicked under the name of Christian abuse evangelical freedom,
carry on their rascality, and insist that they were Christians
subject neither to law nor sword, as some are already raving and
ranting.

The political witness: Service to others

61. *Commentary on the Prophet Zachariah (1527)**

Thus there are three kinds of external government and three
methods or means, each with its own divine government in addition.

*WA 23, 513, 36ff.

In the secular government, it is the sword and the fist that count;
in the spiritual government, the Word and the mouth; in the angelic
government, reason and the understanding. These are the three
means: The Sword, the Word, and Human Reason. By the sword, I
understand everything which belongs to secular government, such as
secular justice and laws, customs and habits, manners, estates,
various offices, persons, clothing, etc. By the word, I understand
everything belonging to spiritual government, such as the spiritual
offices(I Cor. 12; Eph. 4; Romans 12) and the sacraments, etc. By
reason, I understand everything that the dear angels require in
order to influence us, either to keep us from evil or to nudge us
toward the good...These three governments are not directed against
each other, nor does the one crush or destroy the other, but rather
all mutually serve one another.

62. *Keeping Children in School* *(LW 46:226)*
I have spoken so far about the works and miracles which your
son does for individual souls, helping them against sin, death, and
the devil. Beyond that, however, he does great and mighty works
for the world. He informs and instructs the various estates on
how they are to conduct themselves outwardly in their several
offices and estates, so that they may do what is right in the sight
of God. Every day he can comfort and advise those who are troubled,
compose difficulties, relieve troubled consciences, help maintain
peace and settle and remove differences, and countless other works
of this kind. For a preacher confirms, strengthens, and helps to
sustain authority of every kind, and temporal peace generally. He
checks the rebellious; teaches obedience, morals, discipline, and
honor; instructs fathers, mothers, children, and servants in their
duties; in a word, he gives direction to all the temporal estates
and offices. Of all the good things a pastor does these are, to
be sure, the least. Yet they are so high and noble that the wisest
of all the heathen have never known or understood them, much less
been able to do them. Indeed, even to the present day no jurist,
university, foundation, or monastery knows these works, and they
are not taught either in canon law or secular law. For there is
no one who regards these offices as God's great gifts, his gracious
ordinances. It is only the word of God and the preachers that praise
and honor them so highly.

Therefore, to tell the truth, peace, the greatest of earthly
goods, in which all other temporal goods are comprised, is really
a fruit of true preaching. For where the preaching is right, there
war and discord and bloodshed do not come; but where the preaching
is not right, it is no wonder that there is war, or at least constant
unrest and the desire to fight and to shed blood.

63. *Major Sermon on Usury (1520)**

I do not consider myself significant enough to be able to advise the pope and all rulers of the world on how to manage every situation, nor do I think that very much would come of this. Still, one must know what is good and necessary, just as the government is obliged to consider and to carry out whatever is necessary for governing wisely over the common people entrusted to their care.

64. *Whether Soldiers, Too, Can Be Saved* (LW 46:121-122)

I am not now teaching what Christians are to do, for your government does not concern us Christians; but we are rendering you a service and telling you what you are to do before God, in your office of ruler. A Christian is a person to himself; he believes for himself and for no one else. But a lord and prince is not a person to himself, but on behalf of others. It is his duty to serve them, that is, to protect and defend them. It would indeed be good if he were also a Christian and believed in God, for then he would be saved. However, being a Christian is not princely, and therefore few princes can be Christians; as they say, "A prince is a rare bird in heaven." But even if princes are not Christians, they nevertheless ought to do what is right and good according to God's outward ordinance. God wants them to do this.

But if a lord or prince does not recognize this duty and God's commandment and allows himself to think that he is prince, not for his subjects' sake, but because of his handsome, blond hair as though God has made him a prince to rejoice in his power and wealth and honor, take pleasure in these things, and rely on them. If he is that kind of prince, he belongs among the heathen; indeed, he is a fool. That kind of prince would start a war over an empty nut and think of nothing but satisfying his own will. God restrains such princes by giving fists to other people, too. There are also people on the other side of the mountain. Thus one sword keeps the other in the scabbard. However, a sensible prince does not seek his own advantage.

65. *Weekly Sermons on John 16-20 (1528-1529)***

In this way, Christ has shown us and has given us a precept, that we should not muzzle the truth before the "big boys" and the nobility but rather admonish and punish them on account of their injustice....

For there is a great difference between these two things: suffering injustice and violence on the one hand, punishing them on account of their injustice on the other.

---

*WA 6, 45, 33ff.
**WA 28, 360, 25ff.

We should suffer injustice and violence, yet we should not keep silent. For a Christian should bear witness to the truth and should be willing to give up his life for its sake....

Now if we should be willing to give up our lives for the sake of the truth and for the sake of justice, then we must confess the truth and justice freely and openly....

The princes and the "big boys" rather enjoy the fact that the entire world is punished whereas only they get off scot-free. But they also have to be punished; whoever occupies an official capacity is obliged to tell them where they have acted unjustly and done wrong, even if they have not yet admitted it....But if the "big boys" are punished, that will really cause a great stir!

PART II:

THE MISINTERPRETATION OF THE TRADITION UNDER

THE INFLUENCE OF NINETEENTH CENTURY GERMAN THEOLOGY

INTRODUCTION

The nineteenth century played a crucial and in many ways
disastrous role in the development of Lutheran social ethics,
especially on German soil. A number of strong social, political,
economic, and intellectual currents threatened to sweep away old
landmarks, and in Germany in particular we see both strong impluses
critical of the established order and unyielding resistance to the
new democratic and reforming initiatives.

Beginning without an adequate awareness of the full range of
Luther's thought, theologians of various persuasions used Luther's
political utterances to support the particular ways they had chosen
to deal with the question of order both in the affairs of society
and in the affairs of the mind. Despite the cries for unity, a
dualism in many ways forgetful if not neglectful of Luther's unifying
vision won the day.

The nineteenth century also witnessed heavy out-migrations of
Lutherans from their European homelands to the United States and
to Latin America, as well as the beginnings of a German Empire in
Africa. In the United States a fairly large Americanized group of
Lutherans dating back to early eighteenth-century settlements
provided a counter-balance to what the immigrants brought. As the
tides of immigration increased, however, the influence of German
thinking on the American churches grew in strength. How these
developments unfolded is more fully documented in Part III below.
What we must note, however, is the strong influence of German
theology upon Lutheran communities outside of Germany itself.

In Central and Eastern Europe, for the most part in the domains of the Austro-Hungarian Empire but also in a few parts of Imperial Russia (e.g., Bessarabia, the Crimean Peninsula), there were two kinds of Lutheran communities. German settlements, varying in size and in socio-economic characteristics (some were urban and professional, others were farming communities, including a number of Pietistic origins) were found in scattered locations, holding fast to the German language and traditions. Typically those communities which were Lutheran (there were also Roman Catholic and Mennonite settlements) looked to Germany for cultural and theological leadership. Most of their clergy studied in Germany.

At the same time indigenous Lutheran churches--Hungarian, Slovak, Polish, and so on--also existed as minority churches in Eastern Europe. Like the Germans these churches looked to the homeland of the Reformation for leadership. The Hungarian situation serves as an illustration of this influence of German theology in Central and Eastern Europe.

The story of Latin America differs only slightly. The German immigrants who settled the southern continent regularly looked back to Germany for guidance and support. The German settlement in Brazil was by far the largest of these immigrant groups. Brazilian Lutherans not only maintained an ethnic identity separate from that of the host country, but in religious thought and in their demands for pastors they remained dependent on Germany.

In Southwest Africa we have an example of German colonial enterprise. German missionaries had also entered this territory, as well as undertaking work in areas which are now part of the Republic of South Africa. Missionaries found themselves relating to and serving white co-religionists as well as the indigenous black population. They quickly faced the problem of relating their work to the interests of the colonial administrators and the ruling whites. How would they use the resources of their German theological heritage to cope with the colonial situation?

To answer this question, as well as to examine the influence of German theological thought in Eastern Europe and Latin America, we must turn first to what happened in nineteenth-century Germany as Lutheran theologians reflected on political questions.

CHAPTER 4

THE GERMAN NINETEENTH CENTURY

INTRODUCTION

The distinction between public affairs and private life belongs
among the important issues of the nineteenth century.[5] In this
sense the Enlightenment's distinction between the religious
institution (which it abhorred) and private faith (which it defended
and encouraged) helped set the agenda for the uses to which Luther's
doctrine was put in the nineteenth century. We dare not forget
either that the French Revolution and the subsequent struggles in
the German states (part of the Revolutions of 1848), the rising
industrialization and urbanization also helped focus attention on
questions of human rights (specifically the rights which the
individual person could claim as given, inalienable) and the proper
activities and responsibilities of "the state." The distinction
between state and society, between the sovereignty which inheres
in the state and the rights which free citizens may claim as
inherently theirs, provided the materials on which political
reflection centered. These distinctions already imply a dualism,
and many of the theologians found in Luther resources for giving
validity and legitimacy to the kinds of dualism they wished to
espouse.

Thus we find that one facet of the debate reflects the concern
for defining the proper role of the state and the uses of political
authority (against the background of a liberal revolution in 1848
which failed) and at the same time describes the proper sphere of
conduct for the individual person, in particular, the believing
person, and for the organized community of faith, the church, to
which he belonged.

What belongs in the realm of public concern and what belongs
in the private must be seen as one understanding of the two realms.
At times, however, one may speak of three realms rather than two:
the realm of nature (the domain of science), the kingdom of God,
and the external communities of mankind, in particular the national
state. For the nineteenth-century German theologian had to deal not
only with the problem of defining the relationships of church and
state, political authority and personal faith, but he also had to
come to terms with the questions of the interrelationships of
science and theology, empirical discovery and divine revelation.
In this situation "the spiritual realm" was alternatively played
off against either nature or the political community. The result
was a pair of related dualities.

Another facet of the debate reflects the underlying similarity
despite some basic differences between liberal and confessional
theologians. Two separate lines of theological reflection, each
clearly critical of the other, nevertheless converged remarkably
in the political conclusions which they reached. Thus we can
argue that beneath the diversity of theological schools in nineteenth-
century Germany, despite the sharp differences between confessional
Lutherans and liberal theologians, both gave largely the same
answers to the central questions of political ethics.

For confessional Lutherans, partly in reaction to the concern
for human rights that spilled over into Germany from the French
Revolution, the *authority* of the state became a central issue.[6]
For it was through the state that *order* in the human community was
to be maintained; what kinds of disorder revolution could bring
one could read not only from the French experience but discern in
even more threatening form from the discontent and revolutionary
outbreaks within the German states themselves.

One drew on the evangelical tradition, therefore, to emphasize
the character of the state as an order of creation, to direct
individual Christians to their vocations of service within the
state, and to free the state from any prophetic warnings which
religious leaders might be tempted to offer.

A thorough-going dualism between secular and spiritual realms
provided an understanding of reality that undergirded this political
advice. Religion became preeminently the domain of the inner life,
of the intimately personal the private. The institutional and the
external, the public, belonged to the worldly powers. Redemption
was solely the province of the church and, although the state was
also to further redemption, such service could best be rendered
through its pursuit of its own ends. The state meanwhile became

the exclusive province of the law. For the external conduct of
human affairs, the law was determinative. Thus, in effect, despite
the insistence that both realms served one another and stood under
the same God, law and gospel were divided from one another; the
outer and the inner lives of the faithful could presumably follow
different directives.

Not all confessional theologians followed this separation
without question. At Erlangen, von Harless recognized the possibility
of changes in political authority. Thus he both qualified the
necessity of obedience, for the Christian "recognizes that no other
order and power of the state could or should ever bring him to act
contrary to the order of Christ's Kingdom," and at the same time
indicated the circumstances under which changes in the existing
political order were legitimate. Von Harless recognized clearly
that an existing regime could in fact be destructive of order;
under these circumstances the Christian response could not simply
be one of uncritical acceptance. The determining value for von
Harless, however, remained "order," and he argued that "even in the
midst of the perversion of the pagan world, there exist creaturely
orders which have preserved themselves in conformity with the
divine will and can therefore be fulfilled by Christians for the
sake of God and of Christ." In short, in a very explicit fashion
von Harless made the ultimate legitimation of political institutions
the existence of an original order of creation itself. Thus he
provided Lutheran theology a new way of conceptualizing the
structures of society, known as the doctrine of the "orders of
creation." While Christians could appeal to this order for criticizing
existing political arrangements, the doctrine of the orders easily
tended to confer divine legitimacy upon the status quo.

In addition, the conception of the Christian role in political
affairs--except for those called to be rulers--is primarily that
of the person who responds to others, not that of the active participant and initiator of action. Only when the domain of the private
rights of the believer is invaded, when "conscience" is at stake,
does the believer have a mandate to act, primarily even then, to say
No and suffer, not to initiate change.

Theodosius Harnack accepted the separation which the confessional
theologians had elaborated and gave further authority to it by
attributing it to the Reformation. In the work of Harnack nineteenth-
century dualism covered itself with the mantle of the sixteenth-
century reformers.

It remained for Christian Eduard Luthard to point out that in
fact Luther's doctrine of the two kingdoms had been ignored, that
his ethical insights had been little used and were not well known.

In more explicit fashion than any other theologian of the nineteenth century Luthard then proceeds to the rehabilitation of the doctrine of the two kingdoms. Luthard's exposition is important because he begins with the dualism of outer and inner. These he fully equates with law and gospel, and thus continues the sharp differentiation of the two worlds of Christian existence his predecessors had begun. The distinction of public and private remained paramount. He also appeals to the orders of creation, still seen in the traditional language of state, home, and church. Luthard seems not to notice that in Luther's day these three institutional complexes effectively encompassed all of the believer's life, for household combined economy and family, and that in Luthard's day economy had become something entirely different. Luther's distinction of outer and inner must necessarily run through all three of these complexes; in the nineteenth century, specifically in Luthard, the private or inner is described as apart from, qualitatively different from the public or outer; the interdependence of these dimensions is overlooked.

In good evangelical fashion Luthard strikes the note of "love," but he at no point relates love to Luther's concern for human freedom. It is striking that in nineteenth-century expositions of Luther, his treatise *The Freedom of the Christian Man* is almost totally neglected.

While confessional theologians centered their political concerns on questions of authority and order, *autonomy* of both social institutions and the natural order served as a central concern for liberal thinkers. In the strongest possible fashion Sohm reduced the church to an invisible spiritual association that has nothing to do with the secular world. "The Gospel frees us from this world, frees us from all questions of this world, frees us inwardly, also from the questions of public life, from the social question."

What confessional theology celebrated as "orders of creation," liberal theology termed autonomous spheres of human existence. In economic affairs only economic considerations determine what is normative; in effect liberal theology (with some qualifications and misgivings) embraced the chief elements of laissez-faire theory. In politics the power relationships of nations, considerations of domestic order, and questions of positive law are determinative. Thus the arenas of major social change in nineteenth-century Germany were effectively removed from the moral scrutiny which a critical Christian social ethic might provide. The consistent effect of liberal ethical reflection was the separation of secular and spiritual from mutual interaction. Theology served only to legitimate authority. For these writers, as for the Enlightenment, religion is a private matter.

If religion is a private matter, the chief foci of ethics can only be on the one hand to provide instructions for the development of personal virtues and for the moral development of the individual, and on the other hand to document and describe the autonomous principles at work in such public spheres as the economy and the polity. The cultivation of moral virtue, the solid bourgeois virtues of the new commercial classes and the civil service, can go hand in hand with the espousal of *Realpolitik*. The uses of power, whether of the sword or of the marketplace, are severed from moral accountability.

The duality of religion and science received similar treatment. In the face of the flourishing science of the nineteenth century and the strong claims of an explicitly deterministic scientific worldview, theology could only accept the autonomy of nature as given. Thus liberal theologians busied themselves primarily, along with their humanist colleagues in the German universities, with finding a basis for continuing their own work. The realm in which the Christian faith could still continue to be active would be found "where moral communication is cultivated among men, where the private life is idealized as so unique a reality that it can no longer be compared with anything else that can be known." The moral claims of Christianity were not demonstrable according to the norms of secular knowledge; its validity depended upon moral conviction.

Thus in the sphere of knowledge as in the sphere of public life, the Christian found himself excluded. His task was limited to the private life, the cultivation of spiritual virtues.

In a striking fashion Ernst Troeltsch read this sharp separation back into Martin Luther. While it is true that impulses in this direction existed in Luther, Troeltsch, with the confessional theologians, ignored major parts of Luther's ethical writings to make his point. Troeltsch was right in indicting the santification of the status quo, for which purpose the confessional writers had used Luther. Troeltsch failed in large measure to see that the conclusions of his liberal contemporaries were no different in political consequences. Liberals and confessional theologians alike believed that they were saying different things. But the consequences of their positions converged remarkably.

Troeltsch is also important for shaping much of the general American understanding of Luther's teachings. While Lutheran theologians in the United States questioned the accuracy of Troeltsch's description of Luther, they did not examine how well he characterized contemporary confessional Lutheran accounts of Luther's

74

teachings. The historical accident of the major role Troeltsch
has played in the understanding of Luther in the United States
make his inclusion here important. Furthermore, as we shall see,
many American Lutheran ethicists provided confirming evidence of
Troeltsch's reading.

Whether the state was seen as the authoritarian guardian of
public order or as an autonomous institution of national power, in
both instances Christians as Christians, whether collectively or
individually, had no apparent choice but submission. In the twentieth
century these admonitions were to have far-reaching consequences.

A. THE KINGDOM OF GOD AND THE WORLD IN CONFESSIONAL LUTHERANISM

Stahl, Vilmar, and Kliefoth

66. Stahl--the External Kingdom of God*

The state always remains merely the institution for mankind's
earthly relationships and merely the instrument for God's earthly
guidance, that is, for the unfolding of earthly events which we
call "history." Man's eternal bond with God, or "religion," and
God's guidance so that His eternal kingdom may come--these certainly
also require an external institution here below to serve as a
community for men and an instrument for God. The institution for
this purpose, however, cannot be the state but must be an institution
in its own right, distinct from the state, namely the church. For
religion differs fundamentally from all temporal relationships and
obligations in that it lacks an external object, finding its
fulfillment solely in the most intimate kind of persoanl union with
God. Also, the activity and guidance of God by which He establishes
His eternal Kingdom here below--that is, the entire economy of the
work of redemption and revelation--differs fundamentally from every
other form of guidance in history since it rests entirely upon the
direct supernatural acts of God, namely upon His miraculous deeds.
Hence the church, as the institution which serves the cause of
religion and the Kingdom of God, must also differ fundamentally from
the state. She differs first of all in the nature of her object.
The state aims at what is external and temporal, the church at what
is inside of a person and eternal. For the state, therefore, the
external institution is a precondition for the inner disposition,
whereas for the church, it is the fruit of the same. The state
exercises authority over whatever falls under its sway; the church,
however, dare never compel anyone to join against his will, just as
the church dare never compel obedience.

---

*From F.J. Stahl, *Die Philosophie des Rechts nach geschichtlicher
Ansicht* Vol. II, part 2 (1833-37), pp. 8-9, 10-13.

The church relates to the state in the same way that the work
of redemption and revelation relates to history. For the church
represents the former, the state the latter. Just as the work of
revelation, as God's super-natural activity, is always distinguished
and set apart from history (which is only a natural phenomenon),
so the church is also distinguished and set apart from the state.
But just as revelation is intertwined with history, and history, no
matter how omnipotent it may appear on the outside, must still
serve as revelation's highest final goal, so the church is also
incorporated into the state and, despite her outward legal subordination, serves as the state's highest goal. And just as history
diffuses the revelation without being able to change its content,
so the state must advance the church without, however, being allowed
to interfere with her dogmatic substance.

The state stands in indissoluble relationship with the law.
Both have as their object the external human community. The legal
code for governing that community's membership is the law; the
institution for its governance is the state. Just as the law
regulates every human relationship, so it provides the state with
the legal code by which the state exists; vice versa, just as the
state governs every human activity, so it provides a government to
interpret and administer the legal code. In this way, state and
law mutually restrict one another.

The state exists only through the law and the law exists only
through the state. But they do not overlap in the sense that the
law merely provides the state with its norms and the state only
governs inasmuch as it administers the law. Rather, the law regulates
all relationships according to their external condition and not
merely for the sake of the state, while the state, as a living
governing body, must not maintain relationships only in accordance
with their own immutable rules but must rather promote the common
activity in conformity with the goal and destiny of these relationships. It is especially this mutually restrictive function of law
and state which must persuade teachers of natural law, once they
have abandoned the proper point of view, to restrict both law and
state with respect to the other, as when they maintain that the
state is the only association that is really necessary or that the
law is the only goal of the state.

Law and state together in this indissoluble association form
the external Kingdom of God; they are the body through which He
works upon men and through which He maintains His order among men
here below as He conducts that order according to His purposes.
Law and state, as has been pointed out before, belong to the earthly
condition and have their origin in man's apostasy from God. If

mankind actually were "in God," then the inner community would reflect His order in all its external aspects, but as the fruit of and not as the foundation of that order. The law, as the special legal code governing external conditions, would then be rendered superfluous and unnecessary by the universal nature of sanctification, and the state, or the governing of an external institution, would likewise be rendered superfluous and unnecessary by the direct rule of God Himself. Man and mankind would no longer stand under two different sets of orders, since in the transformed human being, the spirit would form the body in its own image and would govern according to its own spiritual nature and will. But because of sin, both the law and the state remain necessary--that is the origin of this peculiar intermediate stage in earthly life between the order of nature and the eternal order of human existence. The kingdom of the external community, or the state--since the state is made up of self-conscious human beings, it comes into being by its own activity and manifests its moral will through such activity--is always of a higher form than the kingdom of nature, whose creatures reflect the image of the divine spirit only passively and unconsciously in their material existence. The state, however, occupies a rung on the ladder far below that of the eternal or true Kingdom of God to which human beings are called in accord with their destiny. The eternal kingdom reveals the divine spirit as an inner will and as the free activity which it produces. The kingdom of the external community--the state--is revealed in the results of its activity, in the external phenomena which it continuously produces, while the eternal or true Kingdom of God is revealed in the spirit of God Himself as He pervades human personalities. The state can only be grasped through its effects--law, regulation, and order--to which external phenomena alone are responsive.

67. *Vilmar on Religion and Politics (1851)**

So much is of course true, that...Christianity, which is not of this world, the confession of faith in the resurrected Christ, ought not to burden itself with the petty problems of this world. Certainly, Christianity sets the rules of conduct which determine, for example, that there is such a thing as "mine" and "thine," but neither religion nor Christianity nor the Christian Church has any right to determine what is actually "mine" and what is "thine" or to make decisions concerning these matters. That holds true not only for a transaction between two private individuals, but it applies as well to broader and more extensive relationships

---

*A.F.C. Vilmar, *Zur neuesten Culturgeschichte Deutschlands*, Vol. II (1858), pp. 210-211.

such as the entire inner administration of a so-called state or
relationships between states. In themselves, these actual political
conflicts remain far removed from the Christian faith--important
is only whether or not the persons who participate in such conflicts
are believers in Christ--just as they should also remain far removed
from the church and her servants. The servants of the church have
only to make certain, by the power of the word, the sacraments, and
prayer, that those who are entrusted with the task of conducting
these political conflicts as part of their vocation perform their
function in the name of God and of the Lord Christ. *Whether* or not
they actually do this is their own personal responsibility; *how*
they do this, both generally and specifically, lies completely outside the influence of the church and her servants. In this sense,
the servants of the church not only should not take a political
stand, but they really cannot do so, and least of all can they
interfere with or impose themselves upon secular government.

68. *Theodor Kliefoth on Church and State**

Church and state have a relationship to one another similar to
that of Gospel and Law. In the age of revelation, before the Son
of God had appeared, there was only Law and no Gospel; in the age
of fulfillment, there will be, properly understood, only Gospel
and no Law. Today Law and Gospel are the two powers which should
always remain and work together, yet the one should never wish to
be mistaken for the other. The relationship between church and
state is similar. In the age of revelation, it was necessary for
the coming redemption to take on the form of the state, for only
through the Law could redemption in that stage of development be
preserved in the world against sin. In the age of fulfillment,
where sin and the necessity for laws commanding and forbidding
will be no more, the state as such will cease to exist, since the
transfigured form of the church will sustain the common life of the
new humanity.

The Erlangen Theologians

69. *Von Harless: Renewal and Change in Existing Political Order***

For this reason (i.e. due to the imperfection of all earthly
orders), and because even the best of earthly orders has not been
predestined to immortality, the Christian cannot consider the
existing order to be one that binds him unconditionally. However,

---

**Acht Bücher von der Kirche*, I (1854), pp. 432-433.
**From G.C.A. von Harless, *Christliche Ethik*, 3d. ed. (1845),
pp. 264, 267-268, 270-271.

it is undoubtedly so durable that it would be sacrilegious for him to disregard it or to dissolve it on his own. And even if the convinced Christian cannot conceive the duty of rulers and subjects within the political order to be that of preserving the existing order, he is just as unlikely to see it as his divine calling to destroy it. Rather, the convinced Christian has a collective as well as an individual calling to preserve the political order. Whether he does this by preserving and improving all that advances that order or by warding off all that harms it, he always remains within the limits of his individual calling as well as within the limits of his collective calling as that is defined by law and legal statutes.

But just as the Christian realizes that the norm for service in his individual earthly calling is to place that calling at the disposal of Christ's Kingdom, he also knows that he can only find the strength to truly fulfill his individual calling here on earth as he acts in the spirit of Christ's Kingdom. Therefore the Christian anticipates that the true fulfillment of his collective calling and the collective order of the nations will depend upon the extent to which the Spirit of Christ permeates the popular mentality of both rulers and subjects. By the same token, he recognizes that no other order and power of the state could or should ever bring him to act contrary to the order of Christ's Kingdom, preferring if necessary to suffer for the sake of Christ.

The convinced Christian conducts himself differently in the second instance, namely when the existing political order comes to an end as the result of events outside of his immediate control. If the change is legitimate, that is, either an exchange of personnel occurs among those holding lawful office (through succession, new elections, etc., depending upon the individual political form), or a change is introduced by someone occupying an office with the authority to command and to legislate--as long as the change conforms with the existing law and promotes the public order--then the Christian will find nothing in his calling to keep him from accepting the change and submitting to it as a new order. If this change of an existing order comes about as the result of a national catastrophe, such as the aftermath of a struggle which has broken out over the divinely bestowed calling of a nation, and a new government is imposed upon a conquered people by force, then the Christian does not have to accept either the previously existing order or the new order as something which applies to him unconditionally. If the nature of the new order or the particular nature of the Christian's own calling does not oblige him to oppose the new order for reasons of conscience or to withdraw from it as he carries out his calling, then the cessation of the previous order in and by itself gives him no reason to declare himself conscientiously opposed to the new order. For the Christian knows of no unconditional right favoring one ruler against the other or one nation against the other that would oblige him or even allow him to react blindly against the victorious new order in the name of a former privilege or a former independent status which he may have enjoyed. On the contrary, the Christian finds that chastisements and sufferings, even a national catastrophe, may prove beneficial; hence he must not try to use the suffering itself as a pretext for his avoiding such a catastrophe but must look only to the special nature of his own calling. Similarly, the Christian recognizes that his oath as a citizen and subject binds him only to the existing order and not to some order which has ceased to exist; the fact that such an order has ceased to exist, however, does not invalidate the oaths of those who have previously sworn allegiance to it.

The way in which the Christian, obeying the law and in conformity with his calling, acts to preserve the existing political order has a twofold aspect which is further limited by the Christian's insight into the nature of the existing earthly political order. If it is impossible for him to participate in any kind of new beginning that places itself in absolute opposition to the existing political order, it does not necessarily follow that the Christian conscience has to identify itself solely with preserving what exists. That could only be true if the Christian conviction no longer took note of the *anthropina* (human element) in the existing political order or if everything comprising such an order were but an unchangeable *theion* (divine element). On the contrary, the more the Christian is aware of the fact that much of what goes under the name "existing order" is in fact destructive of order, the less he can identify himself with the notion of "preserving the existing order merely by preserving what exists." If the language of the political parties has turned "conservative" and "reformist" into such an antithesis that the one automatically excludes the other, then, when one considers the abstract concept itself rather than the tendency that lies behind the name, the Christian conviction decides in favor of neither the one nor the other but for both at the same time or, more accurately, for the one *within* the other. It is simply impossible for the thoughtful Christian to imagine that the existing political order could be preserved without the continual renewal and elimination of whatever stands in its way, any more than he could imagine that orderly renewal could ever occur without the preservation of the existing order. Only where no divinely binding

80

authority at all is recognized in the human political order or where
nothing but divinely binding authority is recognized can preservation
and renewal confront each other as irreconcilable polar opposites,
as unrestricted renewal and falsely restricted stability. At any
rate, by limiting himself to what is lawful and within his capacity
to perform, the Christian avoids all unwarranted false political
activity, after moments of renewal as well as after moments of
preservation.

70. *Von Harless: State and Church**

Christianity is not worthy of its name if it does not affect
the whole man and if it is not reflected in every aspect of human
relationships. And the normal human relationships are perverted
to the point of abnormality unless they are so constituted or capable
of modification that a Christian can participate in them for the
sake of Christ, live and play an active role within them, and be
subject to the various orders which are naturally part of them in
harmony with the will of Christ. This however would not be the case
if it could be said about any actual order of this world that it
maintained a neutral position over against Christianity and thus
showed how utterly useless it is, in order to then be complied
with for the sake of Christ and in His Spirit. Now if the New
Testament Scriptures claim that the political order and government
of even a pagan commonwealth ought to be obeyed for the sake of
God and of Christ, this does not mean that the objectives and
representatives of that order have to be regarded as out-and-out
pagan. Even in the midst of the perversion of the pagan world,
there exist creaturely orders which have preserved themselves in
conformity with the divine will and can therefore be fulfilled by
Christians for the sake of God and of Christ, as well as with the
mind of Christ. Should a political society organize itself so that
its members and representatives are Christians, **this** does not affect
the identity of that creaturely natural condition which lies at the
bottom of both the political order and the pagan world in general.
Thus it follows that a Christian dare not regard the political
order as identical with the order of Christ's Kingdom, nor dare he
make this identification in actual practice. It does *not* follow,
however, that the Christian, as he participates in the construction
of the political order, cannot give expression to that vocation
whose strength, far from being opposed to Christ's Kingdom, exists
rather for the sake of the same and is able to serve the purposes

*C.G.A. von Harless, *Staat und Kirche oder Irrthum und Wharheit
in den Vorstellungen von "christlichen" Staat und von "freier"
Kirche* (1870), pp. 48-49.

of Christ's Kingdom and to provide exercise in Christian obedience as well. This divine vocation, which is built into the natural framework of all human orders, is, however, disavowed and trampled under foot wherever it is promulgated as a fundamental principle that the state and its organization have no relationship at all to Christ, His Kingdom, His Church, or that Church's ecclesiastical structure, or when it is implied that one must carefully avoid every statement concerning the formal organization of the state which aims at and arises from a responsible concern that the state keep its own proper function intact. Such principles can only be palmed off as "Christian" by a kind of pseudo-Christianity which considers the order of Christ's Kingdom alone to be the emanation of the divine will, whereas all creaturely orders on earth are regarded as products of a world alienated from God or, even worse, as diabolical orders that are at enmity with Him.

*71. Theodosius Harnack on Church and World**

I now wish to indicate briefly how the Lutheran Reformation also set the relationship between church and world back on its proper foundation. While the Reformation chose to make a sharp distinction between both spheres, it did not cast the earthly ordinances and vocations aside into the realm of the profane. Rather, it recognized them as independent divinely instituted ordinances which, far from conflicting with the Christian's vocation, actually serve as a school for that vocation and are to be sanctified in turn by it. Thus the Reformation opposed every arrogation of power by the church over the state and the estates, restored to them their independence, and developed the golden doctrine of the earthly vocation with an assurance and clarity missing in the church since the third century.

On the other hand, the Reformation did not press the distinction between church and state to the point of completely separating the two. Rather, it upheld the conviction that the church is duty-bound to embrace the nations and to exercise a sanctifying and educational effect upon the national life as long as it is given the opportunity of doing so. Just as little as the Reformation intended that the church should enjoy a theocratic control over the state, so little did it propose to hand the church over to an autocratic control at the hands of the state.

------

*Theodosius Harnack, *Die lutherische Kirche im Lichte der Geschichte: Ein Conferenz-Vortrag gehalten zu Leipzig am 22. August 1855*, pp. 31-32.

Christian Ernst Luthard

72. *On the Role of Luther (1867)**

Luther's significance for ethics and his decisive influence upon the fundamental ethical viewpoints of Protestantism have not always been taken into account or given the appreciation they deserve. A more careful investigation of his basic ethical insights certainly would not harm contemporary research in ethics. In this sense, what follows is intended as a contribution to the task which our discipline lays upon contemporary theology.

Nothing that has any scholarly significance for this theme can be quoted from earlier works. Aside from various anthologies in which dogmatic and ethical sentences taken from Luther's are complied according to pre-arranged categories--such as the dissertations published in the eighteenth century by Schramm and Lehmann, to name only a few--these works offer practically nothing worth mentioning.

73. *On the Two Kingdoms (1867)***

Next to the doctrine of justification, there is hardly another doctrine which Luther treats as extensively and as passionately as this doctrine about the spiritual and inward character and nature of the Kingdom of Christ and the distinction between it and the kingdom of the world (that is, the realm of natural, created life) which it establishes. To begin with, the Gospel has absolutely nothing to do with outward existence but only with eternal life, not with external orders and institutions which could come into conflict with the secular orders but only with the heart and its relationship to God, with the grace of God, the forgiveness of sins etc., in short, with heavenly life. The most characteristic sign of the Kingdom of Christ is the order of grace; that of the kingdom of the world and life in the world is the order of justice. Thus the categories differ completely and do not lie on the same plane; they belong to entirely different worlds. As a Christian, I am a member of the former; as a human being, of the latter. For we stand in two spheres of life; we are simultaneously in heaven and on earth. Both spheres differ from one another in the same way that the sphere of redemption differs from that of creation. The distinction between the world and the redeemed life is not simply one of degree but of essence. Here a quantitative point of view is no longer adequate; only a qualitative point of view will suffice. For the Kingdom of God consists not in eating and drinking etc. but in justice, peace, and joy in the Holy Spirit. This word of the

---

**Die Ethik Luthers in ihren Grundzügen* (1867); pp. 5-6.
***Ibid.*, pp. 76-80, 82-83, 110.

apostle is the basic theme of all Luther's many statements, which in all their diversity still revolve around this single central theme.

This means that it is not the vocation of Jesus Christ or of the Gospel to change the orders of secular life and establish them anew. On the contrary, Christ has nothing to do with this sphere but allows it to go its own way. He does not, for example, have to instruct the Emperor Augustus on how to conduct his government, just as "one does not need the Lord Jesus" for business and commerce, but all of that is subject to its own laws and to reason, "for which one does not need the Holy Spirit." Thus Christ's servants, the preachers, likewise have no reason to espouse these secular matters but are only to preach grace and the forgiveness of sins in the name of Christ. As for secular concerns, "the jurists may advise and help here on how this should function." Even Christianity does not change that; no one is deprived of these orders or of his secular vocation once he becomes a Christian. Christianity wants to change man's heart, not his external situation, as the monastic ethic teaches. For everything remains just as it is until the great change of all things (i.e. on the Last Day). Until then, the Kingdom of God possesses only an inner form and Jesus a dominion over the heart. Thus the Christianity of earthly life consists not in the fact that the earthly life is somehow restricted, outwardly modified, or externally sanctified by the church etc. but in the Christian conviction of a heart that has been renewed by faith; this conviction is what the Christian is expected to carry with him into every aspect of earthly life. This is the true holiness of the Christian life: to believe in Christ and to be faithful in one's vocation without outwardly separating oneself from other human beings or indulging in isolated foolish asceticism or in the monastic life, which leads only to hypocrisy. It is not what is on the outside but what is on the inside that is important, and Christ acted only for the sake of the latter! That alone is the intent of Christ's words as well--especially in the Sermon on the Mount, where he lays down prescriptions for the Christian life (that one should not swear, etc.). It never occurs to Him to lay down prescriptions for the outer life, but He has in mind solely the inner personal attitude. His words do not apply to the external vocation and to the public behavior which it necessarily calls forth but rather to the individual person--to his convictions, to the inner personal disposition of his heart. Otherwise, Christ would overturn the entire world order, were His word to be understood as applying to external behavior. For then outward behavior in the exercise of an earthly vocation and public office would only become hopelessly confused.

Luther makes specific application to individual concrete examples. Thus in reference to the question of marriage, the estate of government, and the military profession, the decisive understanding which he always maintained in these questions was this, that he showed how one ought to distinguish between the Christian's inner personal conviction and his external sense of duty toward his secular office and worldly profession. On the basis of this distinction, both spheres are certainly compatible with one another so that neither is disadvantaged or impeded by the other, neither the Christian life by the secular life or vice versa.

But this in turn assumes two things: The first is that each remain within its own boundaries, so that the Gospel is not made into an external legal code for life in the world--since Jesus has given His Law only for His Christians and not for the others-- nor, on the other hand, should secular power interfere with the inner life of conscience and faith which is reserved for the Gospel. The other assumption is that the secular sphere in which the Christian is to live and be active for the sake of his earthly vocation is not in itself sinful but is one of God's lawful orders. Were this not so, then the Christian would certainly have to avoid it. But this applies as well to the normal worldly professions and occupational groupings. For this secular life that is exercised through a vocation is related to the Gospel in the same way that creation is related to redemption. As human beings in the world, we belong to the kingdom of creation; as Christians in the Kingdom of God, we belong to the kingdom of redemption, which has been established by the resurrection of Christ. Christ has not first established the world and its life and orders through His redemption and resurrection, but this entire sphere "is already there from before, having been instituted from the beginning of the world." Therein lies the justification for its independent status. It does not first receive its right to exist from the Gospel or from the church but already possesses that right through the creative will of God.

For Luther, the moral world and moral behavior come together in these three hierarchies of *church*, *home*, and *state* to form a totality. In this totality, the spheres of creation and of redemption--God's two worlds--unite on the basis of what differentiates them to form the most beautiful harmony.

This service of love determines the eternal relationships of life as well. It is interesting to discover that Luther, even on those occasions when he was deeply depressed on account of inner temptations and melancholy moods, still sought to maintain his

outward good humor, as an obligation of love toward those with whom
he had to deal.

On the whole, his position and judgment concerning the sphere
of social and general human behavior is determined by two points of
view: first, that the natural life as created by God, with its gifts,
joys, and activities, is in itself good and proper; second, that
all of this should enter into the service of love and, ultimately,
of the Kingdom of God.

B. THE AUTONOMY OF THE SECULAR SPHERES IN LIBERAL THEOLOGY

Rudolph Sohm

74. *The Church Is Spiritual* *

The nature of the church is spiritual, the nature of the law
secular. The church wishes to be guided and directed by the
governing of the divine spirit; the law can only produce human
government, and that from a nature that is earthly, fallible, and
subject to the flux of time. The church clings to objective truth,
that is, she proclaims God's Word and His will in truth, offers
herself to the world, and is empowered by Him to be active in the
world. The law, on the other hand, clings to the abstract form
for the sake of principle (*summum jus summa injuria*--the stricter
the law, the more serious the crime) and must cling to the abstract
form above everything else, for only in this way can it rise above
the factions and render a judgment which both of two conflicting
parties, despite their antithetical interests, can accept as just;
it renders this judgment not on the basis of momentary influences
but on the basis of firmly established, traditional, universally
valid principles. Therefore it inevitably follows that the law,
though it does not encourage coercion as an ideal, nevertheless
achieves its goals by means of coercive force, whereas the essence
of the church abhors coercion, since only the free acquisition of
God's gifts is of spiritual value. Above all, the church is--by
virtue of her ideals and reality--Christianity, the people and
Kingdom of God, the body of Christ on earth. It is unthinkable
that the Kingdom of God as such should have human (legal) constitutional forms or that the body of Christ should have a human (legal)
government. The essence of the law is diametrically opposed to the
ideal essence of the church. Just as the legal order is in harmony
with the essence of the state, so the legal order is in contradiction
to the innermost essence of the church.

Kirchenrecht, Band I, Die Geschichtlichen Grundlagen (1892),
pp. 1-2.

75. *The Christian and the Social Order in Public Life**

The Inner Mission and Christianity are unable to solve the questions of public life, the most important of which is today the social question. The Inner Mission has not been called to do this. That is not her office. She would be entering into a completely foreign field of activity. The Inner Mission and Christianity bring the Gospel under the guise of charity. Christianity has nothing else at its disposal. She exists only on the basis of the Gospel. As Christians, we are unable to possess anything more unique, better, higher, or vaster than that. The Gospel frees us from this world, frees us from all questions of this world, frees us inwardly, also from the questions of public life, also from the social question. Christianity has no answer to these questions.

76. *The Relationship to Labor***

It is not as though the Gospel should be handed out to the workers as a kind of opium that should now motivate them to set their sights on the world to come while forgetting the world here and now. No! No!--What a wretched Christianity to be offered to the masses in such false currency! Such a sermon would be doomed to failure from the start. No, the economic aspirations of the working class for freedom and independence, for equality with their fellowmen, should remain untouched by the proclamation of the Gospel, completely untouched. We who presently find ourselves in possession of social power exercise that power not for our own sakes but for the sake of the working class; our desire and efforts are all for your sake, that you may become a true and proper Christian. The earthly goods, as everyone knows, are not enough to nourish a man. And while a certain amount of earthly possessions is undoubtedly a prerequisite for human existence, still, what is earthly is and remains dust for the human soul. What is earthly cannot satisfy a person or give him what he needs to live. Inasmuch as Christianity gives you community with God through Christ our Lord, it also gives you life, true life, inexhaustible vitality, heaven on earth, heaven in the depths of your heart.

77. *The Contribution of the Reformation****

The Reformation left no stone of canonical law standing on top

---

*Rudolph Sohm, "Der Christ im öffentlichem Leben," *Verhandlungen des 28. Kongresses für innere Mission in Posen vom 23. bis 26. September 1895*, pp. 35-36.

**Rudolph Sohm, *Der Arbeiterstand und die Sozialdemokratie: Zwei Reden gehalten in öffentlicher Versammlung des Evangelischen Arbeitervereins zu Leipzig am 27. März 1896*, p. 12.

***Rudolph Sohm, "Weltliches und geistliches Recht," *Festgabe der Leipziger Juristenfakultät fur Dr. Karl Binding zum 7. August 1913*, p. 69.

of another. Not merely the world of faith was transformed, but the
entire world of law as well. A spiritual law no longer existed,
likewise no spiritual authority. No greater revolution of the
entire legal system has occurred since. The world was freed from
coercive spiritual power. The independence of secular law, the
sovereignty of secular authority, the responsibility of all public
power to the state--all of these ideas which have provided the
conceptual roots for the modern state have received their religious
justification from the Lutheran Reformation, and only in this way
have they obtained their power to become fully effective. The
Lutheran Reformation was a renewal not only of faith but also of
the world--the world of spiritual life as well as the world of
law.

Ernst Troeltsch

78. Troeltsch on Luther's View of Natural Order (1911)*

At this point, however, a whole host of other reasons appear
which explain why Luther rejected "sectarian" views. These reasons
are not directly connected with the idea of grace. As a matter of
course Luther regarded secular institutions and natural possessions
as appointed and ordained by God. Nature and the life of the senses,
a humanity almost entirely dependent upon mutual help and organization, government and property, law and oath, war and violence--all
is willed by God; therefore this social order has its good side;
so far as the rest is concerned it is an inevitable state of affairs,
and is necessary, owing to the presence of sin, as the arena in
which the conflict with evil must be fought. The Christian, therefore, is not set in the midst of a social order controlled solely
by the radical Christian ethic of the Sermon on the Mount, nor by
the mysticism which preaches self-denial and detachment from the
world. As an individual, of course, in questions of personal piety
and in the sphere of purely personal relationships, the Christian
is bound to try to obey this higher law. But the Christian also
belongs to the secular order of Nature and of reason.

The third characteristic of the Lutheran ethic, therefore--the
acceptance of the secular institutions of reason--of law, might,
compulsion, and property--which is connected with that universality
which tolerates the non-realization of the Christian ideal, is
also interpreted in a fresh way. It must be admitted, however, that
in the main Luther here carries forward the Catholic ecclesiastical

---

*Ernst Troeltsch, *The Social Teaching of the Christian Churches*,
tr. Olive Wyon (New York: Harper Torchbooks, 1960; 2 volumes
consecutively paged), pp. 499, 502-503.

idea of a Christian unity of civilization as something which is absolutely natural and obvious.

But this acceptance of the natural order is now no longer interpreted in the mediaeval sense, in which the natural order and all its institutions are placed under the control of the Church, in order to serve the purpose of life in the supernatural order. In the Lutheran ethic these secular institutions become pure forms and presuppositions; in themselves they have no meaning. Luther's view is that these institutions have either been appointed by God directly, or by reason, indirectly--that therefore they are implied in the creative order of reason and the Divine Law; it is, therefore, the duty of a Christian to accept them just as he accepts sun and rain, storm and wind. This situation happens to be that which has been definitely appointed as the one within which Christian love ought to be exercised, and Christians have no right to leave this sphere for self-chosen conditions of life. The right attitude towards them, therefore, is not the acceptance of the natural order as of a lower stage of development, regulated by the higher standpoint of the purpose of the Church and the community, but it is that of obedience to conditions of life willed by God, which provide natural opportunities for exercising the Christian spirit of love. The intramundane political and social ethic has thus been changed from a doctrine of relative ethical values which have to be subordinated to the supreme aim of Supernature, into a doctrine of forms and presuppositions of the Christian way of love appointed by God, which lie ready to hand in the ordered and law-abiding life of the State, with its guild and class organizations. These forms can be understood from the natural law of morals, and their apparent inconsistency with the Christian ideal can be explained by their adaptation to the conditions of fallen humanity; the right attitude towards them, however, is not one of explanation and ethical acceptance, but of religious obedience and humble submission.

Wilhelm Hermann

79. *Theology and Secular Knowledge**

The resolution of the problem dare never be described in the form of a compact between religion and knowledge which theology-- with a furtive glance backward at the results of secular knowledge-- would have to mediate. If it is true that the Christian world view does not conflict with secular knowledge because it is not the product of that knowledge, then this fact must become most evident

*Wilhelm Hermann. *Die Religion im Verhältnis zum Welterkennen und zur Sittlichkeit: Eine Grunglegung der systematischen Theologie.* 1879, pp. 450-451.

89

at that point where the Christian world view develops according to
its own laws apart from all secondary objectives. Hence we have
just as little reason to question the grounds for the universal
validity of the Christian faith, with its tendency toward universality
(relying, of course, upon spiritual means)--which it necessarily
must have--with the objection that these principles must first be
verified on the basis of the solid authority of secular knowledge.
Rather, we present these principles just as they are interpreted
by faith itself. At the same time, it is a fact that the universal
validity which the Christian faith claims for itself can neither
be confirmed nor refuted on the basis of secular knowledge. That
claim arises from the assumption that everywhere where moral
communication is cultivated among men, there the private life is
idealized as so unique a reality that it can no longer be compared
with anything else that can be known. But no theoretical knowledge
is able to prove such an assumption; the assumption itself is the
product of an existing moral community, the result of a moral law
that compels us to think morally about those with whom we come in
contact. We hold before others, however, the confidence that the
content of the historical life of Jesus as reflected in the New
Testament and in the Christian community will convince them too
that this is God's own revelation. To be sure, the riddle which
may confront them as selfless workers in the world of experience
will not be solved in this manner. But the Christian revelation
of God holds out to the searcher after knowledge the key to the
riddle of his own being. Inasmuch as he is not morally depraved,
the searcher after knowledge shares a similar desire to preserve
his individual life; this view of life becomes clear to him as he
dedicates himself freely to the moral order in order to affirm it
as a reality that is independent of the world. That this desire
can be satisfied in the world view which is based upon trust in
the historical Christ is the certainty which endows every sound
Christian sermon with its convincing character and its power over
the spirits. As long as dogmatic theology is satisfied with
explaining the inner grounds for this certainty and as long as it
examines only those objects of faith which we can truly establish
in this manner, then it has not the slightest objection to raise
against a secular knowledge whose assistance it most certainly does
not seek.

80. *The State as a Product of Nature**
     The state is the political order that is administered by a

---

     *Wilhelm Hermann. *Ethik.* 5th ed. (1913), pp. 213, 217, 223.

governing authority, by which a group of human beings bound together by common ties of nature and history seek to maintain themselves in a sense of common identity.

The first thing that the Christian must realize before he can participate in a state is that the state is a product of nature and therefore cannot be love but only self-assertion, coercion, and law. The second thing is that the state in its natural form, that is, as God created it, can be used as an agent for the moral purpose, and that this insight has certain consequences. The state is not a product of moral sentiment; but it can and ought to be utilized by those to whom it is entrusted as the most powerful earthly tool for the realization of the moral purpose.

Once the Christian has understood the moral significance of the state, then he will consider obedience to the government to be his highest vocation within that state. For the authority of the state on the whole, resting as it does upon the authority of government, is more important than the elimination of any shortcomings which it might have. Should the Christian, due to moral scruples, be unable to carry out his government's command, he will not preach revolution but will gladly suffer the consequences of his disobedience. For the person who is inwardly free, it is more important that the state preserve its historical continuity than that he obtain justice for himself.

Secondly, the Christian must see to it that the government actually administers the law in the course of the continual trans-formation, expansion, and even contraction of its obligations over against his fellow-countrymen. Yet the form in which the Christian seeks to exert this influence upon the government of his nation as a whole cannot be derived from Christian moral sentiment alone but must be sought on the basis of unique historical relationships.

Thirdly, the Christian must seek to promote patriotism among the citizenry. The joy of the masses at the might of their civilized state can only increase among them as they observe that the state, far from suppressing their aspirations for improving their condition, is actually doing its best to stimulate and safeguard the same. The Christian must desire the government, but he must also desire that it remain, for all its power and glory, only as a channel for the life that is springing up from out of the depths of the nation.

CHAPTER 5

LUTHERAN CHURCHES IN EASTERN

EUROPE, SOUTH AFRICA, AND LATIN AMERICA

INTRODUCTION

In this section three brief examples are offered of the development of reflections on questions of political ethics in three very different geographical areas: Eastern Europe, South Africa, and Latin America. One purpose for introducing these materials into this reader, despite their brevity, is to provide a historical basis for understanding the events of the twentieth century. A second one is to take note of the fact that Lutheran ethical reflection was by no means confined to German theologians, although in the instances here cited German influence remained paramount.

Hungary: Hungarian Lutherans constituted a minority evangelical church in the predominantly Roman Catholic Austro-Hungarian Empire during the period which this reader covers. Because they were not permitted to have their own theological faculty, as well as for other historical reasons, these Lutherans were heavily dependent upon German Lutherans; their pastors for the most part received a German education. Under the circumstances we must not be surprised to discover in the literature the same misunderstandings, the same dualism, and the same servitude to the state which characterized German theological reflection.

South Africa: During the nineteenth century Southwest Africa (today's Namibia) became the scene of German colonial and missionary undertakings. Thus we have a setting for examining another kind of question in Christian political ethics: How shall a mission relate to a colony?

Interestingly, it was not a foregone conclusion that the mission should serve the interests of the colonial power. Indeed in a rather self-conscious distinction from Anglo-Saxon missionary enterprise (which flourished mightily during the great century of missionary expansion) some writers wished to stress both more modest and less political intentions. The dangers of being merely the instrument of secular policy are recognized.

Yet for the mission and for its converts the mandate of obedience to "the governing powers" remained. The possibility of an independent course of development for the indigenous population was not entertained. German tutelage of one's "missionary children" was a must. Such tutelage included instruction in skills serviceable to the colonial power as well as inculcation of submission to constituted authority. Under these assumptions the political ethic of Christian freedom was totally submerged in the requirement of obedience.

The reaction of missionary leadership when the African population rebelled against heavy-handed paternalism and oppression can be read from the last selection; basically it communicates a sense of outrage that one's "children in the gospel" could sin so wickedly. The missionary mind was at one with the colonial.

Brazil: Brazilian Lutherans, as the essay which H.J. Prien has contributed makes clear, are transplanted Germans who for a long time continued to maintain their German identity within the confines of a Latin American, Roman Catholic state. Although a minority in Brazil, the pattern of their settlement made it possible for the Germans to continue not only their Lutheran religious practices but also to preserve their German language and customs. In Brazil we consequently confront a phenomenon, occasionally attempted in North America, which provides another variation in which a Lutheran ethic could unfold, namely, the attempt to survive as a German-speaking cultural and religious enclave. Prien draws to our attention the long continued sense of dependence on German leadership, on a German rather than a Brazilian identity, as these Lutherans struggled for autonomy. For them the nineteenth century can only be a prolog.

A. EASTERN EUROPE--HUNGARY

*81. Istvan Schneller: Concerning Religion**

With the help of the national genius, the moral order of the world has organized in our land a state. This state has set an

---

*"Ueber die Religion," *Protestantische Rundschau: Theologische Zeitschrift* (1907), p. 582.

example in guaranteeing religious, national, social, and individual
freedom. Our various confessions and denominations exercise
sufficient influence to be able to establish intimate contact with
all of the national groups on the intellectual level. On the
cultural level, our national minorities have the attractive vocation
of mediating our cultural treasures to the neighboring nationalities
while in turn interpreting their literature to us; this cultural
exchange serves to promote friendship among the various nationalities.
Such a lively and valuable mutually reciprocal activity enriches all
the nationalities, deepens the noble national feeling, and strengthens
the moral responsibility for the home (which ought to be served
with heart and soul so that it too may strive to serve humanity and
the Kingdom of God). Once we understand the nature and vocation of
our national state in this sense, then our home will become a
microcosm in the midst of a macrocosm, that is, humanity or the
Kingdom of God. Whoever performs his civic duties with this understanding also serves the true God and prays to the Father in spirit
and in truth as his Christian faith requires.

On the basis of such an understanding of our national state,
we can begin to grasp the profound statement of Richard Rothe,
that the church should attach herself more closely to the state so
that faith may then determine our daily life as well as our holidays.
Thus our entire life and activity will be influenced by God's Word.
In this way, believers, even when they are creative citizens, can
become members of the Kingdom of God, indispensable, irreplaceable
organs having an absolute value.

82. *Lajos Csiky: On the Pastor's Role in Public Affairs (1908)**
The pastor's first and foremost obligation is to adapt himself
to his congregation, above all that he make an effort to inform
himself thoroughly about all church matters and become intimately
acquainted with them. It would be completely wrong to expect him
to carry out a vigorous activity in other areas that are unrelated
to his main profession before he has completely fulfilled his own
work-program, clarified his methods and aims, and set his pastoral
activity into motion according to plan. The pastor should not
interfere with public social life but should participate in political
and related public activities only after he has already performed
his duty at home, that is, in his own profession as a conscientious
servant of God, in keeping with the universal high opinion and
recognition which he enjoys. Before he has done this, it would be
completely wrong for him to crown himself with secular laurels upon
the public stage. Public opinion is more inclined to accept a pastor

---

**Theologia Pastoralia* (Budapest, 1908), p. 218.

who places **his** **priority** upon worldly pomp and thunderous applause, who uses his talents and eloquence to make a great impression upon a large audience, than one who devotes himself to quiet and unassuming pastoral care, where the main concern is salvation and peace for the individual soul.

Many believers are seriously upset whenever a pastor takes his official authority and dignity into the whirlwind of political life. If he already plays a leading role in public life, the pastor ought to handle himself similar to the ship at sea, which lies in the water but swims on the surface. In political campaigns, the pastor ought to keep in the background, since such campaigns often lead to muddy paths and contaminated waters. It is of vital importance that he not promote the political program and ideas of any particular party from the pulpit, for by such action he may unnecessarily drive away from the house of God those members of his congregation who share a different political opinion. Those pious people who wish to hear the Gospel in the church and who wish to be strengthened and comforted by God's Word may be irritated by a political pastor, since Jesus did expressly state that His Kingdom is not of this world. On the contrary, political ideas--which are transient, earthly, and usually entirely specious--do not enjoy a long life. Politics is and remains the science of our earthly existence.

How should a pastor decide in the event that the public trust offers him a seat in parliament? In this instance, he should conscientiously consider whether or not his activity in parliament would bear fruit, not only for the fatherland but at the same time for the church and the Kingdom of God. The criterion in this case is obviously that the pastor must make a valuable contribution to the Kingdom of God. Both civil society and his fellow-believers expect without fail that a pastor who is simultaneously a political official should express himself factually in parliament, making his knowledge and influence felt in questions concerning Christianity or his own church body. And if he expresses himself in such a way that a touch of homesickness comes into his voice, this too rises in the direction of the heavenly fatherland and the Kingdom of God!

83. *The Two Worlds (1918)**

Every Christian is a member of two worlds. The just person lives by his faith. Through faith, he strives to become a citizen of eternal life and a member of the communion of saints. In his vocation and through Christian love, he is obligated to serve his neighbor; he must work for and also with that same neighbor.

---

*Dietrich Vorwerk and Jacob Wallrabenstein, *Der Spiegel des Pastors* (Budapest, 1918), p. 34.

The Christian is appropriately compared with the inhabitant of a worldly city whose house lies at the edge of a shady forest. A beautiful blue sea enlivens the landscape. Roses bloom, doves coo, and everywhere is heavenly peace and quiet. The person who lives in this earthly paradise travels by train into the big city every day. There a factory is located from whose chimnies smoke belches forth day in day out. Gigantic machines rustle, rumble, rattle, clatter, and roar. Stains of dust cover the dark windows. Pale, unhappy workers scurry this way and that way. Here the worker must perform his work. This is his home by day.

The fact that the Christian enjoys citizenship in the world to come at the same time that he is active in this world represents a continual paradox between the eternal and the transitory, the divine and the human, the perfect and the perishable, etc.

B. SOUTH AFRICA

Mission for the Kingdom of God or Colonization for the Secular Kingdom

84. *Mission Policy (1885)**

But if we now greet the German colony in South Africa with joyful hearts, it is important that we not close our eyes to the misgivings and dangers which are posed for us by the same. First of all, it is important that we ourselves clarify this matter and not allow the obvious recognition that mission and colonization are two different matters to be obscured by patriotic enthusiasm.

Colonization serves to expand the power and reputation of our beloved German Fatherland, whereas mission work wishes to serve the expansion of the kingdom and the honor of our heavenly king, Jesus Christ. Hence we do not wish to hopelessly mix together **here** things that are actually dissimilar nor to confuse them with **one** another. It will be better for both if they are clearly and distinctly held apart, for history teaches us that nothing good ever comes from missionaries founding colonies or from the colonial power performing mission work. But just as church and state back home are often forced to assist one another and to work hand-in-hand for the benefit of the entire people, the one showing the required consideration for the other, so it is with mission and colonization abroad.

That is what we must desire from the entire heart, and that is the task for which we and our foreign missionaries as well have **warm**ed our entire hearts, that a peaceful and friendly relationship may exist between mission and colonization. Thus, everywhere where

---

*Excerpt from *Berichte der Rheinischen Missionsgesellschaft*, 1885.

it is possible to do so, the one should gladly and willingly support and work hand-in-hand with the other, so that each shows the proper consideration for the other at all times. That this latter development may actually materialize for the German Empire as a colonial power and for the colonial societies as well is the goal to which our every hope and desire is directed.

85. *Missionary Enterprise and the Coming of the Kingdom (1915)**

We no more believe in a gradual progressive development of mankind toward the Kingdom of God than we believe that the progress of culture down through the centuries can be equated with the coming into being of the Kingdom of God. We do not believe that the Christian by his own effort can bring about a condition of universal peace. That would amount to projecting the idea of progress, which the world presently finds so intoxicating, onto the concept of the Kingdom of God and thus revealing a poetically lovely vista of a future golden age. Idealists and utopians who imbibe from this vision are satisfied to be able to lend a hand in realizing it, and they undoubtedly release much honest energy through their activity. But this is no biblical view of human history!...

The antithesis of Kingdom of God and world is becoming a question of conscience for the mission. That is a process of development which--as we heard yesterday--England, North America, also the Netherlands and France, have all passed through in one form or another. The mission activities of these lands have thereby been damaged grievously in their inner life. They have been harmed by an unhealthy fusion with international political and business interests, with Anglo-Saxon cultural expansion, and with American secular ideals. We would prefer to preserve for the life of the German mission the precious jewel of her pure religious motivation. Such concern is justified. But the above-mentioned task that is set before us remains inescapable. One cannot avoid the danger by sticking one's head into the sand like an ostrich; rather, one must confront it with clear vision and a brave heart.

---

*Julius Richter, "Besteht eine Gefahr der Verweltlichung unseres Missionslebens?" Lecture at the Herrnhuter Mission Week, October 14, 1915, *Nationalität und Internationalität in der Mission,* published by the Brandenburg Mission Conference as a result of the First World War, pp. 44, 48.

The Obedience Befitting Loyal Subjects: Mission Support for the
Ruling Colonial Power

86. Christianity Not Utopian (1859)*

It does not help our situation when we indulge in long-range
reform projects or seek to entice and stimulate the Christian world
with impressive and optimistic plans for the future. Such projects
and utopian dreams always end up placing more emphasis upon our
own activity and performance than upon the creative work and activity
of the Lord--even when this is not intended.

87. The Duty of Obedience (1863)**

Let us take note of this very simple and yet very important
fact.... First, the congregation of Jesus--now known as the church--
is in no single time or place under any kind of obligation to ally
itself too closely with any one particular form of government,
especially since governments in this earthly life are of necessity
constantly undergoing change. On the contrary, the only obligation
which it owes to any political authority that has ever existed and
been established at any single time is the active offer of obedience,
the loyalty which is required of a subject, and--in keeping with
Paul's important advice in his first letter to Timothy--the obligation
to conscientiously make intercession for it. Should the Christian's
political obligation extend further, and should he himself or the
church as a whole be permitted in a Christian sense to meddle in
political questions or to choose sides in them, then I really do
not know how it would be possible for one to avoid the reproach
of God's Word that He has left us entirely without advice in this
all-important aspect of life. Indeed, if that were allowed
according to the Scriptures, then the Scriptures themselves would
of necessity have to indicate not only the most ideal form of state
but also which state is in itself morally good and which morally
bad. But there is so very little evidence of such concern; the
Holy Scriptures themselves never directly attack the institution
of slavery--an institution which plays such a vital role in the
entire socio-political life today--no matter how diametrically
opposed the existence of slavery may be to the sense and spirit of
the Scriptures. Thus, even when a political conflict arises over
the question of slavery, a Christian can never substantiate his
occasional solidarity with the anti-slavery party on the basis of
God's Word. With even lesser right can he do so with respect to

---

*Friedrich Fabri, *Ueber den christlichen Staat* (1859), p. 168.
**Friedrich Fabri, *Die Stellung des Christen zur Politik*
(Barmen, 1863), pp. 30-31.

other questions that concern the political parties.

88. *The Mission as Educator (1904)**

   The inhabitants of our colonies cannot remain in their natural condition. They are by nature mostly untamed and warlike, whereas the colonial administration wants people in its territory who are orderly, well-bred, and peaceful. The natives are by nature lazy and work no harder than they must, whereas the German planter wants willing and hard-working laborers. The natives are by nature unpretentious, whereas the trader hopes that they will buy all of the beautiful wares which he lays out in his shop--and as payment for these wares, he wants them to bring him as many products of the soil as possible. If the native population is ever to satisfy these desires, they must be raised out of the childlike state in which they presently find themselves to a higher level. They must lay aside their bad manners, just as they must learn how to extract greater yields from the rich tropical soil in order to pay for the "necessities of life" which they have so recently discovered and in order to develop a resistance against the dangers which the European culture is so rapidly bringing down upon them.

   In short, the natives must be educated. Here is where the mission steps forward and announces: "That is my task. I am prepared to act as educator in our colonies, just as I have done in other of our Lord's lands." That is not the mission's ultimate and highest purpose. Its ultimate purpose is and always remains the obligation to bring the Christian faith to the heathen and the Moslems. But she cannot do this without at the same time setting into motion a great deal of educational energy in other areas. The education of the native inhabitants is, so to speak, a by-product of their Christianization, and it is quite acceptable to the mission that she is able in this way to be of service to the politicians, business interests, and other colonists. For the sake of her higher purpose, the mission should not undertake common activity together with her fellow-countrymen in secular professions. She must rather-- even in individual instances--offer herself as the spokesman for the natives, since she is by her very nature in a better position to gain their confidence. So much the better, then, that the mission has something to lay on the scales in order to do a great service for her fellow-countrymen.

---

*Pastor Paul, "Die Mission als Erzieherin der Eingeborenen in unseren Kolonien," *Flugschriften der Hanseatischen-Oldenburgischen Missions-Conferenz* (Bremen, 1904), p. 2.

89. *Pastoral Letter to the Herero (1904)**

Dearly beloved in Christ Jesus:

It is not easy for us to attach such a title to this letter.
Our love for you has suffered a rude shock on account of the terrible
rebellion in which so many of you took part and on account of the
awful bloodshed, as well as the many atrocities associated with
the rebellion, for which you also share at least co-responsibility,
even if we still hope that only a few of you were directly involved
in these atrocious and murderous deeds. But our Savior's love
never ceases. It pursues the lost sinners to save them and make
them holy. The father continues to love even the prodigal son who
has left his father's house and has trampled upon his father's will,
just as he is prepared to forgive the same son as soon as the son
returns penitently to the father and says: "Father, I have sinned
against heaven and before you and am henceforth no longer worthy to
be called your son." It is in this spirit that we continue to refer
to you as "dearly beloved in Christ Jesus."

We dare not conceal from you that you have made us very unhappy
and have caused us great sorrow. Our heart bleeds when we think
of you, as the heart of the father bled when the prodigal son turned
his back on him. You too have set out upon a path which will
inevitably lead you to misfortune, and you will perish miserably
unless you soon recognize your error and repent. You have raised
the sword against the government which God has placed over you without considering that it is written: "Whoever takes the sword shall
also perish by the sword."

C. LATIN AMERICA--BRAZIL

90. *Historical Overview***

Evangelical churches of the reformed variety first originated
in Latin America as a result of immigration from the German-speaking
areas of Europe. Our restriction of these sources to Brazil is
justified by the fact that Brazil was the first Latin American state
to concern itself with non-Iberian immigrants--the immigration of
German-speaking elements had begun already in 1824--a fact which
led the congregations founded by these colonists to join together
into loosely organized synods at an early date. Following such an

---

*Hirtenbrief der Rheinischen Mission an die Herero-Christen,"
Rheinische Missionsberichte (1904), pp. 349-351.
**Especially prepared for this volume by H.J. Prien of Hamburg,
formerly professor of Church History in the Lutheran seminary in
Sao Leopoldo, Brazil.

unsuccessful initial attempt from 1868 to 1875, Pastor Rotermund, holder of a doctorate in theology, finally succeeded in founding the Rio Grande Synod in 1886. This was followed by the Evangelical Lutheran Synod of Santa Carina, Parana, and other Brazilian States in 1905, the Evangelical Union of Congregations of Santa Catarina in 1911, and the Middle Brazil Synod in 1912. Their joint merger in 1968 is regarded as having formed the largest evangelical church of the Lutheran Confession in Latin America, with a combined membership of some 700,000 members. By comparison, it may be noted that the German Evangelical Synod of Rio de la Plata came into being in 1899 and by the year 1900 embraced just ten congregations.

The unique ecclesiastical situation of the evangelical diaspora congregations of Brazil in the nineteenth century arose from the fact that the majority of the evangelical immigrants came from the simple rural classes and brought along with them a correspondingly rudimentary ecclesiastical tradition. They were supplied in many places by a clergy of non-theologians who were scarcely better trained, with the result that the intellectual and spiritual tone was more or less set by a group of ordained pastors dispatched from Germany in numbers far below what was required. The situation was further complicated by the fact that the Protestants, as non-Catholics who were opposed to the Roman state church, were allowed to conduct private worship services only in buildings which could not be recognized as churches from the outside. The immigrants were second-class citizens in a political sense as well, since they were valued for their labor, as compensation for the reduced numbers of imported slaves. It was not long before they attained a certain social recognition in a slave-holding society which regarded all physical labor as demeaning.

The evangelical colonists scarcely protested against their status quo, since they were unaccustomed to political freedom from Germany and thought in a vague pietistic sense "that the Christian dare not meddle in politics, since politics is corrupt, and if the Christian participates in political life, he too can become contaminated."[7]

The legal achievement of political equality in 1880 was largely the result of personal effort by liberals like the journalist Carl von Koseritz of Porto Alegre, a member of the generation of 1848 revolutionaries. Koseritz and Rotermund joined together for the first time in 1881 "to struggle shoulder-to-shoulder for the strengthening of the German nationality."[8]

The attainment of political equality made the struggle for religious equality appear that much more promising. In a monarchy

101

with state ecclesiastical patronage, comparable in many respects to the legal privileges enjoyed by Protestant princes in Germany, Rotermund attempted in 1885 to persuade the government to form an ecclesiastical consistory for the evangelical congregations, thus providing them with a public legal basis and enabling the individual congregations to unite through official administrative channels. Apparently, he also anticipated a resumption of certain state measures in support of the church as had been customary during the first half of the nineteenth century. Certainly this was analogous with the support enjoyed by the Catholic Church, and the Prussian ambassador Eichmann had engaged himself for such a step already in 1863, but in vain. The government, however, ignored these requests and thus helped the evangelical congregations to avoid what would undoubtedly have developed into a questionable dependency of the church upon the state.

With somewhat more self-assurance, the congregation of Santa Maria ventured in 1886/1887 to construct a church building that was recognizable as such from the outside because of its belfry; this step provoked the intervention of the police as soon as it was completed. The newly founded Rio Grande Synod collected over 8,000 signatures in a petition to the legislature requesting modification of the restrictions which they regarded as being discriminatory. Complete religious freedom had already been successfully pushed through the Senate by the liberal Senator Silveira Martins as a response to this request, but it failed to overcome the resistance of the Chamber of Deputies. The latter had been placed under intense pressure by the ladies of Rio de Janeiro, who had gathered their own collection of signatures in opposition to the demands of the non-Catholics--demands which they considered to be a more or less blasphemous attack upon public morality. The republican constitution of 1891 proposed the establishment of full religious freedom while simultaneously granting to the churches the fundamental right of assembly. This step, however, was not felt to be entirely adequate in terms of the Gospel's claim to the right of open accessibility. On the other hand, the Protestants, in contrast to the Catholic Church, welcomed the separation of state and church, as well as the full religious freedom which was implied in this step, as a victory for their cause. Thus the fiction of a state religion that had restricted all non-Catholics was finally abandoned. The elimination of the colonial patronage system clearly defined the spheres of church and state: On the one hand, it met halfway the fundamental idea of Luther's doctrine of the two kingdoms by granting the church independence and room in which to function; on the other hand, it contradicted the same doctrine with its ideological rationale, in keeping with liberal thought, which limited the church to the sphere of the private and inward, thus implicitly acknowledging a right for political activity to function according to its own built-in laws (i.e. *Eigengesetzlichkeit*).

Granted that Rotermund demonstrated foresight when he warned of a Pandora's box, nevertheless, he too was theologically naive with respect to the problem of German nationality. For him, as for the overwhelming majority of pastors, German nationality, German language, German culture, German virtue, and German character were well-nigh identical with the evangelical church. Since the Kingdom of God always manifests itself in a concrete form within a distinct nationality, for anyone to despise or abandon this nationality was equivalent to heresy. A national church body that defined itself in this way granted to nationality a kind of de facto equality with the confessions by interpreting nationality as a natural order of creation (*Schöpfungsordnung*).

Three observations should be made in closing:

1. In these and other sources from the same time period, reference is never consciously made to the doctrine of the two kingdoms as such. Thus it can be assumed that the doctrine had been forgotten.

2. The struggle for political and religious equality, conducted with political weapons and in alliance with the liberal party, after some initial hesitation, indicates that those forces which asserted that the church and politics have nothing to do with each other did not prevail. The dissatisfaction with the church's prevailing right of assembly on the part of a few far-sighted persons in 1891 indicates clearly that what was peculiar to the church was in no way regarded as something to be restricted to the private and inner sphere of life.

3. A dangerous perversion of the doctrine of the two kingdoms is to be noted, however, in the concept of nationality as a natural order of creation (*Schöpfungsordnung*), that is, as a God-pleasing development in which the natural order operates according to its own inner laws (i.e. *Eigengesetzlichkeit*). This unevangelical de facto relegation of nationality to the Kingdom of the Right Hand was to confront the synod with a difficult test in the course of its subsequent history.

91. *Request for the Establishment of a State Consistory for the Evangelical Congregations (1885)* *

Dr. Wilhelm Rotermund, pastor of the congregations of Sao Leopoldo and Lomba Grande, addressed a request in the name of his congregations to the legislature in Rio de Janeiro on May 30, 1885, asking that a consistory be established for the evangelical congregations in Rio Grande do Sul in order to legally regulate the relationship of the evangelical congregations to the state.

"We want our children to inherit our evangelical faith. We cannot accept that our church should be ridiculed and laid waste as happens now, owing to the lack of a legal arrangement. Therefore we request of you that you regulate the evangelical church in a legal manner." The details of the regulation would be left up to the *assembleia*, or parliament. One significant demand was stated, however: "A governing body is necessary, to be given the name of consistory, church council, or something similar; it must consist of three pastors, two laymen, and one government representative, with the condition that all be members of the Protestant Church."

The Brazilian government did not comply with the request to regulate the relationship with the state that was here so clearly expressed. Not only was the political thinking of that time-- four years prior to the proclamation of the republic and under even stronger influence from positivistic ideas than in 1863-- opposed to such a request, but the further loosening of the ties with European thinking in state-church questions that was to follow the end of the empire, as well as the full incorporation of Brazil into the general American development and into the American way of thinking about the relationship between state and church in particular, lay before the **door.** The order which Dr. Rotermund desired would have result**ed in an** extremely tight bond with the state. It was furthermore completely out of touch with the political thinking that was now gaining the upper hand in Brazil. In 1886, a year after the proposal by the congregations of Sao Leopoldo and Lomba Grande, the evangelical church of the German immigration had to content itself for a second time with a constitution for the Rio Grande Synod that failed to provide the legal foundation by which the synod could have put its relationship with the state on a more satisfactory basis.

With the proclamation of the republic, the evangelical churches obtained their full freedom, something which they could only welcome, now that the church had thrown off the last restrictions upon her effectiveness. But on the other hand, already in 1885

---

*Article by President Dr. Hermann Dohms in the *Sonntagsblatt* of the Rio Grande Synod, Nos. 11/12 (March, 1939).

Dr. Rotermund had correctly designated this as a Pandora's box. With positivistic impartiality, the state of the first republic took no further interest in the church. That was the church's own affair. But in its liberal way of thinking, the state had also granted to the church the right of assembly, thereby relegating the church juristically to the private sphere. That had to inhibit the church's development, since the church is no ordinary "association" and cannot express her true nature constitutionally as an "association" within the state. The church has a public responsibility and hence requires a special legal guarantee of her public status in order to protect her in the fulfillment of her responsibility and to direct her—and here the state on its part must show the greatest interest!—to her appropriate place within the state.

92. *Document 2: Request of the Rio Grande Synod to the Legislature (1887); Legal Regulation of Religious Freedom**

Illustrious and worthy representatives of the nation!

The executive committee of the Rio Grande Synod, as the legitimate representative for the evangelical congregations in this province, presumes to seek your invaluable intercession that Article 5 of the imperial constitution be annulled—inasmuch as it restricts the exercise of non-Catholic worship services—and likewise Article 276 of the criminal code, which follows from the first-mentioned article.

According to these articles, non-Catholic worship services are allowed and tolerated in this empire, but it is expressly forbidden that they be celebrated in buildings having the form of a church or that they be celebrated publicly in any locality. The constitution tolerates the immigration of evangelical colonists, but nothing, nothing at all, is allowed to remind the Catholics that there are citizens who do not profess the state religion. When the building in which the evangelical congregation assembles in any way resembles a church, when the members of the Protestant congregation accompany the remains of a deceased brother in solemn procession to his final resting place, when clergymen pray at the grave of a fellow-believer, or when they come in official dress to bring the holy sacrament to a sick member—in all of these and other cases, they violate the constitution and are punishable according to the regulations of the penal code. The Roman Catholic religion is the state religion, but those in the land who profess another religious faith are not allowed to identify their site of worship by means of the external sign of a church building, as though any other worship apart from Catholicism

---

*From the Archives of the Rio Grande Synod, Sao Leopoldo, Brazil.

were a disgrace and an insult to our land.

Illustrious and worthy representatives of the nation! What
if such a suspicion as is found in the above-mentioned articles is
to be upheld? How wounded must be the feelings of every one of
the more than 40,000 Protestants of this province, not to mention
the feelings of their brothers in the remainder of the empire--your
fellow-citizens!--who engage themselves by their labor and, when
necessary, with their blood, for the greater good of the common
fatherland!

It is true that the stipulations of the constitution and of
the civil code in this province have remained a dead letter for the
past thirty years. The laws lie dormant, and only for this reason
can non-Catholics hold their divine worship services in churches
and in public. What a lamentable situation! At any moment the
laws can spring back to life, and those Protestants who have dared
to demonstrate their faith in public can be prosecuted as common
criminals; at any moment, they can be exposed to the greatest
chicanery by means of the above-mentioned articles, especially since
these articles are completely lacking in any kind of definition as
to what constitutes the external form of a house of worship!

Gentlemen! We are not imagining these things! They are really
happening! They are actual fact! It should be enough to recall
a single incident which occurred recently when the police of the
city of Santa Maria da Bocca do Monte in this province, at the behest
of the chief of police, forbade the members of the evangelical
congregation in the same locality to assemble in their own church--
a decree from this same month and year threatens criminal charges
upon disobedience--and all because the building is adorned with a
steeple!

His excellency, the Vice-President of the province, Dr. Rodrigo
de Azambuja Villanova, however, after he was confronted with the
complaint about the incident, concurred and gave counter-orders.
This is a praiseworthy step in the right direction, since it is
the sign of a fairer, more enlightened, and more tolerant spirit--
yet it still violates the prevailing regulations!

It is unworthy that a part of the Brazilian citizenry should
stand outside the laws and that they should exist only by the grace
and goodwill of the authorities. It is contradictory to the spirit
of our century that one religion be privileged while the others are
merely tolerated under the condition that their worship not be
celebrated before the public. What prevents you, who have so
generously granted to non-Catholics political equality with Catholics,
from approving religious equality as well and expurgating Article

106

5 from the constitution and Article 276 from the criminal code?
These articles, already rendered obsolete by the spirit of the age,
stand in the way of our land's progress, its immigration policy,
and the welfare of Brazil's non-Catholic citizens.

93. *German Nationality and the Gospel**

At the end of my last synodical report, I expressed the fervent
desire that a mighty wave of enthusiasm for what is essentially
German might come in the next instant and wash away all inclination
for non-Germanic languages and customs, that a brightly burning
flame of evangelical heroic courage might consume all indifference
and inertia. When the great struggle suddenly erupted (i.e. the
First World War), I hoped, along with many others, that this desire
would be fulfilled. My present opinion, however, is that we expected
too much from the profound emotion and excitement which this has
unloosed among us also. Certainly, our pride at being German has
soared to new heights, and even many who seemed to have forgotten
this fact now recall with pride that German blood also flows within
their veins. With the utmost singlemindedness, the entire German
colony has voluntarily gathered gifts and has contributed generously
to alleviate the distresses of war among our fellow-countrymen on
the other side of the ocean. Our congregations have also proclaimed
in magnificent fashion their inner solidarity with the fighting,
bleeding, and sorely afflicted German people in the native homeland.
We have not only conducted divine services of intercession in time
of war, but in each Sunday devotion our prayers rise to the disposer
of battles; the events of war are diligently utilized to bring the
Word of God closer to the heart, conscience, and understanding....
However, when we ask whether this gigantic conflict has influenced
the actual convictions of our people in a German-evangelical sense,
then we will probably receive an overall negative answer.... I do
not notice that the preference of so many families and circles for
using the Portugese language has in any way been halted or that
what comprises German culture is cultivated more intensively now
than previously. The news from the theaters of war, in all of its
variety, keeps us constantly aware of what our Lord God thinks about
all the watering down and changing of His Word and Will, reminding
us of the great strength that lies hidden in the sacrificial will
of the unconquerable German nation.... But scarcely anyone can
argue that the contemplation of a faith which is maintaining itself
in powerful struggle, likewise the heartfelt piety and eagerness to

---

*From a lecture by Pastor Dr. Wilhelm Rotermund at the 26th
Synodical convention of the Rio Grande Synod, May 1916 in Santa
Maria, Brazil in *Synodalberichte*, 1914-1958, pp. 16ff.

confess one's faith which have revealed themselves in such an exemplary and touching manner, has actually brought us any farther out of our religious indifference.

We are instructed by the experience which we have made in this respect to acknowledge as true the assertion that the Kingdom of God is built only by the Word of God and the sacraments, and that the external destinies, events, and experiences only serve to promote morality and piety where the church's means of grace have first pointed heart and mind in the proper direction. That Word of God teaches us to perform our vocation faithfully and vigorously and to esteem that office which preaches reconciliation and redemption as the chief factor in the rebirth of both the individual and the entire people.

Wherever in the entire world German loyalty and conscientiousness, German strength and love, are cultivated, inherited, and propagated from generation to generation, there the evangelical church, with all its institutions, must show itself as the indispensable and most effective main spring. That we here in Rio Grande have still managed to retain so much of our German nationality among us is the Gospel's doing; indeed, many congregations have just recently been won back to the German nationality as our church has set herself to work. But if, as is now apparent, German nationality finds itself on the decline, then the fault for that lies in indifference to the Gospel. Whoever ceases to feel and to think of himself as evangelical stops being a German, and vice versa, whoever denies the German language and the German character will also be lost to our church. German nationality and the Gospel are bound to one another in life and in death. That is why the work of our synod is so important and every obstacle that lies in its path so momentous.

PART III:

THE DEVELOPMENT OF DIVERGENT ATTITUDES TOWARDS

POLITICAL RESPONSIBILITY AMONG LUTHERANS IN THE UNITED STATES

INTRODUCTION

The settlement of large numbers of Lutherans, coming from the various German states, the Scandinavian countries, and Eastern Europe, provides us with the possibility of looking at an entirely different context in which Lutherans could articulate a political ethic. The diversity of the experiences of these Lutheran groups, as well as the initial differences among them, provides us with comparative data on the encounter of groups of Lutheran heritage with the problems and opportunities of a new environment. If the dearth of explicit references to the doctrine of the two kingdoms strikes us as strange, the reason for its absence is not in any failure to articulate responsible ethical insights on various occasions.

We must remember that resources for the theological study of Luther, as well as the availability of his biblical commentaries, devotional and other writings, were greatly limited until recently. Lutheran clergy and teachers had to draw on a small range of materials, often on compendia that presented edited excerpts two or three times removed from the original author's work.

To understand what happened we must keep three things in mind:

1. *The newcomers brought differing kinds of religious traditions with them.* Some were German pietists, bringing with them their Bibles and Arndt's *Wahres Christentum*; others were Haugeans, strongly committed to lay initiatives. Still others brought the books of their favorite Lutheran dogmatician. Another group was in rebellion against ecclesiastical oppression. Finally large numbers probably came for economic reasons, often indifferent to the religious

arrangements of either homeland or host country.

2. *The incoming Lutherans arrived at different times and settled in different places.* Some of them were genuine pioneers; among them the strength to survive may have counted more than pious subservience and theological subtleties. Some found homes in the flourishing urban centers of the North, contributing their skills as brewers or musicians, craftsmen or mechanics to the growth of both old and new cities. Still others found the rich soils of the cornbelt and the wheatlands of the plains attractive. They followed no single pattern in the New World, no more than they came from a single homogeneous source in the Old.

3. *The settlement patterns were also quite different.* A few Lutherans succeeded in building closed cultural and religious enclaves; most found themselves living in continuing interaction with neighbors of different religious persuasions. In some parts of the Eastern United States (Southeast Pennsylvania, Western Maryland, Rowan County in North Carolina, to name a few) Lutherans have constituted a major part of the population for two centuries. Along with others of German descent they gave their region a unique cultural quality, that of the Pennsylvania Dutch. We can locate similar concentrations--Norwegian, Swedish, Finnish, as well as German--in Michigan, Wisconsin, Minnesota, the Dakotas, Iowa, and elsewhere. Not all of these settlements were closed cultural enclaves, but in some measure they put a stamp upon their communities of settlement. We could, in addition, list major urban concentrations which differed from the rural ones. Unfortunately most of the sociology of such settlement patterns remains unwritten; we can only point to the important variables we have identified.

Out of the interaction of these factors we can identify, first, two major groups of incoming Lutherans, as well as three different groupings in terms of which we can describe their responses to the American environment. Finally, we may also identify three different models for dealing with the world.

1. *Colonial Lutherans:* One major concentration of Lutherans consists of the descendants of an early migration of Germans which reached its peak before 1750. These Lutherans were part of a larger German migration, including Reformed and a variegated group of believers of Anabaptist and other sectarian persuasions. Many of these Germans, the Lutherans included, were under strong pietistic influences.

These Germans settled in a number of places along the Atlantic coast: in the Hudson River valley of New York, along the Schoharie in the same state, in the Carolinas and Georgia. The majority of them however settled north of Philadelphia and in southeast Pennsylvania, gradually spilling over into western Maryland, the Shenandoah Valley of Virginia, and down into North Carolina. By the beginning of the nineteenth century they were settling in southwestern Ohio and in the east-central counties of that state.

Except where the concentrations of Germans were dense or the population was augmented by new arrivals from Germany (e.g. in Philadelphia), many of these Lutherans became English-speaking by the third generation. They were heavily exposed to revivalism, not only to the awakenings among the neighboring Scotch-Irish but also the movements in the German settlements which led to the Evangelical Association (Albrechtsbrüder) and the United Brethren (Otterbein.)

The colonial Lutherans, even more than the later migrants, had to shape their own institutions and patterns of survival with little help from their homelands. Not only did they often find themselves short of pastors, but as pioneer settlers in an environment whose major institutional structures were still in the process of formation, these early arrivals had to struggle with gaining a livelihood in an unfamiliar world, with problems of education (often a congregational responsibility), the maintenance of good order, the regulation of family life, and so on. While the Germans did not seem to have had as turbulent a frontier experience as the Scotch-Irish, the early journals, diaries, and other accounts indicate that the establishment of orderly communities required considerable effort. One need not be surprised either at the preoccupation with morals nor at their openness to the revivalist "new measures" of their English-speaking neighbors. One can find similar concerns for establishing morality among Swedish and Norwegian immigrants later in the 19th century.

2. *Immigrant Lutherans:* After slowing almost to a halt for almost three generations, migration from Germany picked up momentum again after 1830. These Germans flowed into the cities of the East and on into the Middle West, into the territory of what became the Joint Synod of Ohio, the Buffalo Synod, the Iowa Synod, the Missouri Synod, and so on. These Germans came from various German states; some came for religious reasons, seeking freedom to practice their faith in ways forbidden in their homeland; others were looking for a better economic opportunity; some--most of them hostile to the church--were the exiles of the abortive revolution of 1848. Many of these Germans had been under the influence of the religious awakenings of the nineteenth century; others were simply nominal

churchgoers in their homeland who found cultural hospitality in the Lutheran churches.

The immigrant Lutherans included tens of thousands from the Scandinavian countries, as well as Germans from German settlements in the Austro-Hungarian Empire and the Russian Empire. Slovak and Hungarian Lutherans also began to arrive near the end of the immigration period. The Norwegians were under strong Haugean influences; Swedish Lutherans experienced the separation between the Mission Covenant people and those who remained within the Lutheran fold; the Danes represented both orthodox and Grundtvigian traditions.

While the Middle West received these Lutherans in large numbers, putting a permanent Lutheran stamp on Wisconsin, Minnesota, and the Dakotas, Lutherans found their way to many other states; some of them settled in the industrial cities of the East; others travelled all the way to the West Coast. While the descendants of the colonial Lutherans were largely English-speaking, these Lutherans for the most part worshipped in their native tongues until World War I and thereafter.

Some of these Lutherans were pioneers, taking up land on the frontier, others belonged to the "settlement" wave of newcomers; i.e., they took over the claims of the original homesteaders, purchased land which speculators had partially developed, or became the customers of the Western railroads. Like the colonial generation many of the immigrants experienced a shortage of clergy, suffering the rigors of the new environment with limited provisions, but in the nineteenth century development proceeded at a faster pace; agriculture was clearly a part of the market system; and major institutional patterns were already established. Unlike the Pennsylvania Germans the immigrant generation had little opportunity to put a strong cultural stamp on their region of settlement.

In the responses to the American environment we can distinguish three major groupings: American Lutherans, cultural isolationists and dualists, and moderate confessionalists.

1. *American Lutherans:* Whether as part of the original heritage, a religious style introduced through the work of Zinzendorf or borrowed from more zealous sectarian neighbors, or a style which the effective ministry of Muhlenberg inculcated, the traditions of pietism shaped many of the colonial Lutherans. After the death of Muhlenberg, the Lutheran churches went through a serious decline. Having made America their homeland, these Lutherans moved to the task of shaping their own ecclesiastical institutions. The Lutheran awakening coincided with a renewed revivalism in the American churches.

Into this situation moved a young American-born son of the parsonage, Princeton-educated Samuel S. Schmucker. While his reputation suffered greatly in the controversies which he himself initiated, Schmucker contributed greatly to Lutheran survival. He provided these Lutherans with a seminary, a general organization, and a series of theological works that helped establish a major American tradition.

Theologically Schmucker's work fell short of confessional norms, but culturally he defined what it meant to be Lutheran. Schmucker's strength, however, lay in his recognition of the challenges of his generation. Through his students and friends, through his leadership, and through the columns of the *Lutheran Observer*, he shaped a particular tradition in American Lutheranism.

Whatever Schmucker's theological shortcomings, in political ethics--consciously calling upon the writings of the Reformers--he gave positive content to the political duties of magistrates and citizens. He insisted on the responsibility of government for the public welfare; he underlined Christian responsibility for promoting and preserving just institutions; he stood up to be counted on the question of slavery.

Schmucker's son-in-law, Samuel Sprecher followed loyally, but in his theological reflections we can see the pietistic concern for experience grow into an emphasis on the personal subjective dimension. Thus for him the inner life (consciousness) plays a larger role. But neither in Sprecher, nor in others, did American Lutherans surrender to a sharply dualistic model. Even in the encounter of science and theology the accent in Sprecher falls on the harmony of these domains rather than upon their separateness. Sprecher saw the world as a unity under the sovereignty of God.

American Lutheranism, like many of its Protestant contemporaries, more and more fell prey to the temptations of legalism, attempting to write laws making the United States an explicitly Christian nation. Yet upon occasion, their theologians--like Richards--could recall the essentially Lutheran focus that love finds its expression in service to neighbor. More than other Lutherans, they were open to the Social Gospel.

The response to slavery reveals one facet of the American Lutheran response. While one cannot rule out the continuing influence of their pietistic heritage, the Franckean Lutherans (descendants of Palatinates who had settled in the Schoharie Valley) also lived both in considerable isolation from their fellow Lutherans and in the very track of the sweeping great revival in western New York. Some of their pastors came under the influence of Charles G. Finney, the revivalist. Most explicitly than any other Lutherans, they made a strong witness against slavery.

Unfortunately the Franckean stood almost alone, with only the Pittsburgh Synod offering similar testimony. The impulses probably came from the equalitarianism inherent in the pietist strain of American Lutheranism; most American synods, however, did not stand up to be counted. Indeed it took the Franckeans more than two decades to become part of the General Synod, and their entry helped trigger the conflict out of which the General Council (moderate confessionalism) emerged.

2. *Cultural Isolationism and Dualism:* While the Franckean Synod was forming, another group of Lutherans was landing in Missouri. A conscious Lutheran identification, which more than once led them into quarrels with German benefactors, a sense of separation from the American scene, and a deliberate commitment to the German language led these Lutherans away from involvement in the communities where they had settled. Aggressive missionary effort among immigrants of German origin, thorough indoctrination of their pastors and teachers, and the persistent claim that they were indeed the rightful guardians of the pure Reformation heritage fostered continuing growth with little apparent compromise of their identity. They used a literalistic hermeneutics to establish teachings to which they then clung with a legalistic insistence.

Wilhelm Sihler, in early life a Prussian army officer, then a pastor in Fort Wayne and president of the practical seminary there, expressed the stance of many Missourians in his articles in *Der Lutheraner*. In the midst of the Civil War he could argue that slavery is not anti-scriptural. Not surprisingly he found American ways disorderly; he was at one with many of his German contemporaries in his preference of order to freedom.

The doctrinal quarreling in which many of the German Synods in the Midwest became involved allowed them little time for dealing with the question of the Christian's relationships to the world. The church and the German parochial schools many of the congregations sponsored provided the necessary instruction for the German immigrants. Beyond this, they minded their own business and worked hard to prosper. In this model of political ethics church and state go their separate way.

The response of the Scandinavian immigrants to the new environment finds its chief focus in their attitude towards slavery. When some of the more orthodox Norwegian clergy agreed to an alliance with the Missouri Synod by furnishing a Norwegian professor to help in the preparation of clergy for their needy congregations, they failed to take into account the commitment to freedom which the

Norwegian laity had brought with them. The Haugean strain made its
most remarkable contribution to the Lutheran ethic in the revolt of
the laity against the clergy's acceptance of Missourian views on
slavery. The result may find its typical incident in Claus Clausen's
twofold shift of allegiance: from pro-Missouri to the anti-Missouri
Brotherhood and from the Democratic to the Republican party. Large
numbers of the Norwegian immigrants joined in his political choice,
as did the Swedes, whose ecclesiastical leaders almost took
Republican affiliation as a matter of confessional orthodoxy. The
review of the slavery controversy which Bredesen offers shows clearly
how a doctrine of authority triumphed over an understanding of freedom
in the development of a Lutheran ethical response and how a generation
or more later the old battle lines remained fixed.

The Missouri Synod was by deliberate choice a German-speaking
body. Yet very quickly it had to deal with the fact that some of
its members found English a more congenial language. Obviously,
if the loyalty of these believers and of their pastors was to be
kept, instruction had to be provided for them in the English
language. Parts of the doctrinal and ethical admonition these
Lutherans received are found in the selections from articles with
which A.L. Graebner filled the pages of the *Theological Quarterly*
(later *Theological Monthly*). Here we have straight forward
exposition of the tradition; the continued espousal of the notion
of three major institutional complexes in terms of which human
life is lived and the insistence upon rigid separation of spiritual
and worldly affairs. Graebner and his successors did their work
well; several generations later the ideology of separation still
dominates a large number of the leaders of Missouri Synod Lutheranism.

3. *Moderate Confessionalism:* Even during Schmucker's life
time his program for the revision of the Augsburg Confession called
out opposition. Thus in southeast Pennsylvania, in the very home
territory of American Lutheranism, a separation occurred. Under
the leadership of Charles Porterfield Krauth, himself a student of
Schmucker and American-born, a movement began that sought rather
consciously to reestablish the confessional identity of the Lutheran
church in the United States. Shortly after the Civil War the
General Council came into being with a seminary in Philadelphia,
with strong support from many of the pastors and congregations of
the old mother synod, the Ministerium of Pennsylvania. In the
Atlantic States the General Council attracted into its membership
many of the new immigrant Germans, including immigrant pastors,
some of them educated at mission schools in Germany. In this setting
we discover many Lutheran pastors coming under the strong influence of

Erlangen. Heinrich **Schmid's** *Dogmatik der ev. luth. Kirche dargestellt und aus den Quellen belegt*, translated by H.E. Jacobs and Charles Hay in 1876, became a standard work for seminary instruction; by 1890 thirteen seminaries used it as a text. Thus in many ways, while still claiming its American heritage, the General Council resisted the Americanization of Lutheranism in the United States.

Henry Jacobs and Theodore Emmanuel Schmauk are two of the leading voices. It is immediately apparent that on political questions the American situation remains paramount; here one must speak of citizens, not just of subjects. Here active participation is called for. Indeed, in many ways some of the pietistic heritage shows through, particularly in Schmauk's concern for the poor. Out of the encounter of these two elements arises an interesting amalgam: a recognition on the one hand that the American environment called for a more active Christian response, but with a careful direction of that response into the development of personal character and the support of private charity. The Social Gospel of Walter Rauschenbusch was not accepted. The ethic of R.F. Weidner, a contemporary of Jacobs and Schmauk, provided for an ethic of personal obedience, the development of the moral virtues proper to the citizens of the Kingdom of God without a clear grasp of the freedom of the Christian person. In ethics and public policy the moderate confessionalists probably differed little from their American Lutheran neighbors. Some of the brief selections from the *Lutheran Church Review*, the Philadelphia faculty's theological journal, show how much the influence of legalism, even of a pietistic emphasis upon the new birth remained in this group.

Quite different from the German accent on the importance of authority is the resistance to authority found in American Lutheran discussions of polity. The primary Christian reality is the local congregation, consisting of both pastor and people. The power of government moves from the bottom up through a system of representation and delegation. While we can trace this commitment to democracy in part to the American environment, we must not overlook the theological rationale found in the conception of evangelical freedom, an eloquent exposition of which we find in S.A. Repass' concern for the new being, the Christian person as one set free to live in a new way in the world.

J.H.W. Stuckenberg. No discussion of nineteenth-century American Lutheran reflections on questions of the response of the Christian to the world can omit the work of J.H.W. Stuckenberg. Educated at Wittenberg in the General Synod mold under Sprecher, a parish pastor, a civil war chaplain, then a teacher at Wittenberg (where he introduced one of the first courses in sociology in an

American college), an early pioneer of the social sciences, Stuckenberg spent the most fruitful years of his life as pastor of the American church in Berlin. He was thus clearly at home in the Lutheranism of his native land as well as in that of America. When he returned to the United States, he found himself out of step with growing confessionalism, even in the General Synod. In a climate in which discussion among those who disagreed strongly served largely to fortify previous positions, he could find few Lutheran platforms for his views.

In many ways what Stuckenberg had to say clearly reflected the major biases of his century. Because of his scientific concerns, he was somewhat closer to the German liberals than to the confessional school. Yet it is worthy to note that though he continued to think in the dualistic terms of his age, he drew the lines differently from many of his contemporaries. For him the central distinction was between the natural and the human; the spiritual and the personal had much in common. By bringing the world of human social institutions into close relationship with his understanding of the personal, he found that in fact believers belonged in the world of neighborly obligation. The personal and the social were inseparable. Thus despite continuing elements of legalism and of the General Synod distrust of traditions, Stuckenberg had reintroduced pieces of the Lutheran ethic that had long been forgotten. The individual Christian could not live in isolation from his neighbors.

One can only speculate what might have happened had Lutheran theologians and ethicists engaged in open dialogue with this creative mind. A more adequate response than the increasingly passive withdrawal into the cultivation of personal virtues might have been possible. But it was not to be. While the growing confessionalism had not yet rediscovered the two kingdoms as a doctrinal entity, its proponents clearly rejected a teacher who brought the spiritual and the worldly together in ways unfamiliar to them.

CHAPTER 6

AMERICAN LUTHERANISM

A. THEOLOGICAL VOICES - SCHMUCKER, SPRECHER, AND OTHERS

94. *S.S. Schmucker on Civil Governance (1834)**

In regard to political affairs our churches teach, that legitimate political enactments are good works of God; that it is lawful for Christians to hold civil offices, to pronounce judgment and decide cases according to the imperial and other existing laws; to inflict just punishment, wage just wars and serve in them; to make lawful contracts; hold property; to make oath when required by the magistrate, to marry and be married.

I. *The Confessors do not pronounce any particular kind of governance of divine origin.*

II. In this article the *Confessors clearly represent the welfare of the people as the proper end of all civil governments.* The legislative power is to be exercised in the production of "just laws." The judiciary is to be conducted on equitable principles; "for the judgment to be given is just." "Just punishments" alone are to be inflicted, "the right of property," and "the obligations of contracts to be observed," and "the duties of both civil and domestic life are to be performed in the spirit of Christian benevolence."

All human government is but an approximation to justice; nor is it possible for anything short of infinite wisdom, either to frame a code of Laws, or execute one, in which the various interests of all the citizens and of every section of country can be perfectly

*Samuel S. Schmucker, *Elements of Popular Theology* (1834).

adjusted, and the punishments be minutely graduated to every shade of guilt. Yet the worst government is better than entire anarchy, and the majority of human polities secure to their subjects a far higher degree of happiness, than could be attained without them, whilst some few confer on man all the blessings that he can reasonably ask. Christianity does not prescribe an exclusive form of government, but the observance of its precepts on this subject will alleviate the burdens of the worst, and, fully acted out, will eventually conduct to the adoption of the best form, under which man is capable of living. It clearly points out the security and happiness of the people, as the end to be contemplated; and leaves to the experience and judgment of men the adoption of the polity by which, at any time and in any nation it can best be secured. Had the divine Savior prescribed any form, it would doubtless be the republican; for such is essentially the form of government which he gave to his church, as may be seen in the Formula annexed to this volume. But the grand design of his appearance on earth was not to erect a political fabric, but to redeem the human family, and establish a spiritual kingdom; in which the sons and daughters of men, by nature aliens from the commonwealth of Israel, should be elevated intellectually and morally, and qualified for citizenship in heaven, for participation in angelic felicity in the celestial empire of Jehovah.

III. *The Confessors inculcate the justice of revolution in those governments, which fail to accomplish the just end of their establishment.*

Yet is there a class of our population in regard to which these fervid inspirations of patriotism above quoted, would be the keenest irony. Alas, that in reciting them, the image of the poor enslaved African should rise up to our view, who after the lapse of half a century, yet groans in bondage among us, a reproach to our political system, and a violation of the rights of "equal" man! To the honour of Pennsylvania and the States north of her, be it said, that they have given liberty to their captives. Some Western States have, in constructing their constitution, nobly excluded slavery. Our Southern fellow-citizens are also often unjustly censured; for not only had the present generation no agency in introducing slavery into the land; the great majority of them are in favour of some rational plan of abolition. Himself a native of a slave state, and for many years resident among slaves, the writer is convinced that those who advocate entire, immediate abolition, do not understand the subject. This great work has its difficulties. But it is feasible. The experience of Great Britain has in several instances

demonstrated it on a small scale. Reason and justice demand it;
and the recent glorious resolution of the British parliament, in
regard to their West India Colonies, will, we trust, place it
beyond all doubt. The work, in justice to the master, and in mercy
to the slave, must be gradual; but its commencement ought to be
delayed no longer.

95. *The Church as the Guardian of Public Morality**
    *The Christian pulpit, the rightful guardian of morals in
political no less than in private life.*

    It is our purpose I. *To prove the obligation of the Christian
pulpit to occupy this ground,* and

    II. *To exhibit the prominent instructions which it is her
duty to inculcate.*

    I. The claim of the Christian pulpit, as the exponent of
Christianity itself, to tender some instructions to man in regard
to his political interests and duties, is already implied in the
fact, that Christianity has established her right to sit enthroned
above all science, and especially all departments of human,
responsible agency. There was a time when infidels expected to
entrap the Bible on the ground of its relations to physical science,
and detect its author in blunders; but the progress of investigation
has dissipated all these delusions, and Christianity stands out
before the world, fully vindicated as the handmaiden of universal
knowledge, and as consistent with all truth. Her inspired records
were not designed as a text-book of universal science, physical
and moral, as was formerly maintained by some visionary minds in
Great Britian, such as Parkhurst, Hutchinson, and others, but as a
revelation of moral or religious truth. And as moral relations run
through all the agency of man, physical and intellectual as well as
moral, and political as well as physical; it is obvious that
Christianity, which first placed these relations in their proper
light before his eyes, has some lessons of instruction concerning
all his conduct, and therefore also his political action.

    Again, if man be responsible to God at all for any of his
actions, even for his religious conduct, such responsibility must
also extend to his political agency; for it is undeniable, that
the political institutions of a country exert a vital influence on
its religious condition, and on the progress of the Redeemer's
kingdom on earth.

    II. What are the nature and extent of the instructions of the

---

*S.S. Schmucker, *The Christian Pulpit,* a Thanksgiving Sermon,
November 26, 1846.

inspired volume on this subject.

These instructions may in general be characterized as belonging to the *morals of politics*, and consist in the application of the principles of the *moral law* to the discharge of political duties, both by rulers and subjects or citizens.

To correct prevailing errors on this subject, we shall first specify some supposed political virtues which the Christian pulpit cannot teach:

1. The scriptures contain no instructions on *mere party politics*, and that minister who employs the sacred desk to give utterance to his views, however sincere they may be, on such topics, undoubtedly descends from the high vantage-ground which it is his privilege to occupy; and loses his claim to that deference with which the appropriate instructions of the pulpit ought ever to be received.

2. Nor can the Christian pulpit inculcate *that unprincipled species of patriotism*, or love of country, embodied in part in the motto, "Our country right or wrong," professed by many, which justifies fraud, injustice, robbery and oppression towards other nations, for the benefit of our own...

Let us now pass on, and, in the second place, specify the positive instructions of the Christian pulpit on our theme.

1. She inculcates *the recognition of God, as the Supreme Ruler of all nations, and the precedence of his claims over those of Caesar.*

It seems to be a dictate of reason, that he who is not only the Creator, but also the Governor of the Universe, and by whose delegated authority all lawful rulers on earth govern, should be recognized by them, and the precedence of his claims be conceded alike by rulers and people. This is accordingly demanded in explicit terms, by the work of God, and must be inculcated by the Christian pulpit. "The powers that be," says the great Apostle of the Gentiles, "are ordained of God;" not intending thereby, that God established any one particular form of government; but that it is his will that mankind shall be formed into civil polities and be governed by civil rulers, in short that *government is an ordinance of God.*

But our obligation to acknowledge God in our civil relations does not stop here. We are taught to regard this duty as absolute, we are informed by his word, and therefore the Christian pulpit is bound to teach, *that the laws of God must have precedence over those of man*; that if our earthly rulers command us to do, what our heavenly ruler has forbidden, "He that dwelleth in the heavens," is to be obeyed, rather than the worms of the dust that inhabit his footstool; in short, that we are to "obey God rather than man."

122

2. The second general duty which the Christian pulpit is called on to hold up to the view of our rulers and fellow-citizens in their political action, is *to recognize the universal brotherhood and equality of man in civil rights.*

This relation requires citizens to exercise *impartiality in selecting from the whole body of the community the best qualified men for office,* regardless of family influence, or party spirit, or bribes.

Again, the universal brotherhood of man requires, that *rulers should enact such laws as bear equally on the whole population.* All human legislation is at best but an approximation to equal justice; yet many of the grossest violations of this principle are intentional, and deserve severe reprehension. That such cases should exist in the despotic and regal and aristocratic governments of the old world is not remarkable, for there equality is not professed. But in our boasted republic, where all men are said to have been created equal, and entitled to certain inalienable rights, all unequal legislation is an inconsistency, and, when intentional, is justly condemned by every enlightened and impartial friend of our race. Of this character are the laws of different free States, which withhold from the colored man some of those equal rights which God has designed for him, and especially those laws in the District of Columbia and other slave States generally, by which he is stripped of personal liberty, is deprived of those inalienable rights, which by our own profession, and by the universal judgment of civilized man, belong to him as well as to ourselves. Such laws cannot but be offensive to the Great Parent of the universal brotherhood of man, of the privileges of which they are gross violations, as they also are of some of the precepts of the decalogue and of the fundamental ethical principles of Christianity....

3. The Christian pulpit is bound to *inculcate the obligation of the moral law of God, in all legislative, judicial and executive business of our public officers and all political action of private citizens.*

A few practical *inferences* shall close this discourse.

1. From this subject we learn in the first place, that the Christian pulpit has an important work to perform in preserving and promoting the moral purity of our political institutions.

2. It is evident that Christians generally, and the community at large, have also an important part assigned them, in promoting and preserving the purity of our political institutions. This is supereminently the case in all representative governments. There the people select their own rulers, and thus virtually themselves

make and execute the laws of the land, through their representatives. It is therefore the duty of all parties to nominate men of unblemished moral character for all offices. It is utterly unimportant with what religious denomination they are connected because under our happy constitution all denominations enjoy equal rights; and our legislatures have no power to enact laws giving preference to any religious sect; but all our officers should be men fearing God and loving justice.

Another part of the work devolved by Providence on Christians and the community at large, is to labor for the correction of all immoral, unequal, and oppressive laws. If laws are enacted inconsistent with the public faith, or with the laws of God, or the universal brotherhood of man, either by our State or National Legislatures, they should be repealed. As a patriot and a Christian, I feel bound to bear testimony against the unjust laws relating to our despised and often oppressed colored population.

*96. Duality and complementarity of consciousness and science--Samuel Sprecher**

a) We have thus found the facts of the world-consciousness, the moral consciousness, the religious consciousness, the Christian consciousness, the intuitions of the human mind and the dictates of revelation, to be in vital relation to faith and independent of the processes of science. We have seen that the true position of science is not above, but in the light of these facts. Under the guidance of the intuitions of the mind involved in the experience of the common consciousness, she has a large and fruitful field of operation in philosophy; under that of the dictates of revelation, a wide and rich territory for theology. In the one, she can increase the knowledge and foresight of men in the domain of nature; in the other, she can elevate and enlarge their views, enliven and strengthen their hopes in the sphere of religion, and thus augment their power and extend the range of their influence and activity. There is no limit to her attainments, or end to her progress in the light of the self-evident truths of the soul, and the clear facts of revelation. But it is her business neither to ignore nor to demonstrate the insights of the reason; neither to deny nor to prove the discoveries of revelation; but to test our consciousness by the laws of thought, and thus to find what is the real idea, the actual testimony of consciousness, which will always be found in agreement with the true requirements of the thinking mind. And under this direction and

---

*The Groundwork of a System of Evangelical Lutheran Theology (Philadelphia: Lutheran Publication Society, 1879), pp. 71, 329.

guidance she will find that she is walking in the true light of our being.

The principle of the Reformation which thus makes the Christian consciousness independent of science, is so far from limiting the operations or arresting the progress of the scientific mind in natural or revealed truth, that it has given to this spirit its true starting point and its great impulse. It has given greater power and life to all sciences....

Faith and science should be regarded as complements of each other, and as mutually inviting one another. The religious consciousness gives the fact through experience, and together with this, by an inseparable intuition, the idea of religion; science decides whether the idea of this fact is consistent with the laws of mind and matter. Religion gives the realization of the facts; science the intellectual interpretation, the speculative apprehension of it. In their agreement the truth receives its highest and clearest manifestations.

97. *Christian Good Works (1902)* *

Christian good works consist in serving one's calling with faith in God, and with love to one's neighbor. Hence the Christian must stand in his place, wait on his calling, and do good to others as he has opportunity. "Faith is the actor, love is the act. Faith brings man to God, love brings him to man. By faith he becomes acceptable to God; by love he does good to men." Any work, therefore, that makes our fellowmen happier and better is a good work in the Christian sense, provided it proceed from faith.

B. THE SLAVERY QUESTION

98. *The Franckean Synod on Slavery*

From the Constitution**

6. No minister of the gospel shall be a member of this Synod who shall not sign the pledge of total abstinence from intoxicating liquors as a beverage; or who is a slaveholder, or traffics in human beings, or advocates the system of slavery as it exists in these United States.

---

*J.W. Richards, "The Doctrine of Justification in Its Relations," *The Second General Conference of Lutherans in America held in Philadelphia, April 1-3, 1902. Proceedings, Essays, and Debates.* (Newberry: Lutheran Publication Board, 1904), p. 72.
**Proceedings of a Convention of Ministers and Delegates from Evangelical Lutheran Churches in the State of New York,* Fordsbush, Montgomery County, May 24, 1837; p. 9.

Report on Slavery*

That they have considered the subject of slavery, and cannot do otherwise than respond favorably to our petitioners, "to give our decided testimony against American slavery." Remembering the spirit of Christ, we would speak mildly but decidedly. Truth and love are mighty weapons when rightly used, and they are very suitable in putting down all moral evil. Love, meekness, gentleness, with inflexible firmness, are all victorious in removing prejudice and in suppressing vice. TRUTH, with its keen edge, when wielded with the potent arm of love, will do execution. Every Christian and philanthropist, under the proper influence of truth and love, should feel deeply towards the oppressed of our land, that in heart they might realize, and in conduct express the gospel truth uttered by the servants of God, that we should feel for those in bonds as bound with them, and render unto servants what is JUST and EQUAL. We, as a Synodical body, are averse to American slavery, because it is void of TRUTH and LOVE. What is truth but living facts, realities, things as God made them? Slavery violates the nature and high prerogative of man. God made man free in mind and body; but slavery deprives him of liberty, equality in rank, and the opportunities of elevating character and cultivating the noble powers of mind. Instead of retrieving ruined mind, it only degrades it and reduces it to brutal inferiority. Slavery is opposed to the Bible and its claims. The Bible inculcates the marriage institution; but slavery tramples it in the dust. The Bible teaches certain duties of parents and children, such as "train up a child in the way he should go;" "to train them up in the nurture and admonition of the Lord;" but slavery abolishes parental obligation at its own pleasure and without apparent conviction of doing wrong. It enjoins universal and MUTUAL love; but slavery changes love into a selfish passion, and forbids the master to love the slave himself, and commands the slave to love the slaveholder more than himself. The Bible teaches light and knowledge; but slavery, in its worst and mildest forms, keeps back light, and in some states prohibits under penal sanctions the first rudiments of knowledge to be taught unto the slave. To say that it is imprudent to emancipate the enslaved immediately, is virtually to acknowledge their degradation, and the imperative necessity that something should be done to meliorate their condition; --that the yoke of bondage should be broken, and nothing short of it. To aver that the church should not interfere, is to say, that the church has no right to oppose and reform all moral evil and every heaven-provoking sin.

Journal of the First Annual Session of the Franckean Synod of the Evangelic Lutheran Church June 7, 1838, pp. 15-16.

1851

Your committee, upon whom was imposed the difficult and important task of setting forth the reasons which led to the rejection of the resolution to unite itself with the General Synod, would respectfully and briefly report as follows:...

3. The objection, however, mainly urged, was that the General Synod was *identified* with slavery; that delegates being slaveholders are admitted as members, and that we by uniting become implicated in the sin of slavery. This position, though strenuously opposed, even to the last, finally having excited the minds of same, influenced them to cast their votes against the union, hence the resolution for the union was lost.

1853

Resolved, That by uniting with the General Synod, we do not change our relations or position in regard to slavery, as defined in our printed minutes.

*Richard C. Wolf, *Documents of Lutheran Unity in America* (Philadelphia: Fortress Press, 1966), pp. 93-94.

CHAPTER 7

CULTURAL ISOLATIONISM
AND
DUALISM (MISSOURI SYNOD)

A. WILHELM SIHLER

100. On Slavery (1863) *

The net result of all these utterances from the Holy Scripture
(i.e. concerning slavery) as interpreted and applied in conformity
with the literal meaning and with faith is finally this: First,
the Gospel and the faith in Christ which it produces enables even
the person who is in physical bondage to participate in the forgiveness
of sins and in the reception of the Holy Spirit of spiritual
deliverance from slavery to sin and the devil. In and of itself,
the Gospel has absolutely nothing to do with the circumstances of
his physical bondage, since the Gospel affects only the soul of even
that person who is in a situation of physical servitude, starting
with his relationship to God, that his soul might be rescued from
God's wrath and severe judgment and transferred to the blessed
freedom of the children of God. For this reason, the Gospel has
nothing to do with the outer person and with the physical subjection
of the slave to his master, as though it could offer the slave an
opportunity to raise a legal claim for physical liberation from
bondage to his master and make it stick. Nor can the Gospel stipulate
it to be a matter of faith and of love, that is, a matter of conscience,
that the slaveholder grant his slaves their physical freedom on the
grounds that they too are his brothers in Christ.

---

*Wilhelm Sihler, "Die Sklaverei im Lichte der heiligen Schrift
betrachtet," *Der Lutheraner*, February 15, 1863.

Certainly the state is something entirely different from the church. But Christ, together with the Father and the Holy Spirit, still governs both, though His rule for each one varies, depending on the specific nature of both state and church as He has created and ordained them. He governs the church as a spiritual realm, as a kingdom of grace already here on earth, through His Word and from the inside, namely in the hearts of His saints, through faith and love alone, as kindled and maintained by Gospel and sacrament. The Kingdom of Christ is not of this world, that is, not of a worldly kind and quality, nor is it governed like a worldly kingdom, on the basis of laws and commandments and by a worldly prince or by some kind of papal prince. The Lord Christ alone is and remains the sole king of His Church on earth among all the peoples that exist under the heavens and that live within reach of His Gospel, and He rules among His believers with the upright scepter of His Word. The government of the Lord among the kingdoms of this world, however, is another story altogether. There he has delegated governing authority in every direction so that these same subordinates may render the obedience that is their due. They do this by making certain that their laws and commandments do not contradict those which God has written into the heart of every human being, as the conscience of each person bears witness. Here is a God-pleasing antithesis between those who command and those who obey, between those who rule and those who are ruled, and God is not greatly concerned whether or not those who rule carry out their governing in some degree of conformity with existing historical relationships. How they govern is of no great concern to God. They can rule like patriarchs or as unrestricted absolute sovereigns similar to the present and former princes of the western world whose will is law for their subjects. Or they can govern so that their legislative authority is restricted by a parliamentary assembly. Or finally, their government can be organized in such a way that they merely carry out the will of the sovereign people, who actually hold the reigns of political power....

Christians acknowledge the governing authority even in its harshest form, that of unlimited absolute rule, as a beneficial order of God against the coarser outbursts of the corrupted human nature and against the increasing use of violence against the weak and the poor on the part of the godless rich and powerful. They subject themselves willingly even to those rulers who are tyrants,

---

*Wilhelm Sihler, "Welches ist die Gestalt unsrer Zeit und welche Zukunft haben wir zu erwarten," *Der Lutheraner*, August 1, 1863.

although they naturally do not agree with their views. They do
this first for the sake of a good conscience before God, in accord
with Romans 13:1, 4, and then because of the divine punishment which
the Lord metes out against godless subjects at the hands of severe
princes. This chastisement is both necessary and useful for the
Christian's Old Adam and gives the New Man in him that much greater
opportunity to exercise himself in the blessed school of the cross
by practicing faith, patience, meekness, and humility at the hands
of a strict and harsh government. Ultimately, however, they subject
themselves to such rulers from the heart, out of love for the
neighbor, for without their protection and without the fear of their
mighty arm, everything would fall apart, and no one could be certain
of property, wife, or the security of his own person in the face of
violent interference and intervention on the part of the unbelievers
and the godless, nor could he be satisfied with a so-called "rule
of the fist."

Christians, by virtue of their spiritual nobility through faith
in Christ, are already true lords, even kings and priests, before
God, although their glory is still hidden for a short time under
the cross from the eyes of the world. They remain at the same time
subject in body and will to their secular government inasmuch as it
does not command anything that is in opposition to God's command,
offering the government at all times--in keeping with God's command
in Romans 13--honor and fear, service and obedience, prayer and
intercession, taxes and tribute.

B. THE NORWEGIAN REACTION

102. Claus L. Clausen Joins the Republican Party*

In haste I take my pen to write a few lines. If time allowed
I would write at length and present through the columns of *Emigranten*
the reasons which have prompted me to accept the nomination to the
legislature; but I certainly do not have time for that now. My
chief consideration is the hope of uniting all our countrymen here
in northern Iowa in the Republican party; for the realization of
whose principles I, with God's help, entertain the only hope for
checking the further spread of slavery and for the preserving our
free republican institutions from destruction. Thus far my hope
has not been in vain and as far as my election is concerned that
seems quite certain, even though I have encountered no little
opposition due to local differences of opinion. I also consider it
almost certain that the whole Republican ticket will win ·in this
district.

*Fred Swansen, *The Founder of St. Ansgar* (Blair: Lutheran Pub.
House, 1949), p. 124. The statement appeared in *Emigranten* August
15, 1856.

103. *Adolf Bredesen: New Light on the Slavery Controversy*[*]

I now wish to demonstrate on the basis of American Christian biblical scholars and exegetes that first of all the synodical teaching on slavery as such, as well as on slavery in the Scriptures, is good American teaching. It is a fact that all of the generally accepted or well-known Bible commentaries most frequently used at the time of the slavery conflict and still in use to this day were used by laymen and scholars in the American churches to interpret Scripture in the same way and to express the same teaching on slavery as that of the synodical pastors in 1861 and thereafter. Matthew Henry, Pools' *Synopsis*, the *Comprehensive Commentary*, Bishop Patrick, Bishop Lowth, Bishop Mant, Bishop Wordsworth, Whitby, Gill, Thomas Scott, Adam Clarke, D'Oyley, Devenant, Hammond, Doddridge, Macknight, Alford--Episcopalians, Congregationalists, Presbyterians, Baptists, Methodists,--they all teach with one accord that slavery is an evil but not in itself a sin. All of these Bible interpreters declare, together with the synodical pastors but against Pastor Clausen, that the obligatory servanthood about which the Scriptures so often speak is a real slavery, and that this obligatory servanthood is not in itself a sin. Only in the teaching of Adam Clarke--and possibly also in that of Scott--can one find a few comments which Pastor Clausen apparently uses to his own advantage. The synodical pastors know these things, and whoever does not know them and desires proof can have it for the asking by reading the work of Bishop Hopkins, *Scriptural View of Slavery*, pp. 123-225. Hopkins was an Episcopalian bishop in a Vermont diocese; his book was first published in 1863. On p. 33, the scholar Hopkins says the following concerning all the leading American interpreters whom I have mentioned: "None of them can be found denying the main facts, or imputing as *a sin* in any Christian man to own a slave, provided. . .the slave be treated with kindness and justice, in obedience to the precepts of the Gospel. None of them denounces the *right of property* in the master, nor the duty of obedience and fidelity on the part of the slave. None of them maintains the doctrine of the ultra-abolitionist."

C. A.L. GRAEBNER

104. *Christianity and Social Problems*[**]

But there is still another misconception which pervades the entire work before us. The title of the book is *Christianity and*

---

[*]Translated from the Norwegian, "Slaveristriden i ny belysning." *Teologisk Tidsskrift*, (Decorah, Iowa), vol. 7 (1905), pp. 24-25.
[**]A.L. Graebner, review of Lyman Abbott, *Christianity and Social Problems* in *Theological Quarterly* (St. Louis), vol. I (1897), pp. 102, 110-111.

Social Problems. Now the doctrine of Christianity is properly the
Gospel of divine grace in Christ Jesus; the soul of Christianity is
faith in Christ, the savior of mankind; the end and aim of
Christianity is the *eternal salvation* of sinners and the glory of
God; the signature of Christianity in this world is the *cross of
Christ* borne by the followers of Christ. Of all this, however, very
little is said in this book. On the other hand we hear of the
Golden Rule, of Christ's *law* of the family, Chirst's *law* of service,
Christ's *law* for the settlement of controversies, all of which are
not specifically Christian at all, but simply applications of the
moral law, "Thou shalt love thy neighbor as thyself." If this is
Christianity, then Christianity might have been essentially what
it is without Christ, the Redeemer.

Society, at large, or the State, which is society organized
within a given territory under national and municipal laws and a
government with legislative, judicial, and executive functions, can
consistently deal only with the *materiale* of the moral law, and
with that only as far as it relates to the temporal affairs of the
community and its individual members, while it must leave the entire
formale, according to which the law is the exhibition of the holy
will of God, and also the *materiale* of the First Table, to the
religious life of men and to the religious community, the Church.
Civil laws are reasonable and expedient only as far as they can be
generally enforced. But the love of God and man can never be
enforced and should, therefore, never enter into civil legislation.
The love of God and man is the daughter of faith and, like faith
itself, can be engendered only by the Gospel. And the Gospel is
not an aggregate of social principles, but a means of grace, and
was not entrusted to the State, but to the Church, by him who has
ordained that civil government should bear the sword. However
important the social problems dealt with in Dr. Abbott's book may
be, the thorough theoretical and practical separation of Church
and State is of greater importance for the welfare of both Church
and State.

105. *Sermon on the Christian Amendment**

"Christ Jesus Lord of Nations," this is the title of a small
pamphlet issued by the National Reform Association. The object
of this little pamphlet is to show that we, the people of the
United States, ought to acknowledge the divine authority of our
Saviour Jesus Christ in our Constitution and make His Word, the
Bible, our fundamental law, and its moral and civil code the basis

_____

Theological Quarterly, (St. Louis), vol. 1, (1897), pp. 250,
251, 254.

of all civil legislation. It appeals to all true Christians in the
land to use their endeavors for the achievement of such results,
and points out the great benefits that must necessarily result from
such a change in the character of our Government....

Oh that such people would bear in mind that Christ's kingdom
is not of this world, that the worldly government and the kingdom
of our Savior are two different realms, strictly to be kept apart
and not to be intermingled! They would, then, perceive that they
are not fighting for the Lord, but directly against Him, that they
are constantly mis-applying Scripture in defence of their erroneous
position, that they are actually adopting the principle of the
papacy, which is, to promulgate the gospel not by means of the Word
alone, but by means of the sword and temporal power, and that no
good will result, if they should succeed, but that they will only
rear a race of hypocrites and ruin the church of God. Not in the
sense of a worldly ruler is Christ Jesus the Lord of nations.

*106. Ethics, The Moral Spheres**

All the various states, relations, and acts of men determined
by the moral law may be variously referred to various spheres. They
are the spheres of moral *rights* and moral *duties*, and these rights
and duties are either *religious*, or *domestic*, or *civic*.

The Spheres of Rights and Duties in General

The moral law imposes duties and establishes and secures rights.
God created man and gave him existence and human endowments; he
has established various relations between man and man; he has ordained
that man as moral being should in all his ways and days live in
conformity with the divine will. By the law, the utterance of his
will, God would determine man's relations, disposition and conduct
toward God and toward his fellow-men, and inasmuch as the divine
law is authoritative in all its demands, it is man's *duty* in all
these respects to fulfill the requirements of the moral law. And
in still another aspect the moral obligations are duties. By the
divine law men are also bound to each other. God would have us
serve him by serving our neighbor. St. Paul says, *Owe no man any
thing, but to love one another; for he that loveth another hath
fulfilled the law*. 1) Here the fulfillment of the law is conceived
as a debt which one man owes to another and which it is his duty
to pay....

It should be remembered, however, that the rights as well as
the duties here considered are strictly and primarily moral,

Theological Quarterly, (St. Louis) vol. 3 (1899), 385-436
passim.

determined by divine ordinance and law. No human will can by its own authority impose a moral duty or establish a moral right. Nor can human authority absolve any man from a moral duty or annul a moral right as such. When the secular law makes cruelty a cause of divorce, it does not create a moral right, and he who claims such right and acts in pursuance thereof, commits an immoral, sinful act. When civil government imposes a tax, the payment of such tax is not primarily and by human authority a moral duty, but only secondarily and inasmuch as the powers that be are the *ministers of God*, to whom we must be subject *for conscience sake* and *for this cause pay tribute also....*

What these rights and duties, and those of other men and women in their various ways and conditions of life, really are and have been and shall be, will appear as we consider them under the following heads, the *Religious Sphere*, the *Domestic Sphere*, and the *Civic Sphere....*

Religion, however, is not an act or a series or system of acts, but a personal relation in which God is to the individual human person what he would be in such relation, and man is to God what he should be in such relation....

C. The Civic Sphere

When God blessed the first human couple and said, *Be fruitful, and multiply,* 1) he contemplated more than the domestic sphere; for he continued, *And replenish the earth, and subdue it; and have dominion over the fish of the sea, and over the fowl of the air, and over every living thing that moveth upon the earth.* 2) If man, then, was to replenish the earth, multitudes unnumerable springing from the first ancestors of a race, and if these multitudes were to subdue the earth and have dominion over the multitudes of created things in the air and in the sea and on the earth, all this, unless a *bellum omnium contra omnes* should ensue, implied an established order of things beyond the family circle. And as the words quoted were the terms of a blessing, the order of things and its various provisions must be such as to conduce to the well-being of the beings who should be called into existence according to such blessing, that they *might lead a quiet and peaceable life in all godliness and honesty.* 3) Thus, also, St. Paul indicates a distribution of rights and possessions as contemplated and ordained from the beginning, when, in his sermon to the Athenians, he says that God *hath made of one blood all nations of men for to dwell on all the face of the earth, and hath determined the times before appointed, and the bounds of their habitation.* 4) The unity of the race and the multitude of its individual members with their manifold common and individual interests were only conceivable under the supposition of certain fixed principles and firmly established rules which, though variously applied under various circumstances and complications of circumstances, would secure the continuance of the race and the peace and quietude and prosperity of its members....

The assertion and protection of the civic rights of its members is the chief purpose of that form of human consociation which we call the *State*. A State is a community of persons jointly occupying a definite territory 1) and permanently organized under acknowledged laws 2) administered by an established government 3) endowed with or supported by sovereign authority and power to protect the rights of such community and of all its members. 4) The notions of state and civil government are not identical. Governments are the organs of states for the authoritative performance of the various functions of a state. These functions are legislative, judicial, and executive, all of which have in common the great cardinal purpose of statehood and civil government, the protection of the civic rights of the members of the state, or the subjects of the government, *that they may lead a quiet and peaceable life in all godliness and honesty,* 5) or, that they may securely be what God made them and own what God gave them. The proper province of civil government is not the religious sphere, nor the domestic sphere, but the civic sphere. Its purpose is not the salvation of souls and the control and supervision of religious affairs as such. Nor is it the internal government of the family and the performance of parental duties proper. It is the protection of civic rights as such....

Such, then, are the norms of the *justitia civilis*. It is the will of God, that we should *obey present laws, whether they have been framed by heathen or by others.* 1) When Christians bear civil office and sit in judgment, they are to *determine matters by the imperial laws, and other laws in present force.* 2) It is the majesty of these civil laws which must be vindicated by the punishment of the transgressor, and it is the duty of rulers and magistrates, of the judicial and executive organs of the State, to enforce these laws. It is the duty of jurors and attorneys and judges to do what is in their power that every one who has, and no one who has not, offended against these laws may be promptly convicted and duly sentenced according to law and the nature and circumstances of the case, and it is the duty of the executive to let the law take its course in the execution of the sentence....

II

The temperance question must be viewed either as an ethical question or as a political question. It is either the one or the other, not both.

III

Ethically conceived, the temperance question must be, in substance, this: "Is total abstinence from intoxicants enjoined by the law of God?"

IV

Politically considered, the temperance question must be, in substance, this: "Is it expedient for the state to prohibit the production and sale of intoxicants?"

V

As an ethical question, the temperance question can be definitely and conclusively answered only from and according to the word of God.

VIII

As a political question, the temperance question can not and must not be answered from the word of God, and it is not of the province of the state and civil legislation to deal with intemperance as a sin against the law of God, the moral law, but only as a *malum civile*, whereby the civil rights and temporal welfare of individuals or communities are endangered or infringed. Matt. 22, 21. I Pet. 2, 13. See THEOLOGICAL QUARTERLY, Vol. III, pp. 434 ff.

IX

Forasmuch as the cardinal purpose of the state is the protection of society and its members, it is incumbent upon the state to regulate the production and sale of intoxicants in a manner and measure sufficient to afford protection to society and its members. I Tim. 2, 2. Rom. 13, 3, 4, 6.

XI

Inasmuch as the enactments of civil or political legislations are concerned about the *justitia civilis*, their form and substance is not determined by the word of God, but by the dictates of human reason, and subject to the private judgment of those whose duty it is to contribute toward or assist in such enactments. Luke 12, 14. I Pet. 2, 13.

Theological Quarterly, 4 (1900), 153-154.

CHAPTER 8

MODERATE CONFESSIONALISM

A. THEOLOGICAL PRESUPPOSITIONS: JACOBS AND SCHMAUK

*108. The Nature of the State**

1. *What has the State to do with spiritual things?*

It is not a human, but a divine institution (Rom. 13:1-4; I Peter 2:13, 14), for the regulation of the external life, defining the various earthly callings and their duties and prescribing the conduct of men in their manifold relations to each other. It restrains the violence of the ungodly, and to the godly it affords not only salutary discipline, but also important aid in the discharge of their obligations towards both God and men. While often abused as an instrument of unrighteousness, nevertheless, in its ideal form, as well as in its general effect, it gives the Church protection and a place for the latter's administration of spiritual interests.

2. *Does the Heavenly Citizenship of the Christian (Phil. 3:20) justify him in indifference to the prerogatives of earthly citizenship?*

Paul did not hesitate to avail himself of the privileges belonging to him as a Roman citizen (Acts 16:37; 22:25). To neglect them is to fail to use talents which God has given, and to forsake at least part of one's earthly calling. It is God's order to develop our spiritual capacities through our use of that which is bodily; the heavenly, through the earthly; the eternal, through the temporal....

9. *May we not derive the inference hence, that the precedents of Church government in Europe cannot be applied to the circumstances of the Church in America, except with discrimination?*

---

*Henry E. Jacobs, *A Summary of Christian Faith* (1905), pp. 472-484.

The Lutheran Church has never had the opportunity until in America to apply her principles without interference from the State. In every regulation and precedent transplanted from Europe, the influence of the State Church is to be considered, and adjustment to be made to the diverse circumstances of a free and self-governing Church.

10. *Has any particular form of government higher authority than another?*

With constant recognition of the defect of all earthly ordinances, the existing form is generally commended as the best for the circumstances and degree of cultivation of the people who are addressed in Holy Scripture. The desire for radical change is discouraged, except where consistency with the past cannot be maintained without doing violence to conscience. The course of history, the rise and fall of nations, and the modifications in governments are regulated by Providential forces over which even the most influential leaders have but little direct control. Even where their power has been most effective, it has generally been so unconsciously and without any purpose on their part. The Patriarchal, the Theocratic, the Monarchical, the Democratic or Republican forms of government, when established, have all alike divine sanction.

11. *Is the declaration: "Government of the people, by the people, and for the people," strictly correct?*

Theologically, it is not. It seems to ignore the supreme authority and paramount claims of God. But this, doubtless, was not so meant. Such ideal, however, can be realized only when, by the new birth, men enter into the enjoyment of the Kingship which Christ has provided for them (see Chapter XV, 14). We would prefer "Government of God through the people, by God through the people, for God through the people." The secular power is strong and efficient only when firmly laid upon the foundations prepared by God....

20. *Is the State, therefore, without jurisdiction in regard to ecclesiastical affairs?*

The external affairs of the Church enter within a sphere where they cannot be ignored by the State. The Church has a body as well as a soul; and this body, like all other corporations, falls under the control of the civil government. If it is to have a fixed place of worship, it will not be long before it must acquire property by a legal title, and must be able to enforce its right to that property before the courts. If its various congregations are to have any permanency, it must have officers whose time and labor must be secured by the collection of funds: and these funds must be regulated by law. If it is to distribute alms, and to accumulate means by receiving bequests and donations, it will need at every step the aid of legal provisions. As a promoter of public morality, and the greatest prop whereby to support, by moral sentiment, the authority of the government, it can justly ask certain favors and exemptions. As Marriage has both its religious and its civil side, the State often provides for what is practially a combination of the two offices and constitutes ministers officers of the courts for this purpose, under the strict guardianship and supervision of law. It is the duty of the State also clearly to define the limits of the ecclesiastical sphere, and to keep it rigorously within its own bounds, in order that the authority of religion may not be invoked, as has often been done, for what is clearly an infringement of civil law. It may appoint days of fasting, of prayer and of thanksgiving; and under special stress of circumstances ask that the attention of Christian congregations be called to certain subjects closely connected with its supervision. It is also within its power to adapt its ecclesiastical requirements to the distinctive features of the various Confessions represented among its subjects.

109. The Lutheran Church and Modern Religious Issues in America (1898)

But there is another side to the question, and one which the Lutheran Church in this land has been slow to recognize and consider. Wherever the Augsburg Confession speaks of the "Imperial Majesty," of "Electors," "Princes and Estates," who are the earthly sources of civil power, as distinct from magistrates and judges, who are its instruments and organs, there, today, we must read "the American citizen." The same close connection that existed in those days between the individual sources of civil power and the Christian religion exists today between the individual American citizen and the Christian religion. It is not merely the office-bearers, the President, the Governor, the Judge, that the Church obeys, but it is the office creators and controllers in their individual capacity that the Church touches and teaches. Our Church has scarcely opened its eyes to its responsibility in this matter in our land. It has always spoken out boldly of duties to magistrates and office-bearers, but it has failed to realize, that what Luther was to the Elector of Saxony as elector, that the representative of the Church today is to be to the American citizen as citizen.

*T.E. Schmauk, "The Lutheran Church and Modern Religious Issues in America," in *The First General Conference of Lutherans in America held in Philadelphia, Dec. 27-29, 1898. Proceedings, Essays, and Debates* (Philadelphia: Lutheran Publication Society and General Council Publication Board, 1899), pp. 295-296.

In other words, to speak briefly, *the Christian is the State*. There is to be entire separation between the Church and State, but not between the Christian and the State. The "Let alone" policy which Lutherans are apt to assume and teach with reference to the State is a great mistake. Coming over from the old country, they learn to exercise the elective franchise very quickly as political citizens, but outside of *obedience* to the law, they do not see what it means to be Christian citizens. Trained to obey law, they do not seem to grasp Christian responsibility as to the source of that law. They seem to think the State some outside power which has been constituted from above in a way that does not concern them, and which is to go on by itself, or at least without them as Lutherans. All they ask of it, as Christians, is to be let alone by it, and they feel a right to let it alone as Christians, except when some peculiar interests, language or other, are involved. Such is not their right.

110. Christian Social Concern*

This marriage introduced Jesus as the Saviour to the social life of His day....

The social problems of our day are the problems raised by poverty, unemployment, unwillingness to marry and have children, the break-up of home-life, love of amusement and the streets, drunkenness, and extreme social inequalities. Many men and women are looking forward to a reconstructed society in which the heavy burdens at present lying on them will be lifted, and they themselves will enter a new world of freedom and happiness....

Now what does the example of our Lord Jesus teach us on this great subject?

1. First of all it teaches us that happiness is not to be found in plenty of food, money, comfort and idleness; but in a soul at peace with itself, a soul redeemed by His precious blood; and a life lifted by love and service....

The lesson of His life is not a glorification of poverty, especially such poverty as we see in our American slums. His was a clean, self-respecting poverty. There was sufficient for the needs of the day. What His life teaches is that it is possible to live the fullest, best, and happiest life in very meager circumstances. It does not teach, however, that grinding hunger, hateful, unsanitary surroundings, and wearing one's life out to earn less than a subsistence, is a blessed thing....

---

*Theodore E. Schmauk, "A Social Arbiter," *The Living Christ* (1923), pp. 80-86. This sermon was probably preached before World War I.

4. We must take a deeper look at Jesus' devotion to the outcast and the oppressed. Because they were not respectable, or even because they were public sinners, was no reason to Him for passing them by, and having nothing to do with them. Please notice that what He gave them was not money, but *Himself*....

The average Christian is willing to let this work be done by missionaries and social workers, and then to blame the Church because he is being taxed so often to support them in their work. Jesus gave *Himself* to the weary and heavy laden. He invited them all to come to Him. He was *on the lookout* for men and women who needed Him and with love He tried to draw them up into the hope and faith in which He lived. It is because you and I do not sufficiently do this, because we keep to our own class, because we sit in our own comfortable pews, and do not concern ourselves with what is going on around us, that the Church is blamed as a failure today, and that its enemies claim that it is subsidized by wealth, and only wants the higher and respectable classes in its midst....

6. Jesus insisted further that the Kingdom of God is a spiritual reality. He declared it is not enough to be simply a good man, or even a redeemed man. There is a kingdom here to which we belong, composed of those who are children of the one Father. God's grace works on men and makes them His sons and these sons are united in one kingdom awakened to the Father's love. It is the grace of God, working on the soul, and not merely better wages or the abolishing of poverty, that is going to save the world....

7. And yet this kingdom is a regenerated society, a social system transfigured by love and mutual service. We are to be bound into a brotherhood, instead of being alienated by class feeling, we are to live together trustfully in the peace of God, untormented by care, and each and all contributing to the common welfare as we are able instead of striving for our own personal supremacy.

The Kingdom of God is to be fulfilled by personal service on the part of Christ's disciples. Jesus trained men to live for this kingdom. He put His own Spirit in them. He implanted in their hearts His love for the poor, His unworldliness, His faith; and He sent them out to bring this kingdom into the lives of others,--to the poor, to the sick and to the outcast.

We also are bound to the service of Christ's kingdom and **are** constrained to spread it, to make it a reality, and to carry its brotherhood, joy, holiness and faith, to those who are outside of it. We are to be good Samaritans, to the classes in trouble....

We are to be a leaven amid the darkness and hopelessness of

society. We are to bring our Christian convictions into school
boards, charities, town councils, legislatures, business, and
wherever we circulate. We are at all times to stand fearlessly
for the rights of the down-trodden. We are not to ignore any
appeal for fundamental justice in our civil life....

111. *The Social Gospel (From a letter of Theodore E. Schmauk to
Walter Rauschenbusch)**

We do believe in a vigorous and thorough treatment of social
questions by Christians in the State, but we believe that this work
should be done by them as citizens, and not as Christians. We do
not believe it to be the province of the Church to enter as a Church
upon the problems of society or of the body politic. We believe
in the old-fashioned doctrine, which is good also for America, of
the complete separation of the functions of Church and State, and
in the training of the people in the Church to such a point of
principle and of conscience as that they will carry their Christianity
into the State. We believe that the organization of the Church
for the passage of society measures bears many evils in its train,
not the least of which ultimately is the Roman principle of the
right of the spiritual power to rule legally over society.

B. THE ETHICS OF THE KINGDOM

112. *Moral Life and Civil Righteousness***

THE KINGDOM OF GOD THE HIGHEST GOOD.

God's Kingdom the Highest Good.--The kingdom of God, as the
highest Good, is not merely the sacred realm of liberty and love,
but, moreover, the blessed realm in which man finds his last and
final satisfaction, or his peace.

The highest Good, may be taken in a double sense; (1) as *bonum
supremum*, that which is superior to all other good things, in which
man finds peace and rest, which he can find nowhere else; (2) as
the *bonum consummatum*, the perfect Good, the epitome of all good
things, containing within it the fulness of all perfection.

In both significations the kingdom of God is the highest Good....

We may speak, therefore, of the kingdom of God as the perfect
Good within its earthly conditions, as a typical representation of
the future final condition of the kingdom of God.

It is this kingdom of God upon earth, which, under the postulate

---

*George W. Sandt, *Theodore Emmanuel Schmauk, D.D., Ll. D.,
A Biographical Sketch* (Philadelphia: United Lutheran Publication
House, 1921), p. 279; no date is given for the letter.
**Revere Franklin Weidner, *Christian Ethics* (2d ed.; 1897),
pp. 40-41, 44, 50, 51, 131, 311, 347-353.

of appropriating activity, is the task of ethical *productivity*; whilst the heavenly kingdom of God is the task or problem for ethical expectation and receptivity, since we should prepare to receive the Lord. The glory of God's kingdom will, during this stage of existence, continue to have a veiled presence....

THE KINGDOM OF GOD AND THE KINGDOM OF SIN

The Kingdom of Sin.--As the Good, considered as the destiny of man, is love to God and his Kingdom, the Evil can only be defined as the essential contrast to love, or as Egoism....

THE KINGDOM OF GOD AND THE KINGDOM OF HUMANITY

The Kingdom of Humanity.--On its entrance into history, Christianity not merely discovers an independent kingdom of humanity, but awakens and calls it forth as certainly as it awakens the principle of personality. It plants the germ of God's kingdom, sows the seed of the operations of grace and the gifts of grace, institutes the Church, and the congregation. But at the same time it also plants the germ, sows the seed of an independent kingdom of humanity with the whole affluence of man's natural endowments and natural powers which develop themselves in his worldly relation in culture and civilization.

We designate this moment, which has so great a significance in the divine plan of education, as *Emancipation*, *i.e.* deliverance from the natural bonds of the ancient times. But Emancipation is not Redemption. Redemption makes free to inward communion with God, freedom founded on grace....

Humanity and freedom are the watchwords of the age; and *rightly understood*, these demands are sanctioned by Christianity itself. In face of emancipation, with its immense development of man's natural powers, the Gospel continues to testify: "If, therefore, the Son shall make you free, ye shall be free indeed" (John 8:36).

The Aim of History.--Divine mercy and human freewill, God's kingdom and the kingdom of the devil, these are the contrasts which make up the content of history.

The all-embracing aim of history which should be ever present to our efforts, is the unity of the kingdom of humanity and the kingdom of God--a unity including the completion of the work of redemption and the work of emancipation....

CIVIL RIGHTEOUSNESS

The Morality of the Natural Man.--The historical appearance of morality, as seen in the natural man, in the sphere of the family, the state, and society, we designate as *civil* righteousness. The individual here knows only special duties, he has not taken up *duty itself, the good itself*,--the feeling of duty does not embrace the *whole* life of his personality....

THE FAMILY AND THE MORAL WORLD

The Moral Life of Society.--The moral life of society is developed in the Family, the State, and the Church, which latter is the Communion of Saints. The individual ought to be a member of each of these circles, and to occupy with respect to them a relation at once of cooperation and appropriation, of toleration and devotion, while constantly aiming at his own perfection as well as the perfection of the whole. One essential side of man's destination is displayed in each of these social circles, and the purpose of Christianity is to develop the "new man" within each. It is in proportion as the Christian ideal of human nature is realized in them that the kingdom of God attains a social, and at the same time an individual, appearance of earth....

THE STATE AND JUSTICE

The State is the Kingdom of External Justice.--While the family shows us a kingdom of love and dutifulness, the State, on the contrary, exhibits a kingdom of right and justice, where the individual sympathies which prevail in the family retire, and individuals only count as persons whose freedom stands in prescribed relation to the general law of the State. *Right* is the rule imposed by law upon the human will. *Justice* is the regulating and dispensing power which maintains and defends its enforcement in presence of human arbitrariness. Hence it is not only legislative, but also judicial and retributive. But the State is only the kingdom of *external* justice. Its commands are not directly moral. It says not only, you ought, but, you *must*; and is able to effect the fulfillment of its decrees by *force*.

The State is not a human invention, but a divine ordinance, "for there is no power but of God; and the powers that be are ordained of God. Therefore he that resisteth the power, withstandeth the ordinance of God" (Rom. 13:1, 2). This does not, however, exclude the fact that it is also a human ordinance; for its administration and execution have, by means of a long historical development, been entrusted to the hands of sinful men. The State further proves itself a human ordinance by the fact that it is not, like the Christian Church, of divine institution....

The duty of the State is not confined to prevention and punishment, but includes also that arranging and distributing justice which carries out impartially what is right in every relation of civil society. The State comprehends the entire life of the nation, and not only takes under its protection the rights of the individual,

144

but guards also the rights of the community and its common employments, and consequently the circles and institutions interwoven with them. It should furnish those external conditions by which the family, trade, art, science, nay even the Church itself, may attain their own development, and co-operate in the task of the whole.

The State, as the region of external justice upon earth, has by this very character both an ethic and a physical side. Its physical side is power. A State without power is a nonentity; and States have from all times exhibited a tendency to increase their power. But the State only approximates to its ideal in proportion as the use of its power is determined by justice and law, and it is upon these that all real authority in the State depends....

The necessity for the Christian character of the State is mainly founded on the fact that the State does not exist for the sake of this or that subordinate aim, but for the sake of human nature itself, that its vocation is to furnish and work out all those external conditions which are indispensible to the general development of human culture and prosperity. It is for this very reason that there can be no constitution or government worthy the name which is not pervaded by a thorough understanding of the nature and destination of man, of the history of the race, and the ultimate object of human history. Again, the necessity for the Christian State rests upon the circumstance that the State is the realm of external justice. But external justice cannot be carried out or administered without internal justice; in other words, without a religious and moral disposition, by which alone it can come to pass that the laws are obeyed not from fear of punishment, but for conscience' sake. This again brings us back to Christianity, which, with its heavenly citizenship, makes us truly fit for citizenship in this world.

We may therefore define the Christian State as that form of government whose fundamental moral ideas are determined by the principles of Christianity. In this view, the kingdom of God among men is the centre and aim of history, and the State is a mere instrument for the development and promotion of the kingdom of God and the kingdom of mankind on earth.

C. POLITY

*113. Fundamental Principles of Faith and Church Polity (1866)**

OF ECCLESIASTICAL POWER AND CHURCH POLITY

I. All power in the Church belongs primarily, properly, and
exclusively to our Lord Jesus Christ, "true God begotten of the
Father from eternity, and true man, born of the Virgin Mary,"
Mediator between God and men, and Supreme Head of the Church. This
supreme and direct power is not delegated to any man or body of men
upon earth.

II. All just power exercised by the Church has been committed
to her for the furtherance of the Gospel, through the Word and
Sacraments, is conditioned by this end, and is derivative and
pertains to her as the servant of Jesus Christ.

The Church, therefore, has no power to bind the conscience,
except as she truly teaches what her Lord teaches and faithfully
commands what He has charged her to command.

III. The absolute directory of the Will of Christ is the Word
of God, the Canonical Scriptures, interpreted in accordance with
the "mind of the Spirit," by which Scriptures the Church is to be
guided in every decision. She may set forth no article of faith
which is not taught by the very letter of God's Word, or derived
by just and necessary inference from it, and her liberty concerns
those things only which are left free by the letter and spirit of
God's Word.

IV. The primary bodies through which the power is normally
exercised which Christ commits derivatively and ministerially to
his Church on earth are the Congregations. The Congregation, in
the normal state, is neither the Pastor without the People nor the
People without the Pastor.

V. In Congregations exists the right of representation. In
addition to the Pastor, who by their voluntary election is already
ex-officio their representative, the people have the right to choose
representatives from their own number to act for them, under such
constitutional limitations as the Congregation approves.

VI. The representatives of Congregations thus convened in Synod,
and acting in accordance with those conditions of mutual congregational
compact which are called a Constitution, are for the ends, and with

_____

*S.E. Ochsenford, *Documentary History of the General Council
of the Evangelical Lutheran Church in North America.* (Philadelphia:
General Council Publication House, 1912), pp. 139-140.

the limitations defined in it, representatively Congregations themselves.

A free, Scriptural General Council or Synod, chosen by the Church, is, within the metes and bounds fixed by the Church which chooses it, representatively that Church itself, and in this case is applicable the language of the appendix to the Smalcald Articles, "The judgments of Synods are the judgments of the Church."

VII. The Congregations representatively constituting the various district Synods may elect delegates through those Synods, to represent themselves in a more general body, all decisions of which, when made in conformity with the solemn compact of the Constitution, bind, so far as the terms of mutual agreement make them binding, those Congregations which consent, and continue to consent to be represented in that General Body.

D. DIVERSE VOICES

114. *Law and Grace**

If the state desires to be a truly humble servant of God, then let it work in line with God's principles of government, as He has established it in the dispensation of grace. In other words, let civil government be pervaded with grace the same as the church.

115. *The Church and Social Service***

There are three divine institutions. One is the Family, and its watchword is love. Another is the State, and its watchword is Law. The third is the Church, and its watchwords are reconciliation and righteousness.

116. *J.A.W. Haas: The Centrality of Freedom****

The material and the contents of most works in Ethics leave untreated or treat too cursorily and unsatisfactorily such parts as are of special importance to us in America....

Its plan might be evolved upon the suggestion of Frank. Christian Ethics could be properly described not as the free development, but as the development of freedom. Freedom characterizes the very centre of Christian life.

---

*F. Berkemeyer, "Law and Grace. A Code of Grace in Civil Government." *Lutheran Church Review*, 15 (1895), p. 60.
**George W. Sandt, "The Church and Social Service." *Lutheran Church Review*, 34 (1915), p. 519.
***J.A.W. Haas, "A Suggestion on Christian Ethics," *Lutheran Church Review*, 14 (1894), p. 190.

We need to hold strictly to the presentation just made. The Christian man is not man in a state of nature under the bondage of sin and its condemnation. In other words, he is a new creature, and created in Jesus Christ after His own image. Of such an one, it is said, and is true, "old things are passed away; behold, all things are become new." While there has been no destruction of the nature of the man there has been a renewal, a real and truly new energy implanted, involving a change of his relation to God, and making him who was before a child of wrath, a child of God. This is something more, and, indeed, something other, than a mere awakening of the conscience, giving to him clearer moral perceptions; and something other than the quickening of certain forces before latent, bring these out into the light of consciousness, and imparting to the man earnestness of purpose, and even a better and higher aim in life. We say, and with emphasis, the Christian is something more and other than this. To reach the thought of the New Testament in what it declares concerning him who is born of God there must be included something wholly new, something in no sense belonging to the man in his natural state. This is that given in Regeneration, a birth in its nature, its origin, and its author, from above. In this view of it Regeneration is akin to the Incarnation. To the one, the individual, a new nature is given, this being the condition of a renewed personality; in the other, the person of the Son of God assumes humanity. In both the union is equally real. It is this that makes, and indeed, *is* the Christian man. Education can never evolve it, no matter how complete this may be. Nor can any measure of civilization, however broad and refined, bring man or humanity to this new stage, as truly new to the individual as the Incarnation was a new thing to the race. The Christian man is born from above, is truly a new creature, and possessing a new consciousness, may we not say, a new personality?...

Those who believe are delivered from the condemnation of sin, and truly and really restored to His favor. Without any work or merit of their own, and without any obedience as a condition, except as faith itself is obedience, they are fully accepted as children and adopted as sons of God. And in that relation they yield a free and ready obedience, finding their delight in doing His good pleasure. Their service is a service of freedom, rendered without constraint; and as they have, to use Luther's fine phrase, "a heart of the Law,"

---

*S.A. Repass, "Christian Liberty and Its Limitations," *Second General Conference of Lutherans* (1902),pp. 122-123, 125.

they delight in obeying Him who gave it. The ground or necessity of compulsion is removed, all fear is clean gone, and reconciled in Christ in the spirit of children they render ready and willing service. While they are diligent in obedience, and fear to offend against God, this is in neither case the ground of their hope of acceptance. That is the complete righteousness of Jesus Christ, theirs by faith, and theirs henceforth and forever. This is Christian liberty, the liberty wherewith Christ hath made us free. They who stand in it serve in liberty, and walk at liberty. All things are theirs, and they are lords over all. The law cannot bind the conscience of such, since they are free from its constraints; and whatever service it requires or demands they render freely. They refuse to go under any yoke of bondage, no matter by whom or what this may be imposed. Having taken refuge in Christ they stand in a large and secure place, rejoicing in the victory he has gained for them. In bondage to no one, and to nothing, they walk on high places assured of their liberty and confident in their possession. From the law, from Church ceremonies, from holy days and Sabbath days, and from all compulsory human enactments, they are free, free in the liberty of Christ.

CHAPTER 9

J.H.W. STUCKENBERG

118. The Christian Sociology of J.H.W. Stuckenberg*

Christianity is a mighty social power, and if left to work
out its inherent nature it will establish Christian society. Every
healthy believer feels the social energies working in himself, and
if he follows their impulses he will seek the companionship of
other believers. The formation of Christian society, therefore,
does not depend on the understanding of the social power of Christianty,
but on the working (whether consciously or unconsciously) of this
power.

119. The Kingdom of God**

a) Christ teaches that his kingdom is not of this world,
differing from earthly kingdoms in principles, in character, in aim,
and in the methods of promoting its ends. In distinction from them,
it is spiritual. It is the kingdom of God because he is its author,
and the life that emanates from him is its life. It is the kingdom
of heaven because it is modeled after heaven, being a reflection of
heaven. As a spiritual, divine, heavenly kingdom, it is sufficiently
characterized as distinguished from other kingdoms. Jesus clearly
indicates the aim of this kingdom when he teaches his disciples to
pray: "Thy kingdom come. Thy will be done in earth, as it is in
heaven." God's will is thus to prevail in this kingdom as fully as
in heaven.

---

*J.H.W. Stuckenberg, *Christian Sociology* (New York: I.K. Funk
and Co., 1880), p. 7.
  **The first quotation is from Stuckenberg, *Christian Sociology*,
pp. 92-93; the other is from J.H.W. Stuckenberg, *The Age and the
Church*, (Hartford: Student Publishing Co., 1893), pp. 157-161.

Differing as this kingdom does from earthly dominions in character, so also are the means for promoting it different from theirs. These means are internal and spiritual. Outward forms are not rejected; but they are valuable only so far as they are the manifestation of spiritual power. Divine truth is the principal element for the establishment and promotion of this kingdom. It is significant that Christ, whose aim was so practical, made the very thing which all philosophers have sought the basis of his kingdom. With his claim to royalty he connects the declaration that he came into the world to bear witness unto the truth, and that every one who is of the truth hears his voice; that is, he who is moulded by truth into the likeness of truth will recognize in Christ, as by intuition, a teacher of the truth, and will be drawn unto him.

The stress which Jesus lays on the power of the truth is an important factor in his sociality. The truth is the basis of his social relations and conduct as truly as of his kingdom.

b) This kingdom of God is the whole sphere of God's operations on earth through Christ. In respect to quality, it includes all the influences which emanate from Christ, all the manifestations of His truth and Spirit. In point of extent, this kingdom embraces the world so far as Christ's influence is exerted--the world where the wheat grows beside the tares. Heaven is all wheat; the world outside of divine influence is all tares; in God's kingdom, considered in point of external extent, the wheat and tares are together, but the wheat alone is the kingdom.

In point of influence the kingdom of God includes all who experience the effects of the Gospel. Many are under this influence in a preparatory stage, being taught and trained for full membership. By the schoolmaster they are being led unto Christ. Some not aware of the fact are greatly affected by the truth of this kingdom. The kingdom, as confined to the church, is so narrowed as to lose essential features given by Christ Himself.

There is worship in this kingdom; but what is commonly called "divine service" is, but a small part of the divine service of Christians. All truly divine service is included, all that finds an illustration in Christ's word and work. This service includes all embraced in the immense sweep of love to God and love to man. Nothing done in Christ's name and spirit is excluded. He heals the sick and feeds the hungry; and work like this is not only included in the kingdom, but in Matt. XXV, it is even made the test of belonging to the kingdom. The law of the kingdom is divine and human love and sympathy. All Christian works come under this law. The spirit

151

and work of this kingdom far reach beyond the limits usually
assigned to them.

It is the kingdom of God, but for men; human therefore as
well as divine. Nothing truly of humanity is foreign to it. Christ
came to spread joy, and all pure joy has a home in this kingdom.
Culture, too, here finds the purest soil and the best seed. The
kingdom has room for art, for music, and for poetry, as well as for
science and philosophy. Thus the Christian life and all the Christian's
concerns are divine service; and He who could command that the net
be cast into the sea and be drawn from it has dignified labor. The
business of the Christian is not outside of but within God's kingdom.

*120. Dualism and Man and Nature**

It is therefore evident that the study of our age is concerned
chiefly with the two permanent factors, man and nature. Within
and between these lie all the phenomena which are within reach of
rational interpretation. And since humanity is the object of our
inquiry, it is especially man as our age presents him that concerns
us.

*121. Division of Humanity****

a) According to the Christian view of humanity, society is
divided into two classes--those who have been redeemed by Christ
and are Christians, and those who are sinful and redeemable, but
have not yet been redeemed. That is, humanity consists of the
redeemed and the unredeemed; of those whose sins are pardoned, and
of those whose sins are not yet pardoned. These two classes
constitute what is called Christian society, on the one hand, and
what is called the world, on the other, using the term world to
designate the unregenerate, in which sense it is frequently used
in Scripture.

b) Humanity, therefore, and not merely a part or party thereof,
is the family of God, and he is the Father of all men. But if he is
the Father of all, then are all men brothers. In teaching this
intimate relation of humanity to God, and of men to one another,
Christianity far transcends the particularism of Judaism and the
caste systems and national selfishness and prejudice of heathen nations.
The Gospel lays no stress on race, or nationality, or rank. In every
man it sees a likeness to God, and his child, and a moral nature that
is sinful but redeemable. While it does not put all men on the same
level, it nevertheless sees in all common powers and common sympathies,
common possibilities and common needs. Therefore, its truth and its

---

*Stuckenberg, *The Age and the Church*, p. 5.
***Christian Sociology*, pp. 111, 114-115, 118.

grace, its Saviour and its God, are for all.

c) There is thus a natural sonship and there is a spiritual
sonship. There is also a natural and there is a spiritual family
of God. There is a likeness to God which is only that of nature,
which has its source in creation, and which is greatly marred by
sin; and there is a spiritual likeness to God, that is, a likeness
in spirit, in affection, in deed--a likeness that has its source in
the new creation, in regeneration. In the spiritual sonship the
image of God is restored to its original purity. Of the natural
sonship Adam, "which was the son of God," is the historic head;
of the spiritual sonship Jesus Christ is the historic head. The
former sonship has only nature; the latter has also grace. There
is also a natural brotherhood, consisting of all the members of the
human family; and there is a spiritual brotherhood, consisting of
those who are made spiritual through Christ. Jesus is the elder
brother in the spiritual brotherhood, and those who are brothers
to him must also be brothers to one another.

The spiritual brotherhood is synonymous with Christian society.
This is formed from those who are members of the natural brotherhood;
but in entering this spiritual brotherhood they do not cease to
belong to the natural brotherhood.

122. *Mission of Christian Society**

a) With reference to the world, Christian society has a mission
of the utmost importance. The life imparted to it, and of which it
is the embodiment, is communicative, and is to diffuse itself
throughout humanity.

b) If laws are enacted which are in conflict with the believer's
conscience, then he must submit to the punishment for violating the
laws, rather than violate his conscience. No effort should then be
spared to remove such laws. Indeed, Christian society may do the
State good service in the efforts to secure such laws, and such
only, as are right and will prove a blessing to the community. Even
if there can be no direct religious legislation, the moral standard
of the Gospel may be made the ideal for the State. A Christian
spirit should pervade the laws, instead of the atheistic spirit
which some would infuse into them.

c) So far as worldly affairs are right and necessary,
believers ought to engage in them. In doing this they adapt themselves to the divine arrangement and do God's will. They are to be
in the world, but not of it; not worldly-minded or conformed to the
world, but spiritual in mind in the midst of their worldly avocations.

---

*Christian Sociology, pp. 185, 195, 197.

This leaves a large variety of occupations which the Christian may enter, but there are also many which he cannot enter and yet maintain his Christian character.

More important, perhaps, is the question, how far the believers may enter into relations with non-believers. They can, of course, enter into no relations which can in any way be regarded as a compromise of the Christian character. This is the general rule: Christian society can associate with all, so far as its aims and theirs agree, and so far only.

123. *The Controlling Principle* *

Love to God is not possible, unless there is also love to the brethren. "If a man say, I love God, and hateth his brother, he is a liar: for he that loveth not his brother, whom he hath seen, how can he love God, whom he hath not seen. And this commandment have we from him, That he who loveth God love his brother also."

These clear and emphatic declarations of Scripture leave no room for doubt as to the controlling principle of the believer in his social relations; and writers on Christian ethics generally admit this fundamental character of love....

What right has the Christian to complain of the corruption of politics, if he refuses to hold office, avoids political conventions and primary elections, and refuses to lift his little finger to remove the corruptions?

Nowhere does the Scripture encourage the neglect of the body or of secular affairs. But in attending to these, it wants the right spirit and proper motive to rule. The body is regarded as sacred, because it is the temple of the Holy Spirit; and it is to be treated with great care.

In all his secular, as well as in his religious relations, the believer is to be controlled by the principles of Christ. It is a rule of universal application, never in any relation, by word or deed, by omission or commission, to violate the rules of the Gospel. If the Christian character were perfect, then its spontaneous activity in all affairs would be in harmony with Christ's teachings. But no character is so perfect that it does not need constant watchfulness. The purest and warmest Christian love needs divine grace and the rules of Scripture. The very soul of the Christian's business transactions should be the Golden Rule.

Christian Sociology, pp. 226, 283.

PART IV:

THE TWENTIETH-CENTURY CONFLICT OVER THE

POLITICAL RESPONSIBILITY OF THE CHRISTIAN COMMUNITY

INTRODUCTION

At the beginning of the twentieth century Germany theological scholarship occupied the first rank in the Protestant world community. Although in ethical theory British and American theologians had stated the case for democratic political institutions, even in these arenas German Protestants had supplied the intellectual foundations for liberal theology. For conservative Lutherans German leadership was almost unquestioned.

Thus the events of this century and the ways in which German theologians elaborated the doctrine of the two kingdoms are of crucial importance. The development of this doctrine from its nineteenth-century foundations generally failed to provide theologians with the constructive-critical tools for coping with the changes in German society; instead the doctrine was easily and frequently misused as an ideology leading to silent or explicit legitimation of existing, even reactionary and unjust, power relationships.

In the development of the doctrine of the two kingdoms or some of its individual elements into an ideology, German Lutheranism in its specific historical situation played the decisive role. Not only were the essential theological formulations worked out there, but through emigration and mission German thought-forms and positions were carried to the Lutheran churches of all continents. The primary factor in the development of the political ethic was the fascination which political and military victories had for many theologians, leading to the reactionary union of "Throne and Altar." After the collapse of the Wilhelmian Empire, nostalgia for the past dominated the majority of the Lutheran clergy.

The German romantic defense of the old social order against influences of the French Revolution is related to the above developments. With the help of "orders of creation" understood as eternal, one can block the question of the greater or lesser justice of the public order. Consequently the witness of the church to the newly emerging industrial workers became inaudible. Instead the church--under the additional influence of the new pietistic awakening--withdrew from questions about the structure of public and socio-economic affairs and limited its social responsibility to church-owned caritative diaconia. In the effort to relate the church to the modern world of the late nineteenth century, liberal Lutherans used a dualism of spiritual and secular (presumably derived from Luther) only in order to declare the interests and laws of the imperialistic capitalistic national state to be autonomous and in this way to claim legitimacy for the realm of the private and the inner which they had been able to save for Jesus Christ.

The development of Lutheran political thought took place during the years of the Lutheran Renaissance. The new Weimar edition of Luther's works gave scholars rich lodes to mine. Even the chief Luther scholar, Karl Holl, could not break out of the dualistic interpretation of Luther's thought. Loyalty to the old order seemed paramount. Thus it should not surprise us that during the early years of the Weimar Republic books on the "Collapse of Lutheranism as a Social Formation" could be written. Later Karl Barth and others could sharply criticize Luther, Frederick the Great, Bismarck, and Hitler as members of a single lineage. In fact, it was German national socialism that brought the catastrophe of German Lutheranism into the open, and at the same time provided the impetus for a new self-critical reflection. It is not accidental that at this time, the beginning of the 1930s, the elements of the Lutheran doctrine under criticism were first conceived of as a unity under the technical designation, "the doctrine of the two kingdoms."[10]

The new stance in German Lutheranism after the Nazi years did not carry the field completely either in the Federal Republic of Germany or in the regions under German influence on other continents. In the Federal Republic of Germany large circles accepted the newly discovered necessity of critical-constructive cooperation in public affairs timidly or not at all. On other continents we cite as examples the Lutherans of German ancestry in souther Africa or the Lutherans of the Missouri Synod with their essentially German orientation.

It is interesting, on the other hand, to observe under what historical conditions Lutheran churches and theologians of other than German territories and spheres of influence found their way back to an alternative interpretation of the Word of God and the Reformation. During the Nazi period the Norwegian church had already used the two kingdoms doctrine to establish a basis for the independence of the church from the demands of the German occupation forces. After World War II many theological works coming from North American Lutheranism reflect the collapse of the German Lutheran piety of subordination and the necessity of reading the two kingdoms doctrine in a non-dualistic form. Interestingly, many of these ethicists began with the doctrine of the orders of creation. During the past few years, in the growing crises in the United States itself, the voices increased which emphasized the role of the churches in public, indeed global, affairs. Willing to reflect critically on the basis of their own studies of Luther, these theologians recover Luther's insistence that the realization of Christian love through concern for the welfare of the neighbor belongs properly in the sphere of political action.

A further decisive breakthrough took place in Eastern Europe, particularly in Hungary. Here one acknowledged the guilt of the church through its previous involvement in feudal and capitalistic social systems and developed a new form or theology of diaconic service to society. A reformulated version of the doctrine of the two kingdoms replaces the old dualism.

In South Africa and Namibia major developments occur. Driven by the sufferings of the black populations, church leaders and theologians discover anew that the two kingdoms doctrine in its dualistic form is a "theological crime" (de Vries) and that instead in its authentic form it must teach that God in diverse ways (spiritual and socio-political) desires to serve the entire human being in all social relationships and calls upon humans in these ways to cooperate with him against the powers of evil. Here one notes how Luther's two kingdom doctrine can be interpreted under the aspect of his theology of the cross. Whoever fights together with God for salvation and justice against the powers of evil, as they appear in the conflict with the powers of this earth, is drawn into the suffering of Christ. The conflict of black Lutherans in southern Africa and of a part of the Chilean Lutheran church are actual, dramatic examples of this truth.

These historical documents and discoveries provide a clear working hypothesis for judging the role of the two kingdoms doctrine in the theory and praxis of the Lutheran churches: If churches and theologians attempt, consciously or unconsciously, to legitimate privileges of the church or of definite social groups, the two kingdoms doctrine becomes--generally in its dualistic or as an explicitly unpolitical, in fact highly political, form--a (heretical) ideology. If churches and theologians--de facto generally in situations of crises or suffering--use the two kingdoms doctrine to cooperate with God for salvation and justice for all, concretely working for and witnessing in behalf of the underprivileged and oppressed, they rediscover the biblical and Reformation meaning again.

From these circumstances we understand why Lutheran voices--despite the general amazement of representatives of Western Lutheran churches--seem to echo unheard in the ecumenical arena when they seek with the help of the two kingdoms doctrine to point out that God serves eschatological salvation and socio-political justice in two different ways. For as long as this distinction serves the purpose in wide areas of the Lutheran churches to make the political dimensions of God's activity secondary in importance, the two kingdoms doctrine will be seen as an excuse to leave untouched the privileges of a generally white, Western population stratum. Then Lutheran churches and theologians are widely experienced as accomplices of the powerful of the world. So the Lutheran churches in this century will lose the underprivileged of the Third World as they lost the underprivileged workers in the 19th century, or--stated in a better way, the services of the Lutheran church will be lost to the majority of the world's population. Then, as in the nineteenth century, we will be left one-sidedly with an individualistic proclamation of salvation and a caritative treatment of symptoms.

CHAPTER 10

GERMANY IN THE TWENTIETH CENTURY

INTRODUCTION

When the twentieth century began, both confessional Lutheranism and liberal theology had reached a position in which the spiritual and the secular, the order of the kingdom of God and the order of nature, faith, and politics were decisively kept apart. This separation they applied in heightened fashion to the events of the war.[12] The majority of German theologians distinguished clearly between a private morality, which could follow the love commandment, and a morality of the state, which had to take its directions from the necessity of national survival.

Theologians of diverse backgrounds found common ground in this distinction, as some of the documents we have selected indicate. Friedrich Naumann, the politician, for whom insight into the separation of the spiritual and the secular had led to the forsaking of theology, exhibits with particular clarity the social Darwinian components in this thinking. The liberal theologian Wilhelm Hermann interprets the irrevocable character of political events as destiny. The Erlangen church historian, Hermann Jordan, was, so far as we know, the first to describe the independence of political life from faith as "the autonomy of the state," and thus to introduce a concept which had far-reaching consequences for the later discussions of the doctrine of the two kingdoms.

Jordan's thesis, that insight into the autonomy of the state is the most important fruit of Luther's distinction between the two kingdoms and the two regimens, was subsequently incorporated into Luther interpretation as well as into the political stance of the

Lutheran churches. We can find it in a modified and differentiated form in Karl Holl, the key figure in the Luther renaissance. In his essay of 1917 the distinction between the gospel, which deals only with soul, and the natural order of God, the order of creation, provided a framework within which the war had to appear inevitable.

The collapse of the German social order after 1918 called forth the question whether the ethical foundations of the existing social order had also broken down. In 1921 Georg Wünsch answered this question affirmatively for the Lutheran tradition. Following his teacher, Ernst Troeltsch, he interpreted the Lutheran understanding as a "double morality," which had relinquished their autonomy to the secular spheres. This interpretation, which Troeltsch had already voiced, Karl Holl attacked most sharply in his programmatic essay, "The Reconstruction of Morality." Holl insisted that Luther understood natural law not as something self-sufficient, independent of the gospel, but as the content of the Christian love commandment and that for Luther acting on the basis of reason coincides with acting on the basis of love. The community of love provides the criterion by which the political and economic order are to be tested, and particularly in their structures. Nevertheless for Holl it still remained true that the tension between the laws of the world and the spirit of the gospel can be overcome only in the disposition of the Christian person.

This position is clearly expressed in the criticism which Paul Althaus directed at religious socialism. Karl Barth is the first, as far as we know, who in his answer to Althaus (not reprinted here) defined this position explicitly and terminologically as "the doctrine of the two kingdoms." Barth charged pointedly that this position, with its drastic separation, surrenders the radical and critical quality of the gospel.

To these texts from the beginning of the 1920s we have added one from the early 1930s. Ernst Wolf's survey of the social ethics of German Lutheranism makes unambiguously clear that at this time there was no established, terminologically unambiguous, solidified doctrine of the two kingdoms, which provided a common currency for ecclesiastical discussion. Wolf discusses the "so-called theory of the two spheres" and criticizes it as well as the misunderstanding of Luther in the schemata of the "so-called double morality." The problem of a dualistic misunderstanding of Luther was consequently well known, but the concept of the doctrine of the two kingdoms was not used with either critical or affirmative intent as a settled topic for theological and ecclesiastical discourse.

The documents selected for dealing with the role of the doctrine of the two kingdoms in the church conflict are limited to those dealing with ecclesiastical politics. An attempt to provide a view of the early systematic discussion of the Lutheran distinction between the two spheres would go beyond the limits of this source-book.[13] In the strict sense Harald Diem's dissertation of 1938 begins the discussion.[14] The documents presented here (more fully collected in the corresponding German volume) can make clear that the systematic efforts to understand Luther took place in direct connection with the quarrel over the ecclesiastical-political application of the two kingdoms in the church conflict. This quarrel flared up in 1933 as the Rengsdorf theses on the one hand and Karl Barth's reply on the other side show very distinctly; the conflict was about whether it was theologically defensible to assert that the Christian stands equally without reservations in two orders, the order of the gospel and the order of the German people.

Against this background the Barmen theological declaration acquires signal importance with its assertion that Jesus Christ is the one Word of God and represents God's demand upon our total life. For this reason the Barmen theses belong in the context of the two kingdom's discussion, as do the Ansbach Proposals, in which Lutheran theologians under the leadership of Paul Althaus and Werner Elert contradicted the Barmen theses. The Ansbach document derives the separation of the two spheres from the distinction between law and gospel and asserts that the preaching of the law leads to subordination under the natural orders as a Christian duty. Thus the neo-Lutheran doctrine of the two kingdoms was established as a legitimating ideology for accommodation to the worldview and politics of national socialism; Karl Barth perceived this connection very quickly and with critical decisiveness. We can understand fully the sharp tone of the discussion after 1945 between representatives of the doctrine of the two kingdoms and those of the lordship of Christ only when we understand these facts about the function of the doctrine of the two kingdoms during the time of the Third Reich.

The debate went on vigorously in official declarations and counter-declarations. (Some of these can be found in the German edition.) We offer only one further highly significant document from this period, Peter Brunner's theological-ethical reflections about the war. His reflections show how within the confessing church the attempt was made to take account of Luther's doctrine of the two kingdoms in the explanation of contemporary ethical decisions.

The debate has continued since the end of World War II. The discussions have centered on the one hand on the antitheses between

162

the doctrine of the two kingdoms and the lordship of Christ and on the other hand on differences in the interpretation of Luther. While one group interpreted the doctrine of the two kingdoms by distinguishing the two forms of governance, the other took its point of departure from the two kingdoms as sovereign and personal associations. In the interim it has become clear that the doctrine of the lordship of Christ and the doctrine of the two kingdoms, correctly understood, are not to be seen as alternatives, since both have as their aim to make theologically valid the universal claim of the lordship of God in Jesus Christ. It has become just as clear that an interpretation of Luther's contribution, based on the history of the tradition can and must take into equal account both the distinction of the kingdoms and that of the forms of governance.

These discussions cannot be included in this collection of sources. We have restricted ourselves to one example of the ecclesiastical use of the doctrine of the two kingdoms after 1945, the reflection on the situation of the refugees. In addition, to provide an insight into the underlying arguments, we have included two documents about the "politicalization" of the church. The issue here seems to be that criticism of the preparation for the use of power (rearmament) or its actual use is interpreted as a "politicalization," while the acceptance without reservations of existing political power is seen as unpolitical. Every instance of "politicalization" of the church is also seen as a threat to the unity of the church.

The discussion remains unfinished. Because of the events of the 1930s and of developments since the end of World War II the debate cannot be limited to the Federal Republic of Germany.

A.   THE DISTINCTION OF TWO SPHERES IN WORLD WAR I

Friedrich Naumann

124.   "The Faith Engendered by War" (1915)*

This faith that there actually is a life for which the individual human being gives up his own life can be founded on either a natural or a supernatural basis. The natural argument proceeds from the fact that already in the upper levels of the animal world and among savage primitive peoples the preservation of the species or the family is more highly regarded than the preservation of the individual

---

*F. Naumann. "Der Kriegsglaube," Hilfe, 21, no. 36 (1915), reprinted in F. Naumann, Werke (Cologne/Opladen, 1969), vol. 1, pp. 850-815.

member. The supernatural argument assumes that there are ideals
and life-goals that simply must be realized, regardless of the cost
involved. Both arguments, however, converge in the single injunction:
"Die for the Fatherland!" This phrase expresses first a natural
tribal idea and secondly a spiritual-cultural goal. You die for the
sake of your people because they exist and because they will become
something better; you die for the sake of their common existence
and for their common development....

This is a proper faith in the restricted sense of the term,
since no one dies for what he can grasp, see, or possess. The
names that you give this invisible quality are not really important.
You can call it "the people," "the state," "justice," or "freedom,"
or "humanity," yet everything flows together in a confused way. This
faith believes in what is yet to come, and therefore it sets forth
bravely in the direction of the shooting.

Combatants of every nationality do this, but in different ways.
How great is the obvious difference between the English worker and
the German worker! How completely different is the Russian small
farmer from his East Prussian counterpart! If the faith engendered
by war would be exactly the same for each army, then we would enjoy
fewer victories. It is not just performance and weapons that win
the victory, but the inner self overcoming death. Since this inner
self is present in profusion among our people, and since it exists
in a natural and self-evident manner requiring no world of explanation,
we all receive a powerful and magnificent strengthening which continues
to win more new believers all the time. A faith that must be kept
alive artificially requires a great deal of explanation, whereas
a faith that is truly alive takes effect under its own power. Many
preachers of the faith could learn something from the faith that is
engendered by war.

Wilhelm Herrmann

125. *"The Turks, the English, and We German Christians"* (1915)*

There has been a lot of talk recently about how we can possibly
bring this war into harmony with Christianity. In view of the
frightful things that come to our attention every day, this is a
legitimate question to ask for this as well as for every war. The
same question can be raised concerning competition in society,
where people snatch from each other the necessities of life with a
show of bravado and right that is positively awesome. Naturally,
if we wish to talk about this war, then it is necessary that we

---

*W. Herrmann, *Die Türken, die Engländer und wir deutschen
Christen* (Marburg, 1915), pp. 21ff.

concentrate upon that aspect of it which is unique. But at the
same time we must remind ourselves that much of the horror which
war still possessed as recently as a hundred or even sixty years
ago has disappeared today. We think of the care received by the
wounded, the provisions made for the soldiers, or the treatment
accorded a hostile country. Most important, however, is the fact
that this war is a destiny which is laid upon us.

I continue to maintain that Christianity has absolutely nothing
to do with the fact *that* human beings must suffer such a destiny
but only with *how* they bear up under it. We want to endure our
destiny in a way that enables us to fight this war through to the
bitter end, but we also want to give others free rein to develop
to their full potential in human society. If we are granted eventual
victory, we only can hope that the earth finally will be liberated
from the fantastic madness that one nation wishes to rule over the
others. If this liberation actually succeeds, it will make a
powerful victory for Christianity and a new start for history. Some
pious Swiss have sneered at the notion of a "Christianity for the
42-centimeter cannon."[15] We wish to record our complete agreement
with that strange formulation. For this weapon enables good iron
to fulfill the useful purpose for which God created it. Besides,
such a weapon demonstrates a good bit of the iron loyalty to one's
vocation which also undoubtedly will have to be reckoned to the
account of Christianity.

Herman Jordan

126. *"Luther's Understanding of the State" (1917)**

The clearer we focus upon the issue, the easier it will be for
us to recognize what is historically of greatest importance in
Luther's understanding of the state. Luther's signigicance rests
in the manner in which he picked up and universalized the idea of
the two spheres--the Kingdom of God and the kingdom of the state--
as entities to be distinguished, the one from the other, as each
follows its own autonomous laws. Luther is also important in that
he confirmed this understanding in all of its religious, ethical,
and political ramifications.

Now the distinction between the two spheres--spiritual and
secular, religious and political--is certainly something that Luther
considered to be related to the Gospel in an intimate way. Although
this distinction impressed Luther primarily because it freed the
Gospel from secular elements, his interest in the tendency of political
life to operate according to its own autonomous laws was entirely
self-generated. We can easily follow the train of thought which led

---

*H. Jordan, *Luthers Staatsauffassung: Ein Beitrag zu der Frage
des Verhältnisses von Religion und Politik* (Munich, 1917), pp. 191-197.

Luther from one to the other. The powerful attraction which this notion of the state's freedom to follow its own autonomous laws held for Luther lies in the fact that it follows inevitably from his understanding of the Gospel. For this reason, the idea has always reappeared in the history of Lutheran Protestantism where Luther's thought in all its pristine purity is asserted....

Lutheranism in recent history has continued to serve as the bearer of the notion that religious and political life must operate according to their own autonomous laws. When, as in the example of Bismarck, we find a desire for shaping the national state on the basis of power—by war if necessary—coexisting with the Christian conviction of a believer, that is but a continuation of Luther's line of thought. By way of contrast, the politically active Christian who has lost his ability to make this distinction is always in danger either of losing his way in politics—which follows its own laws— or of watering down the ethical content of the Sermon on the Mount, thus affecting the character of Christianity....

To ascribe Christian motives to a political purpose is only possible where people have not yet liberated themselves from the traditional opinion, which holds that the state exists merely to help spread the Gospel in the world; this, in turn, presupposes the continuing validity of the old theocratic understanding of the state. What makes us so unhappy with the entire English-American religious and political cant is primarily that it tends to confuse spheres which in reality differ enormously from one another. By neatly divorcing the natural life from the Christian life, Luther maintained the pristine purity of both, preserved the Gospel from confusion with secular interests, and protected the state from the hypocritical application of evangelical motives in what is really its own proper sphere. Inasmuch as Luther did not subordinate one sphere to the other, but instead placed them side by side, he described in simple terms the two worlds in which we live, thus making it possible for the Christian to exist simultaneously in both worlds with a clear conscience....

Lutherans do not consider the state to be the highest good in human life, although they do probably view it as the highest form of human obligation on earth, something to which the Christian can dedicate himself wholeheartedly and for which he must sacrifice himself. Here, however, we understand even better that what was of primary importance in Luther's understanding of the state was not so much the idea of a natural love for the Fatherland but rather the fulfilling of an obligation to one's people in the service of God....

At the same time, the state--because of the distinction between the Kingdom of God and the kingdom of the world--can function only as it obeys laws that are particularly tailored to its own nature. Accordingly, Luther made a sharp distinction between personal ethics and political ethics, between the ethics of the state and the ethics of the individual... Thus it became a fundamental axiom for the political development of every state which had some contact with Lutheranism--a judgment now accepted as accurate, at least in principle--that neither the Gospel nor the ethics of the Sermon on the Mount can stand in the way of measures which the state considers to be in its own best interest. Out of the soil of Lutheranism there emerged a point of view which refused to call a policy "Christian" that applied the words "blessed are the peacemakers" to the state and to its political life in such a way as to endanger its internal stability and external security....

Thus Lutheranism was always able to reject the enthusiasts for eternal peace, as well as the false peace that results from struggling on behalf of the cross and Christianity with the aid of secular weapons. The basic character of Lutheranism makes it impossible for this religion to wrap itself in the religious cloak of an imperialistic policy that goes beyond what is considered necessary for the welfare of one's own people; nor can Lutheranism recommend a policy of weakness and complacency that passes under the name "Christian." To this day, Lutheranism has been a consistent motivating force for a national policy which enables every progressive and active nation to focus upon great goals while at the same time striving to fulfill its political obligations at home and abroad.

Karl Holl

127. *"Luther's Understanding of Gospel, War, and the Church"**

Luther distinguished clearly between the order of God's Kingdom--which is based upon love--and the order of the state-- which is based upon justice. The former derives its laws from the Gospel of God's Word and applies to Christians. The latter applies to the natural man, to believers and nonbelievers alike, and obtains its standards from natural reason and judicial procedure alone. Luther insists strongly that the two not be confused. The Gospel offers no prescription for economic and political affairs but is concerned only about souls. That is why Luther refused to allow the peasants to camouflage their cause with the Gospel. For the

---

*K. Holl, "Luthers Anschauung über Evangelium, Krieg und Aufgabe der Kirche," in *Gesammelte Aufsätze zur Kirchengeschichte*, vol. 3: *Der Westen* (Darmstadt, 1967), pp. 150-152, 162-163, and 165-167.

same reason, he opposed waging war against the Turks as a holy crusade. The Gospel has as little to do with this war as with any other conflict. What the Gospel prescribes is the opposite of war....

The government has an obligation to protect its subjects; that is the office to which God has appointed it. Thus the government also is permitted to wage war. In like manner, even while he rejected the way in which the insurgents misused the Gospel during the Peasants' Revolt, Luther never failed to speak forcefully to the consciences of the lords and nobles. For he never intended that everything in secular life ought to remain exactly as it is just because the Gospel never talks about it. Reason and justice, which set the standards in this area, should be seriously applied. How many proposals on behalf of the existing order did not Luther himself set forth, proposals relating to schools, the city administration, and economic life....

Now, if the Christian is a member of God's Kingdom, that is to say, of the invisible church, and at the same time belongs to the world with all its particular relationships, do the two spheres come into direct contact within the individual Christian, without any buffer zone between them, so that his personal behavior differs from his public behavior? That was not Luther's intent. He did not want a double morality. He insisted strongly that the Gospel-- especially the command to love--not only should be maintained as a Christian attitude, but that it ought to serve as the motivating force in determining all of a Christian's individual activity.

Luther also discovered a way to bring the theoretical separation of the two spheres into some kind of inner relationship. Whatever takes place within the world's orders also finally works to the benefit of love. Just as a ruler, whether Christian or non-Christian, establishes the preconditions for the higher fellowship of the church (that is to say, when he produces love) by the way in which he administers justice, so every worker and every businessman also does his part. By their labors, they all create the conditions for the (natural) communal life of human beings in society. This is precisely why the Christian can participate in the world's orders without being untrue to himself. In fact, he is in a better position to do this than other people, for he realizes--as the non-Christians do not--that even this secular activity ultimately serves the purposes of God's Kingdom. This goal is not obscured for the Christian, because each individual action must be performed in accord with the rules considered to be "reasonable" for each sphere. Just as a shoe repairman does not dare to fit a child with an adult-sized pair of shoes, so it is unthinkable that a business could remain solvent unless it demanded a fair price for its goods or that a government could govern unless it took steps to punish wrongdoers. The Christian cannot violate these norms. Here it is not a question of how one soul relates to another, but of preserving the natural conditions of human existence. The more certain it is that the particular activity corresponds to the structure of the entire enterprise, the better it is able to contribute to the maintaining of that enterprise. In the same way, such activity becomes, also for the Christian, a service and a way of fulfilling an obligation to show concern for the well-being of the neighbor. Luther fearlessly carried these thoughts to their logical conclusion. Thus the Christian is allowed to take an oath if the government requires it, or if he can protect his neighbor from harm in this way. What he is never permitted to do for his own advantage, that is allowed him in the service of love. In this way, the Christian goes beyond the letter of the Gospel while at the same time fulfilling its spirit....

In this way, we arrive at a proper standpoint for rendering a moral judgment in the question at hand. Ultimately, we are dealing with powers that lie beyond the will and human consciousness. Or, to express it more accurately, here we come into contact with God's order of creation. It is God who allows some people to expand naturally, others to decline, even as it is God who distributes His gifts to individuals or peoples in various ways, enabling some people to overcome difficulties which cause others to destroy themselves....

Against this background, even war takes on an appearance of inevitability. It is unjust to expect a dying people to inhabit an extensive territory while a fresh and vigorous folk must languish within narrow frontiers. But no people can be expected to declare themselves on the verge of extinction, any more than a person who has been designated to rise and plead his own case is in a position to evaluate his own moral value and worth. No court of law, no matter how neutral it may be, is able to render a trustworthy verdict here. A conflict of forces in armed battle produces a decision--at least temporarily. I am speaking cautiously here, for it should not be imagined that the outcome of a war should be taken as a divine judgment, as though the people enjoying moral superiority always are victorious in the end. Victory demonstrates only that at this time God sees fit to grant this particular people more room to live out their lives. How long this will hold true, and why this ultimately happens, that remains a secret.

When we first recognize this natural divine order, then the question is put to us exactly as it was put to Luther before. Two

mutually exclusive entities stand opposed to each other--on the one
hand, the natural divine order in creation and the legal and
economic order which is based upon it; on the other hand, the Gospel.
The vital point once again is: Will the Gospel, with its unconditional
command to love, ultimately be shown to have been an illusion?...

The Gospel affects individuals first and deploys its entire
strength at this point. But Jesus also equates love for God with
love for the neighbor, and not only in the sense that both are placed
parallel to one another in an external way. Those who set their hope
on God are likewise bound to one another as brothers. This does not
mean, as Loisy superficially expressed it, that all men are brothers
already from the day of their birth; they ought indeed to become
brothers and that Christians ought always to act towards their fellow
humans as if they were surrounded only by brothers. This is the
origin of the question as to whether the community of souls as Jesus
intended it allows for such a transfer to earthly relationships or
even requires it....

What the Gospel requires can always be satisfied only on a
personal level. To speak of "improving the moral climate" in the
relationship between peoples can mean only--if it is not rhetoric--
that one people ought to respect what is unique about another people
and ought to take into consideration what they need in order to
survive. But it is still a long way from "respect" to Christian
love. And even respect for another people as a feeling with a mass
basis only occurs when that people demonstrates some capability and
ability to defend itself. Such respect is limited by one's own
people's requirements for survival....

Similarly, the Gospel only suffers harm when a particular people
attempts to regulate its legal and economic order according to the
precepts of the Gospel.... Law compels the individual to limit his
demands in consideration of his performance and his contribution to
the collective well-being of his entire people. If love replaces
or weakens law--at least in the public order--this means the loss
of the beneficial necessity for people to exercise self-control.
In similar fashion, this would cheapen the Gospel. An economic
order based on the idea of love, that is to say, on the idea of
community, necessarily must transform love itself into an object of
compulsion.... For such an order, like any other, could be maintained
only through the use of force. Work itself, the external service,
would appear then as a form of love, and the Gospel, with the
deepest sentiments that it signifies, could not be distinguished
from the disposition that it requires. Only as the order of law
and the order of love are separated cleanly from each other can the

Gospel be thrown into relief as something special and absolute in itself. Let the individual learn to distinguish between what is important to his natural existence and what is important to his inner being, and let him learn to see in the latter the one thing that is needful in his life. Just as friends who wish to keep their friendship untroubled will never settle any business matters between them on anything but a purely businesslike basis, so love cannot retain her position upon the heights unless she breaks through all relationships that rest upon another foundation,

Luther's understanding, in its traditional formulation, undoubtedly can hold its own, even under present circumstances. Compared with his critics, both old and new, Luther is no bantamweight but rather the clearest and deepest of thinkers.

B. THE BEGINNING OF THE DISCUSSION DURING THE WEIMAR REPUBLIC (1919-1933)

Karl Holl

128. "The Reconstruction of Morality" (1919)*

We should not let ourselves be deceived by the fact that Luther was willing to designate the various estates whose continued existence he accepted, as "natural" and the resulting orders as "rational." Now this does not mean that Luther would have regarded "natural reason" in its generally accepted meaning or the "nature of things" as an independent source to which the Christian is expected to ascribe positive value on account of his relationship with it.[16] We must examine more carefully just what Luther understood by "reason" and "natural law" in this connection. Certainly he emphasizes that there are irrevocable facts established in the order of creation which in themselves help to organize the structures of human life, as can be seen in the relationship between parents and children, the unequal distribution of natural abilities, or the difference which emerges between those who issue orders and those who obey. But Luther does not have in mind this unchangeable natural condition when he speaks about natural law. Rather, he is thinking of the rule by which the law is morally taken account of, a rule which is to be integrated within the total context of social life. He calls this the "natural law" in order to indicate that it has its seat in the immediate human conscience....

Despite this, Luther accepts the fact that the natural

---

*K. Holl, "Der Neubau der Sittlichkeit," in *Gesammelte Aufsätze zur Kirchengeschichte*, vol. 1 (Tübingen: J.C.B. Mohr (Paul Siebeck), 1932), pp. 245ff.

conscience--at least among the sensitive, since not all are so
predestined--immediately recognizes Christian morality, when it
is encountered, to be the only true morality and the fulfillment of
something already planted within itself. Just as no people ever
has been so "impious" that it did not have some kind of divine
worship, since mankind has always been aware of the commandment in
the first table of the Law, so it has given the obligation toward
parents and toward the neighbor a degree of universal recognition.
Moses and the Sermon on the Mount did not proclaim anything radically
new but merely confirmed and clarified what already had been written
into every human heart by nature. Thus Luther could call the Christian
commandments, as well as the Decalogue (which harmonizes with these
commandments in their spiritual sense), a "natural law." This
"natural law" is what Luther has in mind when he attempts to reach
a verdict concerning the form and shape of human life. Luther never
raises to the level of a standard a "reason" which might act in
opposition to Christian morality or which might venture out on its
own to give independent prescriptions for organizing human life
apart from or parallel to Christian morality. Then such "reason"
would become for him only something to be resisted and overcome.
In other words, wherever Luther appeals to "reason" or the "natural
law" as something of direct normative value, he really is always
thinking about a reason with a Christian orientation or, to put it
another way, the Christian command to love. It is a fact that even
where Luther calls this command to love "reason," he takes it with
his usual seriousness. By uniting "reason" with the natural law,
Luther, far from reducing Christian morality to a more modest level,
rather interprets the natural conscience for the Christian conscience....

However, Luther passionately opposed the idea that the Gospel
itself can be transformed directly into an order of society, as
though demands for civic and social freedom and equality can be
derived from the freedom of the Christian man. This solution, the
easiest of all on the surface, struck Luther as too easy and
superficial, even as a misuse of freedom. What he found here was
the same distortion of meaning which he had rediscovered recently
with his understanding of religion and morality. If political
consequences can be drawn directly from the Gospel, that is, from
the relationship to God that has been established through faith, then
religion and morality would no longer be ends in themselves, a service
performed on the basis of free devotion, but something already
verging on becoming a means to a radically different end, that of
earthly bliss. If religion and morality are to remain on the heights
to which Luther restored them, then the proposition must be upheld

that their continued survival is possible under all external circumstances, even the most oppressive.

Luther expounded the principle upon which he really stood with all the clarity that he could possibly muster. When it was necessary for him to answer the question as to what represented a "blessed state" and what a "sinful state"--for that is the form in which Luther always couched his questions, not only with respect to soldiers, as in the title of one of his best-known writings, but also with respect to government and other vocations--he responded by taking into consideration the extent to which the office in question "served the Christian community" or, as he explained it more clearly, the extent to which it was a vocation that could cause love to spring forth from the law. The standard which Luther establishes for constructing a proper social order is the same idea of an invisible community, the Kingdom of God, which he had grasped already in his younger years and from which he had drawn the practical consequences for the reformation of the church already at that time. For him, the idea of community represents the legal basis by which all other forms of social life must be defined, since it represents God's ultimate purpose. If this idea, because of its religious content, proved to be important for the renewal of the church, it attracted attention in connection with the question of the social order because to that aspect which is turned toward the world, namely its claim to represent the most intimate kind of community. But if someone tried to claim that this community of love coincided with the invisible church, then it became obvious that the idea of community could not be forced upon the "world" as a law, as the Anabaptists wanted to do. It was rather a community of hearts, presupposing a freely affirmed relationship to God. It certainly was also just as evident that this invisible kingdom of love could not survive in the world unless certain external conditions were fulfilled. Since the members of this kingdom were also human beings who had to live, were in need of food and clothing, and, wherever possible, deserved to enjoy an undisturbed existence, it can be asserted with certainty that Luther always recognized this "natural law." Yet precious little was said about the way in which it applied to the question occupying Luther's attention. What mattered for him was whether or not the forms which human beings created to satisfy this "natural law" in the course of history were compatible with that community of love. But Luther raises an even more extreme demand. He is not satisfied that these historical forms merely prove compatible, but he demands positive proof that they "spring forth from the law of love." Only when historical forms can be derived from the idea of a loving community and when it can be demonstrated that they themselves make a positive contribution to that community, only then does Luther consider the question answered to his complete satisfaction.

However, he discovered a point of view in that highest idea of community which became his standard for evaluation that caused even this obstacle to disappear. Luther maintained that the state, for all its severity, simultaneously performs an indispensable service for the Kingdom of God. Without this service, Christianity would have no chance to succeed. At this point, Luther's conviction-- which is confirmed by the Scriptures and experience--that in reality the Gospel always affects but a small minority assumes practical significance. For Luther now realized that without the state this minority of the world's finest citizens, because of their basic principle of not resisting evil, would be placed at the complete mercy of unscrupulous violent people. Only one institution could rescue them, not individually--for individuals are able to reconcile themselves to their fate--but as a community and in the visible form of a community, and that is an institution which upholds justice and which possesses the power that is necessary to put justice into practice.

In this way, the state first reveals itself to Luther as a divine order in the true sense of the term, although in comparison with the Kingdom of God it appears to be only a second-rate kind of divine order. The state is the kingdom of God's "left hand," the protective shield which God has established to perform His work in this world. Luther deepens this idea even further by drawing attention to that dual aspect of the state which generally characterizes God's activity in the world. With respect to the punishing of the wicked, the state shows itself to be an agent of divine wrath; but when observed from the standpoint of the Kingdom of God, it takes on a somewhat nobler appearance. Here it shows itself to be part of the divine mercy. For the state actually demonstrates love by taking care of the victims of violence, the weak, and the afflicted. As far as Luther is concerned, this puts the force which the state applies in proper light. He does not view it as an end in itself. It is nothing less than a wild presumption to claim that Luther glorified "force for the sake of force."[17] In Luther's opinion, the state's application of force is just as little an end in itself as wrath can be said to represent God's ultimate purpose. Force is both limited and justified by love, and even the force applied by the state is pressed into the service of love....

Luther scrutinizes the economic order in similar fashion. In this sphere too, the idea of a loving community is the standard by which everything else is to be measured.

Georg Wünsch

129. *"The Collapse of Lutheranism as a Social Formation" (1921)* *

Luther is a thoroughgoing inward-looking man bent on eternity. For him, the goal of all human life is the world to come, just as the value of all human existence lies in our basic disposition. He views the totality of all existence--and here he is being quite biblical--in terms of an absolute dualistic separation between the mundane world and the world above, between the world here and now and the world that is to come, between time and eternity. Each is sharply separated from the other, with its own unique laws, and each is involved in a struggle, the one with the other. The present world is the world of the devil; ever since the fall into sin, it has been entirely lost for divine purposes. The social form, with all its contradictions and injustices, also belongs to this world and is unable to be dislodged by any kind of earthly power; it will always be and remain just as it is. The Christian awaits his redemption first in eternity. Until then, he must suffer and endure patiently what is essentially the devil's world. A chasm separates these two spheres. Only the orders of family, church, and government offer a viable scaffold for preserving the world as it is. But they too are a distinctive part of this present world, an emergency construction which is doomed to disappear with the collapse of the entire demonic establishment....

In politics, Lutheranism was affirmatively conservative, as long as kings were in the vogue, and even today it looks back nostalgically to the Christian principalities that have since disappeared. Lutheran conservatism was not conservative in the sense of medieval Christendom, for which the principalities represented perhaps the single reasonable insitution in a politically undeveloped time, although medieval Christendom knew how to maintain a safe distance from these same principalities. Then, as later, it was still an undiscriminating kind of monarchism, since the monarchy in the popular consciousness had already outlived its day and was showing strong evidence of degeneration among its representatives. Luther's patriarchal attitude was out of place in such a setting; it even became an object of scorn for intelligent people and thereby tended to make Christendom as a whole look ridiculous.

Nevertheless, this derailment of Lutheranism--which caused it to lose contact with the course of historical development in a deeper

---

*G. Wünsch, *Der Zusammenbruch des Luthertums als Sozialgestaltung* (Tübingen: J.C.B. Mohr, 1921), pp. 19, 23-24.

sense as well as with the Gosepl--could have been endured had it
been possible to put a leash on the influence of the monarchy and
the classes which sustained it. What was unendurable was the
behavior of official Lutheranism in questions concerning economic
life.

Here, too, the Lutheran heritage had a disastrous effect as
a result of Luther's separation between the world and the Kingdom
of God, as well as because of his one-sided misplaced emphasis upon
eternity and the inner life. Hence Lutheran theologians have shown
almost complete indifference to economic problems. Today there
still are no useful Protestant ethical treatises dealing with economic
life. The theologians' sole concern was to cultivate the disposition
of the inner man; decisions concerning public life were for them
matters of conscience. A suitable economic order would come into
existence, they thought, all by itself. "Seek first the Kingdom
of God...."

Contemporary Lutheranism as a social formation represents a
degeneration from what it was in Luther's day. Let us not deny
that it provides a means for holding the influence of Christianity
far away from the world and its social life while preventing the
Christian from exercising his principles in this world. We have
already had a Christian state, a Christian monarchy, and a Christian
society, all of which were distinguished by this fact: In the most
critical questions that confronted the state, the monarchy, and the
society, Christianity had nothing to say! As a result, many people
concluded that the Christian religion had become worthless; it
revealed a one-sided moderan Lutheran who had only to swallow the
doctrine of the world as taught by the Lutheranism of his day, and
behold, what a fantastic metamorphosis: he turned out to be a
modern power-hungry despot in a Darwinist sense or in the sense of
Nietzchian philosophy. This is just one example indicating the
extent to which Lutheranism related to the spirit of the age--
unfortunately at the cost of being completely untrue to the spirit
of the Gospel.

The Controversy between Paul Althaus and Karl Barth

130. P. Althaus, "Religious Socialism" (1921)

Let us summarize and offer three objections to religious
socialism: First, the religious socialist is partially in danger
of speaking his part in the complex questions of economic life in
a way that displays an overly hasty brand of Christian dilettantism.
We remind ourselves here how necessary it is to have access to the

---

*P. Althaus, "Religiöser Sozialismus," in *Grundfragen der
christlichen Sozialethik* (Gütersloh, 1921), pp. 58f, 76ff, 88f, 90f.

most precise technical information. We cannot simply use our
Christian principles in order to ignore theoretical economic
formulations and the way in which these formulations attempt to
come to grips with basic social necessities. Secondly, over against
an absolute faith in the possibility of a "Christian" economic order,
we emphasize that considerations of substance and techinque as well
as of history effectively limit the extent to which Christian and
moral principles can be involved in economic life. Ethical
rationalizing is restricted by the process of economic life itself.
Thirdly, many religious socialists appear to derive the norms for
a just economic order directly from the Gospel. In opposition to
such "nomism," we point out the necessity for the decision by a
living conscience arrived at in the midst of economic life.

Over against this, Luther takes a position which on the basis
of medieval assumptions is completely impossible. He questions not
only each of the two standpoints, but also their common foundation.
First he sharply emphasizes the contrast between the love--constitution
of the kingdom of God and the secular orders. The kingdom of Christ
and the state with all its conditions and forms are and remain two
different entities. Second, the Christian cannot and must not change
the world into the kingdom of God; he also cannot set up any compromise
form between the two. He must neither withdraw from life in the
world nor from the unconditional demands of the Serman on the Mount.
This constitutes the rejection of the ascetic ideal--for the secular
orders are also God's orders. And therefore the rejection of a two-
level morality, for the radical words of Jesus are not counsels but
demands upon all.

The historical-natural ordering of life can nowhere be dissolved
through the love-constitution of the Kingdom of God--the world
remains world--but the unconditioned quality of the demands of Jesus
also have no limits of place or time.

Third, Luther's solution is not a compromise, but consists of
the knowledge that the Christian fulfills the love commandment of
Jesus in the midst of his obedient participation in the orders of
the world. In his very participation in justice and property, state
and power under all circumstances he can act out of a selfless
loving disposition and in full inner freedom. Fourth, this solution
is made possible for Luther only by the fact that for him the will
of Jesus is directed not at worldly orders but at the depths of human
dispositions. The kingdom of God does not appear to him as a
particular structure of relations in the world, but as a definite
posture and commitment of the heart. This can be asserted and
maintained in obedience even against the apparently contradictory

177

historical ordering of life. The Christian can, even in undertaking hard, difficult work in the law, government, and war, live completely in the spirit of the Sermon on the Mount.

Luther's solution has its uniqueness, that he establishes the harsh dualism of the kingdom of God and the constitution of the world and then overcomes this dualism in the action of the Christian. The dualism becomes the tension between the constant unchanged disposition of the heart and the works which must be done. In the complete separation of the spheres and their simultaneous and continuing union, through their penetration in the action of the Christian, Luther saw the solution of the difficult question. He was conscious that no one before him had offered this answer....

It is customary to present as Lutheran the doctrine of the autonomy of the historical orders of life. This expression does not cover Luther's position adequately. Luther also recognizes a moral norm for economic and political life. The Sermon on the Mount as such does not generally come into the picture for him; at least insofar as this is understood as a denial of the whole ordering of historical existence through laws and power and as a command for particular actions....

In summary, we can no longer speak of a dualism of a morality of the office and of the person. The moral action of the Christian has unity. Instead of "alongside of" we see interconnectedness. But the Christian again and again experiences the powerful tension between what he must do in the historical orders of life and the disposition with which he acts. Love must carry our many difficult tasks. But this paradox is no greater, no more difficult to bear, than the paradox of God's action. It is noteworthy how Luther places the ethical and theological paradoxes alongside one another. One learns to sense how little his solution of the difficult problem represents a compromise, how deeply his view of God is grounded....

Alongside the constantly present spiritual reality of the kingdom of God there also exists as independently significant the world of living history and the work of culture and state-building, to which we are called. We cannot act only personally, but we must also deal with facts and serve the orders of history, which are something quite different from the kingdom of God. The cultural and world-historical task of humankind is something independent, alongside the kingdom of God, and cannot be subordinated to the kingdom as the means to an end. The same duality characterizes God's relationship to the world. That relationship is not fulfilled with God's sovereignty over individual souls, that is in his community with us in Christ, but also completes itself as creation, structure, dominion over nature, and the development of culture. Who would say that nature and the development of culture are only a scaffolding for the building of the kingdom and not an independent goal of his will? God's sovereignty is not completed in the spiritual reality which we call the kingdom of God.[18]

Formulating a Lutheran Social Ethic

131. E. Wolf, "Toward a Lutheran Social Ethic" (1932) *

1. To this day, there still is no systematically grounded, genuine, living Lutheran "social ethic," either because Lutheran social ethics, like German Protestantism in general, has misunderstood its mission in "individualistic-quietistic" terms or because it--to some extent, at least--has turned Luther's thoughts on the subject, despite the fact that they are limited in applicability by the historical environment in which they arose, into a social theory whose unhappy influence is still with us today. Although the problem of devising an Evangelical social ethic was and remains primarily a Lutheran one (at least in German history this is true), more and more attempts are being made today to formulate a genuinely Lutheran social ethic, one that is based upon the theological principles of the Lutheran Reformation and which uses the existing patterns of life which Lutheranism had a part in shaping. Luther's ideas take on a strength and a momentum never observed before in providing the critical standard and establishing the starting points as well as the guiding principles for a Lutheran social ethic. These efforts (see thesis no. 2) and their Reformation antecedents (see theses nos. 5-9) are surveyed critically here and are related to present-day problems (see thesis no. 10).

2. Three different attempts are presently underway to find both theoretical and practical solutions to the problem of how to formulate an Evangelical social ethic; these efforts involve a more or less conscious (and successful) return to Reformation origins-- ignoring for a moment the critical investigations into the possibility for an Evangelical social ethic on the part of the so-called "dialectical theologians" and the still rather uneven beginnings by those involved in the "young Lutheran" renewal. (The orientation around Luther, as seen in the Reformation emphases, for example, is strong enough to set the tone from time to time in each of the following groups):

A.   Attempts to analyze the Lutheran social ethic from the vantage point of intellectual and legal history endeavor to fit this

---

*E. Wolf, "Zur Sozialethik des Luthertums," in *Kirche, Bekenntnis und Sozialethos* (Geneva, 1934), pp. 52ff.

ethic into the framework of the so-called "double morality" (on the one hand, the personal and subjective morality of the Sermon on the Mount, on the other, the official and legal morality of the social orders in the concrete forms of state and economic life--with the glorification of force that goes with it) and to accommodate it to the theory of the supposed "natural autonomy" (*Eigengesetzlichkeit*) of all spheres of cultural life, which is really only another way of describing the gap separating religion from culture. The goal of this set of attempts is an Evangelical social ethic whose Evangelical aspect is restricted to the "inner conviction of the individual Christian"; one and the same individual thus indicates by his own dual nature a possible solution to the problematical relationship between the Kingdom of God and the kingdom of the world. Theoretically, such efforts are most convincingly represented by Troeltsch and, at least in terms of practical concern, by those men who depended upon him in one way or another, like Naumann (on his way from Christian socialism to political socialism). This is the formalized and secularized form of a Lutheran social ethic "that quietly (!) wishes to leave the social ethos--which is really based upon the modern division of labor--to the kingdom of the natural man"; it is the social ethic that would prefer to recognize in the "concept of social obligation" the Lutheran "principle for a social worldview" and in "service as the spokesman for the neighbor" the Lutheran "maxim for social activity" (according to Joachimsen, *Sozialethik des Luthertums*, 1927, pp. 53-54).

B. Attempts to utilize the Lutheran conservative tradition wish to retain the traditional ideological armor that developed around it in the course of time to aid in solving the problem (Stoecker is an example of this); these efforts are themselves undergoing partial modification in our day as a result of the great many supporting mechanisms provided by the intellectual and cultural philosophy known as German Idealism, which provides polemical yet also justified criticism of the separation that results from the attempts listed under Part A above. Here, in contrast to those first attempts (see Part A), there has been an effort to link up the Kingdom of God with the world, not primarily in the individual and in his Christian-moral disposition but, more particularly, in those forces which play a positive role in the social world (such as the intellect or culture) and which, in harmony with natural laws, serve in either a protective or a creative capacity.

Here we should mention many more recent ideas which attempt to promote the notion of an "order of creation"--really another name for the "Lutheran" rediscovery of the First Commandment!--as a fruitful solution to the problem of formulating a political theology or ethic or even an evangelical economic ethic (see Wünsch); see too the variety of consciously Lutheran appeals to the "orders of creation" in more recent times.

C.   Attempts to overcome the problematical nature of the way in which the Kingdom of God and the kingdom of the world, love and justice, radical moral demand and relative moral possibility are related to one another all enlist the aid of a divine pedagogy.

This critique maintains--

   --with respect to part A: (1) Either it is no longer advisable to speak of a genuine ethic, at least of a Christian social ethic, or (2) the effort to establish a historical foundation for Lutheran social teaching, despite all the weighty and conclusive observations that have been made, remains inadequate and even partially false;

   --with respect to part B: This effort is threatened by a threefold danger: (1) the reconstructed world, for all its alledged relationship to what is happening on a day-to-day basis, remains absolutized to the point that it becomes illusory; (2) to make Christianity responsible for shaping the world or for serving as a basis for effecting change in it ultimately sanctions the world and thus enables it to escape the divine judgment; or (3) both efforts may lead to a false interpretation of the important positive foundation that undergirds this attempt, namely, the Lutheran understanding that Gospel and society ought never to be separated from each other, despite the Lutheran so-called theory of the two spheres.[19]

   --with respect to part C: This opinion, admirably represented today by A. Runestam, probably is closest of all to the Reformation point of departure in terms of history and content, though perhaps partially at the expense of the "hidden reservation"--i.e. the traditional Lutheran pessimism, as well as Luther's basic notion of the world as God's "cabaret"--which means that it can never be brought into complete harmony with Reformation anthropology.

   3. In all of these attempts to provide a "Lutheran" solution to the problem of enunciating a Christian social ethic that have

been made, it becomes rather obvious that there is a major difficulty here or, to express it more positively and more pertinently, an important point of definition. Luther saw the church as the organizing principle for understanding social life from the standpoint of faith, what is more--something that surely ought not to be overlooked--the church as separated from its socio-political anchorage, as the communion of saints (*communio sanctorum*), that is, as the Kingdom of Christ. The church is the representative of Christ's Kingdom in history and the sign pointing beyond itself to the kingdom of fulfillment. The church also exercises a critical function over against the orders of creation, such as marriage or nationality, which have been established by God to preserve the social world, and over against the order of legality or government, which must function within certain fixed limits as a consequence of sin.

4. In my opinion, however, none of these efforts has dealt sufficiently with an even more serious difficulty. There is clear evidence of another important "point of departure" which unambiguously and inescapably locates the ultimate source of Evangelical social ethics in the significant lack of any comprehensive social ethic for mankind as a whole (as well as for conscience) based upon any kind of feasible philosophical anthropology.

5. This means, first of all, that the problem of theological anthropology makes crystal clear--at least for Luther, in his paradoxical formulation, *simul justus et peccator*--that both of these two in part unrecognized but no less original "points of departure" for a Lutheran social ethic (i.e. the church and justification) are objects of faith. They first become visible-- only from time to time and in a relative sense--in the activity that results when divine love is moved by faith to action.

6. Faith refers back to the Word of God, the *logos* which created it. Thus, the genuine Lutheran understanding--something of fundamental importance to both the church and the individual Christian alike--holds that vocation, which extends from creation through redemption and beyond to the Kingdom of God (i.e. the Kingdom of Christ), represents the only real point of contact for a Lutheran social ethic (that is to say, the Christian acts on the basis of his belief that he has been called).

7. Rejecting as it does every merely historical condition as well as every conservative hardening and foreshortening of the Lutheran concept of vocation, the Lutheran social ethic must be formed starting with the concept of vocation itself and proceeding from there to the constituent and normative aspects of Word, faith,

and church--

1) not by falling back upon a principle which originates in the world's understanding of its own responsibility--for that is prevented by the revelatory nature of creation, grasped by faith alone and under the critical norm of the Kingdom of Christ (see thesis no. 3),

2) but also not by relying on an assured directing conscience somehow associated with the human possession of the divine image corresponding to the norm of creation--for that is prevented by the Lutheran understanding of sin and by the corresponding anthropology of the doctrine of justification that results from it (see theses nos. 4-5).

8. On the other hand, Lutheran social doctrine ought never to draw back to hide behind an intellectual warping of the knowledge of the contingent relationship of the justification and the vocation of the Christian. To begin with, the community of the church, as one of the essential and basic determinants of the social ethic, belongs to the Word that has called human beings into their vocations; thus, the Lutheran social ethic has an obligation to raise questions-- if not according to a universally applicable ideal, then at least in terms of universal conditions that apply to the individual in a social setting alone and in terms of the concrete tasks which first make their appearance in that context. Inasmuch as a vocation also points up our involvement in the simultaneously veiled yet revelatory way in which the created world holds together, it likewise places us under obligation to the universal command to offer God obedient service, in the sense that such service, originating in the patterns of created life, is always related in some way to the Kingdom of Christ.

9. Since vocation is both the result of God's justifying love and the effective means through which that love operates, since according to the Lutheran understanding the world and its orders provide numerous opportunities for exhibiting the instructing love of God, and since Luther was of the opinion that the "universal order of Christian love" enjoys a "higher" rank than the three hierarchical orders of church, state, and family--for all these reasons, the order of love is shown to be the ultimate source that lies concealed behind the point of contact represented by vocation. It is also shown to be the power that determines the direction of all social and ethical activity which is performed in the world and its orders out of a sense of vocation. As for the problem of how social and ethical concerns can be put into practice, here special reference should be made to Luther's appreciation for "fairness"

in order of legality. He practically equates *epieikeia* with charity (*caritas*) and indicates that this insight can be realized in practice: "For charity is lord and master of the Law" (*caritas est domina et magistra legis*) (*WA*, 42, 505).

10. The purpose of these theses is to show that the theological foundations of a Lutheran social ethic themselves, in terms of how they function within the forms that they have assumed in the course of historical and intellectual development and in keeping with their concern for objectivity, require--

    1) a loosening-up of the "conservative" viewpoint that misrepresents those theological foundations;

    2) a rejection of the "liberal" foreshortening that ends up transforming them into a private domain;

    3) a liberation from their being used merely as an intellectual construct.

The theses show how a Lutheran social ethic can be made appropriate to serve in a relevant manner the social and political problems of our day.

C. THE TWO KINGDOMS IN THE CHURCH CONFLICT

The Rengsdorf Theses and Barth's Response

132. "The Rengsdorf Theses" (October, 1933)[20]

1. The term "*Deus dixit*" (God has spoken) ascribes to God's revelation an expression that is merely formal and hence inconclusive. It misleads theology into a kind of "existential thinking" that fails to correspond to reality. God's revelation lies enclosed in the phrase "*Deus creavit, salvavit, sanctificavit*" (God has created, redeemed, and sanctified). God is both Creator and Redeemer, the one who gives the Holy Spirit to the world.

2. There is no "universal Christianity." Christianity as such is an abstraction that has no real existence of its own. For the German, there can only be a Christianity that has its roots in the German nation.

3. There is no contradiction between an unconditional allegiance to the Gospel, on the one hand, and a similarly unconditional allegiance to the German national, that is, to the National-Socialist state, on the other.

4. For us Germans, the Reformation brought the Gospel into an intimate relationship with the character of the German people.

---

    *"Die Rengsdorfer Thesen (Oktober 1933)," in *Die Bekenntnisse und grundsätzlichen Äusserungen zur Kirchenfrage des Jahres 1933*, edited by K.D. Schmidt (Göttingen, 1934), p. 91.

History confirms that this proclamation of the Gospel is admirably
suited to the German race.

5. The National-Socialist revolution has molded in the German
people a distinct character that applies with equal validity to both
their faith and their nationality.

6. The national community is based upon those values for which
the German sacrifices his life. These values include, among others:
a healthy family life; his blood and soil; loyalty to his own nation
and state; and in all things, an attitude of obedience toward God.

7. State and church are both divinely ordained orders. Hence
there can be no conflict between them. Should conflict occur, it
is due to one side's encroaching upon the other. The church is
obliged to obey the state in every earthly matter. The state in
turn must allow the church room to carry out her task.

*133. Karl Barth, "Counter-Theses to the Rengsdorf Theses" (November,
1933)* *

1. The formulation "*Deus dixit*" refers to the fact that God's
revelation in Jesus Christ has occurred once for all and is attested
to once for all in the Holy Scriptures. By ourselves, we do not
know what creation, redemption, and sanctification are; God's Word
first has to tell us.

Whoever today opposes this formulation as being "merely formal"
replaces the free Word of God with an arbitrary statement of human
self-understanding and places himself outside the Evangelical Church.

2. The actual extent to which "Christianity" is specific and
concrete on the soil of German nationality cannot be determined on
the basis of what we claim to know about this soil, but it is to
be accepted as the particular form in which the only commandment
and only consolation of the Word is revealed to us in conformity
with that Word's own wisdom and will.

Whoever today preaches "a Christianity that has its roots in
the German people" binds the Word of God to an arbitrarily contrived
ideology, discredits that Word, and places himself outside the
Evangelical Church.

3. The "Christian confession of faith" is the only "unconditional"
allegiance which is offered and allowed us. This is the focal point
from which all other opinions (including those concerning German
nationality and the National-Socialist state) are to be placed under

---

*"Karl Barths Gegenthesen zu den Rengsdorfer Thesen (November
1933)," in *Die Bekenntnisse und grundsätzlichen Ausserungen zur
Kirchenfrage des Jahres 1933*, edited by K.D. Schmidt (Göttingen,
1934), pp. 92f.

critical examination.

Whoever today speaks of two "unconditional" allegiances is talking about Yahweh and Baal, about being able to serve God and Mammon, and places himself outside the Evangelical Church.

4. The Reformation as a renewal of the church and the Word of God is not something that is "brought into an intimate relationship with the Germans" because it corresponds to their national character but rather because it corresponds to the wisdom and will of Divine Providence. It was and remains as suited or unsuited to the German as to any other race.

Whoever today treats the Reformation as a specifically German matter interprets it in a profane historical sense and places himself outside the Evangelical Church.

5. A "character" in a human being that does justice to his faith is to be found in the mystery of his new birth by the Word and Spirit of God. It can neither be "molded" by the National-Socialist revolution, nor can it be identified either directly or indirectly with the national "character" that is molded by the National-Socialist revolution.

Whoever today proclaims that faith is molded by events like the National-Socialist revolution makes faith itself into a perishable human work and places himself outside the Evangelical Church.

6. As for the attitude of obedience to God, Jesus Christ alone has sacrificed Himself vicariously for the disobedience of us all. Being a disciple of Jesus Christ probably can mean that we sacrifice ourselves for the sake of those values which we have received from God, but it can also mean that we renounce them.

Whoever today speaks in one and the same breath and in an uncritical manner of sacrificing himself for the sake of obedience to God and for the values of the German people denies the reality of sin, reconciliation through Christ alone, and the freedom of the divine command--and places himself outside the Evangelical Church.

7. Not the divine orders of church and state but more than likely their human realities must and always will find themselves in conflict as long as history exists under the rule of sin. Just what constitutes the obedience in earthly matters that the church is obliged to render to the state and just what kind of room the state is expected to allow for the church to carry out her task, this always must be the object of continual inquiry on the part of both sides, in mutual submission to God's Word.

Whoever today claims to be able to regulate the relationship of church and state on the basis of universal ultimate considerations obtained by paying heed to the living Word is already arguing in terms of an autocratic state rather than in terms of the promise given to the church (for the benefit of church and state alike!) and places himself outside the Evangelical Church.

In conclusion, the "theology" of the Rengsdorf Theses is clearly no theology at all but rather a prime example of the Gnosticism that is rampant today and that operates with Christian concepts. This Gnosticism neither understands nor considers the First, Second, or Third Articles of the Creed as a confession of the Word of God but rather understands and considers all three articles as an explication of man's own self-understanding (as in the emphasis upon the national component that is so common today), which has gone so far as to usurp external authority in the church. For both these reasons, it cannot be taken seriously as a universal ideology but instead has to be opposed energetically, precisely for the sake of Christian love!

The Barmen Theological Declaration and the Ansbach Response

134. *The Barmen Theological Declaration (1934)*[*]

In view of the errors of the "German Christians" of the present Reich Church government which are devastating the Church and are also thereby breaking up the unity of the German Evangelical Church, we confess the following evangelical truths:

1. "I am the way, and the truth, and the life; no one comes to the Father, but by me." (John 14:6.) "Truly, truly, I say to you, he who does not enter the sheepfold by the door but climbs in by another way, that man is a thief and a robber...I am the door; if anyone enters by me, he will be saved" (John 10:1, 9).

Jesus Christ, as he is attested for us in Holy Scripture, is the one Word of God which we have to hear and which we have to trust and obey in life and in death.

We reject the false doctrine, as though the Church could and would have to acknowledge as a source of its proclamation, apart from and besides this one Word of God, still other events and powers, figures and truths, as God's revelation.

2. "Christ Jesus, whom God made our wisdom, our righteousness and sanctification and redemption" (I Cor. 1:30).

As Jesus Christ is God's assurance of the forgiveness of all our sins, so in the same way and with the same seriousness he is also God's mighty claim upon our whole life. Through him befalls us a joyful deliverance from the godless fetters of this world for

---

[*]Reprinted from A.C. Cochrane, *The Church's Confession Under Hitler* (Philadelphia: Westminster Press, 1962), pp. 239-242.

a free, grateful service to his creatures.

We reject the false doctrine, as though there were areas of our life in which we would not belong to Jesus Christ, but to other lords--areas in which we would not need justification and sanctification through him.

3. "Rather, speaking the truth in love, we are to grow up in every way into him who is the head, into Christ, from whom the whole body (is) joined and knit together." (Eph. 4:15-16.)

The Christian Church is the congregation of the brethren in which Jesus Christ acts presently as the Lord in Word and sacrament through the Holy Spirit. As the Church of pardoned sinners, it has to testify in the midst of a sinful world, with its faith as with its obedience, with its message as with its order, that it is solely his property, and that it lives and wants to live solely from his comfort and from his direction in the expectation of his appearance.

We reject the false doctrine, as though the Church were permitted to abandon the form of its message and order to its own pleasure or to changes in prevailing ideological and political convictions.

4. "You know that the rulers of the Gentiles lord it over them, and their great men exercise authority over them. It shall not be so among you; but whoever would be great among you must be your servant" (Matt. 20:25-26).

The various offices in the Church do not establish a dominion of some over the others; on the contrary, they are for the exercise of the ministry entrusted to and enjoined upon the whole congregation.

We reject the false doctrine, as though the Church, apart from this ministry, could and were permitted to give to itself, or allow to be given to it, special leaders vested with ruling powers.

5. "Fear God. Honor the emperor" (I Peter 2:17).

Scripture tells us that, in the as yet unredeemed world in which the Church also exists, the State has by divine appointment the task of providing for justice and peace. (It fulfills this task) by means of the threat and exercise of force, according to the measure of human judgment and human ability. The Church acknowledges the benefit of this divine appointment in gratitude and reverence before him. It calls to mind the Kingdom of God, God's commandment and righteousness, and thereby the responsibility both of rulers and of the ruled. It trusts and obeys the power of the Word by which God upholds all things.

We reject the false doctrine, as though the State, over

and beyond its special commission, should and could become the single and totalitarian order of human life, thus fulfilling the Church's vocation as well.

We reject the false doctrine, as though the Church, over and beyond its special commission, should and could appropriate the characteristics, the tasks, and the dignity of the State, thus itself becoming an organ of the State.

6. "Lo, I am with you always, to the close of the age" (Matt. 28:20).

"The word of God is not fettered" (II Tim. 2:9).

The Church's commission, upon which its freedom is founded, consists in delivering the message of the free grace of God to all people in Christ's stead, and therefore in the ministry of his own Word and work through sermon and sacrament.

We reject the false doctrine, as though the Church in human arrogance could place the Word and work of the Lord in the service of any arbitrarily chosen desires, purposes, and plans.

The Confessional Synod of the German Evangelical Church declares that it sees in the acknowledgment of these truths and in the rejection of these errors the indispensable theological basis of the German Evangelical Church as a federation of Confessional Churches. It invites all who are able to accept its declaration to be mindful of these theological principles in their decisions in Church politics. It entreats all whom it concerns to return to the unity of faith, love, and hope.

135. *"The Ansbach Proposal as a Response to the Barmen Theological Declaration" (June, 1934)*[21]

The divisions that have arisen in the German Evangelical Church since its formation in the year 1933 oblige her entire membership to reflect upon the basis and the extent of their own relationship with the church. In particular, all those who hold pastoral office are obligated by the authority of their teaching office to be able to answer and help those members of our church who are asking questions or who have become confused. For this reason, we attach ourselves in faith to the promise of our Lord for all who have gathered together in His name for the purpose of common theological effort.

We therefore differentiate between the principles and the tasks of our effort as follows:

---

*"Der Ansbacher Ratschlag zur Barmer Theologischen Erklärung (Juni 1934)," in *Die Bekenntnisse und grundsätzlichen Ausserungen zur Kirchenfrage des Jahres 1934*, edited by K.D. Schmidt (Göttingen, 1935), p. 102ff.

A. The Principles

1. The church of Jesus Christ, as the workshop of the Holy Spirit, is bound to God's Word. Therefore her members are obligated to be obedient to that Word.

We find in the confessions of our Evangelical Lutheran Church the pure exposition of the content of Holy Scripture. Therefore members of the church are obligated to be obedient to these confessions as well.

We agree with Löhe's understanding of the Reformation: In its doctrine it is complete; in the implementation of doctrine it is incomplete.

We also agree with the words of the Erlangen theologian, Gottfried Thomasius: "In the house of my church, I consider myself not at all a servant but a child and find in this condition both the obligation of piety and the freedom of a child."

2. The Word of God addresses us as Law and Gospel.[22] The church's proclamation must adjust itself accordingly. The Gospel is the message of Jesus Christ, who died for our sins and was raised for our justification.

3. The Law, "namely, the immutable will of God" (Formula of Concord, Epitome VI, 6) meets us in the total reality of our life, as it is illuminated by the revelation of God. It binds everyone to the station to which he has been called by God and obligates us to the natural orders to which we are subject--such as family, people, race (that is, blood relationship). Furthermore, we are associated with a certain family, a certain people, a certain race. Moreover, inasmuch as the will of God always confronts us in our here-and-now world, it likewise binds us to a historical moment in the family, the people, or the race, that is to say, to a certain distinct point in its history.

4. The natural orders reveal to us more than the demanding will of God. Inasmuch as they establish our entire natural existence by means of their relationships, they are at the same time the means by which God creates and preserves our earthly life. Whoever becomes certain of the Father's grace by faith in Jesus Christ experiences also in the natural orders "pure, fatherly divine goodness and mercy."

As Christians, we give thanks to God for every order, also for every government--even in distorted form--as a tool for realizing God's purposes. But as Christians we also distinguish between good and eccentric masters, between healthy and deformed orders.

5. In recognition of this fact, as faithful Christians we give

thanks to God the Lord for bestowing the Führer (i.e. Adolf Hitler) as "a pious and faithful chief of state" upon our people in their time of need, just as we thank God for desiring to grant us "good government," a government with "discipline and honor," in the form of the National-Socialist state.

For this reason, we recognize that we are held responsible before God to assist the Führer in his work through our respective vocations and professions.

B. The Task

6. The church has a threefold relationship to the natural orders:

First, she must proclaim the law of God. In this respect, her task is the same in every age. This means that she confirms the majesty of the natural orders and reminds them of their God-given task.

Second, the members of the church themselves are subordinated to the natural orders. Inasmuch as church members always are associated with a certain people and with a certain moment in time, their obligation to their own nation receives a definite content at the hands of the present national political order. In this respect, the relationship of the church's membership to the natural orders is subject to historical modification. Only the fact of their obligation remains unaffected by this change.

Third, the church herself bears distinguishing characteristics which resemble those of the natural orders. An example of this can be seen in the extent to which the church's proclamation conforms to the diversity of national languages. In this respect too, the church's order is subject to similar historical modification.

7. Because the church has her relationship to the particular orders modified in the third sense above, she finds herself confronted with the necessity to re-examine her own order constantly.

The standard that is absolutely binding for this examination remains the commission which the church has received from her Lord. This commission extends to the fulfillment as well as to the content of the church's proclamation, to the administration of the sacraments and the office of the keys by the responsible preaching office.

All other factors which characterize the church's historical appearance--above all, her constitution and her cult--are to be measured against this standard. In this sense, the task of reforming the church always appears anew in every historical moment.

8. The accomplishment of this task in the church of our day
should also help us in our theological work and our ecclesiastical
efforts.

At the Beginning of World War II

136. "A Theological-Ethical Reflection on War" (October, 1939)[23]

A theological-ethical reflection on war must begin by
distinguishing between Christ's spiritual Kingdom and the secular
kingdom of sovereign authority. If all human beings were true
Christians, the secular government of sovereign authority would be
unnecessary, for then it would be possible to guarantee an ordered
social existence for individuals and nations alike without having
to resort to compulsion or force. Secular government is just as
unnecessary for Christians themselves. The Christian suffers
injustice and does what is right joyfully and gladly. But, whoever
is ready to suffer injustice and do what is right with such a joyful
spirit really does not need an authority appointed to help him
obtain justice whenever he suffer injustice--for it is not justice
that he desires--nor does he need such an authority to punish him
whenever he commits an injustice--for he does not commit any
injustice that deserves to be punished. That is why there can be
no power in Christ's spiritual Kingdom to compel justice and peace
by force. It is impossible for a human being to be beheaded in the
name of Christ or for a war--even a purely defensive war--to be
waged in His name, for Christ says: "My Kingdom is not of this
world."

But the number of true Christians is very, very small. Even
in a nation where a vast majority of the inhabitants have been
baptized into Christ's name, scarcely a single Christian can be
found among thousands. And whoever is not a Christian is subject
to the rule of sin and the devil. Human beings who are under the
rule of sin and the devil must necessarily tear one another apart
unless they come under some other restraining power. In order to
place an external restraint upon those persons who have come under
the power of sin and the devil, God, out of pure goodness and mercy,
has established the secular kingdom of sovereign authority, "just
as one ties a wild animal with chains and ropes so that it cannot
bite or snap as it usually does, no matter how much it would like
to continue doing so." God does not want the earth to become a
field of bleached corpses, even though that is what the earth deserves.
God wants to preserve human beings and the earth alive, since He

*[Peter Brunner], "Theologisch-ethische Besinnung zum Krieg"
(Oktober 1939)," in *Kirchliches Jahrbuch, 1933-1941*, edited by
Joachim Beckmann (Gütersloh: Gerd Mohn, 1948), pp. 351ff.

wants to communicate with them. God communicates only with living personal beings. God communicates with human beings only through Law and Gospel, in order to bring them to salvation. Ultimately, God wants to communicate with human beings in judgment at Christ's return. In order to meet Christ in His Gospel and upon His return, human beings—who destroy themselves when left to their own devices—must be kept alive. That is why God has established sovereign authority. This is the point of contact between the secular .kingdom of sovereign authority and Christ's spiritual Kingdom. The establishment of Christ's spiritual Kingdom by the preaching of the Gospel presupposes that living human beings are dwelling upon the earth. This precondition for the establishment of Christ's spiritual Kingdom makes the secular government of sovereign authority possible. This secular government prescribed by sovereign authority is transitory, just as the earth is transitory. But Christ's Kingdom is eternal. Hence, the secular government of sovereign authority also is limited in its ability to operate; its function is not to redeem mankind but only to hold back sin. Sovereign authority by itself cannot free human beings from the dominion of sin and the devil. Only the Gospel can do that. Therefore, Christ's Kingdom alone is the kingdom of redemption. All that sovereign authority can and should do is to prevent the dominion of sin and the devil from affecting the external actions of human beings in such a way that one human being takes the life of another. Although the Christian does not require the restraining power of secular government for himself, having been freed by the Gospel from the dominion of sin and the devil, and thus being free of the necessity to be compelled by force to do what is right, yet he freely subordinates himself to the secular government of sovereign authority out of love for the neighbor and for the sake of the common interest. Thus, the Christian considers the secular government of the state to be a gift from God, not for himself but for others. The Christian knows that he himself is completely under the rule of the Sermon on the Mount; but for his part he never places his neighbor under that rule. On the contrary, precisely the command to demonstrate love requires that the Christian seek, establish, confirm, promote, and gladly submit himself to the gift that is represented by the secular government of sovereign authority, for the sake of the neighbor.

In positively affirming secular government, the Christian really cannot go wrong, since authority itself is the means by which the sovereign authority is expected to accomplish its task, namely, the threat and the use of force. The Christian affirms the proper use of power in the hands of the secular government all the way down the line. A proper use of power occurs when its application makes possible the preservation of communal life for those human beings who are placed under the control of that authority. Such a proper use of power includes as its *ultima ratio* the taking of human life....

The question as to when circumstances actually require the sovereign authority to resort to the *ultima ratio* is for those exercising sovereign authority to decide for themselves. But the holders of sovereign authority can never escape the question as to the propriety of their decision, nor the question concerning the proper use of that power....

It would be good for those who hold sovereign authority to be true Christians; then the danger of a misuse of sovereign authority would be minimized. That is why Christians should and can pray fervently for a pious and trustworthy government, even though the gift of a pious and Christian government unfortunately constitutes one of the great rarities of world history....

Apart from the possibilities afforded by a political constitution, theological-ethical reflection does not admit any possibility for subjects on their own initiative to teach the sovereign authority responsibility. The theological ethic cannot write a blank check for tyrannicide any more than it can do so for a revolutionary war. In these instances as well, the theological ethic reminds us of the passage: "Vengeance is mine, I will repay, says the Lord." If the sovereign authority allows its subjects to become involved in exercising a mutual responsibility through a fixed constitution for the way in which sovereign authority is applied, then the Christian too will be expected to make use of the opportunity that is set before him. He cannot pray for those who exercise sovereign authority and then evade all responsibility for the proper use of sovereign power when and inasmuch as he is invited to participate in such cooperative effort....

a) The subject is expected to act within the limits of the possibilities allowed him by his constitution. Thus he should entrust only those persons with the exercise and execution of sovereign authority about whom he can say on the basis of the best knowledge and conscience that a misuse of sovereign authority seems most likely to be excluded if placed in their hands.

b) In the event that a misuse of sovereign authority must be admitted, the subject is expected to act within the limits of the possibilities allowed him by his constitution in obtaining redress, whether it be by means of a constitutional removal of the current officeholder from office and the installation of new persons to exercise sovereign authority or by means of a constitutional amendment.

Yet it will always be necessary to proceed with the utmost caution and care in such a situation....

Thus we have listed the most important presuppositions for discussing the problem of war. Just as the sovereign authority can resort to the *ultima ratio* of executing people in the interest of preserving the lives of its subjects, so it can also resort to the *ultima ratio* of war for the same reason. War is the official action undertaken by a sovereign authority to maintain and secure the lives of its subjects. It presupposes a threat to the existence of its people. Three things can be mentioned here:

a) Peoples usually fight wars but they do not wage them. Only sovereign authorities, only governments, can wage war. Peoples can wage war with other peoples only through the governments that rule over them. Even though in the example of the Prussian *levee en masse* of 1813 the initiative came from what we would call "the people," those people who fought in that instance could wage war only through the command of the person possessing the sovereign authority. The only--and most essential--subject in waging war is the person who possesses the sovereign authority, not the peoples themselves. This maxim applies to a thorough-going parliamentary and constitutional state as well as to an authoritarian state.

b) War presupposes a genuine threat to the existence of a people by a foreign power, just as a death sentence and what has led up to it presupposes a real threat to the existence of a society by one of its members. In a situation where the death penalty is not the answer to such a previous threat, the execution is hardly a God-pleasing action but, purely and simply, judicial murder. In a situation where waging war is not the answer to an actual previous real threat to the existence of a people, the war that results is not war but a predatory incursion.

c) There can be no question that in the opinion of our theological-ethical reflection the sovereign authority is justified in waging wars that are really wars in the usual sense of that term. Whoever affirms capital punishment out of conviction must also affirm war in principle for the same reason.

The Refugee Question

137. "The Situation of the Refugees and the Relationship of the German People to Their Eastern Neighbors" (October, 1965)[25]

The theological discussion involving questions like the right of a people to their homeland and the German eastern boundaries differs remarkably from the deliberations of international law. The discussion concerning justice has raised a variety of opinions about the legal situation, the possibilities for future legal development, and the legal relevance of moral and political postulates. There still is a broad consensus in the evaluation of what international law actually is able to accomplish. This consensus establishes the offense against the law that has occurred, explains the present legal situation, and offers forms and critiques for establishing a peaceful order among the peoples involved. The concrete shape which that order will take, however, depends upon a great many additional factors....

Theological reflection can make an effective contribution to the human and political aspect of the problem concerning the German eastern boundaries only if it has made the effort beforehand to achieve as much as possible a degree of common agreement. This means that the church must exercise caution in involving herself in a dispute of political opinions; she should limit herself only to those statements that she can and must make out of a sense of theological and ethical responsibility.

Thus, the questions concerning German eastern policy (*Ostpolitik*) are considered to be relevant applications of a theologically motivated ethic to a concrete situation. Hence, it should come as no surprise that the resulting discussion has led back to the dispute over principles that has characterized questions of political ethics in Evangelical theology during the past decade-and-a-half. On the one side are the theologians who from the start (and in greater measure) wish to concentrate their ethical thinking upon the reality of this sin-ridden world. In the structural forms of this world's fallen existence they see orders which God has established as a kind of preservative or emergency measures; as long as we respect these orders, we can restrain the power of sin and make decisions in every concrete situation. On the other side are the theologians who express doubt about the possibility of relating moral decisions

---

*"Die Lage der Vertriebenen und das Verhältnis des deutschen Volkes zu seinen östlichen Nachbarn (Oktober 1965)," in *Die Denkschriften der EKD: Texte und Kommentare*, edited by K.-A. Odin (Neukirchen, 1966), pp. 87ff.

to alleged principles of organization or to immutable relationships that are said to exist in the world. Where that happens, they contend, gaps appear, free spaces for moral decisions possessing an immanent, autonomous nature all their own; human beings are able to retreat into these orders and thus avoid rendering total obedience to the rule and claim of Jesus Christ, which always has to be renewed each day; the preaching of concrete Christian forms of obedience must replace the search for a definite system of norms.

The characteristic attitudes of both these groups which are locked in dispute with each other are thrown into sharp profile like the reflection from a mirror as we listen once again to the criticism which each group makes of the other. Whoever wishes to establish the form of human communal society upon a foundation of solid structural relationships opens himself up to the charge of lapsing into an ethics of resignation toward the task of giving shape to the world and to human life; such an ethic lets the world stay as it is at the given moment; it refuses to place at the world's disposal the powers of reconciliation that flow from the Christian faith; it justifies its own passivity by calling upon the divine will for support. The second group then is charged with concentrating upon the ever-changing requirements of a given situation without, however, presenting any clear criteria for doing so; this creates an impression of arbitrariness; the optimism about the possibility for obedience that is revealed here cannot be maintained all the way to its final conclusion; rather, it must fail due to the broken condition of all human activity under the dominant power of sin; the resulting effort to anchor moral and political decisions in the center of faith similarly fails to allow enough room for a divergency of opinions within the Christian community.

The dispute over ethical principles of which we have just found it useful to remind ourselves was conducted with particular passion in the debate over atomic weapons.... The discussion now underway concerning questions of the right of people to their homeland and the German eastern boundaries sounds on first hearing like a return to the old style of argumentation. That still can be seen in some of the concrete details. But the experience gained in the debate over atomic weapons ought to prevent the moment of truth from being absolutized in the future, as well as to preserve ethical considerations from falling prey to a doctrinaire attitude that has nothing to do with real life....

Ethical considerations have their necessary consequences: mutual guilt must be admitted openly without sanctioning injustices that ought not to be sanctioned; the relationship between the German and

Polish peoples in particular must be given a new orientation; the idea of and concern for reconciliation must be introduced as an indispensable factor into political negotiations....

Theological reflection confirms the realization that it is not the church's task to formulate political goals and solutions for every individual situation. But the political service which Christians perform does have an obligation to represent moral and humane conditions for a political course that serves human life and preserves the peace. In doing this, the church's word to political life dare not shrink back from calling by their proper names the sources of wrong political decisions or omissions if she desires to address the conscience concretely. The discussion about the "right of a people to their homeland" and about questions of *Ostpolitik* suffers under an emotional pathos as well as an inadequate factual content. Many public speeches on the subject give an impression of lacking true inner conviction. Thus, the church must step into the breach so that the basic questions of *Ostpolitik* can be given the most careful examination and, in some instances, reformulated....

Which concrete steps will best promote the goal of reconciliation and a new relationship is not something that can be discussed in this memorandum. It is certainly not enough to insist stubbornly and one-sidedly upon the German legal position, but on the other hand, no one can expect a German government to abandon its legal position unilaterally and as a matter of course either. Rather, an atmosphere first will have to be created, among the German people as well as abroad, in which individual acts of reconciliation with the eastern neighbors will become possible, one small step at a time.

This, of course, presupposes that a desire for reconciliation exists or can be awakened among these peoples. The crucial question must also be raised as to whether they will want to maintain their attitude of self-righteousness toward Germany that has been displayed so often in the past. But the dialogue about *that* problem can take shape only if the German people themselves make the first move to indicate that they will resist the temptation to harden their hearts in self-righteousness.

This memorandum thus does not claim to prescribe the path of negotiations for those who are delegated to take such political steps. But it does see an opportunity for the church to make the German people more aware of these all-important goals than usually has been true in the inner-German discussion as well as to eliminate the resistance to such goals that has been demonstrated so frequently

198

in the past. If the operating room for political negotiations has been expanded by this activity on the part of the church, then it is up to the politicians to use their opportunity wisely.

Politicizing the Church

138. "The Church and Politics" (May, 1968)*

I

The episcopal conference agreed that Christians and churches have to assume political responsibility for the sake of peace and justice in the world. The service of Jesus Christ applies to the total human being in all his life-circumstances, hence also in the social and political sphere. In undertaking their political responsibility, Christians and churches ought not to allow themselves to be impeded by those who limit faith to the inner life and thus exclude social problems from consideration, or by those who, for a variety of social and political reasons, wish to prevent the church from speaking. The Word of God, faith, forgiveness, and prayer all serve to preserve the world.

II

Christianity's only task is the proclamation of the Gospel of Jesus Christ. The more determined the church is to accept this task, the stronger is her power of persuasion. Political responsibility dare not lead to the politicization of the church. Such a confusion corrupts both political life and the church.

III

Christians and churches who wish to serve their Lord and mankind recognize that the world and the congregation, much as they are related to one another, still are subject to different laws. God is Lord and Redeemer. For the Christians, Law and Gospel apply. In the congregation, God rules by means of the Gospel. In the world, God rules by means of His Law, which serves as the foundation for human laws. This also means that the service of Christians and churches--who are obligated by God to serve in the world and in the congregation--has a form that is different for each sphere.

IV

In the episcopal conference, it was evident that a variety of questions still have to be thought through anew on the basis of these presuppositions. It was established that:

---

*"Kirche und Politik (Mai 1968)," in *Kirchliches Jahrbuch, 1968*, edited by Joachim Beckmann (Gütersloh: Gerd Mohn, 1970), p. 98.

a) Christians must participate in shaping and changing the
social and political order.

But it was emphasized strongly that it is up to human beings
and the Holy Spirit to fulfill the orders of life.

b) Christians affirm within the order of a constitutional
state the authority and the responsible use of power that is necessary
to protect that state.

However, they keep critical watch over authority. Authority
cannot be established solely on the basis of the political order.
The question concerning the true nature of authority confronts us
daily in all areas of life.

c) The church preserves peace and community among the various
members and groups of people with differing opinions who comprise
her membership.

The individual Christian, however, is bound to his own
conscience. He is obligated to use his political reason. He must
make judgments on the basis of more precise information and take
a stand.

The church cannot absolve him from this task. It can remind
him of his God-given responsibility. In doing this, the church
at the same time frees him to make individual decisions.

d) The utopia of a perfect political and social order is
forbidden the Christian.

The church provides a realm free from ideologies and prevents
the Christian from discriminating against those who think differently
from himself and from labeling them as heretics.

Churches and Christians make intercession for politicians
and their task. They are obligated to provide them with pastoral
care.

139. *"Right and Wrong Intervention of the Church in Politics"**

1. We must refuse to accept the alternative of having to
choose between, on the one hand, the "true" task of the Church,
which consists of proclaiming the gospel of Jesus Christ, and on
the other hand the perception of political responsibility. The
Church has only to do what belongs to its essential task, and nothing
that it really has to do is "inessential." Here the distinction is
not one between matters of primary and of secondary importance,
but at the most a distinction between the centre and the periphery.
In the centre stands faith, on the periphery you have works; in the
centre the gospel, politics on the periphery; in the centre
salvation, on the periphery the well-being of our neighbour.

---

*Helmut Gollwitzer, *The Rich Christian and Poor Lazarus*, tr.
David Cairns. (New York: MacMillan, 1970) pp. 22-23, 26-27.

Between the centre and the periphery our human life revolves, on the periphery is decided and revealed what has happened at the centre....

Works in comparison with faith, sanctification in comparison with justification, are not "inessentials," matters of secondary importance, but the articles dealing respectively with justification and with sanctification stand, as the Lutheran fathers said, in relation to each other as *articulus fidei constituens* and *articulus fidei consequens*.... Similarly, in my relationship to my fellow-man, my service done for his welfare is not a secondary matter in comparison with my service done for his salvation. The two are inseparable. If his physical misery can bar his way to salvation, his hearing of the gospel, then my service can become a hypocrisy if I concern myself only with his soul and make no sacrifices for his body....

The Church has not become political in the bad sense when it thus says yes or no in political questions, but when this yes or no does not follow from a careful listening to the gospel as an attempt to do justice to its contemporary challenge, but is based on other reasons, drawing its inspiration from other sources and other attachments, which will then certainly be "godless attachments".... The only refuge from this bad type of meddling with politics is responsible political action, the perception of political responsibility in a carefully tested and critical, above all, self-critical, fashion. But this will always involve taking sides. The credibility of the Church does not depend upon its neutrality.... Its credibility follows from its independence, from the fact that in supporting a party, i.e., taking sides, it does not belong to a party....

In my opinion the following principle can be enunciated to guide the Church in legitimate political participation (here I mean the Church's official representatives and organs). The interest guiding such participation must not be that of the Church's self-preservation and the preservation of its privileges, but the interests of peace (i.e., of co-operation and the avoidance of violence and bloodshed), the interests of those who are deprived of secular justice (i.e., equality before the law and a fair share in the products of society), and civil freedom (i.e., the opportunity of responsible self-determination in activity and in helping to shape the forms of society).

140. *Creative Discipleship in the Contemporary World Crisis**

The co-responsibility of Christians in today's concrete crisis
is something which I do not derive simply from the current mentality.
Instead my thesis is: By creating freedom and love, the gospel
affords us criteria with which reason can find its orientation
and free itself from false priorities. The reason of which we speak
is not reason in the abstract, but in that form which it has assumed
through its incarnation in our present, scientific-technological
world.

How is that related to the doctrine of the Two Kingdoms, such
as is operative in Lutheranism? Does not this doctrine tend to
partition off the gospel, the spiritual realm, precisely from all
things earthly, and thus relinquish the world to its own self-
interests? Does not this doctrine separate the message of love
from the necessary ordering of this world and the secular reason
which corresponds to it? This kind of static-dualistic use of the
doctrine of the Two Kingdoms is unfortunately widespread. Such
use is made of it when one advocates conservative quietism in public
matters and emphasizes individual salvation in the private realm.
But, I am afraid, in doing this one misses completely the truth and
sense of the doctrine of the Two Kingdoms and appeals wrongly to
Luther. One can conclude this from Luther's own attitude even
without complicated theological investigation. Luther certainly
opposed mixing together the spiritual and secular realms. He fought
clericalism as strongly as he fought religious authorization of
secular-political offices or of political action. For example, he
felt that he could not tolerate for this reason the peasants who
proclaimed their revolt in Christian terms as a concern of the
gospel.

Luther felt obligated as a doctor of theology to enter into
the secular events of his time with demands, recommendations and
advice to remind Christians of their specific responsibility. From
them, this must be strongly underlined today, he expected non-violence
and the waiving of rights in personal matters, strictly corresponding
to the requirements of discipleship in the Sermon on the Mount.
His theology enabled him to demand publicly a new law of peace as
a replacement for the medieval laws governing feuds and the
protection of one's own interests. In his exposition of the
Magnificat, in 1520-21, he virtually taught the people a lesson in

*Heinz Eduard Tödt,"Creative Discipleship in the Contemporary
World Crisis," *Lutheran World*, 17 (1970), pp. 325-326. An address
to a plenary session of the Fifth Assembly of the Lutheran World
Federation, Evian, France, July, 1970.

law. He repeatedly demanded the establishment of schools and development of an educational system and interpreted these things to be the proper consequences of evangelical preaching. In the famous "Sermon on Keeping Children in School", from 1530, there is the sentence: "Therefore, to tell the truth, peace, which is the greatest of earthly goods, and in which all other temporal goods are comprised, is really a fruit of true preaching."

If temporal peace is a proper fruit of preaching, there is tied to this ministry of preaching an eminently critical task. It is almost inconceivable to me how it was possible that Luther's sharp, public accusations against the rulers of his time, against "tyranny and suppression" of the poor have been forgotten, and how views in favor of a general and uncritical legitimization of those in power have been derived from Luther's doctrine of the Two Kingdoms. That it has been the subject of so much attention is really only understandable in the light of the tragic event of the Peasant War.

Luther very strictly measured the practical action of rulers over aginst the gracious will of God and the concrete needs of man according to which both reason and love should function. Politics, law, economics and science-regardless of all distinctions of competence-do not exist for him self-sufficiently in an isolated realm, but need critical instruction. Doing this is the obligation of those who on the basis of renewed thought inquire about what is now the good and perfect will of God (Rom. 12:2). If, therefore, we now orient ourselves according to Luther's own behavior as a competent interpretation of the doctrine of the Two Kingdoms, we will then recognize our obligation toward analogous responsibilities in our own time.

E. THE GERMAN DEMOCRATIC REPUBLIC SINCE 1949

Introduction[25]

The Christians and churches in the socialist German Democratic Republic, as they looked back on German history in general and their own recent experiences in the church's struggle (*Kirchenkampf*) against the National-Socialist State in particular, found themselves confronted from the very beginning with two equally extreme expectations: either to knuckle under completely to the new state as it existed or to continue a policy of total opposition to it as in the days of the Third Reich.

In the first document both alternatives are hinted at as possible courses of action. The official demand made by the government that the church honor her obligations according to Romans 13 reveals the dilemma in which the Lutheran Church finds itself, since this church in its past history often tended to apply that text uncritically, as a legitimation for existing power relationships. On the other hand, it soon became apparent that the fathers and children of the Confessing Church (*Bekennende Kirche*), far from opposing the socialist state completely, were making an attempt to determine carefully just what was good and what was bad about it.

The Lutheran Church leadership, meanwhile, sought to chart a more careful course, aided by the doctrine of the two kingdoms. The most interesting feature of these efforts has been the drawing of a clear distinction between the social, economic, and political structures of society--which are regarded as being more or less neutral and therefore acceptable in their various historical guises --and the ideological-atheistic components of socialism as practiced in the German Democratic Republic--which must be resisted passionately. Regarding the first aspect, the lessons which the church learned in its struggle under National Socialism clearly have been retained, inasmuch as God's Word is said to apply to all areas of human life (see the Barmen Theological Declaration). The church has never admitted that the socialist criticism of the injustices which occurred under previous social systems might possibly be justified, injustices for which the church might also be responsible--either by its silence or by the way in which it legitimized and supported the social systems which produced them. The documents betray a spirit that is willing to accept the new social order, but only with extreme reluctance, as something to be patiently endured rather than fervently embraced. This holds true for all except the final document from the year 1974, which explicitly acknowledges the positive achievements of the socialist society. Nor are the possible consequences of the new recognition of Christian responsibility for the world reflected in their implications for the structures of the church.

On this point, several theological commissions within the German Democratic Republic go one step further than the official church organs. They call special attention to the church's guilt for past omissions as a factor that prevents it from offering a credible and effective Christian witness or a relatively free Christian service within socialist society. New church structures are also required if the new understanding of Christian responsibility for the world is to be realized in practice. In view of the history of the two kingdoms doctrine, it is interesting to observe that the theological study committee of the Lutheran World Federation's National Committee in the German Democratice Republic has related

these new accents explicitly to the intensive ecumenical discussion
of the same questions. Certainly the daily reality to which
Christians in the German Democratic Republic are exposed and which
they in all honesty accept can be said to have contributed to a
situation in which they can intensively appropriate and make their
own experiences from other churches throughout the world.

Traditional Expectations

141. *Subordination to the Existing State* *

It has been reported to me that Heinrich Vogel has explicitly
refused to make a declaration of loyalty on the grounds that it
cannot be the task of the Evangelical Church to sanction any single
social system or state above another. I am in complete agreement
with Heinrich Vogel's viewpoint that the church cannot and should
not sanction any particular social order. This point of view has
always been emphasized by our side. The declaration of loyalty to
our state in reality should be nothing more than a declaration:

1) about how Romans 13 is to be observed, especially with
respect to our state (and this the synod has done), and

2) about the extent to which the church disassociates herself
from the charges made by Western propaganda that the Evangelical
Church is the only center of resistance against the new social order
in the German Domocratic Republic: up to now, this disassociation
has been made only by General Superintendant Jacob, and even here
on this decisive point where our demand for loyalty has been made
in the past, the synod has left a loophole open.

I believe that it is important to keep this loophole in mind,
just as I consider it urgently necessary to close the loophole in
the future in order to pave the way for a truly fruitful reorganization
of the relationships between church and state in the German Democratic
Republic.

Ecclesiastical Pronouncements

142. *The Christian in the German Democratic Republic* *

This proposal investigates the question as to the possibility
for a Christian in the German Democratic Republic to demonstrate
in his personal life that he belongs to Christ. This possibility
for a Christian lifestyle is placed in question by the fact that
life in the German Democratic Republic is determined by a socialism
whose philosophical foundation is dialectical materialism and whose

---

*Otto Nuschke, "Letter to Provost Grüber," July, 1956, found
in *Kirchliches Jahrbuch*, 1956 (Gütersloh, 1958), p. 27f.
**A Proposal by the Episcopal Conference of the United
Evangelical Lutheran Church of Germany (VELKD) in *Kirchliches
Jahrbuch*, 1961 (Gütersloh, 1963), pp. 198-208.

integrating factor is atheism.

The Christian confesses his solidarity with all mankind. All human beings are in the same way lost sinners for whom Jesus Christ died. This latter solidarity which exists between Christians and atheists dare not be lost sight of or denied in instances where political and philosophical discussion is unavoidable. It prohibits the Christian from superficially painting everything in black and white or from running down his opponent as is customary in political propaganda. Christian brotherhood, for which the Christian also opens himself to the atheist, follows other laws than those that govern the building of political fronts. But the solidarity with all men who are sinners and who have been called by Jesus Christ to forgiveness dare not conceal the special nature of the community of believers in Jesus Christ. This message applies to the atheist inasmuch as the Christian has an obligation to witness to him about Christ in a way that is not separated from the preaching of God's judgment upon all sinners who do not repent.

The conflicts that affect Christian life in the German Democratic Republic, however, do not really take place on the personal level, that is to say, between men who do not think the same way. This is why they cannot be overcome or even reduced by a mere appeal to human solidarity. Rather, we are faced with the fact that an atheistic brand of socialism has taken possession of the means of exercising state power in the political, social, and economic spheres of life. In such a state with a distinctive ideology, the question of belief is not, as it ought to be, a matter of free discussion between equal partners but becomes a question of one's very outer and inner existence.

1. The Basic Christian Attitude Toward the State

A. The Biblical Doctrine of Government and Earthly Rule

In this situation where political, economic, and social life is totally immersed in an atheistic reality, the Christian is tempted to act too hastily in moving into opposition on the political and moral level or to allow his relationship to the world around him to be influenced by political ideas formed in an earlier age. But the Christian understanding of the world in general, as well as his criticism of a particular form of government, must proceed from the fact that God is the lord of history, governing the world of today just as he has governed the world of yesterday and will govern the world of tomorrow. Earthly government is part of this divine governing of the world.

We find the most pertinent guidance for our behavior toward earthly government in the thirteenth chapter of Romans. Here the

Apostle Paul talks about those who occupy offices of secular power as the "higher powers" whom everyone is obliged to obey for the sake of conscience, because through their activity God preserves the world. The sword is given into their hands so that they can carry out their official function of protecting the good and punishing the evil with force if necessary. Such a legitimate use of power exists in a world in which sin must be defended against and a chaotic struggle of all against all prevented. Neither the church nor the Christian sets about first creating order in the world. There are merciful ordinances of God which have been in existence from the beginning of the world and which function even in places where the ultimate origin of these gifts remains unknown and where the power that God has given to human beings is misused. This theological evaluation of secular government is completely independent of that government's historical origin, both with respect to its particular form and to the manner in which it actually operates.

Ever since the time of Luther, the German language has equated these "higher powers" with "government." Recent discussion has shown that most theologians believe this concept--regardless of its original meaning--to contain so many essential theological elements applicable to every sovereign power that it continues to provide a useful point of reference until a better concept can be found. The word "government" is transparent enough for the divine component and brings the secular government out of its anonymity by uniting the institution with the person occupying the seat of power.

The theological point of departure for a critique of government is the vantage point provided by faith. That government exists at all is an assertion of faith. Hence it is impossible to determine whether or not government exists in a theological sense by humanly observing and reflecting upon fixed criteria. Where that happens, there the heart of a theological understanding of government has been eliminated. Earthly government is to be accepted on faith as part of God's governing in the world, even where outer appearances may argue against it.

The Reformation classified its understanding of government under the doctrine of God's two kingdoms, thus anchoring it in the broad and deep biblical understanding of the world and of history. The conflict between the power of God and the tyranny of evil can be endured at all only in the eschatological preservation of this world. This has been instituted as a provisional measure in anticipation of the return of Christ--whose victory has already been won. A correctly understood doctrine of government imposes upon us an obligation to obey earthly tyrants as part of the Christian life. It enables us to recognize even an oppressive earthly government as God's good gift and gives us the strength to endure the miseries and horrors of this present world.

The Holy Scriptures teach us that earthly governments can pervert their origins and their tasks so much that they degenerate entirely into instruments of Satan and take on the features of government as described in Revelation 13. The tension between obedience and disobedience under which the Christian lives in every state receives its acid test at this point. Whether or not a particular state has become demonic in this sense is really a question that can be answered only by critically examining the particular situation from a spiritual point of view; this holds true as well for the question as to the kind of practical Christian behavior which is required here. No doctrine of government can relieve an oppressed and troubled conscience of its burden and doubt concerning the kind of obedience which is called for. In no case, however, dare the comfort of the Gospel be withheld from such a conscience: "Here is the endurance and faithfulness of the saints!" (Revelations 13:10).

B. The Significance of the Biblical Understanding of Government for the Political Preaching of the Church and for the Christian's Position in State and Society

This is how the Holy Scriptures instruct us to live in the world: We are to take an active part in working together to shape its life even as we patiently endure its reality. At the same time, it will become obvious that an evaluation of secular government from an eschatological point of view excludes all possibility for a distinctively "Christian" organization of the state, the economy, and the society. This gives the Christian a great amount of freedom, inasmuch as he can actually involve himself in a variety of political, economic, and social structures as a co-worker from the ground up. As a result, he must be prepared to recognize the hand of God in revolutionary upheavals as well, even when they have been intermixed with injustice and acts of violence, accepting them as an opportunity for new human life in society. Love obligates a Christian to work for the welfare of his fellowmen in his vocation and in society, even when he knows that all labor invested in the earthly human society is placed into question by the shape of the Kingdom of God to come. Just as the church lives by virtue of her own particular commission, which is to proclaim salvation in Jesus Christ, so the Christian abides in the hope which sustains him, independent of all earthly success and human progress.

The Christian's disassociation from the world, together with his simultaneous cooperative effort to give it shape, as well as the fact that congregations of Christ exist with their commission to proclaim to men by means of Law and Gospel the will of God for the preservation of the world and for salvation in Jesus Christ-- all these factors provide some basic principles for public life in society which the church and her members dare not keep to themselves:

1. Salvation in Jesus Christ reaches human beings only through the preaching of God's Word and the administration of the sacraments. The mere fact of the church's existence, as well as the activity which she performs according to her divine commission, deprives political, economic, and social matters of every redemptive quality.

2. The fact that congregations of Jesus Christ exist on earth effectively restricts the competence of the organized state to earthly matters. A claim on the part of the state to embrace the totality of life leads to the self-idolatry of the state and to a corresponding socialization of human beings that glosses over the unique significance of each individual.

3. The temptation on the part of the state to aim for total power finds its proper limitation in the proclamation of the Gospel. The church demands no special position for her service, but the Gospel requires that she be allowed to proclaim the Gospel and live out her life of earth. An organized state that remains within the limits which God has set for it leaves here the necessary room for decisions of faith as well as room for the church to serve free from state intervention. To that extent, the effective recognition of religious liberty and the liberty to proclaim the Gospel only enhances the good opinion which an organized state desires for itself.

4. The church dare not make false claims upon the state. There can be no "Christian state" in the sense that this state would be empowered and equipped to spread the Christian faith by its own unique methods or to guarantee the formation of a Christian content in the lives of its citizens. A state that is "atheistic" in the sense that it propagates its own atheism by extracting from its citizens an atheistic confession in word or in deed and by depriving them of the possibility for Christian obedience--must also be opposed. It is at this point that the necessity for the Christian to obey God rather than men begins.

5. Historical experience shows that a restriction of Christian religious liberty compelled by state power never remains isolated but is connected to further restrictions on liberty. Religious

liberty therefore, is the door to a more comprehensive Christian co-responsibility for public life, a co-responsibility which leads the Christian to intercede for an effective limitation in the exercise of state power and for the preservation of distinctive and essential human liberties.

6. In this connection, it is possible to imagine a multiplicity of political constitutions as well as a plurality of economic and social structures which could easily satisfy the Christian critique. What ultimately matters is that the Christian be enabled to place his life in the service of the divine providence in a way that allows him to retain that dignity which is founded upon freedom of religion and of conscience. It is at this point that the church's preaching of God's Law becomes effective for earthly structures.

7. From these general considerations, it follows that the Christian cannot avoid making political, moral, rational, or historical judgments about state forms or political decisions. The church's preaching combines the demand for obedience to the government established by God with the reservation that she is free to remind those who wield power in the state that God has set limits for them. The Word of God, prayer, and suffering--these are the Christian's weapons in the event that a conflict erupts with the earthly power over a question about the will of God.

Historical situations are imaginable where the church and her members will be prevented by force from exercising any cooperative effort on their own initiative and out of a sense of Christian responsibility within a particular state and social system. It may also come to pass that such cooperative effort will be made impossible by the very way in which that effort is organized. But it is unthinkable that the Church of the Reformation on her own volition should refuse to address the world and its structures with the Word of God in the form of Law and Gospel. She can ill afford to do this since the credibility of her preaching and the strength of the comfort which she gives depend upon it.

II. The Basic Attitude of the Christian Toward the German Democractic Republic

Thesis 1: The Evangelical Christian's biblically grounded faith does not tie him to any particular social structure. Hence there is nothing to keep him from respecting the political and social structure of the German Democratic Republic.

Thesis 2: The Evangelical Christian's faith likewise does **not** prevent him from respecting the socialist economic structure of the **German** Democratic Republic.

210

Thesis 3:   The Evangelical Christian's faith in God through Jesus Christ compels him to reject dialectical materialism because and insofar as it denies God and replaces his commandments with mere human norms.

Thesis 4:   Carrying out a vocational life, as well as performing civic and social functions, has become deeply problematical for the Christian in the German Democratic Republic.   The situation with respect to the Christian education of the young is almost hopeless by virtue of the fact that this workers' and peasants' state is a state with an atheistic ideology; its social and economic policy always serves simultaneously to build an atheistic and materialistic consciousness.

Thesis 5:   Although the government of the German Democratic Republic allows only atheistic dialectical materialism to exert influence over all sectors of the state and all areas of intellectual life as the predominating ideology, the Christian (in accord with Romans 13 and in the light of Revelation 13) views the government of the German Democratic Republic as the governing authority placed over him by God, to which he owes allegiance and which he is to serve by fulfilling his civic obligations.

Thesis 6:   Because social and political goals in the German Democratic Republic are to be carried out only in relation to the atheistic and materialistic ideology, the Christian is prevented from actively participating in political and social life above and beyond fulfilling his general obligations.

Thesis 7:   The Christian can only accept and endure the fact that he must live in a state with an official atheistic ideology. But he cannot approve of or advance that ideology.   This attitude calls for the Christian neither to undertake political resistance nor to flee from the republic but rather to endure to the end with Christian faith and Christian patience in the situation into which God has placed him.

Thesis 8:   As he endures to the end with faith and with patience, the Christian is to bear witness in word and in deed that the will of God is his highest ethical standard, even when this brings suffering or death: "The world passes away, together with its allurements, but he who does the will of God abides forever" (I John 2:17).

Thesis 9:   In a practical sense, the basic attitude of Evangelical Christians signifies that they too are able to work together in the factories which are publicly owned, in the producers' cooperatives, and everywhere else to build up the state and the common economic life of the German Democratic Republic, inasmuch as it is possible to do this without making a confession of allegiance to atheism and without directly promoting the atheistic ideology.

Thesis 10: The Christian cannot help along wherever a procedural or administrative measure is tied directly to a confession of allegiance to atheistic materialism or to a propagation of the same. This applies also to participation in the rite of dedication for the young, as well as to socialistic and atheistic name-giving festivals or ceremonies which the state has introduced to serve as substitutes for marriages and funerals.

Thesis 11: The Evangelical Christian is obliged to reject methods and means which are opposed to God's commandments.

Thesis 12: Apart from general suggestions, the Evangelical Christian can expect to find no individual instruction in the Bible telling him how to conduct himself in the German Democractic Republic. In most instances, he is called upon to maintain his Evangelical existence by making his decision in conformity with the will of God and in responsibility before Jesus Christ, in the assurance that his sins will be forgiven.

Thesis 13: In all conflict situations between the demands of the state on the one hand and the commandments of God on the other, the Evangelical Christian places his trust in the validity of the biblical word: "We must obey God rather than men" (Acts 5:29).

143. *Ten Articles on the Freedom and Service of the Church**
The conference of the Evangelical Church leadership in the German Democratic Republic sees in the "Ten Articles on the Freedom and Service of the Church" the guidelines which an interpretation of Scripture and the Confessions provide for the contemporary church.

"Let us look to Jesus, the author and finisher of our faith, who for the joy that was set before Him endured the cross, despising the shame, and is seated at the right hand of the throne of God. Consider Him who endured from sinners such hostility against himself, so that you may not grow weary or fainthearted" (Hebrews 12:2-3).

There is only *one* Lord: Jesus Christ. Through Him, God has created us, together with all creatures. By His death and resurrection, God has reconciled the world to Himself and has made Him to be Lord of all lords. Through the Holy Spirit, we are God's children. We wait patiently for the fulfillment of His kingdom in

**Kirchliches Jahrbuch, 1963* (Gütersloh, 1965) pp. 181-185.
The article came from a Conference of the Evangelical Church Leadership in the German Democratic Republic.

glory and know that we must all one day appear before the judgment throne of Christ. In this confession lies the freedom of the Christian congregation, its service, and its future.

I. The Task of Proclamation

Jesus Christ has sent His congregation into the world to proclaim God's reconciliation to all men and to witness to them of His will in every area of their lives. Whoever accepts God's Word is not placed under an oppressive coercion but comes into a magnificent freedom. Whoever refuses it remains under God's condemnation. God wants us to preach His Word confidently, without fearing men and without flattering them.

II. The Life of Faith and Obedience

God wants the new man who is created in His image. Therefore He has reconciled us with Himself in Christ. He has renewed the dignity that man lost by the fall into sin and has given our life purpose and fulfillment. For this reason, He admonishes us to give up all godless relationships, to bear witness to the power of reconciliation in our own life, and to be of service to our fellowmen in all areas of life. We have to discover in our existing social relationships what it is that God desires to have from us and are to do good in agreement with His will.... In the freedom provided by our faith, we are allowed to distinguish from the start between accepting the opportunities for service in the preservation of life that are offered us in the socialist society and rejecting the atheistic aspects that go with it.

We act in disobedience when we confess God as Lord in our worship services only to expose ourselves in daily life to the claim of an absolutist ideology as we eliminate ourselves from the universal applicability of God's First Commandment. We act in disobedience when we allow ourselves to be bound to the distinctive morality of an atheistic ideology which makes the human being without God the goal of all education and learning. We confuse consciences when we fail to oppose the claim that the commandments of God and the "Ten Commandments of Socialist Morality" both tend toward a common humanistic goal....

IV. Justification and Justice

In the crucifixion and resurrection of Jesus Christ, God has declared lost man to be justified and has called him to live in His kingdom as the new man of God. To this end, God preserves the world in His providential goodness and also protects man in his humanity by the institution of earthly justice. It is doubtful whether legal precepts of eternal validity can be derived from God's justice. But the justice of God demands that all earthly justice respect the dignity of the human being who has been created and redeemed, that it preserve the equality of all before the law, that it assure protection for the weak, and that it guarantee the proclamation of the Gospel and the life of love for the neighbor.

In spite of sin, man is able to design useful laws. But his contradiction to God--who demands justice--always leads him to succumb to the temptation of misusing the law for his own selfish interests or of subjecting it to the claim of an absolutist ideology, thereby destroying it. Where there is no mercy, there is also no justice!

The evidence of God's justice and the command to love the neighbor obligate the congregation to share a concern for good earthly justice. Such concern is demonstrated when we bear witness to God's commandments, preserve our basic humanity, work in our earthly vocation, and show that we are willing to suffer injustice rather than to act unjustly....

We act in disobedience when we accept in silence that justice is misused or destroyed for the sake of political or economic interests and when we fail to intercede for and suffer with the neighbors who are deprived of their rights and threatened in their humanity.

V. Reconciliation and Peace

God has made peace with the world through the crucified and resurrected Jesus Christ. Christ is our peace. His Gospel proclaims the beginning of a new humanity in which enmity between human beings and nations is brought to an end. For this reason, Christians are to serve the cause of reconciliation in the world.

This service obligates us to seek peace also in our earthly relationships....

The service of reconciliation obligates us further to act honestly and earnestly for peace among nations. In view of the massive means of destruction that exist today, war is less than ever a live possibility for the solution of political and ideological tensions between peoples and power blocs.

The church intercedes for the legal protection of the person who refuses to serve in the military for reasons of faith and conscience, just as she takes care of her pastoral responsibility for those members of the church who do become soldiers.

Whoever must suffer because of his service on behalf of reconciliation can be assured of God's faithfulness and should experience the intercessory love of the congregation.

We act in disobedience when we confuse the peace on earth with the peace of God and when we expose our efforts for earthly peace to the standards of human ideologies, political utopias, and thoughts of revenge,, or when we give way to despair in our efforts to achieve peace.

We act in disobedience when we fail to oppose the misuse which occurs when political or national self-interest is equated with service on behalf of peace....

VII. Government

The church confesses that Jesus Christ, the Lord to Whom all power in heaven and on earth is given, is also Lord over those who administer power in the state. According to divine decree, these people have the obligation to promote justice and peace. We honor this gracious ordinance of God by praying for the government and by respecting its authority.

Those who administer power in the state remain in the hand of God and under His authority, even when they ignore this, make themselves rulers over conscience, and interfere with the ministry of the church. In the certainty of this conviction, we bear witness to the government of the truth, even when we must suffer for it.

We give way to unbelief when we fail to acknowledge the ordinances of God with gratitude or, vice versa, when we suppose that a state which ignores its responsibility would ever escape from God's control and no longer be obliged to serve Him.

We act in disobedience when we fail to determine where we could serve the state in a God-pleasing manner for the preservation of life. We act in disobedience when we do not stand up for the truth, when we maintain silence before the misuse of power, and when we are not prepared to obey God rather than men.

144. *The Christian Encouraged to Participate**

How important the sentence from the resolution of the general synod in 1969 is has already been seen. This resolution pointed out that doctrinal conversations which touch upon the social and political engagement of the church and of Christians must deal with the doctrine of the two kingdoms and the doctrine of Christ's kingship. Here the Lutheran Church must always refer to the biblical insights of Martin Luther and the Lutheran Confessions concerning the present state of the world between the ascension of Christ and his eventual return. This reveals clearly that the distinction between Law and Gospel must be maintained.

From this, there emerges a sober opinion as to the possibilities

---

*From a report of the Church administration to the First General Synod of the United Evangelical Lutheran Church in the German Democratic Republic, (VELK/DDR), 1972.

afforded the church in accord with the will of God for effecting
a transformation of relationships in the world. From this, it
also follows that the individual Christian should be encouraged to
participate actively in our society on the basis of his faith. No
matter where he is, a Christian is subject to the claim of God,
who sets for him both the possibilities and the limitations in all
the areas of his life.

145. *A Church Within Socialism**

It must be acknowledged openly that in the German Democratic
Republic provision has been made for the social security of every
individual, health services have been expanded to a high degree,
and the level of school and educational life has reached an
impressive niveau, even when--and this point must be emphasized--its
ideological and atheistic direction is troublesome. After a quarter
of a century of the German Democratic Republic's history, a time
which has corresponded to the longest peaceful period in Europe
during this century, what was mentioned as a formal opinion at the
federal synod in Eisenach in 1971 should be given consideration now:
we exist not against or beside socialism but rather as a church
within socialism. Here, as in defining the concept of "the socialist
citizen with a Christian faith," we must proceed from the biblical
insights of Luther's doctrine of the two kingdoms. This maintains
that the church and her members are obliged to accept the social
situation and the political reality in which they live in the German
Democratic Republic as coming from God. For He is the Lord over
church *and* state, and as Lord of history He has established the
social and political reality of the German Democratic Republic as
the arena in which the faith of the individual Christian and the
church is to be tested in obedient discipleship.

Confessions of Guilt and Freedom to Serve

146. *The Freedom of the Church to Serve***

For some years now, the churches in the German Democratic
Republic have initiated a series of efforts to determine the witness
which the church of Jesus Christ is authorized to provide in a
socialist society, so as to give her congregations some guidelines
in this confused world. Although it is certainly encouraging that
such efforts are being made, yet we must confess that the results
to date have proved unsatisfactory. Many such attempts bespeak more
a spirit of defensiveness or accommodation than the spirit of the
Gospel that makes us free.

---

*From a report of the Church Administration to the Second
General Synod of the VELK/DDR, 1974.
**Junge Kirche*, January 10, 1964, p. 29.

Hence we have drawn up these theological propositions in an attempt to introduce the message of the humiliated and exalted Lord more clearly into the list of problems discussed in earlier opinions and guidelines. We ask that our theological propositions be checked with the Scriptures. We are aware of the fact that these few propositions can indicate only possible future directions. We hope that they help to clarify the closely related questions of importance, starting from the heart of the Gospel, namely the cross of Jesus Christ, so that one day the church can provide satisfactory guidelines for the searching, questioning, and doubting Christian.

We confess Jesus Christ, our Lord, to be the Savior and Lord of the world. Because He did not come to be served but to serve, the entire world lives by the grace of God. For through Him, God has created the world; through His death and resurrection, He has reconciled it with Himself and has called it into the service of His Kingdom. That is the decisive reality for the world and its history, even when the world remains unaware of it.

The church is the assembly of Jews and heathen, the law-abiding and the lawless, the pious and the impious--in short, the church is the assembly of all those who daily hear, believe, and confess anew in the Word of the everpresent Christ God's love for the world as a means for overcoming their own godlessness.

Jesus Christ frees us to confess our guilt: that instead of living according to God's Law, we have used it to condemn the world; that we have often related God's love only to ourselves, the church, while applying God's wrath on account of sin to the world. Thus God's Holy Name is misused and slandered for our own purposes.

At the same time, Jesus Christ frees us to confess our faith in the forgiveness of sins and in repentance. God's faithfulness upholds us despite our faithlessness to the task of bearing witness of His grace to all mankind. Should we who believe in His forgiveness not hope for those who do not believe in it?

Thus Jesus Christ frees His church, not to keep her justification by faith to herself but to address herself in a confessing, loving, and serving manner to the world whose sins Christ bears. In this authorization for selfless service, the church discovers her freedom.

I. The Task of the Church

Jesus Christ sends His congregation, the church, out into the world in order to bear witness to all men in all areas of their lives of God's buring love for sinners. This task prohibits the congregation from placing the world, as the kingdom of the Law, under the Law's demands while placing herself, as the kingdom of

grace, **under** the consolation of His grace. He addresses all mankind
only under the consolation of His grace. He denies Himself and
loves the world in Jesus Christ. The church that denies herself
and loves the world in discipleship to Jesus is distinguished from
the world through her self-denial and is bound to the world through
her love. This freedom to selfless love is given her by God in every
social structure. No social structure can either give to her or take
away from her this freedom.

In the obedience of faith, the church resists the temptation
to seek her salvation by cutting herself off from the godless world
in a self-seeking manner. She will find her salvation only as she
seeks the salvation of the world.

II. The Life of the Church

The church receives her life from Jesus Christ alone. It is
He who gathers men to Himself in the Holy Spirit and through His
Word in the preaching of the Gospel, Baptism, and the Lord's Supper,
sending them out into the world as His witnesses. When the church
carries out the task which her Lord has given her, she is taken up
into His service and is broken like His own body as she is privileged
to bear witness to the disgrace and death of her leader. In doing
so, she will proceed along her way, comforted and rejoicing in the
temptation that comes to her from pious unbelief and in the threat
that originates in impious unbelief. Thus she provides evidence
that God's Word creates the necessary room for the church to operate
without outside aid, preserves His church for the world, and obtains
justice and the final victory through the resurrection of Jesus
Christ.

In the obedience of faith, the church resists the temptation
of wanting to protect God's Word. Without concern for her own fate,
she can seek fearlessly for new ways to operate in those instances
where her influence is limited and her rights are contested....

III. The Structure of the Church

The church is also obliged to bear witness with her structure,
as with her message and life, that she belongs to her Lord alone and
is obedient to Him.[26] She will subordinate her entire activity to
the service of her lord. She will distinguish her structure--which
is intended for service rather than for power--from the structure
of the political community, without hatred and without indulging in
polemics. She will organize her work in such a way that congregations
and their members are free to give credible witness to God's love
in every word and activity. Thus even the church's structure will
bear witness to the world of God's will that Jesus Christ may be
our Lord and that we may all be brothers.

In the obedience of faith, the church will never forget that it is not her structure that establishes and secures the fulfilling of her task but her task that establishes and secures her structure. She will then give up her traditional privileges, ward off interference into her inner organization, and alter her legal structural form if this handicaps her in the fulfilling of her task. Thus she will be defended most advantageously against being placed in situations where she could be bribed or blackmailed.

IV. The Hope of the Church

The promise of God that Jesus Christ will come to reveal openly the victory of God's grace over all sin and enmity provides the basis for the church's hope for the world. This hope strengthens her in service for the world, enables her to endure the suffering of this present time patiently, and fortifies her for calm and essential action. Thus the congregation waits, watching and praying, in the hope that is based upon the good work of Jesus Christ her Lord, who will come to judge her according to her works and not according to her words.

In the obedience of faith, the church knows that she has been called to accomplish God's good work of reconciliation until Christ is revealed in His glory. Secure in this confidence, she does not set her hope on her own works. Rather, she allows herself and her fellowmen to be comforted by the promise of God's merciful presence. In the expectation of a redeemed world, the church takes courage to heal wounds and create better living conditions for all men. She bears witness to the eternal and perfect justice of God that places the glory of all human kingdoms and all human self-fulfillment into the shadows.

V. The Freedom of the Christian

The church cannot be the accuser, defender, or even judge of political parties in the world when she bears witness to the free grace of God for all mankind. Actually, she cannot even organize herself into a political party of Christians opposed to non-Christians. On the contrary, we who are her members have a concrete social responsibility to act in the free obedience of faith, a responsibility which we are obliged to acknowledge in thought, work, and political activity. Hence we stand before the obligation to make ourselves spokesmen for human life, justice, and peace, without however setting up a Christian political front.

In the obedience of faith, we can be certain that nothing is able to separate us from the love of God. Therefore we confront the non-Christian society without anxiety or hatred, in an attitude of helpfulness and reasonableness, and in this way we can live together responsibly--even in a socialist social order. In so doing, we are to discover--free from anti-Communism and opportunism--what it is that God wants from us and how we can carry out His good will. In this way, we will serve the preservation of life by means of our cooperative efforts and critical counsel, warding off everything that endangers life. We can bear witness to the love of God for the world which has been revealed in Jesus only when we are no longer fixed on the ideological and philosophical polarity of theism and atheism. Thus we live daily, by the grace of God, in carefree assurance and in obedience to God's Word of friendship toward mankind, free in relation to all ideologies and systems of thought and free in relation to all human--also socialist--codes of morality....

VII. The Obedience of Faith in Political Life

1. The State

We confess Jesus Christ as the Lord to Whom all power is given in heaven and on earth, under Whose gracious rule we therefore stand, together with all who hold positions of power in the life of the state. Since it is of divine institution, the state has been assigned the task of looking after justice and peace according to the measure of human insight and human ability that has been granted it, using the threat and exercise of force wherever necessary. We honor this gracious institution of God when we pray for all who exercise political functions in the state, help them to do their duty, let ourselves be influenced in our political activity soley by concern for justice and peace and not by selfish interests, and finally when we decisively oppose all that endangers justice and peace....

2. Justice

All human justice remains imperfect and provisional in comparison with the perfect and eternal justice of God. God's justice justifies the unjust; human justice, even at best, can only render justice to the just and injustice to the unjust. God's justice alone is merciful.

In the obedience of faith, we, in cooperation with non-Christians, try to organize justice under this mercey of God in such a way that the community and the individual can live peacefully with each other, work, enjoy the fruits of their labor, and help one another to find happiness and contentment. We respect the existing law as such an attempt to regulate this mutual coexistence. We help to change the law where that serves the law's purpose; but we do not break it without a concrete command from God, misuse it for selfish ecclesiastical, economic, or political interests, or absolutize it. In this way, we remain aware of one important fact: human justice has need of human mercy.

3. Peace

All earthly peace remains imperfect and provisional in comparison with the perfect and eternal peace of God. God's peace is higher than all human rationality; human peace is the condition created through reasonable agreement that enables human society to live in prosperity, security, and freedom.

In the obedience of faith, we, in cooperation with non-Christians, try to establish a preacful order where war is abolished as a weapon for use in power struggles, armaments are rendered superfluous, armed forces are reduced to police forces for the preservation of public order, and conflicts of interest will be settled in peaceful competition without weapons.

We are of the opinion that peace is the normal situation, war the abnormal! Therefore it is not the absence of force but the application of force, not disarmament but armament, not refusing to serve in the armed forces but serving in the armed forces which is in need of explicit justification to demonstrate how it serves to promote the peaceful mutual coexistence of states and social systems. We oppose the spirit of revanchism, and we are willing to go to any lengths to establish peace. Here too, it is important not to slander the opponent but to convince him by rational arguments and actions.

We consider the psychological or military use of weapons of mass destruction, together with their manufacture and testing, to be not a legitimate application of force by states but a sin, just as we consider any legitimation of them by the church or by the Christian to be a false doctrine against which we must protect ourselves....

We beseech our Lord Jesus Christ to enable all those who do not yet know Him to come to the realization the He has died not *against* them but *for* them. Then both we and they will hear these words, not as a triumph of the church *over* the world but as a testimony to His victory *for* the world: "The kingdom of the world has become the Kingdom of our Lord and of His Christ, and He shall reign forever and ever" (Revelation 11:15).

147. The Christian in a Post-Christian Context*

In the light of the intensive ecumenical discussion that is

_____
*"The Christian in a Post-Christian Context: A Study Document from the German Democratic Republic," in Ivar Asheim, ed. *Christ and Humanity* (Philadelphia: Fortress Press, 1970), pp. 141-153. The Theological Commission of the National Committee of the German Democratic Republic prepared this study.

being carried on, we have become conscious of the fact that for a long time our churches have not adequately faced the question of the Christian's social responsibility. In their proclamation our churches have for the most part drawn social relations into the area of Christian responsibility only via the individual dimension.

The theological efforts of the Lutheran World Federation to relate the doctrine of the two kingdoms to the doctrine of the lordship of Christ we see as a step forward. The two positions have their basis in the Scriptures. They are valid not as correctives to each other but in interpretation of each other. Both are relevant to our socioethical action. The community of Christ Jesus bears witness to the word and deed of Jesus of Nazareth, to his death and resurrection as the act of God which gives hope. It is the hope that the lordship of Christ, who justifies the sinner, will again and again take hold of men and free them for a new life, the hope that the lordship of Christ will gain victory over all resistance and extend--though in a hidden way--into all dimensions of history, the hope that God will bring to fulfillment his kingdom of justice and righteousness. There is no sphere in the world in which God through Christ is not Lord. Christ exercises his lordship in that we, as justified sinners, follow him in faith. This happens in daily service to our neighbor, both within the close fellowship of the family and in the larger structures of society. This is how our responsibility in the world is exercised. Even though we realize that we ourselves cannot create the new world that God wills, we shall not regard men and the conditions which exist as unredeemable. As they act, Christians will always remember what God is doing, and still intends to do, with the world and with men. They see history through the perspective of hope. This hope always functions both as critique and stimulant.

The lordship of Christ will remain hidden until his coming again and must consequently be believed contrary to empirical evidence. A theocratic misunderstanding of the lordship of Christ, which would make it into a matter of law and which would deceptively pass off our works as his works, is therefore out of the question. God's realm "on the left," through which a sinful world is protected and preserved by means of the law, must remain until Christ's return. It must not, however, be identified with his lordship. Insofar as we oppose his lordship, he will assert it over against us in judgment. Since God holds us accountable for everything that we do in our private and social lives, our daily actions take on ultimate significance. It is precisely for this reason that we are free in our relationships to all institutions and persons who may come into competition with Christ....

Faith acknowledges that the world is God's world which he creates and shapes. At the same time it is the world of man which is subject to the creating and shaping action of men. The believer sees in man's creating action the realization of God's commission, while the man who does not believe thinks of himself as responsible to himself for such creating. This situation raises the question as to how to relate the creative activity of God to that of man....

Since the event of Jesus Christ, the law is no longer a road to salvation. This must be acknowledged without qualification. But our concentration on the tension between law and gospel has often prevented us from recognizing the preserving function of the law of God. The community of the new covenant is not released from the law of order and of life but is rather directed to it. Certainly, the law cannot become a means by which we can get into God's good graces, but it does oblige Christians, together with all men, to strive for the well-being of mankind....

The theological approach which we have been considering enables us to take seriously the society in which we live as the context of our discipleship. The concrete shape of the service we can render must be reconsidered from situation to situation. In seeking to fulfill our social responsibility we cannot, even with the best of intentions, escape the danger of error and guilt. Power tactics and conflicts of interest are, even with sufficient information, discernable as such only to a degree and render any objective judgment difficult. Moreover, we ourselves are so intensively involved in the actual circumstances of society that we cannot free ourselves from them, and therefore we share in its failure. This tension of Christian life in the world must not, however, lead us to abandon the helping word and the helping deed. We are conscious of the fact that we cannot declare as universally mandatory that which to us seem essential statements and decisions. We have to bear the burden of being imperfect. The courage to err, yes, even the courage to incur guilt, belongs to the existence of the Christian. This is neither an excuse nor the ground for self-satisfaction. Anyone who speaks and acts in this world is in need of forgiveness. The gospel which offers us this forgiveness in Christ does not give security; it makes free.

We have lost large areas for social involvement. In order to rediscover and reenter the area which we have been guilty of neglecting or from which we have been consciously barred, it will be necessary to take many small steps. Although we know that suffering, too, can be a service to society, we do not feel that we may judge every hindrance to Christian social service as such suffering in discipleship of Christ. The question we are asking ourselves, rather, is to what extent, by these circumstances, God is judging our lack of faith and our pride of years gone by. At the same time, the hope that is given to us in Christ promises us that suffering and limitation from outside will not be experienced without his guidance and without opportunities of service remaining or even entirely new opportunities opening up. Therefore we must not focus on suffering. We have every reason to trust that in our situation, too, the word of God will prove itself to be the power through which responsible Christian action in our society will be made possible.

Being a Christian without community is unthinkable. This becomes especially clear in the face of the responsibility of Christians in a "post-Christian" society. The Christian life (*nova oboedientia*, Art. VI of the Augsburg Confession) and the Christian community (*ecclesia*, Art. VII) belong together. Common responsibility for the various services to be rendered in society demands that the community itself be prepared constantly to reexamine its structure in regard to the effectiveness of its work. We have to ask, for instance: Where do we find groups in the congregation in which the members take responsibility, in partnership and commitment, for their service in society? Especially in a "post-Christian" context, Christians need groups which, in listening to the word of God, in prayer, and in dialogue, discuss the problems of their Christian existence in society and which support them with critique, encouragement, and forgiveness. Life in the Christian community should at the same time open up opportunities for the practice of responsibility in partnership within society. The congregation must be so structured and live in such a way that it helps the individual member toward independent responsible action in society. This holds true also for children and young people, who in a special way need community to help them to live as Christians in society. In order for this to happen, a change in the structure of our congregations is necessary. In bringing this about God's Spirit must lead our deliberations and choices. For this we ask, and this we await.

Our churches' many-faceted diaconic work, which is intended for those in need without regard to what a person is or what ideology he holds, is a service in society which has been laid upon us. This service which is focused on the individual is not made obsolete by the responsibility of the Christian community for the entire structure of society. God has given us an area in which to minister, which according to our understanding is a necessary form of our social responsibility. The Christian community accompanies with its intercession the service of its members in society. Its priestly prayer is itself a decisive service to the world. The situation may even exist in which prayer is the only possibility for exercising responsibility for the world.

Precisely because of the undeniable responsibility for social action, the role of the Christian community in the task of the Christian in a "post-Christian" context must continue to be determined by the word. The congregation in its proclamation--in preaching, teaching, pastoral care, and group dialogue--will testify to its members that social responsibility is also a personal task. It will give them the courage to demonstrate the freedom of the Christian through service within society. Only where the word of God within the Christian community grants ever anew the grace of forgiveness and the power for new life will such freedom become effective.

CHAPTER 11

EASTERN EUROPE--HUNGARY

INTRODUCTION[27]

The following texts, taken from Hungarian Lutheran church literature, indicate a radical change in the theological thinking of this church during the past century.

Behind the first three texts, selected from the years between the two world wars, there still lurks--either implied or clearly formulated--the theological assumption inherited from the nineteenth century that the church's proper sphere of activity is confined to the salvation of the soul and to the inner life. Politics, or the life of secular society, collectively designated as "the world," was felt to be something foreign to the church and to the congregation.

This notion is encountered chiefly in a kind of pietistic thinking of the Lutheran variety which tries to draw an especially sharp dividing line between the twin realities of the world and the congregation of believers. According to this point of view, it is better for the church and the believers to hold themselves completely separate from the world, since every act of solidarity with the world carries with it the fatal danger of disloyalty to the gospel (see, for example, the selections from Farkas and Szikszai).

In the other branch of Lutheran thinking dating from this period of time, the dividing line between the "two kingdoms" of church and world, though never as sharp in its ethical consequences, nevertheless proved just as fatal. This school of thought, which can be characterized as "conservative Lutheran"--illustrated in our anthology by the second text (Várallyai)--certainly relegates the church's primary function to the realm of the inner life, but it also recognizes the world and human society as God-given realities, designating their "orders" (state, family, vocation) as important secular spheres of activity for the individual Christian. The division occurs at that point where the actual ethical task begins. In the "spiritual kingdom," the Christian stands immediately under God's rule. In the "secular kingdom" of government, however, his "sole duty" consists in obeying that government. An exception is made only where the government interferes in "matters foreign to it," for example, in matters pertaining to faith.

The historical context for the textual examples referred to above is the aristocratic half-feudal Hungarian society of an earlier day, a society in which millions of workers and landless peasants had to suffer every day the consequences of an unjust social order. The churches either dismissed their socio-political responsibility as something "not related to their real mission" or let it go with a few verbal protests on the basis of a quoted "theological" formulation. Was it any wonder that the Marxist critique designated this Christian attitude as "otherworldly," as a recipe for socio-ethical and social inaction that provided useful support for the privileged classes holding wealth and political power in that society?

The ethical consequences of this false interpretation of the Lutheran doctrine of the two kingdoms revealed themselves more clearly during the period of growing fascist influence and in the discrimination against--and later persecution of--the Hungarian Jews in the late 1930s and the early 1940s. Apart from a few courageous exceptions, the churches and Christians kept silent before the inhumanity of increasingly severe legal measures that led up to and culminated in the removal of hundreds of thousands of Jews to concentration camps and gas chambers; or they limited their protest to "verbal pronouncements" alone. This separation of the church from the world in the Lutheran camp, as inherently false as it was, provided the tragic accompaniment to the "Christian ethical bankruptcy" of this historical epoch.

Following the collapse of the old social order and during the succeeding years of completely renewed consciousness and a new context for our churches in a Marxist society, there developed in the Hungarian Lutheran Church a theological point of view which is usually designated as "diaconal theology" and "diaconal Christian life-style." It involves a radical transformation in the relationship of the church and the individual Christian to the world, precisely-- and that is perhaps what is most interesting about it--on the theological basis of a reinterpretation of Luther's doctrine of the

two kingdoms, the same doctrine that was so fatally misunderstood
and misinterpreted throughout the nineteenth and in the early part
of the twentieth centuries.

Due to spatial limitations, we can offer only three textual
examples for this theological reinterpretation. These examples
come from the period of time in which this theology--after many
difficult inner struggles within the churches--had already ripened
into maturity. Bishop Zoltán Káldy's inaugural address in 1958
provides what might be called the first clear evidence of this
theological effort at renewal. Gyula Nagy's work on theological
social ethics in 1967 attempts to demonstrate the theological
connecting links which bind this theology of socio-ethical
responsibility to a corrected understanding of the Lutheran doctrine
of the two kingdoms. And finally, the theological point of view
represented by the theological statements of the Hungarian Lutheran
Church at Evian (in the plenary assembly of the Lutheran World
Federation in 1970)--otherwise a joint work of theologians and
pastors--already indicates the multifaceted practical consequences
which this reinterpretation of the doctrine of the two kingdoms
evokes.

Since Evian, Hungarian Lutheran theologians have been busy
demonstrating the concrete areas and concrete human tasks of
"diaconal theology" in a Marxist society and in the human world.
They hope to insure, on the basis of the biblical Word and the
newly understood Reformation heritage, that faith does not leave
us socio-ethically inactive in the world and in society, but that
it is precisely out of the Christian faith that there stream forth
continual and unceasing impulses for showing helping love to the
neighbor and social and political responsibility to the world.

A.   BETWEEN THE TWO WORLD WARS (1918-1945)

148. Serving the Kingdom of God*

Our task consists in serving the Kingdom of God....Ever since
Golgatha, we are allowed to believe and to risk everything. For
the Lord loves not the unassuming person who shrinks back but the
one who risks everything for the totality of the Gospel. He loves
the person who petitions the Holy Spirit that there be people upon
the dry, withered, pagan Hungarian soil who, once they have been
roused from the deadly sleep of sin, speak jubilantly of the grace
that has come to them and who seek one thing above everything else,
namely that they and their fellow human beings may obtain eternal

---

*Zoltan Farkas, "The Third Year" (A harmadik ev), *Emmaus felé*,
1931, I, 3.

salvation. That is the entire Gospel!

149. *Distinguishing the Kingdoms**

This higher unity of the orders and vocations that embrace all earthly forms of human life and undergird them all is what Luther refers to as the "secular kingdom"....

Luther distinguishes the "spiritual kingdom" rather carefully from the "secular kingdom".... This "spiritual kingdom" is realized inside the world of subjectivity, free of every organizational form. It is the most precious of all the treasures of Lutheran piety. The life of the person in whom this "spiritual kingdom" begins to grow appropriates to himself, through faith, the forgiveness of sins which God offers him, gives his heart to God unconditionally, loves his neighbor, recognizes that the earthly vocations and orders are of divine origin, and freely makes use of them....

The only duty that the subject has toward his government is to obey it.... This obligation for subjects to be obedient ceases only when the government issues commands that go beyond its God-given sphere of activity, as, for example, when it interferes in matters pertaining to faith....

It can, of course, come about that the government passes under the control of Satan, thus producing tyranny or anarchy.... Another government is permitted to fight against the tyrant with armed force. Subjects, however, are not allowed to resist with armed force but must endure tyranny until God sees fit to free them from it. The ecclesiastical order likewise must endure the tyrant's violent deeds, but it does have an obligation to protect vocally and decisively against them.

150. *The Christian's Relationship to the World***

Somewhere and sometime the conversation touched upon the subject of the Christian's relationship to the world, that is to say, upon the connecting link. We naturally declared ourselves to be in agreement with the point of view that a believer ought not to enter into any kind of solidarity with the world. He ought only to have enough to do with it to be able to recognize that the world of creation is yearning and waiting for the children of God to be revealed. The believer participates in God's mission, but he dare never entrust himself to the world or make common cause with her works and endeavors.... For that reason, whenever the children of God accept what the world offers or what is of value in the world,

---

*János Várallyai, "Luther on the World, State, and Government" (Luther a világról, Allam, felsőbbseg), *Belmisszioi Munkaprogram*, 1937/1938, pp. 97-98, 100, and 105.
**Beni Szikszai, *On the Fallow Field of Hungary* (Magyar ugaron). Györ, 1944, pp. 102-103.

they must always pay a high and bloody price for it, concluding an unfavorable treaty which is advantageous only to the world but which always signifies a breach of faith over against the Gospel.

B. AFTER THE SECOND WORLD WAR (1945-1974)

151. *A New Direction**

I understand by the term "political worship of God" that the church, as well as its members, must participate actively in the effort to establish a just world order. What is at stake is the exercising of a political responsibility before God that is rooted in love for the world. Diaconal service, viewed in this light, is really an inextricable part of divine worship.

In years gone by, the claim was always made by members of our church that the church ought to avoid getting mixed up on political questions entirely, that she should maintain her purity in this respect. In other instances, this argument was phrased in such a way that our church should cultivate an attitude of strict neutrality in political matters since, when all is said and done, the shape of the world in which the church finds herself is not of any concern to her; instead, the church should carry on her own life completely independent of the world.

Concerning this notion, let me emphasize that under no circumstance dare the church and her members stop exercising their Christian responsibility in the political sphere, since to do this would be to do injury to the diaconal service to which God has called them. The theology of the Reformation, grounded as it is in the Word of God, most decidedly repudiates every renunciation of this political responsibility.

The church in every age has been tempted (and frequently deceived) by the thought that she could retreat from the world. In this connection, the biblical word "Love not the world, neither the things that are in the world," has often been given a false interpretation. There are other instances where the basic idea of a retreat to the inner sphere of church life has been dictated by a conviction which holds that the individual Christian's "peace of mind" is his most important consideration, something over which the external order ought to exercise no influence. These efforts on the part of the church to pull out of political, social, and economic life are derived not from a healthy theology but from a state of enthusiasm, from a betrayal of the Word of God, and hence

---

*Zoltán Káldy, "Bishopal Inaugural Address" (Püspöki szekfoglalo beszed), 1958. From the collection of his addresses and articles entitled *On a New Path* (Új uton), 1969, pp. 22 and 24.

they represent a flight from responsibility. Such a Christian attitude that dwells high in the clouds and occupies itself solely with its own "peace of mind" while abandoning one's fellow human beings in their fate is an unfortunate point of view, for it demonstrates a denial of the incarnation of Christ, the mission of the church, and the great command to love which God has given....

How can the church and her members carry out their political responsibility?

First, by preaching Law and Gospel. If the proclamation appeals to modern man in questions arising from his daily life in community, condemning his egotistical "Old Adam" that expresses itself in lovelessness toward others and pushes aside the interests of society as a whole, then political responsibility has already been exercised in every direction. Nevertheless, we must strive consciously to draw from the Word of God the connecting links which apply to social sins as well.

Prayer for the state and for the government also belongs to the exercise of political responsibility. A great responsibility weighs upon those who direct the life of the state, and power has many temptations. Thus prayer represents a great service. In exactly the same way, the exercise of political responsibility among Christians also takes place whenever they fulfill their earthly vocation in a true and honest manner.

Therefore our church and her members must go forth--in a spirit of responsibility for the entire world--doing all that is humanly possible for world peace, for the removal of opposition between the races, and for the liberation of all colonialized and half-colonialized peoples.

152. *Two Kingdoms Revisited**

There is probably no other portion of Luther's theology which has been exposed to such a pointed and multifaceted critique--in the past as well as in the present--than just this doctrine. After the Second World War, it was even asserted that the same doctrine had contributed substantially toward solidifying the spirit of Hitlerism in German lands by removing political life from the applicability of God's revealed commnad to demonstrate love and by educating the German people, as it were, in the direction of an uncritical subservience toward the emperor and toward Hitler himself.

---

*Gyula Nagy, "The Contemporary Critique of Luther's Doctrine of the 'Two Kingdoms'," *The Church in the World of Today: A Theological Social Ethics* (Egyház a mai világban: Teologiai szociáletika). Budapest, 1967, pp. 158-162.

Let us now ask the following questions:
1. Are these accusations justified?
2. Are there certain portions of this doctrine which should be opened to criticism?
3. Does this doctrine possess sufficient inherent strength so that we today--exercising the necessary criticism--can still regard it as a correct and necessary socio-ethical foundation?

1. The strongest accusation against Luther's doctrine is that it represents a "double morality," or an ethical dualism (E. Troeltsch, W. Köhler). As a counterweight to the misuse of this doctrine in the Middle Ages--the critics charge--Luther separated the Kingdom of God from the kingdom of the world so greatly that he handed the world over to the worship of power and to the unrestricted rule of sin while at the same time depriving the church of responsibility for the ethics of the world and for any ethical activity in the world.

Now it cannot be denied that in the course of church history there have always been those who have misunderstood and distorted Luther's original intentions in this way. But Luther's own doctrine protests powerfully against that, since he contended that both kingdoms adhere together in the hand of God. God is the ruler of both kingdoms! God's command to love is the motivating power in both modes of exercising rule. And similarly, both are bound together in the individual Christian conscience. It is impossible to assert that Luther abandoned the world to its own fate or that he proclaimed another ethical law for the world than that which applies to the church. It is simply not true that he restricted the Christian's ethical responsibility to the narrow confines of parish life and thus deprived the Christian of his ethical activity in the world. Such an accusation against Luther reflects either an intentional distortion of his doctrine or else a sorry ignorance of the same!

The charge is frequently made that Luther's doctrine of the two kingdoms lacks the necessary eschatological tension, that it faces, to be sure, toward this life but fails to take into account the opposition between the coming Kingdom of God and life in this present world, that it overestimates the degree of harmony between the two kingdoms (H. Thielicke, H. Gollwitzer).

It is an indisputable fact that this doctrine of Luther's desires only to explain the dual nature of earthly life, the dual functioning of divine love and activity in the church and in the world. Thus it is a partial and by no means a universal theological

232

explanation. Certainly it does not contain the entire New Testament message concerning God's present and future rule. But one cannot blame this doctrine on the one hand for having forgotten God's coming rule, on the other hand for ignoring the tension between God's rule and man's sinfulness. No, the doctrine of the two kingdoms never loses sight of the real face of this world, as contradictory as that may be! In addition to the homogeneity of both kingdoms (i.e. their harmony), Luther points quite clearly to the danger of human misuse in the "secular" as well as in the "spiritual" realm.

The third indictment made against Luther is one that is especially vocal from the corner of the dialectical theologians, namely that in place of the revealed divine law, he regarded the human understanding and man's natural conscience as the means by which God exercises dominion over the world; in this way (they claim), he restricted the sphere of validity for the Word and Christ's reign to the church (K. Barth, J. Ellul). It is incontestable that Luther--correctly--ascribed to natural human reason and to the human conscience an important role in the life of the world. What would have become of the world without these two elements? It is equally undeniable that he fought bitterly against every interpretation which would leave the "reign of Christ" visible and open in public life, no matter what its form, and which might attempt to "rule the world from the pulpit" (Trillhaas). This, however, indicates not the failure but rather the merit of Luther's doctrine. Christ's rule, according to the New Testament, is an exclusively spiritual rule. His power and glory remain hidden in this world until the end of time; they will never become part of any revealed "Christocracy" or reign of Christ. Behind Barth's interpretation already mentioned lie conceptualizations which simply cannot be justified on the basis of the New Testament!

2. However, one can validly express some critical reservations about Luther's doctrine, especially in view of the changes in society that have occurred since his lifetime. Luther's view of the state and the world--like that of the Apostle Paul--presupposed social relationships where the ruling classes alone exercised power in the give-and-take of public life, while the mass of the people were subject to them, possessing no broader rights and responsibilities in public life. Since then, the image of human society and also of the world has undergone vast alteration, even in this respect. The role and responsibility of the man in the street has been expanded, in society as in the state. The antithesis between ruler and ruled has been replaced by the common tasks of the politically active citizens who participate in power and responsibility. "We

233

must always evaluate Luther's doctrine of God's two kingdoms in the most intimate association with the historical situation of the age in which it arose; and if we, in our altered spiritual and social situation, come back to this doctrine, then we must apply it properly and boldly to the new historical situation in which we find ourselves" (Miklos Palfy).

Today we must think this doctrine through carefully and apply it in response to the new situation; we must place greater emphasis upon the responsibility of the individual Christian and the church in public life as well as upon their cooperation in transforming the fate of the world than was conceivable under the social relationships of the feudal Middle Ages or at the beginning of the new age.

3. In order to judge this doctrine of Luther's properly from a theological vantagepoint, it is necessary above all--as Heinrich Bornkamm has observed pertinently--that one not try to understand it apart from the total context of Luther's theology. For this will merely increase the likelihood of its being misunderstood and distorted. If we investigate it according to its actual intent and full meaning, however, then we will discover its great value, its true modern theological meaning--which is indispensable even in our day, despite the fact that we are so far removed from the conceptual world of the sixteenth century. We see its strong points in the following conclusions:

1. First, this doctrine of Luther's necessarily draws a sharp line of distinction between the church and the world; in this respect, it also shows itself to be thoroughly modern in that it lays bare the role of reason and the natural conscience in the life of the world. "Luther did not want the world to be ruled on the basis of a papal word; but neither did he wish to have the world governed from the pulpit" (Trillhaas). In contrast to the omnipotence of the medieval church, that is of course a severe "loss of prestige" for many today. On the other hand, now we can understand much better how correct Luther and the Augsburg Confession (Article 28) were in speaking of the possibility that the world might live its life independent of the church--but never independent of God and of God's command to love! This doctrine of Luther's enables us today to conduct a dialogue on the same level with the world, without harboring any open or secret illusions about "Christianizing the world," as we recognize in the world the "other mode of God's rule," his providential care. At the same time, however, the special task of the church, diverging as it does from the world, can also get underway.

2. In the second place, the "two kingdoms doctrine" makes us aware of the true role of Law and Gospel, of faith and good works in God's governance of the world. It exhibits the proper place for the Law in the world and for the Gospel in the service of the church. It exhibits the place for faith in the relationship between God and man and the place for love, as well as good works, in the relationship between man and his fellowman. In this way, Christianity preserves itself from transforming its "heart," the Gospel, into a new Law, just as it also preserves itself from letting the Law and works interfere in the sphere of justification, that is, in the relationship of grace between God and mankind.

3. In the third place, it restores "the honor of the world" to its proper place in Christian dogma by demonstrating the great gifts of divine providence and love in the institutional arrangements of the world--in family, state, occupation, economy, and culture. At the same time, it draws attention to the multifaceted possibilities and ethical tasks by which the Christian can demonstrate love for his neighbor in the various dimensions of life in the world. The Christian responsibility and the Christian service in maintaining the world within God's providence--and that is truly one of the chief themes of this doctrine of Luther's--take on added importance in the age of modern technology and atomic weapons. This we dare never forget!

4. To summarize, the doctrine of God's "secular and spiritual rule"--given critical reconsideration and applied to our new state of affairs--can still serve as a perfectly legible guidepost for theological social ethics, having great significance as well as great practical benefit for our modern world.

153. The Diaconia of the Church as a Whole for Man and Society *

We wish to make the point that diaconia for the whole of man in the whole of society is not only the "worldly service" of individual believers in the sense that they, by doing this service, would so to speak leave the realm of the church. On the contrary, this service is just as genuine a ministry of the church and of the congregation as the preaching of God's Word.

It is high time to shake off at last that false churchliness which confines the "service of God" within the walls of the church, to the altar, to the pulpit, to prayer, while refusing to do the difficult yet joyful work of love in the world as the essential mission of the church.

---

*Our Commitment in the World(Budapest, 1970),prepared for the 1970 Assembly of the Lutheran World Federation, pp. 108-109.

Beyond the theological arguments already advanced, we must also point out the impossibility of such thinking also from the sociological viewpoint. For the church is at the same time the people of God and a sociological entity which, willingly or unwillingly, is an economic, social and political factor in the world. The only question is concerning the influences that issue from her upon the life of society and its communities. Is she a barrier, an obstacle in the way of historical development as God wills and of true humanity? Is she helping the progress of the world and society, the evolution of a full humanity which is according to the will of God in all the fields of social life?

In view of the complicated nature withal unity of our world today, the works of neighbourly love, too, have become complicated and comprehensive. Let me give two concrete examples. If I want to help a hungry man, I share my bread with him. But, if we want to help the hungry millions of India, the methods of classical diaconia can provide but a tiny fraction of the help needed. Effective help depends on the transformation of the economico-social structures of the developing nations and, at the same time, on the changing of the structures of the international economic life. And, considering now only the help of Christians, this is more than an individual task; it also calls for the economico-social activity of the whole church, of the whole world of Christianity as well.

Today's churches, including ours, face the profound decision whether they recognize and implement in their service, without vacillation and uncertainty, these perspectives of the church's social diaconia which affects the destiny of millions of suffering people, or they become disobedient to God and--what is inseparable from this disobedience--also inhuman in this hungry, suffering world which lives under the threat of an atomic holocaust, declining to do the new, social tasks of Christian love on a world scale, using some specious but theologically false arguments to justify their inaction. The latter would be the tragedy of Christianity on the road which leads towards the future.

CHAPTER 12

SOUTHERN AFRICA

A. REPUBLIC OF SOUTH AFRICA

Introduction[28]

Until early in the 1960s, only a few pastors in the white
Lutheran congregations and churches formulated precise statements
concerning the idea of the two kingdoms and its role in legitimizing
existing relationships between rulers and subjects. In the Afrikaans
Reformed Church, too, only a small minority of the pastors questioned
the national Christian philosophy held by the white population. On
the whole, the predominant thinking in both the white Lutheran and
the white Afrikaans Reformed congregations was surprisingly similar.
The same fundamental interest had assimilated itself to the most
diverse theological traditions. Even the organizational model for
the relationship between white and black churches was almost identical
for both confessions. Separate churches were established for the
various ethnic groups.

For a long time, the Lutheran missionaries who worked in South
Africa were rooted in the Neo-Lutheran Awakening. After the middle
of the nineteenth century, a Neo-Lutheran piety and theology exercised
a deep influence upon the white Lutheran congregations. After 1880,
as a result of contact with the Reformed Church in Holland, the white
groups and the Reformed Church in South Africa in turn were influenced
strongly by Neo-Calvinist theology. The elements of romantic
philosophy helped Neo-Calvinist as well as Neo-Lutheran congregations
to justify social attitudes among the whites. Their great preference
for God's activity in creation and history can be traced back to
romantic elements in both theological traditions. Some people claimed

to be able to recognize this activity in preordained organic laws of nature and of history. The course of these laws cannot be changed. Rather, one must guard against interfering with them in any way. The missionaries who were rooted in this piety thought very highly of the traditional culture. Traditional values were to be upheld as long as they could be brought into harmony with Christian principles. Ethnic identity was credited with having a dignity all its own. This dignity was granted by God and therefore had to be maintained. Ethnic identity had to develop according to its own divinely preordained laws. Since the identity of ethnic groups was assigned an ultimate value, the unity of the church by necessity was spiritualized. The special worth of each individual ethnic group had to be developed in accord with its own autonomous laws. The church had no right to cast doubt upon these laws, since they had been preordained by God.

In the light of this, it is understandable that assertions arose that the church is non-political, that her assigned task is to preach the Gospel and to obey the government while the state follows its own natural laws. These assertions are in reality highly political, inasmuch as they support the existing relationships of power and privilege among the whites. Only a few scattered voices arose to point out that in doing this the church shared a responsibility for massive injustices that rendered the Gospel incapable of inspiring belief.

In the black churches, the concept of the two kingdoms drew little attention for many years after World War II. Only as the ELCSA-SER became an independent church body were theological considerations raised concerning the political witness of the church and the significance of organizational form for the inner life of the church. Traces of these considerations can be found in the constitution of the ELCSA-SER.

The increasing harshness of the legislation for "separate development" called forth appropriate reactions from the black pastors and members of the black Lutheran Church. They objected to attempts by white Lutherans to use the concept of the two kingdoms in a way that glossed over the church's obligation to apply the Gospel to political and social problems. At the same time, they raised objection to ethnic separation as the guiding principle in church organization. Doubt was expressed about the persistent tendency to explain away matters of church structure as being of no importance for the proclamation of the Gospel.

In the middle of the 1960s, missionaries from Europe began to point out to the white churches and congregations in South Africa

that their "non-political" political attitude and method of
argumentation was based upon a falsely understood doctrine of the
two kingdoms. These efforts initially culminated in the pastoral
conference of Umpumulo in 1967. Further seminars and church
leadership conferences related to this theme were conducted by
the Federation of Evangelical Lutheran Churches in South Africa
(FELKSA) and the Christian Academy. Here the voices of black
theologians began to make themselves heard, as well as those of
Lutherans from various lands who had been put on their guard and
sensitized by the catastrophe which had overtaken large segments
of German Lutheranism under National Socialism.

The church leadership and the official organs of the white
churches then attempted to speak of the political responsibility
of the Christians, but in irresolute statements. De facto,
resorting to the doctrine of the two kingdoms meant that the church
held herself out of political life as much as possible and thus,
either explicitly or implicitly, supported the government's policy.
On the other hand, there has been a massive reaction by a movement
inside the congregations, similar to a development in the West
German church, called "The Emergency Society of Evangelical Christians
in South Africa" (NELKSA), which argues on the basis of the doctrine
of the two kingdoms for restricting the Gospel to the individual
soul and which explicitly supports apartheid as an order of creation.

"Non-Political" Lutheranism

155. K. Hohls: *"Letter to the Missionaries of the London Mission"**
We members of the Hermannsburg Mission are so out of our
element as politicians (and we prefer to remain that way) that we
cannot even begin to question the sovereignty of the Republic of
South Africa over the Tsawana tribes. We observe the admonition of
Romans 13: "Let everyone be subject to the government, for there
is no government unless it be from God."

156. E. Harms: *"Thoughts Concerning the Role of the Mission in
Relation to Emancipation Efforts in the Black Population"***
The mission in South Africa stands before a difficult task.
She must set about her work very carefully so that she cannot be
reproached with having strengthened the natives' revolutionary
efforts by means of imprudent activity. On the one hand, we must
seek to meet the justified wishes of our Christians, showing them
in every way that we really mean well by them and have a warm heart

---

*K. Hohls was the superintendent of the Hermannsburg Mission.
Letter, J. Mackenzie to Dr. Tidman, Sept. 8, 1864, Archives, London
Mission.
  **E. Harms was director of the Hermannsburg Mission.
Hermannsburger Missionsblatt, 57 (1910), 205.

for them. On the other hand, however, **we** are obliged to judge
according to conditions as they are. It is written: where
government exists, it is ordained by God. The Europeans rule over
the land and control the government. It is not our business to
help the natives obtain political rights or to put immature political
ideas into their heads. We have to teach the people that it is a
Christian duty to obey the law for the sake of God, that they can
win the goodwill of the rulers only through good behavior and true,
honest work. Then the rulers certainly will not withold from them
the rights that are due to them.

*157. G. Asmus: "The Racial Question in South Africa"**

It is my own personal opinion that the racial question can
be brought closer to a proper solution only when each race begins
by conceding to the other the right to examine what it is and how
it developed to that point. Similarly, each race must be conceded
the right to continue developing in its own distinct way. This is
the God-given foundation upon which it must continue to build if
there is to be no loss of the inestimable values that are absolutely
essential for the advance of just this race. The African should
remain African; he can and should remain so to all eternity.

*158. J. Kistner, Sr.: "What Does It Mean to Be an Evangelical
        Lutheran Christian?"***

This is the majesty of every Christian service which is
performed out of love for the neighbor, that in this way one sees
God standing behind the neighbor and serves Him by serving the
neighbor. This joy in serving is beneficial to the state. The
Lutheran Church considers it her duty to sharpen the conscience
of the tribes within the state and to make them aware of their
responsibility before God. But she does not interfere in the state's
affairs. By virtue of her distinguishing between Law and Gospel,
the church is prevented either from establishing political systems
or from disavowing them. Lutheran Christians see in secular
government an ordinance of God. Government has an obligation to
provide discipline and order. It also must hold in check the powers
of chaos. For this purpose, God has placed the sword into the hand
of government. Government is placed in the service of the divine
order of preservation. The church, however, has a spiritual office.
It is her task to point the way to salvation. Word and sacrament
are the means by which she operates. The Church is placed in the

---

*G. Asmus was a missionary for the Hermannsburg Mission.
Hermannsburger Missionsblatt, 76 (1929), 54-55.
**J. Kistner, Sr., Pastor of the Hermannsburg Church (ELKSA-H),
unpublished lecture, December, 1963.

service of the divine order of redemption. In this way, Lutherans distinguish between the spiritual and the secular realms.

In the critical examination of the "apartheid" policy which troubles consciences in our land, the church occupies a unique position. The governmental system described by that term cannot be justified on the basis of the Scriptures, but neither can it be disproved by the Bible. The Holy Scriptures provide no book of recipes from which to select political programs, but they present the Gospel of Christ. In this case, it is a question of judgment. If "apartheid" is a means for holding back the powers of chaos and for introducing order and prosperity into the land, then a Lutheran Christian can tolerate it so long as law and justice are maintained. The Lutheran's concern is to give to Caesar what is Caesar's and to God what is God's. He takes seriously his obligations to the government, and he never forgets to pray for it. Obedience to secular authority, however, has its limits. The Christian's obedience comes to an end when the state interferes in his life of faith. Then the axiom holds true: "We must obey God rather than men."

159. *Karl Dedekind: Report from the Year 1913**

Unless I am mistaken, the situation is as follows: Paganism does not have enough to offer our blacks. They realize that they lag far behind the whites. The mission, as well as the missionary, brings them something new, something previously unknown--like education, reading, and writing. From the missionary, they learn all kinds of useful work. Their horizons are broadened. They awaken as though from sleep, but their vision is not yet clear. The missionary preaches about freedom and release, naturally freedom from the yoke of sin and of Satan. But they would like to make use of the missionary to free themselves from a different yoke, that of the state, and because he cannot, is not allowed to, and does not want to do this, they very easily come to regard him as an ally of their oppressor. Mistrust, suspicion, and--among a few--even enmity and hatred arise.

The mission is confronted here with a problem that defies easy solution. Originally this land belonged to our blacks. The whites, however, have enslaved them and therefore it is not surprising that they regard the whites as oppressors, as obstacles to their freedom. And an impartial observer is compelled to agree that the black has not always experienced satisfactory justice. Although the slave trade has been abolished, there are still enough people among the

---

*Karl Dedekind was a missionary with the Hermannsburg Mission. *Hermannsburger Missionsblatt*, 62 (1915), 110. See the statement made by the regular mission director, E. Harms, concerning this same question (No. 156).

present white population who regard the blacks only as slaves and
therefore treat them accordingly. Presently, laws are being considered
which would restrict the freedom of the natives even more. The goal
is to maintain a "pure race" and wherever possible press the blacks
together into an isolated corner. The black man senses that, for
he is not entirely devoid of feelings, and he revolts against it.
He is strengthened in this resolve by the example of certain Europeans
who are without conscience and without tact as well as by the wave
of strikes on the part of white-collar workers and laborers presently
sweeping over our land which puts all kinds of "bad" notions into
his head. It is probably to be expected that we are approaching
a difficult time, perhaps a time of insurrection, revolution, and
rebellion. The mission and the missionaries must then take a stand
on this question.

*160. S. Knak: The Role of the Mission in Politics**

Whoever thinks of the mission as something that is concerned
only with the individual soul can fall prey to the delusion that he
can close his eyes to political events, occupying himself solely
with proclaiming the Gospel to the individual and with joining
individuals together for mutual edification. But whoever thinks
of the mission as something which "creates a new Bantu society" so
as to integrate them into the ranks of "civilized" humanity must
apply all of his energy to getting control of the legislative
process. Only in this way can he create the political preconditions
that are indispensable for this purpose. Indeed, the chief interest
of the mission must then lie in this direction. A mission that is
based upon Lutheran principles does not camouflage her goals with
either of these two points of view. Such a mission wishes to
proclaim to the Bantu the Gospel of the children of God and nothing
more. But the Gospel must be proclaimed in such a way that the
Bantu can understand it. Therefore it is proper for the mission to
teach the Bantu to seek and to confirm their calling as children of
God in organizational unity with their own national, tribal, and
family colleagues, with their fellow workers and their neighbors.
The object of Lutheran mission work is not the individual in his
isolation but the individual as member of a group, hence the entire
people. For without a living organism, there can be no members.
Thus, because the mission has an obligation to the entire people,
it is unable to ignore political questions....

The mission must have a word that applies to the Bantu race,

*S. Knak was the director of the Berlin Mission. *Zwischen Nil
und Tafelbai: Eine Studie über Evangelium, Volkstum und Zivilisation,
am Beispiel der Missionsprobleme unter den Bantu* (Berlin: Heimat-
dienst Verlag, 1931), pp. 310 ff.

a word that fits the present situation. For God's Word always applies to the here and now. That is the work of the Spirit, that is the biblical Word in the present, translated into each contemporary situation. And the church exists for the purpose of speaking that Word!

Even a mission which convinces itself that it works "only" with souls and "only" proclaims the Gospel cannot possibly ignore having a say in political questions. The politics of the African natives today has to do with two tasks: economic questions and education. Is there really any mission in Africa which holds the opinion that the Gospel does not concern itself with the kind of education that the natives receive in school? Actually, all missions are involved either directly or indirectly in winning some kind of influence over the school system. But then they are involving themselves in one of the most important political questions!

But does not the mission have equally good reason requiring it to occupy itself most energetically with the second of these two chief questions of native politics: with the natives' economic conditions? Was not K.E. Phillipps entirely correct when he emphasized, on the basis of his impressions and experiences from Johannesburg, that the natives cannot immediately harmonize the Gospel of the love of God with the facts and hence are unable to accept it when the mission restricts itself to preaching the love of God? The mission tells them about God, that He is a God of love Who loves the black people too, and yet--here doubt arises--why is it that this God, if He really loves them as the missionary claims, does not take an interest in their food and drink or does not find them a decent place to live? "This God of the missionary's provides you with good things, but only when you are dead," they say. The individual missionary can help individuals, but the people as a whole can be helped only by changing the laws and by improving the lot of their entire race. For this reason, the preaching of God's love can be understood and believed by the natives only when the mission openly protests against such economic oppression in a way that is intelligible to everyone. How much the mission actually achieves by this really is not as important for the understanding of the Gospel as the fact that it declares these conditions to be incompatible with the Gospel which the white race professes to believe.

With that, we come to the most powerful reason why it is necessary for the mission to take up the political question. When the mission preaches the Gospel to Bantu Africa, it preaches it not to a free and independent nation, not to a race that enjoys a prosperous peace, but to a class of people who are grievously

threatened by another class of people, in their external existence
as well as in their inner individuality, and this other class of
people professes to believe in the same Christianity as that which
is proclaimed by the mission. The black race has no room to breathe.
On the one hand, they are oppressed by force, held back, and restricted
intolerably in their opportunities for life, while on the other hand
their strength is absorbed entirely in the service of an economic
system that is completely foreign to them, all this with a promise
that eventually they will enjoy the honor of belonging to civilized
humanity as equal members. At the same time that the earthly home
is taken from their race, their phychical home is taken from them
as well. Notwithstanding that, both groups comprising the white
element profess to believe in the same Christianity as that which
the missionaries offer. Thus the mission, because it stands in
the midst of a connected chain of historical developments, is in
itself partially interwoven with those aspects of European civilization
which deprive men of their freedom and alienate them from their
souls. Under these circumstances, how would it ever be possible for
the mission to restrict itself solely to preaching to the natives?
It is much more logical to argue that the mission can proclaim its
message properly only as it raises its voice loudly against this
confusion of the Gospel with Western Civilization, against this
camouflaging of a self-seeking economic policy in the guise of an
idealism that goes by the name "Christian."

If Paul Schütz's book *From the Nile to the Caucasus* justifies
any one basic emotion, it is surely that of outrage when one sees
the sort of relationship with European and American imperialism into
which the mission gradually has slipped in the world of the
non-Christian peoples....Everywhere the mission is in foremost danger
of serving as an outrider for the imperialist cause. This is the
real danger for the mission today, and the demand that Christ not be
allied with Caesar remains the cardinal demand placed upon the
contemporary mission. In Jerusalem, people saw in "secularism" the
opponent to be taken most seriously for the time being. But the
enormity of the danger can be recognized only when we make clear to
ourselves that secularism is to be found inside our own camp, within
the mission itself. Schütz surely was not the first person to see
this or to say it. But he has said it in such a way that many people
can hear it today who were deaf to the message before. For this,
he should be congratulated.

The only proper conclusion that can be drawn from the facts,
once they are properly seen and understood, is this: The church
must recognize the false spirit within her own camp, the fateful
intermingling of imperial interests with the cause of Christ, and

she must call down the divine word of penance upon herself as well as upon others, upon others as well as upon herself. If the church wishes to protest against this intermingling--not just in Christian periodicals and theological lecture halls but so that the world listens attentively--this cannot be done without political action. For the politics of the native is the only platform upon which black men as well as white men can hear this "Gospel" of the church.

Criticism and Critical Reinterpretation of the Two Kingdoms

161. P. Beyerhaus: Lecture on the Lutheran Message in Contemporary Society*

Thesis 17: Although the church has no political obligation related to its administrative tasks, she does perform a service as a prophetic corrective in urging government authorities to respect the will of God--who is the determiner of all human relationships-- in its secular domain.

Thesis 18: If the church's warning voice is not heeded by the secular authorities, the church is entitled as well as obligated to undertake civil disobedience against laws which oppose the rule of Christ.

Thesis 21: The political witness of the Lutheran Church in South Africa is greatly handicapped by virtue of the fact that her church structure is subject to the same universal fragmentation of races and tribes that characterizes South African society as a whole.

To summarize, we must insist that the obvious standstill of our Lutheran Church's missionary effort in South Africa is caused to a great extent by the fact that neither we nor our hearers perceive the Gospel in its social significance. The old Lutheran message that man is declared justified before God through the death of Jesus contains social dynamite.

162. Memorandum from the Pastoral Conference of Umpumulo**

The Lutheran doctrine of the Two Kingdoms has given our Church freedom to proclaim the gospel of forgiveness of sins and righteousness of God, but it has often been misinterpreted to mean that the Church has no responsibility for the state. Temporal government is sometimes understood as an entity in itself with its

---

*P. Beyerhaus (Instructor, Lutheran Theological College, Umpumulo), Lecture on Fellowship Day, Durban, 1966.

**These are excerpts from the results of a pastoral conference of approximately seventy pastors in the theological seminary at Umpumulo in Natal, 1967. The speakers among others, were: E.E. Mshana of Tanzania; Aalen and Lislerud of Norway; also H.J. Birkner of the Federal Republic of Germany. See K.-M. Beckmann, ed., *Die Kirche und die Rassenfrage* (Stuttgart, 1967), pp. 138ff. The English text is from Lutheran World Federation News Service, 14/67, pp. 5-6.

own laws and ordinances which the citizen must accept in obedience, and it is said, as long as the Church is allowed to preach the gospel, she has no right to interfere in the temporal government, her task is to preach the gospel of an eternal righteousness of the heart. Having reviewed this doctrine of the Two Kingdoms biblically and historically, we came to the conclusion that the Church has an active and responsible service to the state and society: the Church shall protest to the temporal authority when evident injustices have been committed. She is also entrusted with the positive function to interpret and counsel the temporal authorities in terms of the ordinances of creation given for the support and performance of human life, namely: matrimony and family, civil community and culture, state and government (Apol. XVI). This entails intelligent and responsible political participation on the part of the believers....

In its practical implementation this Policy of Separate Development limits human rights of the non-White citizens as to the right of labour, the right of buying and owning property, the right of free and full education, the right of freedom of speech and of full participation in political and social life. We, therefore, reject the Policy of Separate Development.

163. Conference of the Church Leadership in Hammanskraal:
   The Political Dimension of Christian Theology *

The central issue of theological thinking with regard to our present situation is the Christian freedom as given by God. The Christian concept of freedom may give us a deeper insight in the structure of the world. The world is not in a fixed shape, set up by nature, but is God's creation, who made it and wants us to participate in his creative work. The aim of his creation is man's communion with him and with one another through the bond of love. There are no natural divisions among men which are of ultimate value.

The relation between Church and State is based on the fact that both have to fulfill their functions for the sake of man. Therefore the division of competence and authority is founded on the common ground of their mandate to serve man. The Church, although powerless in comparison with the State, has its own power of proclaiming the Gospel and educating the people and communicating the Christian understanding of the world to them. The Church should

---

*This conference was sponsored by the Federation of Evangelical Lutheran Churches in South Africa (FELKSA) with the support of the Lutheran World Federation's Department of Studies in 1971. We present here only an excerpt from the "Findings." See K. Kremkau, ed., *EKD und Kirchen Südlichen Afrika*, vol. 12 of *epd Documentation* (Bielefeld and Berlin, 1974), pp. 276-278. The English text is from Lutheran World Federation News Service 53/71, pp. 3-4.

be clearly aware of its power and use it to help shape the world according to God's will.

The dignity of man concerns us as Christians in Southern Africa very much. Man suffers in his dignity not only because of his weaknesses and shortcomings, but in our country especially because of the structures set up in our society. We should make use of the general concept of human rights as a criterion wherever people are suffering.

God's grace is open to all men without regard to their achievements, their social or racial status. Full mutual acceptance of all men should be our answer to God's grace, leading to full participation in society. Diversity within unity should correspond to diversity within full citizenship. There can be no self-realization of any man other than within community.

We as Christians do not seek human rights for ourselves but are concerned with the rights of our fellowmen. We should be more outspoken and articulate as to the need for these rights for they provide for responsible citizenship.

Defense of Traditional Positions

164. Evangelical Lutheran Church in South Africa--Hermannsburg (ELKSA-H): Statement to the Problems Thrown Up as a Result of the Umpumulo Memorandum

The synod is disturbed, not only by the one-sided and hence unfactual evaluation of the political situation of South Africa in this memorandum but above all by the questionable theological basis which underlies this declaration. Although the Holy Scriptures and the Confessions are cited in support of the concerns that are presented, the train of thought in the memorandum is based in the first place upon an ideological point of view. Because of the alleged limitation of human rights for the non-white population, the policy of "separate development" promoted by the South African government is rejected. The Gospel, however, does not permit the publication in the name of a church group of such a tendentious political statement which is ideologically grounded and which does not take into consideration the unique situation in which South Africa finds herself. The practical result of this is that another truth is recognized as a source for the proclamation of the church in addition to the Word of God. It is therefore extremely thought-provoking when the "sin of disunity" inside the church is discussed

---

*Since the discussion concerning this theme had been conducted primarily in the Hermannsburg Church (ELKSA-H), the documents selected from their report can stand as an example of the discussion in the entire white church.

247

at the same time that a critical judgment which is by no means unanimous is being cast upon South African government policy.

In this connection the synod wishes to disassociate itself from all expressions on the part of certain church groups which intermingle the Gospel of Jesus Christ with extra-biblical viewpoints, falsify concepts from the Holy Scripture like "the justice of God" and "Christian freedom" by transforming them into ideological slogans like "social justice" and "democratic freedom," or hold that certain social structures and forms of government are to be approved or disapproved by the church solely because they do or do not correspond to the dominant spirit of the age. In no way does this relieve the Lutheran Christian of his political responsibility. Rather, his political judgment and activity cannot be determined by an ideology but must be informed by facts which the Christian must then take into account in carrying out the command to love his neighbor.

The South African government's policy of "separate development" proceeds from the realization that South Africa is unable to imitate the forms of government found in the relatively homogenous Western states at this time, due to the great disparity between the races that inhabit the country. The great differences of race, culture, civilization, and society among the various groups making up the population appear to make it impossible for them to live together harmoniously. A form of government based upon universal and equal suffrage would enable a race possessing a majority to rule over the numerically weaker races. The history of the African continent in recent years demonstrates beyond the shadow of a doubt that even the most elementary human rights of minorities are respected only too seldom by the people who happen to be in power at any given time. The result of such a form of government for South Africa would be economic decline and, in the end, bloody disturbances leading to chaos. In order to prevent that, the government is attempting to settle the various groups which comprise the total population into special areas. In this way, the danger of a larger racial group's outvoting the national minorities and the disturbances which would result from this are banished for the most part, whereas the universal human rights which apply to each citizen of the land would be respected in these special areas.

This policy of "separate development" admittedly cannot be justified on the basis of a single passage of Scripture--something that holds true for every other form of government as well--but neither can it be condemned on the basis of the Bible. Since, however, this policy represents an attempt to prevent chaos among the people entrusted to the state's care, it can be endorsed wholeheartedly by the Christian on the basis of his sense of responsibility for the world. A Christian at least can be more certain of exercising his political responsibility when he supports a form of government that grants to the broad masses of the population peace and growing prosperity--despite the fact that it stands in contradiction to the dominant spirit of the age--than when he struggles against this form of government in the name of an unrealistic ideal without being able to provide a sensible alternative.

165. *Excerpts from a "Statement by the Church Leadership of the ELKSA-H" to the Topic "Does the Church Have a Political Responsibility?"**

The Christian's sense of political responsibility leads him to work unsparingly to promote a proper attitude toward government:

a) Since government is a part of the exercise of rule in the secular world, the Christian has an obligation to obey it. This precept is valid chiefly as an admonition for the individual Christian and not as his counsel for others.

b) Government has to rely upon people who live in the state to assist it in carrying out its tasks. For this reason, Christians are obliged to help it. Government consists of people who are sinners like ourselves and who make mistakes. For this reason, Christians have an obligation to intercede for it.

c) A governmental policy is not "good"only when it brings personal benefit, nor is it "bad" when it brings personal disadvantage.

d) A governmental policy dare not become a pretext by which the Christian excuses his actions. No government that is serious about the welfare of the state wishes to limit the responsibility of the individual citizen but on the contrary wishes to educate him for responsible action.

e) No governmental policy can please everyone, and each law has its required severity. Thus there will always be those who have experienced disadvantage or suffering, either in their political activity or in carrying out the laws. The Christian has an obligation before God to help these people by his personal involvement. In this way, he performs an important service for his state and for his government, inasmuch as he offers help with labors of love in areas of life which the state no longer is able to reach with the law.

f) The obligation to obey the government has its limit in the obligation to obey God: We must obey God rather than men. This

---

*The document is signed by President Hahne, Bishopstowe, May, 1969. *Mitteilungsblatt der ELKSA-H*, 31, No. 8 (August, 1969), pp. 5ff.

situation occurs when the government offends against the revealed
Word of God, when it places restrictions on the proclamation of
the Gospel or allows the Gospel no room to be preached, when it
claims jurisdiction over the totality of human life or arrogates
to itself divine authority by requiring obedience to itself that
properly belongs to God alone.

Both church and state hold positions of responsibility. They
should perform their functions in the place to which God has appointed
them. Each should take care that the other does not overstep its
bounds.

We beseech our congregations and their pastors that they always
esteem the community of faith higher than common political convictions
and that they show respect and patience in their dealings with one
another.

We beseech the members of our congregations that they recognize
their political responsibility properly and perform their service
in South African political life conscientiously. We beseech them
at the same time not to expect more from their church officials
than the service which God has committed to them, namely proclaiming
the Gospel, administering the sacraments, and providing pastoral
care. We encourage all members of our church to place their hope
in Jesus Christ alone and not to expect salvation from political
programs or earthly powers.

We remind all officeholders in our church of their obligation
to practice the preaching of God's Word by means of Law and Gospel,
without diminishing it or changing it, just as we ask them not to
shirk their pastoral obligations even in this question. We warn
against causing offense through false political zeal and encouraging
confusion in the church's holy task by means of distinctly partisan
political programs. We encourage all who occupy the difficult office
of government or other public offices to recognize their service as
a part of the governing of the world which God has instituted and
to fulfill the same out of responsibility to Him. We are fully
aware of the difficulties and tensions which arise in the course
of this service and wish to help make them bearable by calling
attention to these things in our congregational intercessory prayers.

B. NAMIBIA (SOUTHWEST AFRICA)

Introduction[29]

    The Rhenish Mission began its mission work in Southwest Africa in the year 1842. The Finnish Mission followed in 1870 but restricted its efforts to the Ovambo people in the northern part of the land. Two self-sufficient indigenous churches grew out of the work begun by these two mission societies. The Evangelical Lutheran Church of Ovambokavango was formed in 1954, the Evangelical Lutheran Church in Southwest Africa (Rhenish Mission Church) in 1957. In 1972, both churches merged to form the United Evangelical Lutheran Church in Southwest Africa (VELKSWA).

    The history behind the origin of these two indigenous churches that have developed parallel to each other indicates great differences, conditioned on the one hand by the diverse theological background and origin of the missionaries, on the other hand by the fact that Finland was never a colonial power, so that the problem of having to come to terms with the colonial government did not exist for the Finnish missionaries. The question as to who deserved their first loyalty--the colonial government or the people whom they wished to missionize--was never put to the Finnish missionaries as clearly as it was to the missionaries of the Rhenish Mission. For this reason, documents presented in this collection will reflect primarily the tense relationship of the German missionaries with the German colonial government, something which in turn presupposes a theological analysis of the Rhenish Mission's entire history.

    In his dissertation, "Mission and Colonialism in Southwest Africa," Dr. L. de Vries, President of the black Evangelical Lutheran Church in Southwest Africa (ELK) noted that the missionaries of the Rhenish Mission have never come to grips explicitly with the two kingdoms doctrine, although theological strains indirectly related to it have exercised a great influence upon the mission. This assessment is accurate and has historical roots as well as theological causes.

    After the First World War, South Africa took possession of the former Germany colony of Southwest Africa as a mandate territory in the name of the League of Nations. Thanks to the intercession of the loyal Lower German Reformed Church, it was possible for the missionaries to resume their work and to make a new beginning. The story was much the same following the Second World War, when the missionaries were released from the internment camps and allowed to return to their labors. The conciliatory gestures on the part of the South African government were repaid with pledges of loyalty on the part of the mission. The relationship which the missionaries enjoyed with the government did not allow critical questions concerning the relationship of developing countries to the state even to arise.

Time and time again, the dominant position of the missionaries in the mission churches had an adverse effect upon the congregations and, for a variety of reasons, led to three secession movements (i.e. the Nama, Herero, and Rehobothian Baster uprisings) which caused extraordinary difficulty for the missions and delayed their formation into full-fledged churches. Thus the problem of gathering together into one church body congregations comprising six different peoples stood in the forefront of the missionaries' efforts. In addition, the missionaries in the past had neglected to establish a more sophisticated relationship with the government. Thus they accepted as a matter of course the assumption that the governing bodies of the native peoples could never exist on the same level as those of the whites. A feeling of cultural superiority and a mission goal aimed at educating the black man prevented the development of political self-consciousness among the native peoples.

Theological attempts to translate the implications of the Gospel into an African context cannot be confirmed. Questions concerning the inner life of the church, such as the exercise of church discipline, the overcoming of African cultural residues in Baptism, Confirmation (the initiating rites!), or congregational government, stood at the center of the church's concern. Matters which were considered extraneous to the church, such as the pacification and development of the land, were left to the government, whose interest was almost entirely identical with the interest of most missionaries. Hence it can be maintained that during this epoch, which extends into the 1960s, the mission never had to face a challenge that called into question its uncritical attitude of friendliness and loyalty to the government.

From the standpoint of theological history, the nineteenth century came to an end for the mission in Southwest Africa on a date set by the white government--1962/1963--when a government commission published a report known as the "Odendaal Plan." This lengthy report contained a program which the government had drafted and which indicated a readiness to accept and introduce South Africa's "apartheid" policy into Southwest Africa. The plan, analogous to the Tomlinson Report in South Africa, projects the dividing up of the land into homesteads for the various tribal groups. It was recognized immediately that this government program was diametrically opposed to the movement favoring church unity, and hence the "Odendaal Plan" was rejected. In 1964 and 1967, the Evangelical Lutheran Church (ELK) drew up a memorandum referring to the program of "separate development" and pointing out its inhumane and unjust effects. This faint-hearted protest, which marked the first time that the young church actually took a position on an acute political question, remained without apparent effect. Nevertheless, it signaled a development that was to confront the church, both internally and in its political stance, with enormous tensions and trials.

As the influence of the missionaries diminished and the young church discovered the extent to which blacks had been oppressed by them, one of her special pastoral services to society was to do her part for the ultimate liberation of the blacks. Meanwhile, the church found that the heavy German emphasis in the theology which the missionaries had brought with them to Africa rendered it irrelevant to the African context. The theological discussion of the traditional two kingdoms doctrine grew more intense as the church began to accept her political responsibility. The consequences of this development were:

1) Complete incomprehension among those missionaries still active in the young churches who--either theoretically or in practice--were unable to give up their doctrine of obedience to the government;

2) Increasing alienation from the German Evangelical Lutheran Church in Southwest Africa (DELK) which had been formed in the meantime and which continued to preserve unbroken (apart from a small but influential fringe group) the theological tradition inherited from the pioneer missionaries;

3) Confrontation with the state, which reacted by issuing threats, deporting white church workers, and sharpening laws directed specifically at church activities, etc.

Both of the black Lutheran Churches, which have united to form the United Evangelical Lutheran Church in Southwest Africa (VELKSWA), are prepared to use their theological insight and pastoral responsibility as they set out on the path of suffering. They are combatting the way in which the German Evangelical Lutheran Church (DELK) misuses the doctrine of the two kingdoms to legitimize white interests and structures of political power. They are struggling against a state which oppresses the majority of its population and which attempts with the aid of harsh administrative measures to beat the church into submission. In the case of the German Evangelical Lutheran Church (DELK), these efforts seem to have succeeded without noticeable opposition.

ELK = Evangelical Lutheran Church

ELOK = Evangelical Lutheran Ovambokavango Church

VELKSWA = United Evangelical Lutheran Church in Southwest Africa

DELK = German Evangelical Lutheran Church in Southwest Africa

VELKSA = United Evangelical Lutheran Church in South Africa

FELKSA = Federation of Evangelical Lutheran Churches in
South Africa

RM = Rhenish Mission

VEM = United Evangelical Mission (Finnish Mission)

Christian Responsibility in a Segregated Society

166. Mission and Colonialism in Southwest Africa*

From the sources available it becomes clear that there was no great prominence given to the theology of this doctrine in the mission. Yet one must presume that the theological tendencies of that time must have had considerable influence in the work of the mission....

But is it in fact not just this lack of exposition that indicates to what an extent these missionaries hid themselves behind a twisted version of the two-kingdoms teaching, which demanded their total obedience to the government? As will be shown later on in this study there are two worrying questions that must be asked here:

1) What did the missionaries really understand by the concept "government"? Did it only mean a European Government, and did they thereby fail to recognize the governments that they met in this land as authorities appointed by God to rule over their people?

2) Was their fear of confrontation with the two-kingdoms teaching linked to a fear that their whole theological system might fall to pieces?

It cannot be denied that the Mission and her Missionaries, by their close association with the Colonial Government, neglected their socio-political responsibility towards their congreations and so greatly hindered the progress of the Gospel in this country. The boundary between State and Church became so indistinct that a state of confusion entered mission theology, and after a time could not be rectified....

It should be said here that a discussion on the implications of

---

*Lukas de Vries, *Sending en Kolonialisme in Suidwes-Afrika*. Dissertation, Wuppertal, 1971, pp. 78, 82. Dr. de Vries, a colored Namibian churchman, is the president of the Evangelical Lutheran Church in South-West Africa (Rhenish Mission).

the doctrine of the two kingdoms, especially with reference to the future of the young churches in South and South West Africa, has begun....But until now it has been of far too much a theoretical nature. The churches want a practical exposition, and that means that the churches want to confront the government of the land and are prepared to face up to whatever consequences there may be. To do this they do need the help of their white fellow-workers, but the time has also come for the Churches of Southern Africa to themselves accept their socio-political responsibility. It will be a difficult and dangerous road, but it cannot be avoided if the Church is to gain the trust and respect of the members of its congregations, and if the Gospel is to be proclaimed in all its clarity. We believe that it is only the tireless and fearless labour of the Church that can save this country from a great tragedy and that can make it possible for the different races of this country to live in peace with one another. Some people say that it is already too late, but we believe that there is still hope if the Church will act *now*, come out of its established walls and penetrate the world with the message of true peace. Nobody in Southern Africa who wishes to be honest with himself, will deny that beneath the show of peace a mighty monster of unrest is preparing to rear its ugly head. It will cost tact and patience to pull the Church-State relationship into proper shape, but it is an unavoidable commission that the church can no longer neglect.

167. *Christian Responsibility in a Multiracial Land**

It is apparent from the history of the United Evangelical Lutheran Church in Southwest Africa (VELKSWA) that the church will not be able to ignore the political situation. In a land where the non-white race is brutally oppressed, the church cannot exist in a vacuum and preach around the distress of her members. Every person has a political opinion, whether he is conscious of it and seeks to exercise influence politically or not. Political participation then means trying to change the existing political relationships--be it in a democratic or in a totalitarian state. The goal of such political participation will be to enable everyone to share in "the fruits and in the process of decision-making." In a situation where a dictatorial minority holds power over a helpless majority, precisely there it will be of enormous importance that the church become "the spokesman for those who cannot speak."

The struggle to achieve "justice for all" is no more excluded from the program of the church than it ever was excluded from the

---

*L. de Vries, January 29, 1973.

program of Jesus of Nazareth. That some people have pictured Jesus as having been an "unpolitical preacher" is a distortion of the Gospel facts. He is the one who first began the struggle for those without any rights--the oppressed, the frustrated, the subjugated, and the suffering. Jesus thinks in the comprehensive dimensions of the coming Kingdom of God--a kingdom in which justice will be victorious, where the poor, the exiled, the downtrodden, the despised, and the guilty all will take their rightful place. If it is true that the kingdom of this world should reflect the coming Kingdom of God, then these characteristics of God's Kingdom must find an echo already in the kingdom of the world.

We often hear the notion expressed that "Politics has nothing to do with the proclamation of the Gospel." I would rather express it differently: "The Kingdom of God must penetrate the world like yeast."

Here we can speak of a dialectical relationship between the Gospel and political activity. I repeat once more that the Gospel is not proclaimed in a vacuum but has to do with existing conditions.

168. *The Church's Responsibility in the Political Situation of Southwest Africa (Namibia)**

The Gospel in the situation of Namibia has to mean that a theology is developed which has some meaning for the black man, a theology which is in a position to help the black man understand his situation. I do not call this theology "black theology." I think it is rather a question of interpreting the Gospel so that the black man receives answers to the questions which trouble him in his daily life. Proclaiming the Gospel, in effect, means putting love and faith into practice.

It may sound superfluous for me to suggest that the Gospel proclamation should have as its content faith and love. You may ask: "Isn't that just what we have always said?" The fact is, in the past the black man has always been asked to love the white man, without ever experiencing much of that love himself. The whites defined love as an attitude of obedience to the white man, being subject and subservient to him. That love also involves a relationship in which two people approach each other on an equal level was ignored. The same could be said about the kind of faith that was shown. Therefore the church's chief responsibility consists in witnessing to the Gospel. Only secondly, in my opinion, does the church have an obligation to exercise a prophetic office. In

---

*Albertus Maasdorp, lecture before the main mission assembly of the United Evangelical Mission (VEM) in *In die Welt--fur die Welt*, 2, 1974, p. 28 ff.

support of this second point, we can cite the word of the Old Testament prophets: "Thus says the Lord."

These were the words which the churches used when they spoke with the Prime Minister of South Africa in 1971 and said: "Thus says the Lord." And they will be surprised when Prime Minister Vorster reacts in such a way as to say: "When the church comes to me and says 'Thus says the Lord,' then I am ready to listen." What is the meaning of "Thus says the Lord"? It may be that Vorster completely lost sight of the fact that "Thus says the Lord" means that he too stands under the critical judgment of God. For it was the situation in the days of the prophets that whenever it became necessary to distinguish between right and wrong, the prophets stood up and announced: "Thus says the Lord." The prophetic office has always zeroed in directly on the distinction between right and wrong. As far as the churches in Namibia are concerned, this means that they must take a critical stance in the situation in which they find themselves if they wish to fulfill their prophetic office.

Here we are dealing with one of the most difficult problems and one of the most difficult tasks confronting the Namibian churches. It is so difficult because we are dealing with a black church which, whenever she has anything to say to the whites, always must hear the judgment: "Whatever she says is stupid and irrelevant!" That is why it is so important that both the state and the white population understand that it may so please God to make use of the blacks today in order to say: "Thus says the Lord." Thus God's criticism against the white man and his system can also be spoken out of a black mouth. That is why I have said that it is a difficult task for the church. And it can be that this is an obligation which demands too much from the church as she is and as she exists among the blacks. Perhaps this has been just the reason why the church so often in the past has elected to take a neutral position. It can be that just because she fears to say a word the church will opt once more to become a still and a silent church.

169. *Response of Prime Minister Vorster**

While Bishop Auala is reading his "Introductory Remarks," the Prime Minister interrupts to protest sharply against Point No. 4: "The conscience of the church compels her to reject a policy that encourages whites to place obstacles into her path and that prevents the church from functioning properly."

The Prime Minister explains that this is not government policy **and never has been, that** the government does not want to have anything

*Excerpts from the Protocol of the Conversation between Prime Minister Vorster and Representatives of the United Evangelical Lutheran Church in Southwest Africa (VELKSWA) on April 30, 1973.

to do with the church if it is going to get mixed up in political matters. He adds that every kind of cooperation can be expected from him as a good Christian as long as the church sticks to her duty, which is preaching the Gospel. But if the church, to the contrary, understands her chief task to be getting involved in politics, then the cooperation is likely to suffer as a result.

170. *Response of the German Church in Namibia**

1. Christian responsibility in a multiracial land is no different from what it is in any other land.

2. Christian responsibility in a multiracial land requires various activities which cannot be the same for every land.

3. Christian responsibility in a multiracial land is determined by the Law of the Lord. The relationship of universal human rights to God's commandments as they are recorded in the Holy Scriptures requires intensive theological investigation. For that reason, the matter will not be considered here.

4. Christian responsibility in a multiracial land is always concerned about the well-being of that land.

5. If we wish to exercise Christian responsibility in a multiracial land, we must subordinate ourselves to the acknowledged rules of conduct of that land.

171. *Gospel Without Ideology***

Surely that is an irreconcilable ideology which is unwilling to let bygones be bygones (as a result of all the disappointments, bitterness, dissatisfactions, and complaints on the part of the blacks), but which expresses itself in only one way: by condemning the policy of "separate development." Now no one in Southwest Africa thinks that "separate development" is heaven on earth, not the government and not even the membership of the German Evangelical Lutheran Church (DELK). But to consider "separate development" as something absolutely evil in itself can be done only with the help of a preconceived ideology. The only reproach that can be lodged against the German Evangelical Lutheran Church (DELK) is that it does not share this ideology....

This is the way in which the German Evangelical Lutheran Church

---

*K. Kirschnereit, "Christliche Verantwortung im 'vielrassigen Land,'" *Lutherische Monatshefte*, XII, 4 (April, 1973), p. 211. Kirschnereit is the head of the small white church (DELK) in Namibia.
**K. Kirschnereit, "Evangelism ohre Ideologie," *Erneuerung und Abwehr*, monthly periodical of the Emergency Society of Evangelical Germans, May/June, 1973, published in the *Allgemeine Zeitung*, Windhoek, No. 132, July 12, 1973, pp. 3ff.

(DELK) approaches the Gospel that is being offered on the open market in this land. She most certainly approaches it without ideological blinders! That does not at all mean that the German Evangelical Lutheran Church (DELK) would prefer to speak a Gospel word without any investment of active love and caring mercy. The doors for active love and caring mercy stand open, even under "separate development." The membership of the German Evangelical Lutheran Church (DELK) has here a gigantic field for Christian activity. Their sacrifices always must and will be greater than the sacrifices of the "soldiers of the cross" who have retired from the front lines, even greater than those of the people who are always drawing up resolutions. The church members will have to take into account the fact that their sacrifice will be downgraded as having solely an "alibi function" or something similar and that their efforts on behalf of brotherhood will not be taken seriously.

172. *Politics, Racism, and Our Church**

Should it be impossible for the church to give either an unqualified Yes or an unqualified No, then she has to remain silent. Her proclamation dare not bind the consciences of her members or burden them with one-sided advice. Of course, the church's silence with respect to definite concrete problems is at the same time a form of speaking. This silence transfers the responsibility for decisions which must be made away from the church and onto the shoulders of the responsible, mature citizens, both Christian and non-Christian. Thus the church removes the problem of "separate development" from consideration as a question of faith requiring a theological answer and restores it to the competence of the politicians, who must render a decision on the basis of factual considerations and in responsibility to their own consciences. To express it yet another way: the political decision deserves to be placed on the same level as a theological decision of faith.

Much conscious and deliberate refusal to understand is required to misunderstand the Lutheran doctrine of the two kingdoms in the sense that the state and its political life are turned over to their own autonomous laws if the church decides not to exercise influence directly or to intervene directly in political matters. The doctrine of the two kingdoms, of course, never has maintained that God rules only in the "kingdom of the right hand"--through the proclamation of the Gospel and the offer of salvation and the forgiveness of sins--whereas in the "kingdom of the left hand" he does not rule at all but has withdrawn, as it were, from the field.

---

*K. Kirschnereit; the texts are excerpts from various hectographed open letters circulated during the years 1972-1974.

This much can be said: God rules differently in the world and in its history, over nations and states with their leaders and rulers; there he rules in a "hidden" way. The doctrine of the two kingdoms merely wishes to differentiate between the ways in which God rules, while providing a cogent theological explanation for such a distinction; but it does not give the slightest cause for concluding that God does not rule at all in the world. The "hiddenness" of God's rule in this world makes it absolutely imperative that secular decisions not be raised to the level of decisions of faith....

The guiding principle that one ought to keep silent where the Holy Scriptures do not speak must be revived again in the church so that she does not become a forum for solving all the world's problems. But when the church keeps silent about questions directly related to her proclamation, this is not to say that she abandons the world to its own devices. On the contrary, she restores the right to decide to her members who must live out their lives as citizens. She esteems and values them as her members regardless of whether they have made a political decision for or against rearmament. [The reference is to the rearmament debate within the Evangelical Church in Germany (EKD).]

This is the course which the church also must follow in the question of "separate development." She dare not elevate a political decision to the level of a decision of faith, thereby rejecting all those who share a different political opinion....

Since the church's officials exercise a special responsibility for the task of proclaiming the Gospel, they are required for this very reason to demonstrate an extraordinary amount of self-control....

Let us summarize: The question as to whether injustice ought to be called by its proper name is to be answered neither with an unequivocal Yes nor with an unequivocal No. In states and lands with greater freedoms, it is easy to fall into the temptation of casting one's glance upon injustice and then directing one's preaching against it. This also applies for South Africa. That is why this temptation should be resisted. In states and lands where freedoms are drawn more narrowly, where political life and the guidance of the state are based upon an ideological program, the exercise of the prophetic office automatically will require greater care and restraint, since the exercise of this office then impinges upon one's very existence. It will always be necessary to call injustice by its proper name, just as it will always be necessary to exercise restraint. The prophet in the church has a more difficult task: at least he had better know what he is doing! The church is no agency for the criticism of public affairs, and her proclamation cannot be a moralistic drumbeat for the alleviation of abuses for which she is unable to claim responsibility. Her concern is for God, for His claim and promise, His judgment and His grace. When the church knows how a matter concerns her, she speaks; when the way in which a matter affects the church remains unclear, she is better advised to keep silent.

Consequences for Church and State

173. Synodical Report, 1960*

The church frequently is judged--and just as frequently condemned--on the basis of her activity and attitude toward the world, and she must be able to state her case clearly whenever she is questioned about what is happening in the world. We as a church, among other things, also are called to make political decisions without pursuing a course of political action. We all know how we as Christians--non-whites as well as whites--are confronted with political problems and are entreated to give answer both for ourselves and for the church. At the present time, politics has taken possession of the non-whites too and has stirred them up. People no longer take an interest in God's Word or His commandments but only occupy themselves with politics; efforts are even being made to involve the church in political activity. But it is our opinion that the church must keep herself out of the political arena unless particular events affecting the proclamation of the Gospel require her to make her voice heard. For example, the disorders in Windhoek on the tenth and eleventh of December 1959, in which twelve non-whites were killed, have shocked us to the core. And there are congregations (or at least there is one congregation) where the church leadership was asked to direct a word to all our Christians about this. We have discussed it at length with our church leadership and yet have decided to disassociate ourselves from it. Our opinion was that the church workers' conference ought to be heard from first, and only afterward, if it is thought to be necessary, should the synod then address a message to all the congregations, perhaps even to the white congregations. Such a message will not be and cannot be a political word, nor can it imply any criticism of the investigatory commission's report (i.e. the "Odendaal Commission"), but it can be only a spiritual word that clearly announces in all directions the will of God on the basis of God's Word. In any event, we regret very much that circumstances led to such shootings, and it is our earnest prayer that something like this may never occur again in the

---

*H.K. Diehl a missionary of the Rhenish Mission was president of the Evangelical Lutheran Church until 1972. This text out of the missionary tradition provides a link with the nineteenth-century materials.

261

future, either in our land or anywhere else.

*174. Open Letter to the Prime Minister of South Africa**

His Honour,
The Prime Minister,
Mr. B.J. Vorster,
P R E T O R I A

His Honour,
      After the decision of the World Court at the Hague was made
known on 21st June, 1971, several leaders and officials of our
Lutheran Churches were individually approached by representatives
of the authorities with a view to making known their views. This
indicates to us that public institutions are interested in hearing
the opinions of the Churches in this connection. Therefore we would
like to make use of the opportunity of informing your Honour of the
opinion of the Church Boards of the Evangelical Lutheran Church in
SWA and the Evangelical Lutheran Ovambokavango Church which represents
the majority of the indigenous population in South West Africa.
      We believe that South Africa in its attempts to develop South
West Africa has failed to take cognizance of Human Rights as declared
by U.N.O. in the year 1948 with respect to the non-white population.
Allow us to put forward the following examples in this connection:

(1)   The government maintains that by the race policy it implements
in our country, it promotes and preserves the life and freedom of
the population. But in fact the non-white population is continuously
being slighted and intimidated in their daily lives. Our people
are not free and by the way they are treated they do not feel safe.
In this regard we wish to refer to Section 3 of Human Rights.

(2)   We cannot do otherwise than regard South West Africa, with all
its racial groups, as a unit. By the Group Areas Legislation the
people are denied the right of free movement and accommodation within
the borders of the country. This cannot be reconciled with Section
13 of the Human Rights.

(3)   People are not free to express or publish their thoughts or
opinions openly. Many experience humiliating espionage and
intimidation which has as its goal that a public and accepted opinion
must be expressed, but not one held at heart and of which they are
convinced. How can sections 18 and 19 of the Human Rights be realized
under such circumstances?

---

    *The text is from Lutheran World Federation News Service
31/71, pp. 5-6.

(4)   The implementation of the policy of the government makes it impossible for the political parties of the indigenous people to work together in a really responsible and democratic manner to build the future of the whole of South West Africa. We believe that it is important in this connection that the use of **voting** rights should also be allowed to the non-white population (Section 20 and 21 of the Human Rights).

(5)   Through the application of Job Reservation the right to a free choice of profession is hindered and this causes low remuneration and unemployment. There can be no doubt that the contract system breaks up a healthy life because the prohibition of a person from living where he works, hinders the cohabitation of families. This conflicts with sections 23 and 25 of the Human Rights.

The Church Boards' urgent wish is that in terms of the declarations of the World Court and in cooperation with U.N.O. of which South Africa is a member, your government will seek a peaceful solution to the problems of our land and will see to it that Human Rights be put into operation and that South West Africa may become a selfsufficient and independent State.

With high esteem,

Bishop Dr. L. Auala
Chairman of the Church Board
of the Ev.Luth.Ovambokavango Church

Moderator Pastor P. Gowaseb
Chairman of the Church Board
of the Ev.Luth.Church in S.W.A.
(Rhenish Mission Church)

Windhoek, 30th June, 1971

175. *Pastoral Letter**

We want to also inform the members of our congregations that we are determined to inform the Government of this state of affairs and of our conviction of what changes must occur. We appeal to you to maintain the peace and with a peaceful disposition to continue seeking our brothers in all racial groups. We want to advise you also to build bridges and not to break down contact.

Dear Congregations, we as your Church Boards do not intend sowing seeds of animosity, discord and strife. Our purpose is to stand for the truth and for a better future for our people and races,

Ibid., p. 4.

even when it involves suffering for us.

May the Lord be with you in His Mercy and give you guidance through His Spirit. Let us continue praying for all authorities (I Tim. 2:1-2), so that they may be prepared to alter the grievous circumstances and to take cognizance of the true interests of this country and its people.

On behalf of the two Church Boards

(signed) Dr. Leonard Auala
Chairman of the Church Board
of the Ev.Luth.Ovambokavango Church

(signed) Paulus Gowaseb
Chairman of the Church Board
of the Ev.Luth.Church in S.W.A.
(Rhenish Mission Church)

Windhoek, 30th June, 1971

176. *Response to the Open Letter**

The church leadership of the German Evangelical Lutheran Church (DELK) in Southwest Africa hereby informs the public that she feels obliged to disassociate herself from the "Open Letter" to the Prime Minister and also from the declaration made from the pulpit by both of the non-white independent churches, the Ovambokavango Church (ELOK) (i.e. the Finnish Mission, whose bishop is Dr. Auala) and the Evangelical Lutheran Church (ELK) (i.e. the Rhenish Mission Church). This applies in particular to the conclusion of this declaration, which obviously oversteps the bounds of the church's competence.

While the church leadership of the German Evangelical Lutheran Church (DELK) takes this step of disassociating herself before her own church membership as well as before the general public, at the same time she would prefer to remain open to all questions of a purely ecclesiastical nature which are of concern to the non-white churches. The German Evangelical Lutheran Church (DELK) finds herself surprised by what she views as purely a political action that, in her opinion, cannot in any way be brought into harmony with previous utterances by either of these two churches.

We would have welcomed it if the questions raised in the letter had led to a dialogue with the responsible authorities and we express

---

*Declaration of the German Evangelical Lutheran Church (DELK) to the "Open Letter" of the United Evangelical Lutheran Church in Southwest Africa (VELKSWA).

264

our hope that new possibilities for dialogue with the state
authorities can be found and utilized for the well-being of our
entire land.

177. *Deportation of Pastor Eichholz**

This step which the government has taken comes as no surprise
to the Evangelical Lutheran Church (ELK), for it has become evident
in the recent past that those who stand up for the truth are
considered dangerous to the so-called "security" of the state.

The order to deport Pastor K. Eichholz is a clear sign of the
Christians of this land of the persecution that is suffered by all
Christians in South Africa.

Struggle for a United Lutheran Church in Namibia

178. *The Black Position***

If there is to be any talk of unity between the United
Evangelical Lutheran Church in Southwest Africa (VELKSWA) and the
German Evangelical Lutheran Church (DELK), then we must try from
both sides to discuss our problems on the same level. Political
neutrality in a society where part of that society is oppressed
is a sin, for it is precisely this neutrality which serves to
increase the injustice. And it is just the white church that can
accomplish much because she possesses the ear of the government.
Therefore it is precisely this church which is called to preach the
Gospel of truth into the ears of the politicians.

179. *The Response of the German Church Leadership****

The synod of the German Evangelical Lutheran Church (DELK),
in its "Statement" to the congregational members, has issued a
further explanation:

In this connection, we must call attention to the "Open Letter"
of the Evangelical Lutheran Church and the Evangelical Lutheran
Ovambokavango Church because it causes division between the members
of our respective churches. We recognize today that the "Open
Letter"--despite the fact that it has had strong repercussions in
the political sphere--was inspired by the pastoral obligation of
these churches.

The church leadership regrets today that she first disassociated
herself from the "Open Letter." She recognizes that the church has
the right and the duty to express herself on political and social
questions of vital importance. The General Synod of the United

---

*Excerpt from Explanation of the Evangelical Lutheran Church
on the Deportation of Pastor Eichholz, April 4, 1974.
**From L. de Vries, "Christian Responsibility in a Multiracial
Land," January 29, 1973.
***From *Evangelische Presse Dienst Dokumentation*, p. 191.

Evangelical Lutheran Church in South Africa, of which the German Evangelical Church is a member, has already confessed in her "Statement to the Congregations" from October 4, 1971, her mutual responsibility for those people in South Africa who suffer from prejudice and oppressive legislation. The acceptance of political and social responsibility by the Evangelical Lutheran Church and the Evangelical Lutheran Ovambokavango Church, already united in the United Evangelical Lutheran Church in Southwest Africa, ought not to prevent their union in the above-mentioned body, even when that responsibility is expressed in a manner and method that differs from that of the German Evangelical Lutheran Church.

Thus it is just those people who urge an inadmissable politicization of the church who are trying to prevent the union of the German Evangelical Lutheran Church and the United Evangelical Lutheran Church in Southwest Africa by arguing that the political goals of the black and colored population groups in the land stand in contradiction to those of the white population.

CHAPTER 13

BRAZIL

INTRODUCTION[30]

The limitations of space have made it necessary to restrict our survey primarily to the paradigmatic German emigrant church in Brazil. We can assume from the start that the doctrine of the two kingdoms is far better known now than was the case in the first half of the twentieth century. This has been true especially since the end of the Second World War among the younger pastors sent out from Germany as well as among the theological faculty established in Sao Leopoldo in 1946. Just the same, the doctrine has played no apparent role in theological discussion to date, not even to legitimate a retreat on the part of Christianity into a realm of inner privacy as a means of demonstrating solidarity with the military regime in power since 1964. Such a tendency is more likely to be observed in the Missouri Synod sister church (see no. 192). To be sure, similar currents exist in the lay-organized "Evangelical Legion" (see no. 193), and these most certainly are derived not from reflection upon the doctrine of the two kingdoms, but rather from a formal model such as that provided by Article 7 of the Augsburg Confession.

In a situation resembling the uproar that followed the relocation of the Lutheran World Federation Assembly from Porto Alegre to Evian in 1970--something which, together with the accompanying press campaign against Brazil, was considered by Brazilian Lutherans to be an intolerable defamation of their fatherland--representatives of some 18 congregations of the Evangelical Lutheran Church in Chile protested at the Synod of Frutillar in 1974 against what they

267

considered to be defamatory statements issued by their Bishop Frenz concerning the Chilean military government; they justified their withdrawal from the synod in the name of "the authentic, Christian, and Lutheran tradition" which, in accord with Article 7 of the Augsburg Confession fatefully restricts genuine Lutheran thinking concerning the church's sphere of activity to two minimal requirements: "the preaching of the Gospel of Jesus Christ and the correct use of the sacraments."[31]

Of course, ever since the nineteenth century Brazil has never lacked for pastors who, either as dropouts from mission seminaries or as missionaries for the Lutheran Association for God's Treasury (*Der Lutherische Gotteskastenverein*), shared a weakness for combining spiritual subjectivity with political abstinence, as in the sense of the recommendations made by the Secretary of the Committee for Protestant Germans in South Brazil, Dr. Fabri, who suggested that: "The Christian as such has no immediate political duty...whenever he entertains inner doubts as to what he should do in a particular political situation, he is best advised to do nothing...if he remains in doubt as to what his attitude should be, let him stay quietly in his place and commend king and fatherland to the protection and mercy of God."[32]

This quietistic tendency was vigorously opposed by men like Hermann Dohms, who headed the Rio Grande Synod from 1935 until 1955. He and others like him have promoted and advanced the anchoring of the synod--which is not recognized as a church by the Brazilian state (see no. 190)--within the context of Brazilian reality. To be sure, the expectation that the church leadership participate actively in every respect in the life of the state and speak the appropriate word to it (see no. 191) has not been pursued by the church leadership in a really satisfactory way up to the very recent present, as is shown by the demand for a more effective exercise of the church's prophetic office in the year 1970 (see no. 194). The strong identification of the church with German nationality, especially in the 1920s and 1930s, as well as with National Socialism, was a significant handicap that prevented the Lutheran minority church from ever taking its political responsibility seriously, even though the texts do indicate that it is an inacceptable over-simplification of the historical facts to speak of the synod as having "isolated itself."[33]

The Declaration of Curitiba (see no. 195) may be regarded as a kind of turning point on the path toward a conscious grappling with Brazil's political and social problems. The danger exists, of course, that the manifesto of Curitiba may serve a kind of alibi

function for the IECLB over against critical voices from within
the ecumenical camp.[34] Socio-critical elements inside the IECLB
apparently felt that the manifesto did not speak out clearly enough
about the problems. They assembled a short dossier from the
Brazilian press concerning incidents of torture. Now the church
leadership stirred itself to action and investigated cases of
torture, in order to silence those who would admit only to isolated
encroachments on human rights while dismissing everything else as
exaggeration on the part of the foreign press. But no official
clarifying word on this matter ever reached the congregations. The
discussion was limited to a closed circle comprising only the
political commission and the church leadership.

The year 1972 saw the 150th anniversary celebrating Brazil's
independence, which featured the transfer of the body of Emperor
Pedro I from Portugal and other festive arrangements intended to
serve as a propaganda bonanza for the ruling military regime. The
church leadership felt called upon to direct a word to the
congregations. At a preparatory symposium held in June 1972 at
Sao Leopoldo, the lecture given by Telmo Lauro Mueller, the school's
director, on the subject of "The Church and the Fatherland" indicated
that the process of raising social and political consciousness hardly
had made an impression since 1970, even among those who regarded
themselves as "educated laymen." It was symptomatic that in the
course of a presentation made by a lawyer, doubt was cast upon a
widely distributed report from the pen of Archbishop Helder Camara
on the grounds that it had not been signed by him but only stamped
with his office seal![35]

To be sure, the 25th anniversary of the Declaration of Human
Rights in 1973 saw a pastoral group draft a comprehensive paper on
Brazil's political, social, and economic situation, but the church
leadership took offense to so many statements that it kept the
document under lock and key without any public explanation; at the
same time, two regional Catholic episcopal conferences in May 1973
published well-documented and extremely critical pastoral exhortations
to their flocks.[36]

While it is impossible to speak of the IECLB as entering into
coalition with the existing political structures in any way that
could ever be legitimated on the basis of a falsely understood
doctrine of the two kingdoms, it remains true that the critical
consciousness of broad segments of the church's membership--many of
whom would gladly see their church limit herself to proclaiming
the Word and administering the sacraments--ought not to be over-
estimated. Up to now, this church has been spared the serious

testing that was experienced by the Evangelical Lutheran Church in Chile in 1974.

THEOLOGICAL TRADITION AND POLITICAL RESPONSIBILITY

180. The Situation of the Brazilian Church*

The situation of the Evangelical Church in the First Republic (1889-1930) can be summarized briefly in a single sentence: the state took no cognizance of the church! The possibility for a change in their relationship appeared first after the revolution of 1930, which witnessed the demise of the world view that had dominated the First Republic. In 1931 the Rio Grande Synod clearly expressed her opinion of the new situation. In the synodical convention that year, she unanimously approved statements by the current president concerning "church and state" and further resolved to publish them as an official synodical opinion. In this way, the synod has stated clearly that every limitation of religious freedom is to be rejected as a violation of time-honored law and of the true Brazilian tradition. On the other hand, the synod has upheld the necessity for the church to organize herself properly within the state in which she lives, even in times of tranquility when the problem of church and state does not arise!...

The Rio Grande Synod's petition to achieve recognition as a corporate body according to public law (presented in 1934 with the signatures of over 53,000 members) was rejected by the Constituent Assembly. This has led to the situation in which the Rio Grande Synod finds herself today. With respect to her existence as a church, she receives no legal or even sufficient actual recognition from the state. Thus she has but one recourse against all efforts to neglect her or to deprive her of those characteristics which make her a church, and that is to take a firm stand upon the fundamental right of assembly that confirms her spiritual nature. Internally, she must go beyond the associative nature of her church life and establish ordinances to govern herself (as has already occurred in the "Organization of Ecclesiastical Life" from the year 1937), ordinances which preserve the spiritual integrity of the church and constantly remind the congregations, both her servants and members alike, of this fact. At the same time, we must hold firm to the hope that the state and the public at large will one day appreciate as a church the Evangelical Church of the German Immigration that has now existed in her midst for some 115 years

---

*Hermann Dohms, "State and Church Among Us: Some Historical Observations" *Sonntagsblatt* of the Rio Grande Synod (March, 1939), Nos. 11 and 12 (Original in German).

and thus offer the church the full legal protection to which she is
entitled.

181. *Church and State**

In principle, the Rio Grande Synod has never been anything
other than a Rio Grande Evangelical Church. But not always has she
been treated as such. Nor has she paid sufficient attention to the
welfare of the state, inasmuch as this meant taking into consideration
the political and social problems of this state through independent
action and on her own initiative. Has the synod ever participated
intimately in public life as an inner power, conscious of possessing
strengths within herself that work in silence but which should also
penetrate public life and help shape it--similar to the Brazilian
Catholic Church, yet in an entirely different fashion? Certainly
it is due to the youthfulness of our church, as well as her inner
and outer poverty, that we cannot simply answer a happy "Yes" to
this question.

182. *A Response to LWF Action***

Yesterday afternoon, Mr. Peracchi Barcellos received a
commission from the Evangelical Church of Brazil consisting of
Deputy Romeu Scheibe, Pastor Elmer Reimnitz, Amandio Altmann, Pastor
Norberto Ott, and Johannes Engels. The commission voiced its regret
that the Assembly of the Lutheran World Federation would not be held
in Porto Alegre and at the same time assured the Brazilian government
of its complete solidarity.

[*Note:* This short article from the newspaper with the largest
circulation in the southernmost Brazilian state of Rio
Grande do Sul follows the lead article on the first page,
which reported the relocation of the Lutheran World
Federation Assembly from Porto Alegre to Evian under the
title: "Lutherans Suspend World Congress Because of
Opposition to the Presence of Medici." Peracchi Barcellos
was at that time governor of Rio Grande do Sul; Elmer
Reimnitz was president of the Brazilian District of the
Missouri Synod.]

183. *The Evangelical Legion Protests****

In view of the abrupt cancellation of the Fifth Assembly by
the Lutheran World Federation's Executive Committee, the Evangelical
Legion (*Legiao Evangelica*) had felt constrained to publish an
energetic protest against the Lutheran World Federation for violating
its own political neutrality in bowing to the wishes of a minority

---

*Hermann Dohms, "Church and State". Report of the Synod of
Cai, 1931, pp. 28-37 (Original in German).
**"Lutherans Declare Their Solidarity with the Government of
the Land." *Correio do Povo* (Porto Alegre, Brazil, June 6, 1970)
(Original in Portugese).
***"From the Presidium of the Evangelical Legion." *Folha Dominical*,
LXXXV, No. 33 (August 16, 1970), p. 4 (Original in German).

that has stirred up a witch hunt against our Brazilian fatherland.
This protest has been published by many Brazilian daily newspapers,
thus rendering any further proclamation unnecessary. However, as
president of the Evangelical Legion, I do not at this time wish to
forget to thank all those who have paid me their respects. Among
others, I should like to mention these people: Federal Deputy
Milton Cassell, who made the publication of this protest in the
annals of the Federal Congress possible; State Deputy Oscar
Westendorf; our coordinator for the Third Region, Dr. Ernesto Keller;
the Evangelical community of Sao Leopoldo; and countless others
who have extended to me their congratulations either in person or
by telephone.

(signed)   Dr. Paul Franzeck.

184. *A Protest to the Church**
The questions which, according to our understanding of the
General Council of the IECLB, cannot afford to be overlooked include
the following:
1) Pastors and congregations have perceived repeatedly the
absence of a pastoral word from the IECLB, as well as a lack of
information from the church leadership pertaining to the serious
problems which confront us in situations that are challenging us
to make decisions. Past examples of this practice have been:
a) the complaints reaching us from abroad concerning the disrespect
for human rights in Brazil; b) the cancellation of the Lutheran
World Federation Assembly; and c) the efforts on the part of
authorities concerning the celebration of the "Week of the Fatherland"
in our churches. In the future, no more such oversights can be
allowed to occur!

2) The IECLB must exercise her responsible prophetic office
far more actively and effectively in public life, especially in
those areas concerned with the respect for human rights and the
problems which confront the masses of underprivileged people in
our fatherland....

September, 1970.

(signed)
Pastors: Martin Hiltel, Dietrico Krause, Erdmann Goertz,
   Godofredo Boll, Harald Maltschitzky.
Professors: Dr. G. Brackemeier, Dr. J. Fischer (Rector),
   Dr. N. Kirst, Dr. H. Alpers, M. Berger, B. Weber.

*"Manifesto." *Orgao de Debates*, No. 3, 1970, p. 11. Reproduced
from a journal for theological students and pastors of the IECLB.
(Original in Portugese)

Students: Breno Dietrich (in the name of the president of the CADES, the student representation on the theological faculty).

[*Note*: The manifesto refers to the Seventh General Council of the IECLB which met in October, 1970, in Curitiba and which was over-shadowed by the relocation of the Lutheran World Federation Assembly. It is significant for the advance of the socio-critical forces in the IECLB that Pastors Boll and Maltschitzky were elected in 1973 as presentative regional pastors for Regions IV and II respectively, also that the church leadership entrusted the sociology professor Manfredo Berger with the chairmanship of the political commission. A region corresponds to a supervisory ecclesiastical administrative district, similar to a bishopric.]

185. *The Curitiba Declaration**

Part II. Matters Giving Cause for Concern in the Church

I. The Unique Nature of Christian Worship

. . .Divine worship has political consequences because it awakens political responsibility, yet it dare never be used to favor distinct political tendencies. Fatherland and government are objects of intercession on the part of the assembled congregation, and congregations are always grateful to their Lord for these valuable gifts. The fatherland is to be honored and esteemed--in most legitimate fashion. Its symbols are to be respected and used with the deep appreciation that the state can rightfully expect from its citizens. Yet the Christian cannot speak of the fatherland in idolatrous categories. The dialogue between church and state can be honored as a vehicle which enables both to accept a mutual responsibility for organizing the national days of celebration by which the fatherland is to be honored.

[Fatherland, government, justice, and especially social justice are all objects worthly of Christian intercession]....

(*Omitted final paragraph*)--[Worship services conducted before an "altar of the fatherland," flags that are placed upon church altars, and other frequently well-intended customs can become occasions for fatal errors. They can cast Christians who are honestly filled with patriotic motivation into severe conflicts of conscience. In

---

*"The Curitiba Declaration of the Seventh General Council of the IECLB." *Folha Dominical*, LXXXV, No. 49 (December 6, 1970), p. 1. The full title of the original document is: *Manifestacao da Igreja Evangelica de Confissao Luterana no Brasil* (Manifesto of the Evangelical Church of the Lutheran Confession in Brazil). The original draft has never been published. The text used here is from a German translation in *Lutherischer Rundschau*, XXI (1971), pp. 371-73. The parts in brackets differ from the original draft, written by the theological commission of the church.

order to avoid every error in regard to the questions that have been
raised, it would be perfectly acceptable for priests and pastors
to involve themselves in such a program of national celebration in
a spirit of cooperation so that they can present proper proposals
for worship services in their own churches and can also plan and
carry out in good conscience the worship services that are in the
planning stage.]....

III. Human Rights

Countless Christians have been thrown into confusion by the
flood of alarming news about inhumane practices (such as inhumane
legal and judicial practices) which are said to be taking place
in our land, above all with respect to the handling of political
prisoners. This creates an atmosphere of unrest [foreign press and
radio reports have given rise to an atmosphere of moral discomfort
and uncertainty], sharpened by the lack of exact and objective
information on the subject. Although the news that is spread abroad
often demonstrates a tendentious character, and even though official
sources in this country have maintained repeatedly that these reports
are all unfounded, there remains a climate of unrest caused by
undenied reports in the national press about instances in which
[individual] police organs have applied inhumane methods, be it in
the handling of habitual prisoners [criminals], political terrorists,
or people who are [only] suspected of subversive activity.

As a church, we maintain the opinion that not even an official
state of emergency can justify measures which violate human rights
[even such extraordinary times as those through which Brazil is
passing at this moment can in no way justify any kind of arbitrary
activity on the part of official police organs--not even in individual
cases--which prove incompatible with a profession of adherence to
viable legal guarantees]. As a church, we consider it necessary to
speak with the government about these matters, first to make clear
to the government the extreme seriousness of this question that
allows ethical principles to be trifled with, secondly to engage
ourselves so that steps might be taken against such abuses as are
being committed [as well as to announce our unconditional support
for those public officials who demonstrate that they actually are
seriously concerned about halting whatever abuses have occurred].
Only then will even the lowliest Brazilian citizen--including the
person who holds an opposing political opinion--be afforded the
absolute certainty that he will indeed be treated in accord with
the principles of that same law with which he possibly has come
into conflict.

The conservative groups suffer from an overestimation of the sinful structures in this world by saying that salvation creates a new world, without any influence over the existing one, which has to be accepted both as God's will and His punishment of human sin. On the other hand, the radical groups do away with the wrath of God with regard to human sin, by reducing the biblical God to a political agent and by forgetting about that particular dimension in biblical thought which considers man's inner change as one of the fundamental promises of the eschatological time. Conservative groups see too much creation in the existing order (even if it is disguised as punishment of God); progressive movements see too much sin in it. Progressive groups interpret salvation too optimistically, and think that the new order can easily win numerically. Conservative groups see it too pessimistically by forbidding any entrance of God's new time into the old one. Conservatives put too much emphasis on John 1:11, the first part "He came unto his own" and progressives too easily forget the second part, "and his own received him not."

Both trends suffer from the same deficiency. They don't produce any working program for the coexistence of creation and salvation. Or, they stand isolated and don't touch each other. Or, one absorbs the other and does away with it. Conservative theology sees the history of salvation as a totally new thing which does not have contact with secular history; progressive theology identifies both histories. In ethical terms, conservative theology thinks that moral man can organize a moral society; progressive theology holds the opinion that a moral society will produce moral men.

In summary, I think that Luther's distinction between the two realms could help radical theology to an important degree. It gives the material to demythologize the revolution and make it exclusively man's business in his response to the proclamation of the kingship of God in Christ. It contributes considerably to speaking in a worldly manner about the significance of much-needed transformation, and it invites the avoidance of a religious language, which is foreign to the nature of Jahweh and also to the content of this transformation.

I think that an adequate use of Luther's theory can help to find a golden mean between the two extreme positions of conservatism and progressivism. This theory sees the good elements in both of

*Lambert Schuurman, "Some Observations on the Relevance of Luther's Theory of the Realms for the Theological Task in Latin America." *Lutheran Quarterly*, 22 (1970), pp. 86-91. Lambert Schuurman, professor of Systematic Theology at the Evangelical School of Theology in Buenos Aires, is a Dutch Reformed theologian.

them. Conservatism, with reason, sees in this world much of the creation of God and rightfully insists on the distinction between this world and God's new world. Progressivism is right in pointing out that the renovating forces of the kingdom of God not only have a future nature, but want to exercise their function here and now. Luther's theory also makes clear that there should be human activity in keeping this world away from chaos. At the same time, it does not allow us to fall in a scheme of anticipation, which gives human activity absolute value.

In other words, it is the eschatological tension in Luther's theology which, on the one hand urges us to activity, and, on the other hand, gives a motive to the expectation of the great deeds of God. I think that this tension is inevitable. It is the key to come to grips with the problem.

I would be quite willing to consider Luther's position as outdated, if a good alternative would be offered to me. I have not found it yet. Sooner or later one has to use the concept of the two realms in order to do justice to the one kingdom. Otherwise, absolute standstill or a theocracy are the only alternatives, and I don't like to have to choose between the two parts of this unacceptable dilemma.

PART V:

THE AMERICAN REFORMULATION OF LUTHERAN

POLITICAL RESPONSIBILITY IN THE TWENTIETH CENTURY

INTRODUCTION

Ethical reflection on political questions among Lutherans in the United States in the twentieth century falls very easily into two distinct periods. The first two decades after the end of the first World War largely continue what preceded. With the triumph of Hitler in Germany, the severe economic depression in the United States, and the outbreak of World War II, Lutherans in the United States found themselves confronted with new conditions and new questions. Beginning during the war years and gaining strength in the decades that followed, a generation of Lutheran theologians teaching in the theological faculties and in the colleges provided a new creative and critical accent.

The influence of American Lutheranism, of which the General Synod had been the major prototype, waned as an important factor. The pietistic accent, which the General Synod has fostered, showed up elsewhere, however, in a highly personalistic concern for services to needy individuals through the agencies of the church. The American social gospel also found a representative voice in the work of A.D. Mattson, for many years professor in the Augustana Theological Seminary. Mattson drew on some elements in the Lutheran heritage, insisting particularly on the interpenetration of the two spheres, but in many ways he spoke as an independent voice; the biblical concern for justice rather than the two kingdoms doctrine was paradigmatic for his thinking.

The moderately confessional view, perhpas with an increasingly individualistic-pietistic thrust, found its expression in the works of a number of writers. The distinction between the two spheres is invoked, usually in terms of the dualism of spiritual and secular, and most often in order to affirm the separation of church and state. At times the American conception of the Christian state is also affirmed. In the work of J.M. Reu, for whom Erlangen was normative, one notes that the two spheres are distinguished, the duty to obey enjoined, and the inner realm of grace reserved for the empowering work of the church.

In a retrospective work (*What Lutherans Are Thinking*) published shortly after World War II, C.C. Rasmussen showed that Lutherans in the United States had come to a full awareness of Luther's teachings. Critical reflection was still in the future.

In more conservative circles the old isolationism persisted. Rasmus Malmin, editor of the Norwegian Synod's theological journal, was clearly conscious of the sharp separation between the spiritual and the secular. He noted how the kingdoms overlap, but he emphasized how different the spiritual and the secular are. The Missouri Synod's J.T. Mueller flatly asserted that the gospel is not social but spiritual. Thus, if Christians are to engage in organized works of charity, they must establish their own institutions both philanthropic and educational. The ideal could be to create enclaves of Christian diaconia in the midst of a secular and condemned world.

At the very beginning of the post-war period Harold C. Letts struck the theme for a new and independent American position. Letts was to be the key figure and editor of a pioneer work on *Christian Social Responsibility*, which the United Lutheran Church in America commissioned in 1946; it came to fruition in three volumes in 1957. Many of the significant teachers of ethics in the post-war period were involved in the conferences that preceded and followed its publications, as well as among its contributors.

These volumes also revealed to what degree leadership in social concerns was concentrated in the United Lutheran Church in America and in East-coast Lutheranism. A number of the contributors had studied under or worked with Reinhold Niebuhr, America's foremost exponent of a realistic and responsible Christian political ethic.

During the same years another student of Niebuhr began his fruitful career as a Lutheran theologian and ethicist. Like many others, George Forell found his starting point in the doctrine of the orders, and from the beginning affirmed that the secular should be recognized as under God. In a more explicit way Conrad Bergendoff called for a responsible lay involvement in government. Martin Heinecken, still uncritically accepting some elements of the Erlangen theology, found it important to stress the necessity of civil righteousness. Edgar Carlson in a book significantly entitled

The Church and the Public Conscience stressed the same necessity in
more positive tones. T.A. Kantonen in his contribution to *Christian
Social Responsibility* made clear the necessary involvement of
Christians in the world. That involvement, Heinecken insisted in
another essay, was to be on the basis of evangelical freedom not
code-morality. Unanimously the American writers, while often quoting
Erlangen theologians, shifted away from the emphsis on obedience
to the necessity of Christian participation.

Outside the circle of Lutherans who were later to unite in
the Lutheran Church in America, the most significant although little
known work is Carl Mundinger's review of Luther's doctrine of the
orders in a Missouri Synod study on *The Church and Modern Culture*.

The official documents of the churches eventually reflected
the new accent. As members of church commissions William Lazareth
and Martin Heinecken laid a solid basis for involvement and commitment
to justice in human affairs. Both the American Lutheran Church and
the Missouri Synod took cognizance of the newly recognized implications
of the doctrine of the two kingdoms, but for the Missouri Synod, a
good deal of hesitation accompanied the venture out of isolation.

Indeed, as the crises of the 1960s challenged Lutherans to
involvement in local projects in community organization, the other
accent also surfaced in the Missouri Synod. The work of Martin
Scharleman reflects, as William Lazareth carefully points out, a
Neo-Calvinist theocratic impulse foreign to the Lutheran affirmation
of the secular. Thus the Americanizing influences of Lutherans in
the United States in a strange way completed their migration from
Gettysburg to St. Louis; at the same time political attitudes
shifted from the left to the right.

The new generation of Lutheran ethicists did not content
themselves with a simple restatement. For this reason we present
a series of amplifications, emendations, and criticisms that indicate
responsible independent wrestling with the issues. Bergendoff
challenged the simple dualism of law and gospel. Ziemke recalled
Luther's demand for service to the neighbor. Hertz set the dualism
into the larger context of intellectual history, as well as noting
its ideological uses. The work of Franklin Sherman in a very
creative way moved in the direction of bringing together the various
elements, including the apparently opposing themes of the two kingdoms
and the lordship of Christ.

More strongly than Lutherans elsewhere, in this sense reflecting
both their own personal involvement in the American political process
and the particular American contribution to the interpretation of
Luther, the American ethicists stressed responsible participation

and initiative as part of the Christian's service to the neighbor.
Increasingly, too, there was impatience with limiting participation
to ecclesiastical channels; to do so is in fact to negate the full
thrust of Luther's doctrine of the orders.

Not all Lutheran ethicists, however, were in agreement that
the way to effective political participation could be charted by
the doctrine of the two kingdoms. Phillip Hefner and Carl Braaten
both found the doctrine inadequate for the needs of the twentieth
century.

While the theological and ethical discussions were going on
and even as the various church bodies passed resolutions, some persons
asked whether the newly discovered involvement in public affairs
had any measure of lay support. Under sponsorship of the newly formed
Lutheran Council in the United States of America a research project
in the Detroit area examined "the Lutheran ethic." The research
design unfortunately took as representative of Lutheran teaching
the most conservative dualistic statement of the two kingdoms. What
Kersten found was quite clearly that not all Lutherans, laity or
clergy, subscribed to this version. The existence of at least two
divergent streams--one fairly quietistic, the other concerned for
participation--seems clearly to emerge. Kersten's work indicates
how thoroughly the Troeltschian stereotype of a double morality had
become lodged in the thinking of American scholars; it also indicates
that the dualistic version had its adherents particularly in parts
of the Missouri Synod and in the even more conservative Wisconsin
Synod. Hertz called the adequacy of Kersten's understanding of
the Lutheran ethic into question in a lengthy review.

More recently another Lutheran sociologist, Samuel A. Mueller,
has reviewed a number of research findings. Mueller sees the bent
for participation as a function of the saliency of faith for the
individual church member. Not surprisingly, he finds greater
saliency among the clergy. His work indicates that the remaining
agenda is to convince large numbers of U.S. Lutherans that faith
does indeed include servanthood to the neighbor. Put in another
way, the participation in the world to which the doctrine of the
two kingdoms points has not yet become the viewpoint of the majority
of Lutherans. The heritage of generations of dualism will not fade
away overnight.

CHAPTER 14

INTERIM: OLD THEMES AND NEW

A. THE SOCIAL GOSPEL IN A NEW PLACE

187. *As Response to the Social Crisis**

Social welfare begins with the first commandment--my at-oneness with God--so that when I pick up the man who has fallen among thieves, it is no longer I who pick him up, but it is Christ in me, and that makes or should make all the difference in the world.

We begin, therefore, with the admission that the social problem is primarily the problem of the individual....Just how much less devastating would the recent depression have been if we had each taken some poor soul apart and become a big brother or a big sister to that one person. My first definite plea, therefore, is that each Christ-filled Christian become the big brother or sister of some prodigal son or daughter, that each Christ-filled Christian become the champion of the Christian interpretation of every present-day problem.

Lutheranism, sociologically conceived, is a Christocentric universe in which He who is King of kings and Lord of lords lives and reigns to all eternity in the lives of His people. It is with this last-named solution of the social problem that we are chiefly concerned in this article.

Luther built his program of spiritual social relations on three foundations:

(1) the person of Jesus Christ.

---

*E.P. Pfatteicher, "The Gospel Approach to the Social Question," *Augustana Quarterly*, 14 (1935), pp. 196, 197, 206, 207-208.

(2) the Communion as the means whereby this person is imparted.

(3) the connection between this world and the life to be.

As Lutherans we feel that we must get every convert to experience in turn the three stages through which Peter passed in his own attachment to Christ. First, it was a case of *Christ with him* during which time, preceding the crucifixion, he looked upon himself as the manager of Jesus. The weakness of our day as reflected in much of the literature and talk about Jesus is that so many speakers and writers have not gotten beyond the manager stage. Peter's bitter experience during the time from Good Friday to Easter Sunday was necessary, for it taught him the meaning of the cross--*Christ for him*--Christ for his sin. He learned to know the power of the cross to atone for man's sin. But Peter, never forgetting the Christ for him, advanced to the third stage so beautifully exemplified in his first epistle it has become foundational for Luther's meaning of the second article of the creed. Peter learned to know a new power--*Christ in him*. This is Lutheranism's sociological motive--a new Peter, a new Paul, a new Augustine, a new Luther, a new (put your name here and see whether it belongs here) because Christ is in him, energizing him for life's daily tasks in easing the world's stress, ready with the most fanatical visionaries of our day for prison or death, if need be, that the masses be saved.

*188. A.D. Mattson: Advocate of Social Responsibility**

The heirs of Luther have a contribution to render to the church universal through their insistence upon the fact that Christian activity must always be founded in the divine grace. On the other hand, Lutherans need to learn from some of the more activistic Protestant groups that the church cannot remain satisfied with a mere private type of piety but must insist that the will of God be done not only in the private but also in the public affairs of men.

Christianity is not a new law but a spirit. Jesus never gave us a code of laws as regulative for conduct, and He never outlined any program for His followers. He did give us a spirit, and that spirit we are to apply to our various social problems. That spirit is applicable to all times, all problems, all conditions....That spirit is a spirit of love and involves everything that Christianity

---

*The first selection is from A.D. Mattson, "The Church and Society," in Edward C. Fendt, *What Lutherans are Thinking* (Columbus: Wartburg Press, 1947), pp. 468-469. The second is from A.D. Mattson, *The Social Responsibility of Christians*, "The Knubel-Miller Lectures, No. 15" (Philadelphia: Muhlenberg Press, 1960), pp. 4, 9, 17, 40-41, 46, 68, 80.

means by the word love. Christians are not called to an outward
imitation of Christ but to obedience to Jesus' inner spirit. Jesus
is our model in disposition in relation to God and man. The chief
characteristic of the Christian spirit is the experience of God
pressing in upon human conduct and exerting His influence upon it.

Because of the very nature of Christianity the message of
the church must become, for the Christian, an integrating center
for all life. With its gospel the church must reach out and touch
all of the relationships of society.

As "God is love" so also is the Christian life one that is
lived in love to God and the neighbor. Love to God and love of
fellow man belong together. According to the First Epistle of
John, "If any one says, 'I love God,' and hates his brother, he is
a liar; for he who does not love his brother whom he has seen,
cannot love God whom he has not seen." The ground of the Christian
ethic is not to be found in any kind of hedonism, utilitarianism,
eudaemonism, or in that which makes for good human relations, but in
the love and will of God. This love cannot be separated from the
love of fellow man, for love is a unity. Any such separation is an
illusion. A lack of ethical love separates man from the life which
is in fellowship with God. Failure to love our neighbor cancels our
love to God because God is love. If God's nature is love, then we
must love in order to love God.

The New Testament is replete with a sense of social responsibility. As we become aware of this fact, the meaning of our social
responsibility becomes clear. The relation of the Christian to God
involves more than a dual relationship. God and the individual soul
are involved, but our relationship to God involves a trinity: God,
the individual soul, and our neighbor. As our relationship to our
neighbor enters the picture, we find ourselves in the realm of the
social and social responsibility. As the consciousness of our
relationship to God develops, the sense of solidarity with our fellow
men increases.

There is a dualism in Luther's thinking about spiritual and
temporal power and life which has deeply influenced Lutheranism.
It may be the least satisfactory aspect of Luther's thought. However,
his doctrine of the "two realms" is not a dualism which manifests
a consistent parallelism, but the relationships of the two realms
is one of interpenetration, in Luther's thinking. The spiritual
and the temporal, the religious and the secular, do not run in
parallel lines which never meet. H. Richard Niebuhr says, "Luther's
answer to the Christ-and-culture question was that of a dynamic,

dialectical thinker. Its reproductions by many who called themselves his followers were static and undialectical. They substituted two parallel moralities for his closely related ethics....It is a great error to confuse the parallelistic dualism of separated spiritual and temporal life with the interactionism of Luther's gospel of faith in Christ working by love in the world of culture."

There is a theological concept in the scriptures which inevitably leads to a sense of social responsibility. This concept is the "kingdom of God." When the meaning of the kingdom of God is grasped, religion immediately becomes social in its outlook because the kingdom of God is, in itself, a social concept. Many years ago I determined to find out what those who manifested a sense of social responsibility had, theologically, that was absent in those who failed to emphasize the social responsibility of the Christian. The answer was not difficult to find. Almost invariably a sense of social responsibility was connected with an insight into the meaning of the kingdom of God.

The law of God is a description, in concrete terms, of the will of God. God reveals himself and his will, and man describes his experience of revelation in the form of law or principle. The law and its relation to Christian living have been subject to a great deal of debate in theological circles during the last quarter of a century. The so-called third use of the law, which has reference to the relation of the Christian to the law, has sometimes been denied, sometimes minimized, and sometimes included in the first use of the law, which has to do with civic righteousness. A certain antinomianism in modern theology is apparent, also, in this attitude and attacks the very foundations of Christian ethics. The Christian faith is something more than a "consolation for the misery of sin"-- to us Harnack's phrase. The law of God, as a description of his will, is significant for the Christian.

Christian social responsibility requires of us that we try to find some fundamental principle which may be used to determine the direction social living ought to take. We need a standard by which to judge social phenomena. We offer no apologetics for this statement, for we have good precedents in the biblical emphasis on law, justice, mercy, and love. We must seek what is essential for a Christian social order. Biblical religion has given us such a principle in its recognition of the sacredness of human personality. This means that, in the realm of social relations, human personality is the highest value we know. The welfare of men and women, boys and girls, is the supreme goal of all social endeavor. Men must never be used as means for other ends but, in the realm of social relations, must

always be considered as ends in themselves. Human values are the
supreme test in the realm of social living. Human personality is
unique. It is sacred in the sense of being set apart. It is sacred
in the sense of the original meaning of the word holy. Sin does
not alter this fact in any way.

B. MODERATE CONFESSIONAL ETHICS--TINGED WITH PIETISM

189. *The Christian State**

    That the spheres of Church and State are distinct is pointed
out by Christ in His command to render unto Caesar the things which
are Caesar's and unto God the things which are God's (Matt. 22:21).
This principle is recognized in America by the separation of
Church and State....Neither the State nor the Church has the right
to interfere in the affairs of the other. The State is concerned
with the temporal welfare of men and the maintenance of outward law
and order; while the Church is concerned with the spiritual welfare
of men and the maintenance of genuine religion and morality in the
heart.

    In spite of this proper separation of Church and State, however,
we may nevertheless speak of a State as being a Christian State, if
the major portion of its citizens professes to be Christians, and
its legislation and administration are controlled by Christian ideals.
In this sense the United States of America is a Christian State,
and should become more and more so by the increasing Christian
character of its people. While the name of God does not appear in
its constitution, the American state recognizes Christian morals
as the basis of its laws, dates time in the year of our Lord, sets
Sunday apart as a legal holiday, takes oaths upon the Bible, prohibits
blasphemy, and appoints special days of prayer and thanksgiving.
There is, however, no discrimination against non-Christians. Liberty
of conscience is granted to every man, and Christians and non-Christians
are guaranteed equal legal rights.

    The duty of obedience to the State is enjoined in Scripture
(Matt. 22:21; Rom. 13:1-5; 1 Pet. 2:13). Insurrection and rebellion
are forbidden (Rom. 13:2). Changes in the forms and methods of
government are to be obtained by legal means. Resistance is
justifiable only when those in authority persist in violating the
basic principles of the State, and when resistance therefore is really
a defense of the State against those who are seeking to revolutionize
it from above. Refusal of obedience is justifiable and necessary
when the commands of the State conflict with the commands of God

*Joseph Stump, *The Christian Life: A Handbook of Christian
Ethics* (New York: MacMillan, 1930), pp. 265-266; 267-268.

(Acts, 5:29), in which case the Christian must be ready to endure the penalty for disobedience.

It is the duty of the citizen to pay his taxes without any attempt at evasion. He should willingly pay his share of the costs of government. At the same time he has, as a citizen, a right to expect that the funds of the government shall be properly and economically expended. He should be patriotic and have true love for his country....The Christian patriot will pray for his country, for all who are in authority over him, and for the true well-being of all his fellow citizens. He sees the highest good of his country in the growth of right Christian character in its citizens, and in the regulation of the activities of the individuals and of the State itself by the principles of Christianity.

190. State and Church*

It is obvious from these considerations that state and church are two entirely different bodies, each having an individuality of its own and distinct from that of the other. They are not to be considered as one entity with perhaps two differnt modes of operation or manifestation, but as two distinct organisms. They may occupy largely the same territory, and they may embrace largely the same individuals in their membership; but they are not in any way to be confused or confounded with each other.

Since the state and the church are two entirely distinct bodies, each having a definitely circumscribed divine purpose and a divinely established mode of operation, it is evident that a conflict between state and church can arise only when they go beyond their own sphere and meddle with things that do not concern them. The sphere of the state is the natural life of man; it deals with him as a human being only; and its duty is so to order the social life of human individuals in the community of the state that each individual may enjoy to the fullest extent the inherent rights with which the Creator has endowed him, without at the same time interfering with the enjoyment of those rights on the part of others. The sphere of the church is the spiritual life of man; it deals with him as a sinner who needs the grace of God; and its chief duty is to administer the means of grace, by which sinners are made children of God and live as children of God. In its own sphere each is supreme and must tolerate no interference from the other. The difficulties arise in those fields where the functions of state and church overlap to a certain extent. The practice of his religion according to the dictates of his own conscience is an inalienable

---

*Johann Michael Reu, with the assistance of Paul H. Buehring, *Christian Ethics* (Columbus: Lutheran Book Concern, 1935), pp. 343, 346-348.

right of every citizen and it is one of the functions of the church
to guide and
state, on the other hand, to safeguard and protect him in that right,
even though a person's religious performances should appear false
and foolish in the extreme to most of his fellow-citizens....Again,
it is the function of the state to make laws and ordinances for
the orderly life of its citizens, to enforce such laws, to curb
and prevent crime and disorderly conduct, and to administer the
government honestly and effectively. But the state cannot, by such
external means, produce true morality; which nevertheless is necessary
both to the conception of good laws and for their wholehearted
support and execution. It is the function of the church to cultivate
this morality, and it does it through the regenerating power of the
means of grace, by which new motives are implanted in men. Accordingly,
the church must not encroach upon the function of the state, the
making and enforcing of laws; and the state must not attempt to
displace the church by undertaking to do that which it has not the
power to do. Thus in every case of conflict between state and
church, let each remind itself of its own proper sphere, object,
and means of operation, attend to that, and the conflict will be
solved.

191. The Lutheran View of Christian Ethics*

To differentiate the Lutheran concept of Christian ethics
(and it is not meant to imply that what we here call "spiritual
ethics" is found only among Lutherans) from nomos ethics is not
to deny a proper place to law but rather to affirm that a Christian's
highest ethics takes him beyond the mandate of law, code, or
principle....

The respective ministries of law and gospel find expression
in Luther's view of the two kingdoms to which the Christian belongs--
the kingdom of law and the kingdom of grace. In the latter man is
ruled only by the Word of God; in the former he is constrained by
the enforcement of law.

It is by the will of God that the two kingdoms coexist in this
fallen world. The worldly kingdom is not redemptive; but if it
were not beside the spiritual kingdom, the unrestrained wickedness
of unregenerate man would destroy all order and make the ministry
of the Word impossible. Worldly government thus exists by the will
of God. The legal order in which God has set man is both penalty
for man's sin and opportunity for man in the midst of sin.

---

*Carl C. Rasmussen, "The Lutheran View of Christian Ethics,"
in Fendt, *What Lutherans Are Thinking*, pp. 443-446.

The proclamation that the gospel sets man free from the law is misunderstood when it is construed in an antinomian sense. Luther's discussion of the Ten Commandments show this clearly enough. And Melanchthon's affirmation that "the law ought to be begun in us, and be kept by us more and more," finds many iterations in the Lutheran Confessions.

God is Himself the author of the natural law on which the political order rests. He has made this law of nature as inclusive as the cosmos. His universe is not morally neutral. It imposes its consistent moral imperatives. The state must ever be summoned to make its positive legislation true to this God-made law. The body politic is not within its rights if, in violation of this law, it enacts statutes for the reason that they seem desirable to the sovereign be that an individual, a class, a party, or a majority. The sovereign stands under the judgment of the law of nature which God has built into existence.

This is properly called a natural law, for it is true of the behavior of the created order--and that whether man apprehends it or not. Indeed, man's sin dims his eyes so that this law, of divine origin, is often seen but darkly.

It would be false to say that, because this is natural, it is not revealed. It is both natural and revealed....There is manifestly no inclination on the part of Lutheran ethics to ignore the mandate of this all-pervasive law. Christian ethics speaks for both kingdoms.

But the point which it is particularly important to stress, in view of the persistence with which ethics is legalistically conceived, is that no ethics which stops on the level of law, or code, or principle is sufficiently Christian. There is a higher ethics. The kingdom of God never rests on a basis of law but of grace....

When Christian ethics speaks to us about the Christian's highest ethics, it is, of course, the ethics of the kingdom of God. It presents the quality of the conduct of the man who is "in Christ," and, because he is in Christ, in the relation of love with all who are Christian. It is not that he does not love those who are not Christians. He does. Love is not exclusive. But the mutuality of relationship which is true of all who are in the kingdom of God is refused by him who is without even while he is himself the object of the fellowship's love.

The Christian's action is action in the spirit and the fact of the *agape*-relation. He who lives in this relation is in the kingdom of God, and he who is in the kingdom of God does live in this relation. The quality of the action is regulated, not by law or rule, but by the fact that the regenerated person has become a participant in a new relationship.

C. THE CONTINUATION OF ISOLATION

*192. The Lutheran Attitude on Social Questions**

The Confessions draw a very distinct and even sharp line between this civic rule and the spiritual rule, which is also called the Church....

Since the two kingdoms work in different spheres and with different aims, they also employ different *means*. "The power of the Church is exercised *only* through the preaching of the Word and the administration of the Sacraments," while the secular government uses "the sword and bodily punishments" (Aug. XXVIII). And the Confession adds: "Therefore the power of the Church and the civil power must not be confounded."...

But while the confessions thus keep the two kingdoms apart, the do not separate them as two territories or as f. inst. two adjoining houses, each covering absolutely its own ground with one or two walls between them, each house with its own set of inhabitants.

In the first place the two kingdoms have in whole or in part the same membership....

But since both Church and State have to deal, at least to a great extent, with the same individuals, it is self-evident that the two must have a *common interest*, which may be designated as: *human conduct*. Looking at it from the point of view of the Church, it is also obvious that a Christian is a Christian in all his life and in all his contacts....

The three uses of the Law are called 1) the Usus Politicus, 2) the Usus Elenchticus, and 3) the Usus Tertius. The last named is the usus which has to do with the true members of the Church, the converted and believing Christians, and the Confessions have much to say about this usus. Among other duties mentioned we find also those of a Christian toward human society....

We may now be in a position to state briefly what is the attitude of the Lutheran Church toward social, political, and economic problems.

    1) The Church *is* a spiritual kingdom; the state and all civic institutions *are* secular.

---

*R. Malmin, "What is the Attitude of the Lutheran Church Toward the Social, Economic, and Political Problems of This Country?" *Theological Forum*, VII, 1 (January, 1935), pp. 2-18.

2) The *aim* of the Church is to give eternal things, an eternal righteousness and eternal life. The *aim* of the secular kingdom is not to defend our souls, but our bodies and bodily possessions against outward molestations and maintain civil righteousness and peace.

3) In *spiritual things* man's understanding and will power can accomplish nothing. A new birth and the work of the Holy Spirit are necessary. In *secular things* man has "reason and judgment concerning them, and the liberty and power to render civil righteousness."

4) The Church has no other *power* than that of the Word and the Sacraments, while the state has "the power of the sword and bodily punishments."

5) The church knows no other *authority* than that of the *Word*, while the secular kingdom is under the rule and authority of human reason and natural law.

6) "Therefore the power of the Church and that of the civil government must not be confounded; and the Church must not interfere with civil government nor prescribe laws to civil rulers concerning the form of the government."

7) As the agent of the Holy Spirit in preaching the Law of God, the Church has the duty of enjoining upon her members also those commandments that apply to the duties of every day life, and to the duties of rulers as well as of subjects....

But where draw the line? How far may the Church and those who speak for the Church, go? We answer: As far as your authority will carry you. But your only authority is the Word. Where the Word of God has **spoken**, the Church and her spokesmen may speak. Where the Word of God is silent, the Church and her spokesmen have to be silent....

If, however, the State should violate the spiritual interests of the Church, the word of the apostles about obeying God rather than men has its application. The State has, to take a concrete example, no right to prohibit Christian schools. The State has no right in its own public schools to teach, or tolerate that the teachers introduce such doctrines as are subversive of Christian religion or morals. In such cases the Church has a right to call her members to arms in order to defend both the rights of the Church and the spiritual interests of the people. If the Church then would seem to enter the field of politics and political

campaigns, the fact of the matter is that she has not "entered,"
she has been dragged into the fray.

193. *The Business of the Church**

I. It is the business of the Christian Church to proclaim to
mankind perishing in sin the spiritual Gospel of the crucified and
risen Christ, and not the so-called "social gospel."

II. However, by preaching the spiritual Gospel of Christ it
will, under God, and so far as God blesses its mission, also effect
a solution of many of the social and economic problems which are
confronting us because of man's utter sinfulness and perverseness.

As a Church of Christ we shall preach kindness and charity
and the relief of suffering in the spirit of helpful love.

194. *The Church and Social Problems***

What the Lord says in Mark 14, 7: "Ye have the poor with you
always, and whensoever ye will, ye may do them good," and when He
enumerates some of the least of His brethren in Matt. 25, 35, 36,
and what He implies in Matt.10, 42: "Whosoever shall give to drink
unto one of these little ones a cup of cold water only in the name
of a disciple, verily I say unto you, he shall in no wise lose his
reward," has ever been taken by Christians for their guidance in
taking care of the poor, the sick, the orphans, the aged and infirm.
The institutions which have been erected and are being maintained
by Christians, such as hospitals, children's homes, sanatoria,
schools for the blind, for the deaf and dumb, for feeble-minded
and epileptics, for old folks, bear witness of the fact that good
works are being practised in keeping with the Word of God.

But social work does not confine itself to the relief of such
as are in trouble. It has a wider field of activity, and prophylactic
measures are employed by social workers quite as largely as remedial
measures. Educational sociology sponsors the thesis that it is
far better for society to have all its members, young and old,
become well-integrated units in the social fabric than to carry out
elaborate programs for the removal of maladjustments and the
rehabilitation of social misfits. In other words, the former programs
of indiscriminate giving and even of planned relief have been
supplemented, and in part replaced, by a new objective, that of
developing well-adjusted and integrated personalities. The prime
function of the Church in this connection is to take care of the

---

*J.T. Mueller, "The Spiritual, Not the Social Gospel in the
Church," *Concordia Theological Monthly*, 14 (1943), 684, 693.
**The first quotation is from Paul E. Kretzmann, "The Church
and Social Problems," *Concordia Theological Monthly*, 8 (1937),
pp. 669-670 and the second from the same author's, "The Social
Implications in the Gospel and the Book of Acts," *ibid.*, 4 (1940),
pp. 401-402.

spiritual needs of men, to apply the means of grace, and to apply them properly to each individual case. Its program of education, however, need not be confined to the informational side alone, to the imparting of the truth of salvation. For it is clear that the ethical contents of the Holy Scriptures may be brought out in a much more systematic fashion than that which is usually observed.

One fact must be kept in mind throughout this discussion. Contrary to the opinion voiced by exponents of the social gospel, the teaching of Jesus was primarily concerned with matters of doctrine, of creeds.

CHAPTER 15

A New Impetus--From Orders Of

Creation To Public Participation

A. THE AFFIRMATION OF THE SECULAR

195. *A Reformulation of the Lutheran Ethical Position**

In this concept of Christian liberty we begin to find the
ethical consequences of the doctrine of justification by faith.
Primarily, Christian liberty is, in Luther's thought, a concept of
spiritual freedom from the threats and penalties of divine law,
from the bondage of fear and remorse before God. These threats
and penalties were a necessary part of the preaching of God's
Word, for they set forth the moral structure of life. Justification
does not set aside this structure, but it transforms our relation to
that structure by removing our fear and leading us in thankfulness
for the atonement to conform our lives to that structure. In other
words, God's Law condemns us as sinners, but justification takes
away the threat of that condemnation. The Law is set aside and
yet remains.

It is no wonder that preaching often fails to hold such a
paradox in equilibrium and that laymen and preachers have taken
advantage of this concept of liberty to relax the moral tension in
their lives. This tension is always difficult to maintain. For
Lutherans it has often been cut by an unwarranted use of justification
to remove the significance of sin, rather than to remove the fear
and remorse resulting from sin. The ethical struggle is even more
likely to be relaxed in Lutheranism because social and ethical values
are definitely subordinated to the personal spiritual value of faith

---

*Harold C. Letts, "Toward a New Lutheran Ethic," *Lutheran
Church Quarterly*, 17 (1944), pp. 16-17; 21-24.

and justification.

This much for the general ethical tone of the Reformation.
Its political concepts were drawn chiefly from the Pauline conception
of the divine ordinance of government found in the thirteenth
chapter of Romans, which harmonized well with the doctrine of
justification by faith....Certainly, then, we must attempt a
reformulation of our ethical position in order to keep in proper
focus the whole Gospel and make more effective the special values
of the doctrine of justification.

In this reformulation, one of the crucial issues is the relation
of "faith" and "love." Luther was concerned to emphasize the primary
value of faith and always suggested that an active vital love would
grow out of the joy in justification. The love commandment was
emphasized only in personal relationships, or as an ultimate judgment
upon all human life and all schemes of justice, and then with such
pessimism that little ethical tension or power was created by the
judgment. In our reformulation, it must be made clear that "faith"
and "love" stand in a dialectical relationship to each other.

We live in a day of man's "easy conscience." There is little
humbleness or repentance about our social relationships. Unless
the law of love is rigorously asserted, we shall have no consciousness
of sin and guilt. Without such a consciousness of sin and guilt,
our teaching of faith and justification will seem rather irrelevant.
But if, through the love commandment, we can be made aware of our
inhumanity toward man, then perhaps the immensity of our pride
before God will be shattered and we shall be made aware of our need
for His healing grace. That is one part of the dialectic between
"faith" and "love." The second part is Luther's familiar insight
that real "faith" is ever active and working through "love," stooping
to serve one's neighbor. But through a new understanding of the
relevancy of the love commandment to the social and political aspects
of life, this traditional insight will be broadened and sharpened
in meaning. In this refocusing of the love commandment, its rigor
and tension must be established in three relationships.

In the first place, it must be emphasized as a law of judgment
upon all life, and upon all political concepts or schemes of justice,
revealing their inadequacies when measured against love's standards.
"Be ye therefore perfect, even as your Heavenly Father is perfect"
(Matt. 5:48) is no idle word. It is the ultimate law of life;
anything less than that is imperfect and often destructive of other
life. The message of the First Epistle of John must be in the
heart of every man to make him forever dissatisfied. Luther applied
the law of love in this first way as a judgment upon all life, but,

as he did not apply it in the following two ways, he drew only
pessimistic conclusions regarding the problem of politics from it.

Secondly, the love commandment must be used as a means of
discriminating between different schemes of justice. If Lutherans
had not been so obsessed by the inadequacies of all arrangements
of politics, they might have seen that there is a significant
difference "between the justice, moderation, and equity of Titus
or Trajan, and the rage, intemperance, and cruelty of Caligula, or
Nero, or Domitian," as Calvin once pointed out. Love should be
the means of pointing out this difference and choosing between the
various schemes of justice. The failure today of many Christians
to see any difference worth fighting to preserve between the fascism
of Hitler's new order and the democracy of the United Nations is
partly a belief that all politics are equally corrupt, and partly a
belief that no political scheme, unless perfect, may be supported
by the Christian. The first belief fails to discriminate properly
between fascism and democracy by means of this law of love. The
second belief fails to see that no politics can ever be perfect when
judged by love's standard, and that the only choice ever offered
is between relative goods and relative evils....

But to continue, the third way that love must be affirmed by
Christianity is as the source of, and inspiration for, higher and
more imaginative schemes of justice....

It becomes clear that the three applications of the law of
love--(1) as a law of judgment upon all life lest we accept any
achievement of justice as a final good and sanctify it, (2) as a
means of discrimination between different schemes of justice lest
we fail to make effective our Christian conscience, and (3) as the
source of, and inspiration for, higher schemes of justice lest we
accept present achievements as the only possible arrangements of
life--must be used together and considered in toto if we are to
avoid the various pitfalls into which the Christian ethic has fallen
in the past. Particularly must we stress the second and third if
we are to avoid the conservatism of the Lutheran Church's past.

Furthermore, love must be translated into the terms of politics
if it is to avoid the almost purely personal connotation it had for
Luther. Some such reinterpretation in terms of the Stoic idea of
the natural law of justice and equality as the following one must
be made: "Since the law of love demands that all life be affirmed,
the principle that all conflicting claims of life be equally affirmed
is a logical approximation of the law of love in a world in which
conflict is inevitable." The affirmation of life would mean its
freedom to develop into its highest self. But since in this finite

world, this results in conflict with other persons, the only feasible
good would be the equal opportunity for development along with
others. Thus the interrelatedness of love and equality brings the
Christian ethic into contact with life. Equality seems to be much
closer to the love ethic than does the concept of obedience to
authority. Therefore it must become the dominant political goal
of Christianity.

196. The "Natural Orders" According to Luther*

According to Luther, man is always a member of two realms
simultaneously. Every man is a member of a secular realm and of a
spiritual realm. It is important to realize the difference between
these two realms and to keep them separate. Luther claimed that
Jesus (Matt. 22:21) had emphasized the separation of the two realms
when He said: "Render therefore unto Caesar the things which are
Caesar's; and unto God the things that are God's." Luther himself
pointed frequently to the difference between the two and reiterated
the need for a clear separation. But although the spiritual realm
is separated from the secular realm, ultimately they are both God's
realms.

Luther considered it one of his important contributions to
the ideology of his time that he had separated the two realms of
existence, and yet had emphasized the divine origin of both. In
his explanation of Psalm 82 he wrote that "the secular realm has
too long been subjected to the clerical giant and tyrant....The
reason was that nobody seemed to know the task of the secular
authority, and in how far it is separated from the authority of the
church." And he continued: "Now the Gospel has been revealed and
has shown the obvious difference between the secular and the clerical
authorities, and it teaches us that the secular authority is a
divine order, to be obeyed and honored by all."

Although Luther had separated "secular"and "spiritual" authorities,
he claimed divine institution for the secular realm. This secular
realm is subdivided into a multitude of "offices," "vocations," and
"ranks." The three main groups of orders within the secular realm
are the family or society (family is used in a wider sense than at
the present time), the **gov**ernment, and the church. These orders
are divinely instituted. "All ranks and professions of society are
instituted by God to serve Him." Luther insisted upon the divine
institution of marriage against the "popish heresy" of celibacy.
And his repeated and vehement insistence upon the divine character
of the order of government is generally known....

---

*George W. Forell, "Luther's Conception of 'Natural Orders,'"
Lutheran Church Quarterly, 18 (1945), 166-167, 177.

For Luther the natural orders are real, they are administered
by sinful men, they exist for the sake of sinful men, and they punish
sinful men. Within these orders human reason rules. But this reason
is itself sinful. Christians, too, stand within this realm of the
natural orders. As far as they are members of these orders, they
have to obey their rules. Therefore they may be forced by the
sinful situation and orders to do things that are not Christian.
However, this fact does not in any way lessen the demands of Christ
upon the individual Christian. These ethical demands are eternal
and directed to man in a sinful situation. They do not, in some
miraculous manner, change the sinful character of the natural orders.
But the ethical norms of Christ and His Word must enlighten the
reason of the Christian. This believing reason then becomes a
beautiful and mighty instrument and tool in the hands of God. In
that manner Christ transforms the natural orders through the medium
of the Christian individual. The natural orders will never extricate
themselves from sin; however, used by men who know what is right
and wrong through the revelation of Christ, they may be used to
preserve the world from chaos and self-destruction until the day
of Jesus Christ.

197. *The Lutheran Christian in Church and State**
This Law of God forbids us to worship the deified governments
which seek to occupy the thrones of Caesar. Christians in the first
and second centuries gave their lives rather than submit to this
kind of authority. We must challenge the pretensions of the modern
secular state which knows no limitation to its power or claims.
The state is not a being. It is composed of men and women who make
up society, and when we or they serve the state we serve no
impersonal idea but each other. Back of the mechanized Frankenstein
which we have created in the name of government are only people, and
we need to redefine the functions of government in terms of persons.
Then we can confront these people with the Law which is directed not
to systems or bureaus or machines but to men and women, who love or
hate, sacrifice or steal, are honest or deceitful, chaste or
adulterous. The Law of God must reveal the truly personal character
of those who administer government, and the church must reach these
people with its message of right and wrong....
It is important to distinguish between the vocation of the
clergy and of the laity in this question of relationship to government. More than we are aware the Protestant churches have inherited
a clericalism from Rome which has affected their thinking on the

---

*Conrad Bergendoff, "The Lutheran Christian in Church and
State," *Lutheran Quarterly,* 1 (1949), 421-422.

participation of Christians in matters of government. We have so
much identified the church with the clergy that what we say about
the impropriety of the church mixing in politics really refers
only to the ministry and not to the laity. With their particular
function the clergy are not to instruct the leaders in political
life what measures these should take, for political representatives
are responsible to God on the one hand and to the people who choose
them on the other. But one cannot deduce from this that Christian
laymen are not responsible for the way public affairs are conducted.
There is not in Christianity any good ground for the charge that
politics belongs to the world from which Christians are to separate
themselves.

*198. The Natural Orders as the Place of Service**

It seems quite clear from the above that Luther's teaching
concerning the natural orders does not establish a secular source
of ethics for society, but that the natural orders are deeply rooted
in God's will for the world. However, so far it would seem as if
there were no connection between the ethical principle of the
Christian individual, faith active in love, and the divine natural
law that governs the orders of nature. But Luther explains that a
point of contact between the secular realm and the spiritual realm
exists in the person of the individual Christian. In this point
the spiritual realm penetrates the secular, without, however,
abolishing it. The Gospel itself cannot be used to rule the world,
because it is the Gospel and demands a voluntary response from man.
It would cease to be the Gospel if it became a new law. But
through the person of the believer, who is related to Christ
through the Gospel and who is at the same time a member of the
natural orders, the faith active in love penetrates the social
order. Of the Christians Luther said: "The citizens of the kingdom
of Christ are earthly, transitory, mortal men, live and dwell
scattered here and there in the lands of this earth and are
nevertheless at the same time citizens of heaven." Only they truly
understand the divine character of the natural orders. And it is
for the sake of the Christians that God maintains the world so
patiently. "He has indeed created all that the world contains and
produces for the sake of pious Christians; He gives and maintains
all only for their sake, as long as the world stands, in order that
they should richly enjoy these things in this life and have no need."
Christians alone maintain both realms through their prayers. Luther
asserts: "We as Christians ought to know that the entire temporal

*George W. Forell, *Faith Active in Love* (Minneapolis: Augsburg
Publishing House, 1954), pp. 148-152.

rule and order stands and remains as long as it does only because
of God's order and commandments and the prayers of the Christians.
These are the two pillars which uphold the entire world. When
these pillars are gone, everything must collapse, as will be seen
on the day of judgment. And it is even now discernible that all
kingdoms and governments are weakened and are beginning to topple
because these two pillars are about to sink and break. For this is
the way the world wants it because it does not tolerate the Word
of God (which honors and upholds the world) and persecutes and kills
the innocent Christians and does not cease to rage against the very
pillars which support it." Yet God desires that the Christian take
his full responsibility in the world. He may become a leader in
secular affairs and even bear the sword. If he attains political
power he will at the same time govern his people and serve God.
Through the Christian in the world his faith active in love
influences the social structure. This Luther stated in the
conclusion of his famous *Treatise on Christian Liberty*. He said:
"The good things we have from God should flow from one to the other
and be common to all, so that everyone should 'put on' his neighbor,
and so conduct himself toward him as if he himself were in the
other's place. From Christ they have flowed and are flowing into
us: He has so 'put on' us and acted for us as if He had been what
we are. From us they flow on to those who have need of them....We
conclude, therefore, that a Christian man lives not in himself, but
in Christ and his neighbor. Otherwise he is not a Christian. He
lives in Christ through faith, in his neighbor through love; by
fiath he is caught up beyond himself into God, by love he sinks
down beneath himself into his neighbor; yet he always remains in
God and in His love."

Luther could describe eloquently how under the influence of
the Gospel a Christian ruler could make the institutions of secular
authority the means of service. He suggested to the Christian ruler
that he should imitate the example of Christ in his rule. Far
from seeing in government merely a means of repression, he portrayed
it as a glorious instrument of Christian service.

199. The "Orders" and Creation*

Luther's doctrine of the "orders" should be understood from
his doctrine of creation and the manner in which God reveals
Himself to His creatures.

For Luther the creation as such was good. It is in and through

---

*Martin J. Heinecken, "Luther and the 'Orders of Creation' in
Relation to a Doctrine of Work and Vocation," *Lutheran Quarterly*,
4 (1952), pp. 396-400; 412.

the creation that God comes to man and blesses man. The created world, therefore, is not a lower order of being but is itself the instrument of the divine goodness. When now God chooses to reveal Himself, He does so in and through the creation itself.

Luther insisted over against the Enthusiasts (Schwärmer) that Christ actually was present in the created thing. Here was his best bulwark against a spiritualizing of the God-relation. "The Enthusiasts say: he (i.e., Christ) is present spiritually in us, i.e., speculatively, while in reality he is *above*. But faith and Christ should be joined. This is not a matter of speculation but of actuality." (WA XL, I; 546, 5.)

"Therefore it is a poor wit which says that Christ is ascended into heaven. But it is not in mundane or temporal beings ...the Enthusiasts say, he is not in the world, therefore he is not in the sacrament, in baptism, and the external word." (XXVIII, 142, 9f.)

This is connected with the hiddenness of God in His revelation. God in His naked transcendence cannot appear to man.

"We are not able to deal with God with uncovered face" (WA. XL, I, 174, 2).

God, therefore, deals with men through a medium. In this medium He must, however, be conceived as directly present and active....

Really, God reveals Himself then in two ways. In the Word become flesh and in creation and its orders, both of which, however, constitute a creative activity. Such revelation is, in both cases, in one sense a direct and in another sense an indirect, mediated, hidden revelation. All revelation is indirect, mediated, and hidden....

Creation is not an act of the past but it is God's activity now. It refers to the creative way in which God brings forth all things out of nothing constantly and continues to sustain them so that they do not disappear into the nothingness from which they came, like the light of a candle when it is extinguished by a vagrant breeze. It refers also to the creative way in which God brings order out of chaos and governs his world and makes it possible for men to live together in community and finally also in the right God-relationship.

It is at this point that the "orders" come in.

> "All created orders are masks or allegories with which God illustrates his theology; they are, as it were, to contain Christ" (WA XL, I; 463, 9).

...For Luther, Elert insists, the order of creation is not some ideal state which ought to be and which still needs to be

brought into being. It is something which already always is. It
is clearest with respect to the family. This is not something a
man can evade or change, least of all, does he have to bring it
into being. Every person born into the world is either male or
female. Without going back to first origins, at any given moment
every person *is* either a parent or a child. Beyond that he is also
already either ruler or ruled. By the limitations of his capacities
as well as by the situation in which he finds himself, everyone
also has a place assigned to him in the economic order. Of course,
they are personal relations, involving the freedom of the person.
They can, therefore, at any time be broken, but it must be clear
that they need not first be legislated, as e.g., in the ten
commandments. The ten commandments presuppose the structure of the
"orders of creation." They are the presupposition of all legislation
as part of God's creative and gubernatorial activity. They
constitute, therefore, to cite Elert, *ein creatorisches oder
gubernatorisches Seinsgefüge*, i.e., "a creative or governing order
of being."

> "There is, therefore, this great glory with which the
> divine majesty invests us, that he works through us
> in such a way that he says that our word is his word
> and our actions are his actions, so that he can in
> truth say: The mouth of the pious teacher is the
> mouth of God, the hand which you reach out in order
> to relieve the brother's need is the hand of God"
> (XLIII; 70, 5-9).

This should avoid the mistake of supposing that Luther conceived
of the stations of life as certain classes in society. Nothing
could have been further from his intention....

We have said then that the "orders of creation" are an
already existing order through which God creatively rules the world.
This is God's kingdom on the left hand in which men by properly
conforming to that order attain to a civil righteousness. There
is thus no profane sphere and in his daily life a man is called of
God to do his will. This will of God is a will of love for all men.
The world in which men live, however, is a sinful world and the
people in it are sinful. They are rebels. In the world demonic
powers strive to frustrate God's will. Man himself is a rebel
against God's unconditional will of love and does not practice it.
As a result, living together is impossible without the restraints
of law, without all kinds of conflicts, the toil of work, the
calamities of nature, etc. This imposes upon man the necessity of
practicing love in those conditions. He must practice love within
the framework of the existing orders and manifests a civil righteousness
without ever supposing that this is the righteousness that avails
before God. In the kingdom on the right hand he has a different

righteousness and here force and sternness have no place. All this is not to result in a fixation of the status quo, but existing evils are always to be corrected. Luther was conservative. There is no doubt about it. But one who sees how he tried to preserve what was good--the existing order (the guilds) as over against the growing capitalist spirit which violated what for Luther was the order of creation--can appreciate his conservatism as a genuine radicalism which went to the root of the difficulty.

200. Serving the Purposes of God in the Structures of Society*

To summarize briefly, then, Luther asserts that there is a divine "giveness" about the basic structure of society. It is as it is because God wills it to be that way. The real demands of life are God-given. They are an expression of the divine law and human obedience must be offered within the framework of that social structure. Every man is called to serve God within the orders, offices, and stations which are part of this functional pattern of society. Every man stands in a twofold relationship toward this total environment. On the one hand, regardless of his station, he stands directly under God, wholly dependent upon him and wholly responsible to him. In this relationship, he participates in the spiritual regime, or, as Luther often spoke of it, "the kingdom of the right hand." On the other hand, he stands in a relationship of responsibility and authority toward his fellow-men. Here he acts as an instrument of God in conferring good upon his fellows and is acted upon by others as instruments of God in conferring blessing upon him. In this relationship he participates in the worldly regime, or as Luther also called it, "the kingdom of the left hand."

It is also an intrinsic part of this whole pattern of ideas that man is called to serve in one of the stations involved in the social structure. He does not merely choose a way to get his expenses paid; he accepts a commission. In doing useful labor, in being productively employed, in fulfilling the duties of citizenship,he is serving the purposes of God by contributing to the well-being of men. Luther's emphasis at this point is well known. God can only be served by serving one's neighbor. The way to piety is not by isolation of oneself from the world but by engagement in its necessary toils and by acceptance of the ordinary responsibilities of earthly existence. The only vocation about which he entertained serious doubts was the vocation of the monk, and this because the monk sought to practice his piety in isolation

---

*Edgar Carlson, *The Church and the Public Conscience* (Philadelphia: Muhlenberg Press, 1956), pp. 32-33, 64-65.

from the normal demands of life as these were confronted in the workaday world. It is apparent that Luther had in mind the organismic character of the medieval community, with its differentiation of functions in which each contributed to the well-being of all and profited from the productivity of others. The craftsmen, the farmers, the soldiers, the maids, the professional people, the rulers, and the pastors all had their distinctive and socially important roles to fill. The opportunity for mutual helpfulness afforded by this interrelatedness of assigned tasks constituted the primary channel for fulfilling the law of love....

It has already been indicated in the previous chapter that we are not willing to conceive of this salvation in wholly negative terms. Men are saved for a life that is abundant, for fellowship that transcends anything which can be exclusively defined in terms of the remission of sins and which includes the whole and original purpose of God.

The rejoinder to be promptly anticipated is that this implies an indifferent and disinterested view of the world with all its needs and problems. It is after all a "vale of tears" from which one must be saved ultimately by death or by the coming of our Lord. The answer must be a complete and positive denial. The meaning and significance of our physical and social environment derives precisely from the fact that the created orders are intended to be an instrument in the hand of God for the conquest of man, one of the regimes through which he establishes his dominion. They are related to the ultimate purpose of God as the law is related to the ultimate purpose of God. All the orders, offices, and stations are "masks of God" (*larvae Dei*) through which God approaches man whom he would bring into the saving fellowship of submission and trust. To say that it does not matter whether the social order is characterized by order or disorder, by justice or injustice, by good or evil, is to say that since what matters is that God shall succeed in establishing his dominion in the human ego it doesn't matter whether he has the best or the poorest means at his disposal.

Bear in mind that the function of the created orders in achieving this purpose is only that which belongs to the law, not that which belongs to the gospel. We must, however, take the first article of the Creed seriously. God has spoken in creation, and what he has spoken is law. It may be said that the law bears the same relationship to the created orders which the gospel bears to the church. It is as inappropriate and illogical to profess unbounded respect for the law of God and have only contempt for his creation in which that law is embodied, as it is to profess unbounded devotion to his gospel and have only contempt for the church to which the gospel gives rise and through which it is proclaimed.

201. *Christian Faith and the Political Order**

In the light of this scriptural teaching it becomes impossible to comply with the demand: "Keep the church out of politics." This is indeed what the enemies of the church are shouting. In praying "for kings and all who are in high positions" the church makes itself responsible for secular authority. And while Caesar has a realm of sovereignty limited only by the sovereignty of God, in proclaiming the will of God to all men and in all areas of life the church has the duty to define what belongs to Caesar. The church betrays its mission to the world if it accepts the role of a mere special interest group or pressure group fighting for its own interests. It is to such a status that it can easily be relegated in the present "pluralism of multi-associational society."

This result is hastened when Luther's doctrine of the two kingdoms is falsely interpreted as a splitting of life into two spheres, the worldly and the religious. The true distinction between the earthly and the spiritual kingdoms is the distinction between the law and the gospel. The two kingdoms are therefore not two disparate or static realms of being but the twofold activity of God. Through the law and by means of the earthly kingdom God rules all men, heathen and Christians, unbelievers and believers, while only believers are ruled by the gospel. To the one, force, compulsion, and discipline are essential; in the other God is served "with a free and joyful will." In the one God works as Creator and Preserver, in the other as Redeemer and Sanctifier, but it is the same God at work. And whether God works with his left hand, using unbelievers and performing the "strange" tasks of wrath and judgment, or with his right hand, using the church to make known his saving mercy, it is always the work of love. Thus even a godless government in providing security for its people is an instrument of God's fatherly love.

202. *The Freedom of the Christian for Service in the World***

The act of liberation and unification in Christ also frees in the right way from enslavement to a crippling code-morality. What is it that those outside the church critize most often in church people? Is it that they see church people giving way in

---
*Taito A. Kantonen, "Christian Faith and the Political Order," in Harold C. Letts ed. *Life in Community*, "Christian Social Responsibility," Volume I (Philadelphia: Muhlenberg Press, 1957), pp. 136-137.
**Martin J. Heinecken, *Christ Frees and Unites*, "The Knubel-Miller Foundation Lectures, No. 12" (Philadelphia: Board of Publication, United Lutheran Church in America, 1957), pp. 92-94.

false freedom to their inclinations and "sinning that grace may abound"? Or, do they see how straitjacketed, repressed, and unhappy many Christians are by a confining, inelastic code morality, as though the sabbath were made for man and not man for the sabbath? Those who criticize traditional Christian morality with its arbitrary taboos and senseless inhibitions may be much closer to the New Testament than we allow. Jesus was to his contemporaries a glutton and a wine-bibber who did not hold the traditions of the elders, and Paul's greatest struggle was against those who wanted to. reenslave the people with the whole burden of circumcision. "Our peril is the reverse of antinomianism; it is pharisaism. We shall do well to listen to our critics." When Christian bemoan the decay of moral standards it may be that they are only bemoaning the giving up of a tradition to which they themselves have grown accustomed and which they are falsely identifying with God's will. Those who protest against the absolutizing of relative moral standards in the name of the relativity of all moral judgments have a point. In the Scriptures there is only *one* absolute and that is God's will of holy love.

This is Kierkegaard's recognition of the fact that there is a stage beyond the universality of the ethical demand which we enter with a leap, where there is what he calls "the teleological suspension of the ethical" (not to be confused, however, with the Jesuitical principle that "the end justifies the means," because this is still on the level of the universal-ethical), where like Abraham we are under the direct command of the Lord, to do his will of love in that moment and let him cover in forgiveness, on the basis of the atoning suffering and death of Christ, the sin involved.

This is a matter of fields of personal relationships and not of universal laws and principles. In the Bible we see the distinction between rewards and punishments that issue directly in a chain of reactions from the deed itself, and obedience to the living God whose will is law. Punishments for sin are then viewed as the manifestation of God's wrath who gives man over the the consequences of his deed (Romans 1:18ff) in the same way that the believer sees himself delivered from judgment by the God who makes righteous (Romans 1:16-17). This is surrender to the lordship of God as Judge as well as Redeemer.

The freedom of the Christian, who is no longer under a code morality but under the command of God whose will is love, may be compared to that of the linebacker on a football team whose job it is to follow the opponents line-up, try to diagnose the offense, with freedom to throw himself in where he is needed, just so the ball is not advanced. He is not bound by the same rigid assignments as the other players, yet, of course, he too must play within the rules of the game and can't just do as he pleases. So the Christian's task is to keep the forces of evil from advancing, with freedom to maneuver, while nevertheless bound by the rules of the game which are the structures God himself has provided.

203. *The Significance of the Orders**

Wherein did Luther's *Dreistaendelehre* differ from the *Dreistaendelehre* of the Medieval church? In the thinking of the middle ages the three groups were sharply separated. An individual belonged to one group and to one group only. Since all three classifications were created by God *ex peccato*, the first human beings, say Luther belonged to all three classifications. The ordo politicus includes not only the rulers but also the ruled. The rulers and the ruled form one political organism. Both the clergy and all people engaged in government belong to the Status oeconomicus, the Hausstand, or family relationship. Marriage is the *fons oeconomicus et politiae et seminarium ecclesiae*. The family is the foundation of the state.

Furthermore--and this is very important, according to Luther no particular moral distinction attaches to any one Stand. There is no looking down the nose on the *temporales domini* and the *communis populus* in Luther's thinking. The three classifications are coordinated. All three are holy orders because they have special holiness, which derives from God's creation. There is no special holiness attached to the Status ecclesiasticus, more specifically to the clergy. Luther's antipelagian concept of the nature of man prevented him from joining the Hussites in this opinion. The men engaged in preaching the gospel are sinners in the same degree as the men who spend their life in performing the functions of government. The ethical worth of those who hold office in the church is no greater than the ethical worth of those who hold office in the civil government. The preaching of the gospel is a noble function, but it is done by sinful men. The ethical distinction between clergy and laity in favor of the clergy is anathema to Luther. "The magistracy," said Luther, "has never been so praised since the days of the apostles as by me." His great ardor to combat ecclesiastical encroachment led Luther to make statements

---

*Carl S. Mundinger, "Some of the Contributions of Lutheranism, with special Reference to the Past and European Countries, to Theory and Practice of Government and Society," in John G. Kunstmann, ed. *The Church and Modern Culture*, Proceedings of the First Institute on the Church and Modern Culture, 1951 (Valparaiso, Ind.: Valparaiso University, 1953), p. **61.**

which made him appear to be fawning on princes.

The fact is that servility on the part of the church to the government was anathema to Luther. "The minister is commissioned to be the mentor of the magistrate."...

Luther's *Dreistanendelehre* is tied up with his *Lehre vom Beruf*. This latter doctrine throws real light on the attitude of Lutheranism to government and to society. Although all men belong to all three *Staende* each man has a special call from God to perform special tasks. This call sanctifies all labor. The men who do the tasks belonging to government - Luther includes all lawgivers, administrators, judges, bookkeepers, secretaries--have a call from God to do their tasks. The magistrate has his *Beruf*; the minister has his *Beruf*. Each must serve God according to his office. One *Beruf* is no better than the other. One *Beruf* is no holier, is no more divine than the other. There are temptations peculiar to each *Beruf*. The husband is tempted to lust, the merchant to greed, the magistrate to arrogance.

Besides dignifying every function of every member of a "Stand," the *Beruf* limits the functions of each man. Besides dignifying every function of every member of a "Stand," the *Beruf* limits the functions of each man. The *Dreistaendelehre* itself limits each "Stand." This limitation is fundamental to Luther's concept of the State. He states his basic belief in these words: *Dues vult discrimina ordium*. This is not a prescription but the announcement of a fact. The statement has indeed great ethical consequences. If a large group of people in a given community sincerely believes that God has given certain functions to one group of people to perform and another set of functions to another group, and another set of functions to a third group, this will have a decided effect on their attitude toward the functions of each group.

The preacher is called to preach the Word, to show men, including all men in government, from the king and the five star general to the lowest clerk at the last desk or the buck private in the lowest squad, their sin and to show all men the love of God in Christ. The *status ecclesiasticus* is called by God to wield the Word, to use the means of grace in season and out of season.

The same God who called the men of the church to perform their respective functions calls all men of the *status politicus* to maintain order, to defend the country, to provide for the common welfare, to make it possible for the other two "Staende" to perform their God-given tasks. Each "Stand" is to serve the other two "Staende." A prince does not exist for himself, but for others. He is there to serve, to protect and defend all entrusted to him.

Again: "Whoever wishes to be part of the community and enjoy the advantages of the community, must help bear the burdens of the community, even though he has in no wise caused these burdens."

Wherein did Luther's concept of governemt differ from *Gottesgnadentum*, commonly known as the Divine Right of Kings?

In the first place, Luther did not teach that you are born into a "Stand," nor that you had to remain in the "Stand" in which your father happened to be. The possibility of crossing over into some other "Stand" must always remain for every mother's son. The so-called "Aufstieg" from one "Stand" to another is found in many statements of Luther.

Finally, the *Dreistaendelehre* and the *Lehre vom Beruf* imply that a government must function according to a constitution. This constitution is based on custom and convention and law. Since conditions in one country are not the same as conditions in another and since conditions in the same country are constantly subject to change, governments must adjust to the everchanging conditions in which they find themselves. Luther thinks of political conditions as being in a state of constant flux. There are times when political vision is rare. Then a man of vision arises. He makes suggestions. Conditions improve. ("das es im Lande alles gruenet und bluet mit fride, zucht, schutz, straffe, das es ein gesund regiment heissen mag".) Law must grow out of the needs of the people. The ceremonial law of Moses is not binding on any people except the Jews in the old Testament. His law does not concern us Gentiles ("Sein gesetz geht uns Heiden nichts an".) In the making of laws or customs, reason (ratio) must be the arbiter (Die Rechte aus der Vernumft kommen sind). The fact that Luther insists that all government must be carried on according to law indicates how little support there is in Luther's writings for the Divine-Right theory.

B. EXPLICIT DISCUSSION OF THE TWO REALMS: OFFICIAL AND SEMI-OFFICIAL DOCUMENTS

204. The Heritage of the Reformation*

The classical Lutheran answer to the problem of living "in but not of" this world has been formulated in Luther's doctrine of the "two kingdoms" and reaffirmed in the Augsburg Confession. Now it is no secret that this doctrine, especially as misinterpreted

---

*William H. Lazareth, *A Theology of Politics* (New York: Board of Social Missions, United Lutheran Church in America, 1960), pp. 10-15. (A study document on Christian social responsibility, not an official statement.)

and misapplied by the *Deutsche Christen* in Nazi Germany, has been
a source of keen concern and embarrassment to evangelical Christians
throughout the free world. The wartime propaganda attacks linking
Luther and Hitler need not concern us here since they were generally
refuted as quickly as they were spewed forth. Of far more importance
are those persisting theological attacks (Barth, Niebuhr) which root
the traditional political quietism of Lutherans in the alleged
"cultural defeatism" of Luther. It is commonly charged that the
Reformer advocated an ethical double standard which limited the
impact of Christianity strictly to personal relationships, thus
permitting social institutions such as the state to flourish in
godless autonomy.

If this indictment were true, American Lutherans would be
incapable of making any discriminate judgments in the controversial
area of the current international political power struggle and the
problem of armaments in the nuclear age....Since the purpose of
this study is to lay the theological groundwork for such judgments,
it is first necessary for us to disavow this mistaken "dualistic"
interpretation of Luther's theology of politics as part of the
unfortunate historical mortgage passed on to us by the late nineteenth
century German Lutheranism (Troeltsch via Naumann, Luthardt and
Stahl). That the issues are far more complex than Luther's critics
suggest is borne out by the unflinching testimony of those like
Norway's Bishop Berggrav who answered both the Nazis and traditional
German "Lutheran" servility - with Luther himself!...

Our case rests upon the conviction that Luther's doctrine of
the "two kingdoms" is an authentic restatement of Paul's doctrine
of the "two ages." Luther's intention was to demonstrate God's
two-fold rule of the whole world by law and gospel, and not to
separate the world into two divorced realms of the "sacred" and the
"secular." This has been carefully documented in many theological
studies of the recent Luther Renaissance. Neither Paul nor Luther
advocate any "rigorous dualism" between the two ages of creation
and redemption. Both insist that these two kingdoms must first
be distinguished in principle and then interpenetrated in practice.
We have already shown this to be the case in the political ethics
of Paul and we must now do the same for Luther.

Luther on the "Two Kingdoms"

The foundation is laid carefully in *Secular Authority: To
What Extent It Should be Obeyed* (1523). On first glance, the title
might suggest that Luther found it necessary to protest against
the godless inroads of a secular state so soon after he had challenged

the clericalism of an overzealous church. Actually, the very
opposite is closer to the truth. *Weltlich* meant civil, temporal,
non-ecclesiastical authority for Luther and his medieval contemporaries.
If we translate this today as "secular," we should disavow as
anachronistic any of the irreligious and anti-religious associations
which this ambiguous word currently suggests to us. In attempting
to translate Luther's theology into the twentieth century, we
must always carefully shift the accent in the central thrust since
his chief enemy was clericalism whereas ours is secularism. Over-
simply, Luther had to put the church back under God's gospel; we
have to put the state back under God's law....

Luther charges that it is blasphemous for man to designate
some realm of God's creation as "secular" or "profane," if we thereby
judge it to be unworthy of his divine activity or self-sufficient
in its own autonomy. God alone rules everyone and everywhere. It
is he alone in whom "we live, and move, and have our being" (Acts
17:28). And yet, because not all of God's creatures acknowledge
his lordship, he rules men differently as their Creator and as their
Redeemer....

The key points in Luther's position are these: 1) God is the
Lord of *both* kingdoms, although he rules each by different means
(law and gospel) for different ends (a just peace and personal
piety); 2) every Christian lives in *both* kingdoms simultaneously--
in the kingdom of God insofar as he is righteous, and in the kingdom
of the world insofar as he is sinful; 3) the two kingdoms are sharply
to be *distinguished* from each other, which means that the realms of
law and gospel are to be neither separated (in secularism) nor
equated (in clericalism), but permitted to co-exist in harmonious
interaction and coordination as complementary expressions of God's
creative and redemptive activity among men. Absolutely no "rigorous
dualism" is advocated here either in the actions of God or in the
reactions of men.

Man's Twofold Righteousness

In more concrete terms, this means for Luther that the ethic
of the Ten Commandments is enjoined upon all of God's creatures,
while the ethic of the Sermon on the Mount is addressed primarily
to committed Christians. It goes without saying, of course, that
insofar as Christians remain sinful, they fall with all other men
under the "Thou shalt nots" of the Ten Commandments. It is of
the greatest importance for our understanding of the totality of
Luther's social ethics that we clearly distinguish this twofold
righteousness of man which corresponds to the twofold rule of God

in the two kingdoms of redemption and creation:

1) *Christian righteousness* is the personal piety generated by the Holy Spirit in the hearts of Christians in the form of faith active in love;

2) *civil righteousness* is the social morality of which all God's rational creatures are capable--Christians included--in the form of law-abiding political justice.

Required of the Christian citizen, therefore, is *both* a calculating love which takes the form of justice ("wise as serpents") and a sacrificial love which "exceeds" the demands of the law ("gentle as doves"). In the struggle for civil righteousness, he may join with other men of good will--whatever their faith--in seeking to translate the moral law of God into the civil laws of the nation. But God always asks more of us as Christians than Caesar demands of us as citizens. Consequently, in the exercise of Christian righteousness, the man of faith also goes "the second mile" in offering love beyond justice and sacrifice beyond service to his needy neighbors. Once again it is the interaction of God's law (in justice) and gospel (in love) which is central. Just as men cannot be saved by reason and the law, neither can society be ruled by faith and the gospel. But as the demands of the law break into the consciences of the redeemed (in the church), so too the fruits of the gospel break out to nourish the lives of the unredeemed (in society).

*205. The Place of the State**

This is the point at which Luther's distinction between the two methods of God's rule is clearly relevant. The realm of institutions, of law and justice, is, as Luther put it, God's kingdom on the left hand, where out of love he uses law backed by force. It is not, therefore, a profane realm outside God's Lordship. Its rules and laws exist for the service of divine love, which means "for the good of men." Love must in this sphere of God's domain take the form of law strictly enforced and not be confused with the form of unmerited forgiveness that it properly takes within the church's fellowship. This kingdom of God "on the left" includes civil government but is not identical with it. It is rather the method of divine rule wherever and whenever men live together and need the strong arm of the law to keep order and promote justice and welfare. Therefore, in the kingdom on the left, whether in the home or in some wider circle, whether through unwritten customs

---

*Martin J. Heinecken in Commission on the Role of the Church in Social Welfare, *The Church in Social Welfare* (New York: Board of Social Ministry, Lutheran Church in America, 1964.) pp. 42-43, 50-51. Heinecken is the primary author of the section quoted.

or formal regulations the forms of order must be present to insure justice and well-being. The authority exercised is that of good order; the primary consideration is that habits, customs, and laws be the forms of justice. Thus evil may be prevented and the good things of this life constructively supported.

Nourished and sustained by the word of God, Christian people are to do their work in the world, as active members of society, holding office, serving as soldiers, etc. (AC XVI). They are also under the law and must live under it and further it. Laws and institutions are always impersonal and never themselves loving, although they may be used in the service of love. Only persons can be loving and, therefore, the person-to-person relationship within the framework of the law is all important.

The Place of the State

God's method of rule by means of law finds its paradigmatic expression in the description of the state as the possessor of the God-given power of the sword (Rom. 13). The essence of the political is the possession of legitimate authority to keep order....

If we now return to the assertion that the function of the state is to provide the framework which the other orders can perform their proper function, we have a better understanding of what constitutes justice. Justice means conformity to the law of creation which in turn means the safeguarding of the rights and freedoms just mentioned. It means a realistic care for the needs of the neighbor which safe-guards his basic rights and freedoms. The state exists, therefore, to promote the general welfare, to further constructively the true well-being of every citizen and to secure equal opportunity for full development of all its citizens. Such equality of opportunity does not exist naturally in the world in which we live, where sinful men and pride of power constantly interfere with it. Therefore, it can only be guaranteed and enforced by law the aim of which is maximum justice. Admittedly this will always be only an approximation, but unless the absolute is aimed at, even the relative cannot be accomplished.

No state can exist by power alone. There must be a willingness on the part of the people to submit to its authority, based on the recognition that such submission is in their interest and that the laws which they are forced to obey are actually just. The unjust tyranny will sooner or later collapse (*Sic semper tyrannus!*) from the momentum of its own injustice (see the prophet Habakkuk). Safeguards against the concentration and abuse of power must be provided for, and a system of checks and balances is of vital importance.

We may conclude then that justice requires that the basic needs
of all persons be consistently met. Needs and wants are not to be
confused, neither is the giving of -gifts to be confused with that
to which a man is justly entitled before the law. There is a real
difference between "largesse" doled out and a just distribution of
natural resources.

Children, the sick, the aged, the otherwise incapacitated
through no fault of their own, who have no one to care for them
are in justice to be cared for by the community and are not to be
made objects of charity. There will always be some who are destitute
through their own fault who have no just claim on society's help.
These may properly be the objects of charity, but not those who
are the victims of circumstance. Charity and justice should not
be confused. A Negro who is denied the franchise, or the head of
a family who is thrown out of work because of automation, are not
asking for charity but only for justice under the law.

For the first time in the world's history, man's technical
know-how has made it possible to feed, clothe, shelter, give
adequate health care and opportunity for development to all the
people of the world. Responsible stewardship demands co-operative
planning under law to achieve these purposes. Such planning and
control are necessary not only on a state and national level but
on an international one as well, since this is one world of
interdependency.

There is a vast difference, therefore, between a state which
is regarded as an omnicompetent god freely distributing gifts and
a state whose laws guarantee that human welfare be furthered in
justice to all. A society is unjust to the extent that the structure
of its laws and institutions do not contribute to a just distribution
of resources or provide a just opportunity for the full development
of all its citizens.

So all taxes which are levied for the good of the whole community
must be judged and understood by the criterion of justice, construed
to include positive actions undertaken for the common good. The
willingness to pay such taxes--innumerable referenda demonstrate
that the people do upon occasion voluntarily impose heavy burdens
upon themselves--must not be interpreted as an act of love but as
a manifestation of the fact that the requirements of justice and
public welfare are understood and accepted. The proclamation of
the gospel may indeed have made it easier for men to comprehend the
scope of their public duties, yet the actions remain acts of justice,
and constraint can always be used against the unwilling. Indeed,

if public education, public hospitals, and many similar facilities
had always to wait upon the voluntary gifts of persons endowed with
both benevolence and wealth, many communities would still be waiting
for the most rudimentary facilities.

*206. A Responsible World Community**

The classical Christian tradition views civil authority as a
sign of God's loving activity of advancing human justice and well-
being and of preserving man from his tendency to violence and
self-destruction. Just government performs the double function of
promoting the welfare of men and restraining wickedness.

As each age of history gave birth to institutions of civil
authority appropriate to its needs, so this present age of global
interdependence calls for transnational structures of law and
authority within which human enterprise can be regulated to the
benefit of all and disputes can be settled peacefully. It is of
vital importance that there be established such world and regional
institutions as will encourage social, political, and economic
pluralism productive of genuine human enrichment rather than
perpetual conflict.

It is a hopeful sign that many nations are accepting legal
obligations in connection with their participation in transnational
organizations. These organizations should be regarded as emerging
forms of world civil authority which, insofar as they promote peace
and justice, are worthy of support by churches. Christians should
be encouraged to exercise their vocation through international
civil service.

*207. Bases for Lutheran Social Action--American Lutheran Church***

Luther believed that forgiveness resulted in thankful service,
the justified man freed from self-absorption through faith to become
active in love. The sole concern of this love, this service, was
to meet the needs of the neighbor, not my needs for "self-fulfillment"
or moral justification. But this pure work of love runs into
problems when my station in life calls rather for the exercise of
coercive justice through power. Luther met this problem with the
doctrine of the two kingdoms. God's right hand, which is his "proper"
work, acts in history to bring grace and love through the proclamation
of the Gospel. God's left hand, which is his "alien" work, acts to
restrain sin and disorder through the proclamation of the Law. The

---

*"World Community: Ethical Imperatives in an Age of
Interdependence," adopted by the Fifth Biennial Convention, Lutheran
Church in America, June 25-July 2, 1970.
**American Lutheran Church, Commission on Research and Social
Action, *Bases for Lutheran Social Action*, 1965. (The author is
Pastor Kenneth P. Alpers.)

Christian for himself lives only by the norm of love; but when his station in life deals with the civil kingdom, he must perform God's work of justice.

Ernst Troeltsch interpreted this as meaning that a Christian has a dual morality, a private and a public one, and this view still colors many interpretations. But Luther's view was more subtle and dialectical than that. It is not simply that the Christian acts one way within his family and another when he steps out into society. Luther rejected the Roman dualism between the higher Christian who acts by the "evangelical counsels" and the ordinary one who simply obeys the laws. There can be only one Christian who lives simultaneously in the Kingdom of God and the kingdom of the world, both of which are under the one Lordship of God. The Christian appeals to Spirit-engendered Christian righteousness--guided by the Sermon on the Mount--as the basis for his own personal relations and actions in life. But when, because of his legitimate civil position, he must deal with groups or structures, he cannot expect non-Christians (or weak Christians, for that matter) to live by the Sermon on the Mount. To attempt to impose such standards would result in civil chaos and defenselessness before rampant injustice. So, precisely for the sake of love of the neighbor, the Christian works on the level of civil righteousness--the social justice of which rational men are capable.

*208. Church and State--American Lutheran Church**

9. Both church and state, each in its own way and using methods appropriate to its own function, are to be instruments for accomplishing God's purposes. Our concern is that the church be free to be the church, the state to be the state, each true to its own God-ordained functions. The state, in the performance of its God-given mandate, may not recognize its authority as coming from God but Christians in any event will so see the authority of government.

10. Essentially the church is God's avenue for reconciling man to Himself and for bearing living witness to His divine truth for man's life in community. The state is His instrument for maintaining peace, order, and justice in the community, for protecting the individual's rights, for enhancing his possibilities for personal development, and thus for promoting the general welfare.

11. The church makes its presence effective through changes wrought in persons by the Holy Spirit, working through the Word and

---

*American Lutheran Church, *Church-State Relations in the United States of America*. Approved by the 1966 general convention.

the Sacraments, to effect the dynamics of spiritual growth. The state makes its presence effective through its authority, under law, to pre-empt property and goods, labor, even life, into its service and through the response of identification and loyalty of its citizens.

12. The church looks to the state to maintain the kind of civil order that assures peace, justice, and responsible freedom. As a corporate body the church operates under the laws of the state. Nevertheless, the church retains the right and the duty to proclaim the prophetic Word of God even in opposition to policies of government which are in conflict with the Word. The church counsels its members under every circumstance to obey the laws enacted by the governing authorities except in the rare event that the demands of men's laws conflict with the Christian's higher loyalty to God.

Interrelation of Church and State

13. Both church and state, under God, serve genuine needs of human beings. In so doing, they mutually affect one another. Neither should surrender its independence to the other, nor perform functions exclusively appropriate to the other. Church and state complement one another as they devote themselves to the best interests and well-being of persons.

*209. Principles of Social Action in the Lutheran Church-Missouri Synod**

A. Preface

As a preface to all its resolutions, and stimulated in particular by the concerns expressed in Overtures 9-12 to 9-13 to 9-18, Committee 9 asks the Synod to approve the following statement of principle.

When the church becomes involved in social ministry and action, it needs to understand not only the principle of love but also "the distinction between Christ's kingdom" as defined in the Lutheran Confessions, especially AC XVI; Apol. XVI; XV 43; LC I 274-275; FC XII 17-22. For example Apol.XVI 2-3 states:

> The writings of our theologians have profitably
> illumined this whole question of the distinction
> between Christ's kingdom and a political kingdom.
> Christ's kingdom is spiritual; it is the knowledge
> of God in the heart, the fear of God and faith,
> the beginning of eternal righteousness and eternal
> life. At the same time it lets us make outward use

---

*A Statement of Principles of Social Action, with Special Reference to Corporate Positions, adopted by the Lutheran Church-Missouri Synod at its Denver Convention, July, 1969.

> of the legitimate political ordinances of the
> nation in which we live, just as it lets us make
> use of medicine or architecture, food or drink
> or air. The Gospel does not introduce any new
> laws about the civil estate, but commands us to
> obey the existing laws, whether they were
> formulated by heathen or by others, and in this
> obedience to practice love.

This distinction affirms everything the Confessions say about
Christ and faith, namely that God in the Gospel has declared us
sinners to be His sons and heirs and that we are justified by
nothing more than the faith that clings to this Word of promise.
We believe in Jesus Christ our Lord and come to Him, not by our
own reason or strength but by the Gospel in which the Spirit calls,
gathers, enlightens, sanctifies, and keeps us in the one faith as
one church. In this kingdom we posses the freedom that comes by
knowing the truth, the peace which the world cannot give, and the
hope and life which overcomes even death. Because God our Father
has not only created and redeemed us but also sustains, protects,
and directs us until the day He completes our life in glory, we
are free to trust and obey Him and thus to extend His love to every
neighbor without fear of loss or desire for profit. The mark of
this kingdom is the Word of God, the bread of life on which Christians
feed in worship and sacrament. The church must never be ashamed
of that Gospel or permit the scorn of the world to rob it of its
luster. For it is our life and the ground of our true and eternal
dignity, worth, and power. Heaven and earth shall pass away, but
that Word and that Kingdom shall not pass away.

When the Confessions now speak of the political (secular)
kingdom, they affirm that even the world of fallen humanity is
God's. God does not wish to destroy that world, even though its
ultimate destiny is wrath. On the contrary, God manifests to that
world, even in its enmity against Him, a remarkable mercy, for He
"makes His sun rise on the evil and on the good and sends rain on
the just and the unjust." It is His kingdom. The power of God is
manifest in every force that works in the world, including not only
forces of nature but also government and social pressures which
serve to restrain the lusts of men and thus make peace and civilization
possible. In the secular kingdom God makes men serve His purposes
even though they do not know Him. The very wisdom by which men
pursue their desires and avoid what they fear becomes a God-ordained
force to curb anarchy, to enforce a degree of justice and sometimes
even to inflict God's judgements. Yet the ultimate hope of man
does not lie in this kingdom. For in their common desire to achieve
what they judge to be good for them and to avoid whatever seems evil,

men violate one another. God decrees in wrath that the good they pursue shall leave them hungry even when they attain it, and that the evil they flee shall finally catch up with them. He exposes the futility of the fallen world and signals its final destruction whenever men find themselves enmeshed in conflict, crime, frustration, injustice, guilt, famine, disaster, war, and death.

According to his sinful nature the Christian knows only the earthly kingdom, is fully sympathetic to it, and sets all his hopes upon it. As a saint, however, he is both delivered from that kingdom and yet called right back into it. He is not to seek a higher form of holiness by withdrawing from it. It is the arena in which he is to love and serve his neighbor, even his enemy. In it he is to proclaim God's judgment against every arrogance and independence of man and to offer the world a new dignity, life, hope, and community in Christ. But he is also to participate in its government and economics and in every aspect of secular society, employing all the resources of judgment and common sense, in order that even this fallen world may experience, as a gift of divine mercy, the greatest possible measure of secular freedom, dignity, justice, peace, and joy.

When the Synod concerns itself with the Word of God and the call to proclaim it, it is dealing with what the Confessions call "the kingdom of Christ." When the Synod directs its attention to questions of social ministry and social action, it is responding not only to the call to love but to the call to Christians to participate fully in the "secular" or "political kingdom." These two types of response cannot really be separated, for the Christian remains one person, and his ministry must be to the whole man and even to the whole society of men, as the Mission Affirmations state. Nevertheless, if our Synod is to avoid the tragic confusion into which many churches have fallen, it must also be aware of and maintain a fundamental distinction. Words such as freedom, peace, joy, dignity, life, justice, hope, and love have applicability and meaning in both kingdoms and are indeed gifts of God in both. But the meanings are never equivalent. The history of Jesus Christ crucified dramatizes the difference. For when Jesus died, everything this world treasures as freedom, peace, joy, dignity, life, justice, hope, and love was taken away from Him. And yet as the Son of His heavenly Father, trusting and obeying even to death, all of these were His, and all the forces of devils, death, and hell could not take them from Him. His resurrection reveals which kingdom is eternally true and triumphant.

B. The Resolution

WHEREAS, The overtures here listed raise the question as to
whether it is proper for the Synod in convention to adopt resolutions
which imply taking a corporate position on secular issues and call
for corporate action;...

RESOLVED,

1. That the Synod invite its members to study further the
doctrine of the two kingdoms as well as the ethical principles
affirmed in the Large Catechism on the Ten Commandments and to
consider whether the preface to these resolutions adequately answers
the concerns expressed in these overtures, and invite them to submit
any further questions to the Commission on Theology and Church
Relations;...

C. "CHRISTIANIZATION OF THE POWERS"

*210. The Social Responsibilities of the Church**

We must begin our analysis with a description of the church
as the people of God. Unless we do, we shall miss one of the major
sources of motivation for our work of service. Moreover, without
a reasonably clear conception of the church, not only as a company
of witnesses but as a witnessing community, we shall not find full
satisfaction in our social service. For what we do as Christians,
by way of rendering help to those who are in need, enjoys a dimension
unknown to a mere secular concern for rendering assistance....

We recall that the world as God once created it was intended
to be a place of order. Out of chaos the Lord determined to
construct a universe that would glorify Him as the God of order,
freedom, and justice. But by wanting to be like God, man reintroduced
the "reign of chaos and old night." For, as St. Paul reminds us
(Rom. 8:20-21), all of creation was taken up into man's revolt,
so that to this day and everywhere "whirl is king." Right along
the front of social disintegration our generation is face to face
with these very powers of primordial confusion, let loose among men
to destroy them by cruel and capricious structures. That is one
of the chief reasons why the church must be involved in efforts at
pushing back these forces of disorder and injustice. The latter
are determined to reduce life to the level of a wasteland.

Our God is the Lord of order and justice. Between the fall
and the *parousia* God has chosen to restrain the forces of anarchy
by those orders of preservation to which our theology prefers to

*Martin Scharlemann, *The Church's Social Responsibilities*
(St. Louis: Concordia Publishing House, 1971), pp. 19, 50-51,
54-55, 57, 60, 81.

apply the individual Latin names *imperium, matrimonium,* and *oeconomia.*
These stand, respectively, for the institutions of government and
of marriage, as well as for the general cultural and economic
practices developed within a given society.

These orders of creation and preservation belong to the
distinction between Law and Gospel. On this point our Lutheran
Confessions, in Augustana XVI, make the following observation:
"They condemn also those who do not find evangelical perfection in
the fear of God and in faith but in forsaking civil offices; for
the Gospel teaches an eternal righteousness of the heart. Meanwhile,
it does not destroy the State or the family, but very much requires
that they be preserved as ordinances of God...."

The Biblical teaching on this subject affirms that a Christian,
just like any other human being, lives within certain social and
political structures which are regulated by law. They are binding
on men, including Christians, even when and though they seem to
operate on principles which work in tension with specific commands
revealed in Scripture....

The pattern of God's work, however, did not change. Like
Israel the church came into being by God's grace. That is obvious
enough from our Scriptures. For, as soon as our Lord began His
public ministry, He began to gather around Him the faithful remnant
to have it serve as the nucleus of a new and universal rule of
grace. In Jesus the Word became incarnate and so chose to become
one of us. He asked to be baptized into His mission of involvement
and identification with us. Lest this work come to an end, He
arranged to have God's presence established among men wherever two
or three would thenceforth gather in His name. (Matt. 18:20)

His meat, Jesus once said, was to do His Father's will. He
Himself had come to be the true Israel, to be obedient where the
old Israel had rebelled. He chose His followers to carry on after
Him as the new Israel, a people living in obedience under the terms
of a covenant sealed with blood from the cross. From then on they
were to constitute the sanctuary of the living God. (Cf. 2 Cor.
6:16b)

Every demon under heaven saw the issue for what it was: a
contest for the control of the world. Every word and every act of
Jesus they understood to be an attack by the Holy One of God on all
of their own dark designs. Every miracle they looked upon as another
victory for the kingdom of God. They gathered their forces at the
white-hot center of time, and in wave after wave they assaulted the
Lord of all creation and the source of all redemption. They even
complained when they were sure that Jesus had got ahead of His own

schedule in working at their defeat. As He was about to heal the
Gadarene demoniac, the demons whined, "Have you come here to torment
us before the time?" (Matt. 8:29)

The early morning hours of that long and fateful day, one
might say, had been taken up with the call of Abraham and the choice
of Israel. The time of Joel's grasshopper plague, of the return
from captivity, of the rebuilding of the temple represented the
late morning hours. The day of the Lord had its noon in Christ's
advent to the world, there to be impelled relentlessly toward the
cross and the resurrection. That day's afternoon was completed when
the Spirit of Pentecost came rushing in with the sound of a mighty
wind to prepare the church for her bruising contest with the kingdom
of darkness for as long as history would be permitted to run its
course.

The Israel of the 50th day has never ceased confronting the
assaults of these same demonic forces during every moment of her
experience as she moves forward to undo the works of darkness. At
some points the church faced them in strong concentration. Such
moments called for particularly vigorous counterattacks; and the
Spirit was there to provide strength and endurance for wrestling
with complex social and cultural issues. To be sure, there was
a degree of ambivalence in the work of the church, for she still
belonged also to the old aeon. Yet her life in the new aeon brought
a new hope into the lives of men....

To convince oneself of the transforming power of the Christian
religion, it is only necessary to contrast Gregory of Tours'
description of Gaul under the Merovingians with his statement on
conditions in the empire of Charlemagne. Here is a change that
cannot be charged to technological advance. Christianity did not
convert the barbarians and transform their lives as a mere vehicle
of ancient culture but as the informing spirit of a new civilization
to prepare for the time when men would move to a new part of the
world, to our hemisphere, as a region which needed to be brought
under the sway of an authority greater than that of "powers and
principalities."

Men like Timothy Dwight saw the Christianization of America
as a recapitulation of Israel's conquest of Canaan. We may well
smile at such naive theological exuberance. However, when we reflect
on the beginnings of our nation, we must concede that something
mysterious was at work here, a force that can be subsumed under the
category of divine blessing....

There is only one way out of this narrowing of life. That is
the "Christianization of the Powers," as Berkhof has chosen to call

it. This implies the rejection of ideologies and limiting the state as well as the economic order to being the means of staving off chaos and of ordering human relations, so that social and technological developments will tend to serve rather than to exploit men. In this way alone can our civilization continue to provide what the prophet Jeremiah calls a "future and a hope." (29:11)...

Let the church take on this battle, then, as it once set out to breathe a new spirit into the culture of the Roman Empire and as it once chose to civilize the barbarian. The church is not just the conscience of a nation, educating, inspiring, and motivating individuals to go out as Christian citizens. She is not just an institution that must bring her power to bear where it will make the greatest impact. She is also--and especially--the symbol of God's order and justice. What matters even more, she is the redeemed and redeeming community of the Lord. In the secular city of our day the church has a very special opportunity to help set and keep men free, provided, of course, she is ready to bring the sacrifices which this task entails.

211. *Critique of "Triumphalism"**

I have a good deal of difficulty with the whole section of Dr. Scharlemann's paper. There, on the basis of the experience of God's people in Israel, the "Christianization of the powers" is suggested as the normative stance for the church's mission in the city. For the want of a better term, I will call this a kind of "theocratic triumphalism." We are told repeatedly that this is going to be a "Lutheran approach." But when it comes to documenting the theological stance for the "Christianization of the powers," we are referred to (a) three Calvinistic theocrats--Berkhof, Kraemer, and Mackay, and (b) these Calvinists commenting almost exclusively on two books of the Bible, namely, *Ephesians* and *Colossians*, (c) these two books of the Bible exclusively in terms of their introductory chapters.

Now it would be beyond my competence to try to convert this conference into a hermeneutical seminar. Nevertheless, in terms of the integrity of the biblical foundations of the paper, it should be noted that one of the key debates in social ethics today is the way in which the Lordship of Christ is exercised over the world. A "theology of the cross" holds that Christ is already *de facto* Lord of the church, but he is only *de jure* Lord of the world before his return in triumph. Until then, we must clearly distinguish God's

---

*Quoted from the typescript of William H. Lazareth's comment on the Scharlemann paper.

"strange work" through the law of creation and his "proper work"
through the gospel of redemption. On the other hand, a "theology
of glory" contends that the *de facto* Lordship of Christ is already
exercised directly over the world outside the church in a way
discernible to the people of God. Then, to use the current jargon,
we can know where "God's floating crap game" is taking place and
get out "where the action is" to find out what God is doing today....

I would suggest that this apocalyptic enthusiasm is totally
incompatible with the kerygmatic core of the Paul of *Romans* and
Galatians, and the earliest apostolic proclamation recorded in the
Book of Acts. There it is quite clear that its eschatology is
"Christ and culture in paradox," and not "Christ transforming culture"
on the basis of a realized eschatology rooted in Gnostic hymnody.
This may be somewhat over-stated, but I want to show the basic
contrast between a Lutheran theology of two kingdoms and a Calvinistic
theology of one kingdom. A Lutheran works to "humanize" the secular
realm; a Calvinist has to "Christianize" it.

D. AMPLIFICATIONS, EMENDATIONS, AND CRITICISMS

212. *Distinguishing Law and Gospel**

The distinction between law and Gospel in Luther is of
fundamental importance. But it is not a distinction that can be
extended beyond its context in the Word. It is altogether wrong
to say that the church is the kingdom of God and the world in which
the law operates is the kingdom of the devil. Nor is it correct
to day that the Gospel has to do with the spirit and that the law
belongs to the flesh. All of these terms are ambiguous, and hopeless
confusion results if the distinction between law and Gospel is not
interpreted evangelically.

The Word of God contains both law and Gospel, and the church
is set to proclaim the whole Word, including the law. The believer
who is justified by his faith in the Gospel is not thereby removed
from the jurisdiction of the law. By his faith in Christ he is
saved from the condemnation and curse of the law, but not from its
injunctions. At the same time as he is saved by faith, he is
adjudged a sinner by his failure to fulfill the law. The law,
however, remains good, and it is a gift of God.

213. *The Neighbor's Need and Natural Law***

Between 1521 and 1529 Luther's concepts on love for the

---

*Conrad Bergendoff, "Christian Love and Public Policy in Luther,"
Lutheran Quarterly, 13 (1961), p. 221.
**Donald C. Ziemke, *Love for the Neighbor in Luther's Theology*
(Minneapolis: Augsburg, 1963), pp. 69-74.

neighbor became centered more and more on the needs of the neighbor. Up to this time he had conceived love for the neighbor, as it were, as proceeding from the person of the Christian outward, primarily as an expression of the Christian's faith, either as a result of the nature and structure of faith itself or as a result of the inclusion in the body of Christ begun by faith. Of course, Luther did not deny that the needs of the neighbor determined the structure of the love act. Any other understanding would have meant that the lover imposed on the one loved what he thought was best, and to Luther this seemed like thinly veiled arrogance....

After his return to Wittenberg, however, Luther began to discuss love for the neighbor in terms of the nature of human society (and the church was part of human society) and the natural law. He thus came to think of love for the neighbor both as part of the demand made upon all men by the Law, and as the relationship resulting from fellowship with God expressing the center of the Gospel. The clearest expression of this new approach was in the 1526 tract concerning the validity of the calling to be a soldier....

Thus men are related to each other in a responsible way not only as members of the church but simply as members of society. This responsible relation is not haphazard or subject to human whim--it is an ordinance of God. God has given his law, which to Luther was the concrete expression of his will. In this he followed the change that had been brought to all medieval concepts by the nominalists. Natural law to Luther was not based on nature but rather based on the inclusion of God's law in the hearts of men, which Luther took literally....

The natural law finds expression in the callings and forms of societal relationships that constitute the fabric of human life. This means that God has put men into a series of relationships, e.g., father, son, prince, subject, priest, etc., which determines their lives. Life is to be characterized by service and love, i.e., action for the sake of the other. The calling in which man finds himself is the structure through which God approaches him and demands obedience from him. Therefore Luther could say that God has created the actual social structure in such a way that it functions for man's benefit....

At this point Luther seems to have seen for the first time-- in a way significant for love for the neighbor--the doctrine of creation and God as the creator....Further, he speaks of society as he came to see it in his radical Christological concept of the body of Christ. He regards Christ as the agent of creation, placed over creation, and as the concretion of the will of God, now the pattern

for the life of society. Whereas he previously regarded Christ as
the head of the church and as the pattern for its life, Luther
begins to see Christ as the head of creation including society and
as providing the pattern for its life. That Christ is the pattern
for creation is shown by the frequent use Luther makes of the figure
of the tree, which is useful and therefore "godly" when it produces
fruit for others. This Luther cites as an example of the way men
ought to live in relation to one another.

In all this it may seem that the Law and the Gospel become
strangely mixed, and yet perhaps not so strangely after all. The
Law has the same content as the Gospel, in the sense that what the
Law demands the Gospel makes possible through the exercise of faith.
The Law still condemns by showing how far men are from God's will
for them, and the Gospel still saves by pardoning. But in the
pardon, in the very center of the experience, comes the content
of the kind of life the Law demands, namely the exercise of love
for God and the neighbor, as a natural result.

The divine law is manifest in the natural law because God is
the creator. Since he is a person, i.e., with a will, purposes,
and ability to bring about his goals, God uses the creation as an
instrument to accomplish his purposes. Because it is a matter of
the will, however, which is turned away from God (since revolt from
God is the chief sin) man cannot "naturally" know and understand
God's will in the creation and must be told about it in the Bible.
No analogy based on nature can provide the doing of God's will or
even the knowledge of it, a point which Luther continued to maintain
over against Aquinas. Revelation not only supplies the missing
links and the secrets, it provides the key to understanding the
world. All the evidence which after faith becomes meaningful is
entirely ambiguous, if not misleading, before it.

*214. Problems of Dualism in a Complex Society**

But a problem comes to haunt devout men. For the distinction
between law and gospel, the differentiation of love and justice,
tends psychologically and sociologically to lead to a divorce
between the public and the private, between personal kindness and
official rigor. Pietists in particular follow this logic through
consistently, even to the extent that some of them deny Christians
any proper place in public life. Conservatives, on the other hand,
tend to defend *Realpolitik* on religious grounds.

The practical divorce is also an intellectual one. In the

---

*Karl H. Hertz, "The Social Role of the Man of God," in Phillip
J. Hefner, ed. *The Scope of Grace* (Philadelphia: Fortress, 1964),
pp. 220-222.

dualism of Descartes and in the philosophy of the Enlightenment
the distinction between matter and mind, revelation and reason,
natural theology and Christian dogma, allows men to mark out
"the natural" as an arena in which, paraphrasing Newton, "One
does not make hypotheses," in which only what is empirically given,
or rationally demonstrable, only that which has reality within the
world of space and time, can be taken into account in the ordering
of events in the world of nature.

The differentiation which liberates the scientists, which
spreads into the domain of politics (where the laws of nature and
the rights of man are sufficient ground for good order) and into
economic doctrine (where the free market provides for the wealth
of nations), serves more and more to limit the scope of the man of
God until "pure religion and undefiled" turns into a worship of
God by means of liturgies, hymns, and sermons that extol primarily
an inner "spiritual" life and the personal piety of the virtuous
individual.

The criticism Troeltsch made, so much resented in most
Lutheran circles, has its focus and relevance here. True, Luther
would not have understood these dichotomies, but in the nineteenth
century his heirs in almost all evangelical groups insisted upon
this strange divorce between realm of grace and the realm of nature.

The familiar dualisms of the swords or the kingdoms had
meaning in societies in which church and state towered above all
else as the dominant institutional realities. But even where
"establishment" still exists legally, a pluralistic social order
has in fact replaced the old dual structures. The contemporary
social world is a vast complex of many major organizations and an
almost infinite multitude of minor ones, voluntary or semi-compulsory,
varying from local associations to national and international
corporate bureaucracies.

If a dichotomy is still valid, that dichotomy cannot order
life in terms of church and state--for too much would be omitted.
It must distinguish church and community, but once we make this
distinction, we are in trouble. Two swords and two kingdoms had
meaningful institutional referents; they existed alongside one
another in organized form. But within the community we do not have
church (singular) but churches--of diverse traditions, sizes, and
theological persuasions. We may, if we please, talk about "the
coming great church" but that reality is eschatological, not
institutional.

The options are few and may be briefly stated. We may still,
by some kind of evangelical coalition politics, in memory of a once

327

vital Protestant culture, insist that the community must be ordered under the mandates of God. Given the conservative denial of natural theology, such an order could only be imposed from the outside; it would not grow out of the community in a natural way. In whatever guise it came, the end product would be a theocracy.

We may choose a liberal "way out" and see the churches only as a species of private associations. Then the question remains whether anything legitimates religious demands for social justice; whether the church may speak to the great associations of the public arena.

It is no accident that the founding fathers of the liberal doctrine of the state, Locke and his intellectual heirs, in their pleas for religious tolerance were concerned primarily to get the churches out of their controlling places in the social order. If contemporary religious liberalism now asserts social responsibility, quite often its attempt to legitimate these concerns is grounded in a general doctrine of justice, in a religiously tinged humanitarian impulse, in which the distinction between grace and nature has almost evaporated. Theories of theocracy claim too much; liberalism comes with too little.

In a strange way the liberal doctrine of the essentially private nature of religious associations and the Lutheran doctrine of two kingdoms proved to be functional equivalents under the pluralistic conditions of American life. For the "life of faith" defined a private piety; the public sphere, one affirmed implicitly at least, lay beyond the reach of the gospel. The legislative hall, the courtroom, the market, the ship, even the school, ran on their own inherent principles. The logic of the distinction thus implied the autonomy of the natural, but the compulsive preoccupation of the devout with inner spirituality often led to a practical disparagement of what had been liberated.

One approach to this dilemma is to suggest a new metaphor. Grace and nature do not define two realms of human activity, but two dimensions of a single unity: human existence. They represent different ways in which we are related, not different places in which we stand. Like sight and hearing, both grace and nature serve best to orient us in the world when used together; yet each defines reality in its own way.

Thus positively and constructively we assert that nature and grace must be distinguished, that the unique reality of each must be recognized, and that since every man stands simultaneously in both dimensions, we must understand the relatedness of the two dimensions.

If one common failing of the modern Christian approach to
politics has been utopianism (the tendency to expect too much from
political action), the other has been defeatism (the tendency to
expect too little). At its worst, this latter is no "approach" to
politics at all, but a revulsion and withdrawal. Politics is
regarded as the realm of hypocrisy, of compromise, of self-seeking,
cynicism and the lust for power--in short, of sin; and with such
a realm, the pious Christian obviously will have nothing to do.

In terms of the history of Christian thought, this attitude
might be identified as another out-cropping of Manichaeism: the
public world is surrendered to the powers of darkness, while the
elect retire to their own inner world of religiousness. But in
terms of the more specific history of Lutheranism, one could say
that this gloomy view of politics rests on a modern version of
the Flacian heresy....

This is the aberration that has vitiated the modern evangelical
approach to politics more than anything else, unless it be the
opposite error--equally characterized by the inability to make
the necessary "relative distinctions"--of utopianism. Both
tendencies can lead to the same result: the uncritical acceptance
of a given social order, whether a longstanding or newly-established
one (cf. Hitler's "New Order"),viewed either as ideal or, if
manifestly evil, inevitably so. Within Lutheranism, the pessimistic
heresy has doubtless been the more common one. The accents of
Flacianism are recognizable, even if the terminology is different.
"The history of man," the present writer once heard an American
Lutheran theologian declare, "is the history of sin." Said without
qualification, that is a modern equivalent to Flacius' equation of
original sin and human nature, for in contemporary thought "history"
has replaced "nature" as the primary category in our interpretation
of the phenomenon of man. The repudiation of the Flacian heresy
means, I take it, that we cannot simply identify human history with
the history of sin, but rather must view it dialectically, in terms
of an interplay between sin and "civil righteousness" (speaking here
only of secular history and not of *Heilsgeschichte*). Likewise
with reference to the individual--where we find that, similarly,
the more historical concept of the "self" has replaced that of
"substance"--the avoidance of the Flacian identity means that if
we speak of Christian ethics as requiring self-rejection, we must
carefully distinguish between the self that is God's good creation

---

*Franklin Sherman, "Christology, Politics, and the Flacian
Heresy," *Dialog*, 2 (1963), pp. 208-213.

and the distorted self that is the result of sin. Redemption does
mean the rejection--or rather the healing--of the distorted self,
but it means the re-affirmation and fulfillment of the created self.

When we have said this much about history and about the self,
the implications for politics are obvious, for politics exists at
the conjuncture of these two planes. From the standpoint of the
individual, politics can be described as a realm of (public,
structured) interaction of willing, deciding human selves. From
the other and more macroscopic standpoint, it could be defined
simply as "history in cross section":   today's headlines are politics
(domestic or international), yesterday's are history. If this
definition be charged with universalizing the meaning of politics
and therefore being no definition at all, we may admit to some
exaggeration; but the intention is to suggest that there is a
political *dimension* in all social reality. This is true even in
families, some of which are run as absolute monarchies, others as
democracies or mobocracies, with all of Aristotle's variations in
between. It is true of churches, of universities and of corporations:
in none of these institutions can one avoid those processes of the
choice of leadership, the formulation and execution of policy, and
the development of structures of authority, that constitute the
specifically political dimension. Such structures and processes
appear to be inherent in the very nature of "life together"; which
is to say, they are part of that natural created being which, to
the eye of faith, is "very good."...

But now, if we are correct in our assumption that nothing less
than the whole Christian attitude toward history and toward politics,
as well as toward the self, was at stake in this controversy, then
notice the implication. The implication is that it is *not* true that,
within a Lutheran frame of reference, such social-ethical and "civil"
questions must and can only be argued out on the grounds of the
First Article alone. To be sure, the Formula in what it asserts on
the basis of the Second and Third Articles is still a long way
removed from making judgments on specific political issues; but the
level of generality on which it is dealing is one that, as Niebuhr
and Bonhoeffer have shown, is very important indeed for the ability
or inability of Christians to make a constructive witness in the
social order. Whether one's ethics be more deductive or more
pragmatic, more rationalistic or more existentialistic in character,
whether one work with a complex apparatus of revealed and natural
law or reduce the elements of the problem to "faith and the facts,"
it remains true that one's judgments on concrete issues will faithfully
reflect one's basic judgments on the nature and value of reality as

such. Here it is a question of that secular, social, historical
reality that we call "politics," and the judgment of the Confessions,
as implicit in the repudiation of Flacianism, is that this reality--
sin excepted--is to be affirmed as good. That is not all that
needs to be said in a Christian political ethic, but it is essential
that this be said, lest the whole Christian approach to politics
be vitiated at the outset....

Meanwhile, the contribution of the Formula of Concord at the
most basic level of the problem is clear, from the paragraphs
quoted. If Gregory of Nazianzen's great dictum with which he
combatted the Apollinarian heresy that denied Christ's full humanity
was, "What he has not assumed, he has not healed," the Lutheran
confessors here may be said to be applying the obverse: what he
has assumed, he *has* healed. And this includes the whole of man's
flesh-and-blood, social, cultural, and institutional existence.
This is the mighty Christological confutation of all Flacian attitudes
toward politics.

216. Stand, Amt and Beruf*

The Christian man, then, is to be understood as the locus of
interaction of the forces of creation and redemption; in his own
person, he is the point of unity between the two kingdoms. He will
have an attitude toward the secular that is affirmative, but not
uncritical; and into this secular arena he will bring the energies
of his faith active in love.

We are still faced, however, with the question of what
specifically he is to *do* as he seeks to enact this servanthood.
What shall be the content, and what the means, of the Christian's
work and witness in society?

It is at this point that we may return to Article XVI of the
Augsburg Confession and consider the implications of some of the
categories it employs. There are three of these, closely related
to one another, that are pertinent to our present topic. These
are *Stand, Amt,* and *Beruf* ("station," "office," and "calling" or
"vocation"). I should like to suggest that these categories,
taken together, serve at least three functions in reformation
thought, each of which helps us to move toward a specification of
the content of a Christian's life and witness in the secular sphere.
These are the sociological, the theological, and the ethical functions,
respectively.

By the *sociological* function is meant a purely descriptive,
not a normative, function. Sociology, as most modern social

---

*Franklin Sherman, "The Christian in Secular Society: Insights
from the Reformation," *Una Sancta*, 25 (2), pp. 102-106.

scientists use the term, does not project visions of an ideal
society; rather, it attempts to explain the structure and dynamics
of existing societies. This is just the way in which the concepts
of "station" and "office" function for Luther, I suggest, at this
first or sociological level. It is not that society *ought* to be
structured in terms of a network of interconnecting and interde-
pendent roles--parent and child, master and servant, ruler and
ruled, etc.--but rather, it *is* so structured. It is for this
reason that these are considered elements of the order (or, better,
ordering) of creation; they need not be specifically introduced
by revelation or redemption. Note however that what is in question
here is not the endorsement of a specific form of social order,
but simply the recognition of the inevitability of some such ordering.
Here likewise modern sociology tells us that no society is without
such structures, even if societies differ widely in the precise
configuration of the structures. Some form of division of labor
and some more or less hierarchical arrangement of class, status,
and power is universal....

It should be noted that in Luther's notion of the *Stände*, the
accent fell upon the functional contribution of each *Stand* to the
common weal, not upon the prestige or privileges attaching to it.
Luther's doctrine cannot be used as an apologia for the privileges
inherent in a class society in the sense in which Marxism criticized
it. Luther's period of course antedated the rise of bourgeois
society, and therefore also of the socialist reaction to it; but
his views, rooted as they were in the medieval heritage of an
organic rather than contractual form of social relationships, may
well be closer to the communal emphasis of modern social democracy
than to the individualism of laissez-faire capitalism.

In any case, Luther well understood that social structures
exist to serve social functions, and that when they no longer serve
those functions adequately, they will inevitably be replaced. That
is why he urged the princes so fervently to repent of their injustices
toward the peasantry, lest God's wrath come upon them in the form
of a revolt--even if he found himself unable to endorse that revolt
when it occured. The wrath of God, expressed as the inevitable
reaction to severe disfunction in the social system, is the agent
of revolutionary social change according to Luther's theology.

The Theological Level

In speaking of God's wrath, we have already moved to the second
level upon which these conceptions operate in Luther's thought, namely,
the *theological* level. Here Luther uses the notions of station,
office, and vocation to make theological assertions about creation

and fall, and about the Christian's role within the dialectic of
these two factors.

Certainly the accent falls upon the positive aspect: Christian
are taught to view the whole concatenation of social structures and
their respective functions as part of God's good intent for his
creation. This means that the assumption must be rejected that
social-institutional life as such is evil--an assumption that,
unfortunately, seems to be held by many today, in this admittedly
overorganized age. Just as the line between creation and fall
cannot be made to run between nature and history, so also it cannot
be made to run between person and institution. Institutional life
is a *wahrhaftige Gottesordnung*, and Christians are called not to
"drop out" but to exercise "Christian love and genuine good works"
precisely within this context.

The Ethical Level

Luther, as we have already mentioned, boasted that no one since
the apostles had praised the political office so highly as he; and
he took the same attitude toward a wide range of "secular" occupations.
Karl Holl has shown, in his essay "Die Geschichte des Worts Beruf"
(*Gesammelte Aufsätze*, III, 189 ff.), how in Luther's thought the
theonomous glow of the term "calling," formerly applied only to
the "religious" estate, was now allowed to shine also over the worldly
sphere. Even the word *Beruf*, of course, was not used in a univocal
sense, and frequently is synonymous in his writing with *Stand* or *Amt*.
But a systematic distinction may be suggested as follows: if
"station" signifies the position one holds in the social order (or
in a particular sub-order such as the political, the familiar, etc.),
and "office" refers to the special duties attaching to that station,
then to have a "calling" means to acknowledge one's station as
assigned by God, and to carry out its duties under the aegis of the
divine command. The word *Beruf* and its equivalents in other
languages have of course long since lost their original theonomous
connotation, and have come to mean simply a "job"; but according to
the suggested differentiation of meaning, the specifically theological
meaning would be restored. Everyone, simply by virtue of his
involvement with the social order, has a *Stand* and an *Amt*; only a
Christian has a *Beruf*.

But what of the third, and specifically *ethical* level of the
problem. It is here that the notion of *Stand* plays a prominent role
in Luther's thought. Whenever he was asked, or whenever he put the
question to himself, "Granted that I as a Christian am to let my
faith be active in love, and that this love is to be exercised in the

secular world on behalf of my neighbor's needs, what specifically
am I to do?" He would give a twofold answer: obey the commandments,
and consider your station. These can be viewed as directions as
to how to give concreteness to the command of love.

Agape love, after all, is quite general, in fact universal,
in its scope; but by the same token, it is empty of particular
contents. It no more tells us precisely what to do than does the
well-known first principle of a certain type of philosophical
ethics, "The good is to be done and the evil is to be avoided."
The moral teaching of the Bible and of the Christian tradition
serves to provide such content, and constitutes the element that
the Christian brings with him into every situation. His ethic,
then, is not derived wholly *from* the situation. The Ten Commandments,
for example, serve to establish what may be called the "floor" of
ethics, a statement of the minimal conditions, in *any* epoch or society,
for a decently human life. No society can long exist if it ceases
to observe these elementary prohibitions of the arbitrary taking
of human life, disruption of the structure of the family, or disregard
for the claims of truth. This is to take the Commandments in their
plain meaning, i.e., negatively. When they are reinterpreted in
a positive sense, as Luther does in his Catechisms (which may be
poor exegesis, but is good ethics!), then they function all the more
readily to give content to the love imperative.

The Commandments themselves, however, still are rather general
in character, and it is here that Luther's second injunction becomes
relevant: "Consider your station." The Christian, we have said,
brings something to the situation--namely, a heightened awareness
of the will of God and the inward dynamic of faith dedicated to
servanthood. But he also learns something *from* the situation. The
Christian's "place" in society, in the sense of the particular
station he occupies, is for him the *place of obedience*; but it is
also the *place of discernment*. It is this which makes the ethical
method employed in the Evangelical Academies so appropriate, whereby
those who occupy the respective "stations" in modern society--which,
of course, in this respect has become incredibly complex in comparison
to Luther's time, are themselves allowed to unveil the problematic
of their situation, and to seek for answers. And it is significant
that explicitly "Christian" answers are not insisted upon. The
problem is not to advance from the merely human to the uniquely
Christian, but to advance from the inhuman or inadequately human to
the fully human. These questions, as the reformation well understood,
belong to the realm of the natural.

In emphasizing the contemporary relevance of the notions of

Stand, *Amt*, and *Beruf*, however, we must add one caution. These
categories have often been interpreted as referring only to the
realm of daily work, in the sense of that which one gets paid for.
But the Christian also has his responsibilities as a citizen, a
deputyship with respect to the welfare of the whole society. Luther
himself emphasized that every person is a member of the *ordo politicus*,
the political *Stand*, and has his own special role therein. In our
day, this role cannot be restricted, as it was for the mass of the
people in Luther's day, to simple obedience to what the authorities
command. For in an age of democracy, every man is one of the
authorities, and is called to exercise his own share of political
power, whether it be relatively small or great, in both a creative
and a critical spirit. It is in the realm of the political, above
all, that the struggle for the human is being waged in our day,
and it is here that the Christian must and may bear his testimony
to the reality of God's grace and judgment also in the secular
world.

217. Distinction Without Dualism*

The sum of the matter, then, seems to be that from both sides
what is desired is a recognition of the duality between church and
world, but without a dualism; and on the other hand, sympathetic
identification of the church with the world, but not an identity
between the two. It is this which leads us to propose that, if
a christological social ethic is to be formulated, it is a Chalcedonian
Christology that is required. For it is precisely these two kinds
of error that the Chalcedonian definition of the faith was designed
to guard against: on the one hand, the "Nestorian" dualism between
the divine and human natures of Christ, and on the other hand, the
Eutychian amalgamation of them. Our assumption in saying this,
however, is that the Chalcedonian formula did not, as often alleged,
perform only the negative function of excluding such aberrations,
but is worthy of commendation in its own right as a positive statement
of the faith. From this perspective, Chalcedon is seen as standing
in the great tradition of the christological confessions of Irenaeus
and Tertullian, of Athanasius and Augustine--as indeed it viewed
itself:

The four famous adverbs, on this view, serve not merely to
define the limits of speculation, but to describe a unique and
dynamic form of relationship that transcends both monism and dualism,
and that is applicable not only to the traditional problem of the

---

*Franklin Sherman, "The Vital Center: Toward a Chalcedonian
Social Ethic," in Philip J. Hefner, ed. *The Scope of Grace*
(Philadelphia: Fortress Press, 1964), pp. 241-242.

two natures, but also to the whole problem of the relationship between God and the world, church and society, nature and grace--an applicability which indeed is to be expected, if it really be true that Christ is *the* clue to the relation of divinity and humanity. It is this middle Chalcedonian way, we believe, that Dietrich Bonhoeffer has in mind when he opposes both what he calls "radicalism," which posits an absolute dualism between the ultimate and the penultimate, and "compromise," which simply sanctions things as they are. Though protesting all "thinking in terms of two spheres," Bonhoeffer yet refuses simply to identify with one another the elements that have been traditionally referred to those two spheres.

CHAPTER 16

NEW DIRECTIONS

A. ACCENT ON PARTICIPATION

218. The Augsburg Confession Speaks to Contemporary Involvement*

First of all, it insists that God the Creator is a living God and that his creation continues. "Lawful civil ordinances are good works of God,..." We note that not only the ordinances of the past but quite specifically those of the present are considered *Bona opera Dei*, good works of God. The commitment of the *Augsburg Confession* is not to a static political order either of the first century or of the sixteenth, but rather to the living creator God who establishes order for the sake of man. The structures of government, law, politics, economics and the family are subject to change! The *Augsburg Confession* supports the structures that had evolved in the sixteenth century as functional for its time. Matters would be decided *ex imperatoriis et aliis praesentibus legibus*, by the imperial and other existing laws. It does not advocate a return to the Mosaic law or a legalistic interpretation of the New Testament as furnishing a law binding for all times. By resisting all efforts on the part of certain elements of the Reformation movement to return to the alleged purity of the life of the first century church or of the deuteronomic code, the *Augsburg Confession* makes it in turn impossible to attribute eternal validity to the social order of the sixteenth, nineteenth or twentieth centuries. From the fact that Article XVI allows the princes and citizens of the sixteenth century *politia* to participate in war and to administer the death penalty (*Übeltäter*

---

*George W. Forell, "The Augsburg Confession: Article XVI Civil Affairs," *Bulletin*, Lutheran Theological Seminary, Gettysburg, Pennsylvania, 49 (1969), no. 3, pp. 26-29.

mit dem Schwert strafen) it cannot be concluded that this is
necessarily an appropriate exercise of power for the state in our
time. Article XVI is a commitment to change as well as order.
It rejects any form of restoration or repristination. Its commitment
to order is not a commitment to any particular order. The criterion
for the kind of order envisioned and advocated is spelled out:
"The Gospel...does not destroy the state (*politiam*) or the family
(*oeconomiam*). On the contrary, it especially requires their
preservation as ordinances of God and the exercise of love in these
ordinances (*et in talibus ordinationibus exercere caritatem*)."
Love furnishes the standard for the evaluation of a particular
kind of order. According to the *Augsburg Confession* we must ask,
"Is it possible to exercise love in the particular structures of
our time summarized here under the heading of *politia* and *oeconomia*?"...

    That this concern with the earthly welfare of man is a valid
Christian concern is the second major contribution of Article XVI
of the *Augsburg Confession*....Christians are supposed to engage in
these civil functions! The reverse of the condemnation of non-
participation is the command to participate. The *Augsburg Confession*
calls Christians to responsible participation in the affairs of this
world, to be specific, "To hold civil office, to sit as judges, to
decide matters by the imperial and other existing laws, to award
just punishments, to engage in just wars, to serve as soldiers, to
make legal contracts, to hold property, to swear oaths when required
by magistrates, to marry, to be given in marriage." In short, Article
XVI is a call to total participation in social and political affairs.
The details of this participation which are listed are to serve as
illustrations; they are not supposed to be exhaustive as the *et
cetera* in the German version indicates, and, as we said earlier,
the describe participation in the worldly affairs of the sixteenth
century. Taken seriously, Article XVI demands total participation
in the life of every century, and for us total participation in the
human affairs of the last third of the 20th century.

    It is noteworthy how positively the *Augsburg Confession* describes
this involvement. It speaks about exercising authority, rather than
obeying the authorities, about holding office, not merely obedience
to officeholders; about sitting as judges, not merely accepting
judgment; about deciding matters, not merely submitting to decisions.
There is a profound difference in mood between the position of the
Christian citizen in the sixteenth century and the position of this
citizen in the time of St. Paul. The difference between Romans 13
and Article XVI of the *Augsburg Confession* is dramatic. Paul writes
to the Roman Christians in the First century: "Every person must

submit to the supreme authorities" (Romans 13:1). The *Augsburg Confession* calls Christians to act as authorities. It is written for men and signed by men who have great political and social responsibility. It recognizes the changes that have taken place in the intervening 15 centuries.

Similarly we must recognize the changes that have taken place in the four hundred forty years since Augsburg, changes that are even greater than those which account for the different mood of the *Augsburg Confession*. Faithful to Romans 13 and Augustana XVI, we must define our responsibilities in the light of our situations as citizens of a powerful democracy which happens to have awesome responsibilities for the future of our world. We may not cop out, we must take our full responsibility in the political and social life of our time and make the civil government a more effective instrument of God's creative goodness. Civil office must not only be accepted but reformed. Sitting as judges does not suffice. The laws by which we judge must be rewritten in order to serve the welfare of all men. The whole question of war has to be thoroughly reexamined. It may no longer be possible to engage in just wars and to serve as soldiers in national armies. The flash over Hiroshima in 1945 may have made the notion of the just war obsolete. The notion of private property deserves thorough study. With the advent of private properties like General Motors or Standard Oil of New Jersey the entire notion of property as used in the *Augsburg Confession* may have become an anachronism. Even to marry and to be given in marriage may need a new understanding in the light of the evolving equality of the sexes. Of course, there are also inescapable questions that did not even occur to the writers of the *Augsburg Confession*. The racism which permeates our entire life as a nation and adds a tragic dimension to every one of the above problems was simply unknown to 16th century Germans. Yet it is an issue that has to be faced honestly if we want to take Article XVI seriously. And the same interest in the earthly welfare of all human beings, black, white, brown and yellow must be our overriding concern rather than the defense of white or black ideologies spawned in hate and resentment. Other issues of great importance may not even have been recognized or defined. Article XVI is completely open-ended; the *et cetera* is all-inclusive. Wherever issues may still appear Christians are called to responsible participation.

And finally Article XVI warns against perfectionism as a threat to responsible participation in the affairs of this world. It condemns those who place the perfection of the Gospel not in the fear of God and in faith but in forsaking civil duties. The Gospel teaches an eternal righteousness of the heart, but it does not destroy the state or the family. On the contrary, it especially requires their preservation as ordinances of God and the exercise of love in these ordinances."

219. Emerging Trends*

As a corollary to the prior assertions, it is concluded that the characteristically Lutheran emphasis on obedience to authority ought to be replaced by an emphasis on participation in the secular process for the sake of justice. Efforts have been made in this direction by such persons as William Lazareth and George Forell. The fact remains, however, that Lutherans in America tend to shy away from political participation, particularly when it takes a quasi-revolutionary character.

Finally, any relevant theology of society or social ethics must deal with government against the background of two ever-present and somewhat contradictory realities. There is, on the one hand, the vital necessity of securing some sort of viable world order, of providing institutional structures (both within and between nations) which make for that stability necessary for the preservation of life and the assurance of its continuation. On the other hand, there is the equally vital necessity of taking seriously those revolutionary movements which seek to establish economic and social justice for masses of men hitherto deprived of it. The present task, then, is a double one: to affirm and identify with revolution without thereby becoming enthralled by anarchy, and to search for viable institutional forms without becoming the slaves of reaction.

220. Piety and Politics in Dynamic Tension**

Augustine and Luther in turn took over this view of two realms under God and fashioned it into "the doctrine of the two kingdoms." Handled flexibly, related dynamically to modern society, and formulated in today's idiom, the doctrine provides clues for living responsibly under the gospel in the sovereign democratic nation-state which, while concerned with order and justice, is jealous of its own sovereignty.

Biblical Christianity--rejecting monasticism, sectarianism, and syncretism--provides the ground for the development of the doctrine of the two kingdoms: Christ and culture in tension, church and state in polarity, piety and politics in dynamic relationship.

---

*LCA Task Group on Long-Range Planning, Edward Utne, Director, *Theology: An Assessment of Current Trends* (Philadelphia: Fortress, 1968), pp. 94-95.
**Wallace E. Fisher, *Politics, Poker and Piety* (Nashville: Abingdon Press, 1972), pp. 130-131.

The Christian citizen has obligations to *both* church and state.
His ultimate allegiance, however, belongs to *neither* institution;
it belongs to God. Every Christian is obliged to honor God's
claim on his conscience which, acted on, may or may not alter the
course of the state (Bonhoeffer failed) or the direction of the
ecclesiastical church (Luther succeeded partially). In all seasons
the church's impact on the state is both indirect and direct. The
direct impact is accomplished through the elective processes (in
a democratic state) and through dissent from and resistance to any
state policies which dehumanize society.

B. THE SECULAR ARENA AS THE APPROPRIATE SPHERE OF ACTION

221. Structures for Effective Action*

Existing structures for effective social action through the
churches have fundamental flaws: the ideology of consensus can,
on the one hand, blunt clearcut action in order not to offend a
resisting or apathetic segment of the membership, especially when
that group constitutes a numerical but inarticulate majority; the
same ideology can, on the other hand, through the operating
structures of ecclesiastical hierarchies and religious assemblies
present a "united front" of commitment, for which the membership
feels no ownership, in which it does not participate. Organizational
imperialsim, at the same time, tends to channel such action as
occurs on large-scale social problems into relatively narrow channels
of church-controlled programming. Only in rare moments of a widespread sense of injustice can the religious groups really act
effectively. A better strategy is needed....

It is my fundamental thesis that if church members are
serious about social change, about racism and war, poverty and
blight, *the place for them to be active is in secular organizations
committed to social change, in organizations independent of
ecclesiastical control, budgetary and structural.* Above all, if
these Christians want to be effective, political organizations are
the best available vehicles.

C. ALTERNATIVES

222. Is Luther Adequate for Today's Issues?**

In other words, we can now look back upon the efforts of a

---

*Karl H. Hertz, *Politics is a Way of Helping People: A
Christian Perspective in Times of Crisis* (Minneapolis: Augsburg
Publishing House, 1974), pp. 66-67.
**Phillip Hefner, "Theological Reflections (1)," *Una Sancta*,
24 (1967), pp. 45-50.

current generation of Lutheran theologians who have made an emphatic
reinterpretation of the Two-Kingdoms' dialectic, insisting that it
include the affirmation of Christ's lordship over the entire world.
This generation of theologians is confident that the authentic
spirit of Lutheran theology--to a certain extent going back to
Luther himself again--can overcome the mistakes of the past which
have dampened our passion for the earth. In this vein, one
theologian sounds the hopeful cry that "in brief, there is nothing
so sick about Lutheran ethics that a strong dose of Luther cannot
cure!"

Yet one wonders if this hopeful affirmation is enough. We
can be grateful that the current generation of Lutheran theologians
has expanded our horizons, through the concepts of the interpenetration
of the two kingdoms and the lordship of Christ, but if we do indeed
stand upon the shoulders of these theologians, our vision should
be extended to a still farther horizon, perhaps to a horizon that
Luther himself could not envision, and this farther horizon may
furnish us with an even more helpful understanding of what it means
to be passionate about the things of the earth.

There is yet a note which sounds through the Lutheran dialectic
which does not ring true to the ears of the contemporary Christian.
It is not an easy matter to explain the tone of falseness that rings
in our ears, but perhaps three observations may get us to the heart
of the issue.

1. The passion which the Christian feels for the things of
the earth is dampened by a certain negativity which the Two Kingdoms'
conceptuality applies to the world. The Left Hand Kingdom is
inevitably the realm of God's police work, where he coerces men to
do righteously. The secular order becomes the realm that is to be
tolerated, suffered, the realm where commands alone are given, to
which the only appropriate response is obedience. The world does
not really *inform* faith in any fundamental way. · The secular is to
be judged and ordered, but judgment and ordering do not carry with
them the understanding that God might well do his redeeming work
in creative and imaginative ways within the secular ordering. The
secular realm seems to be that which the Lutheran *reacts* to rather
than that which he "gets with" in order to participate in its
rhythm of accomplishment. This mood is reinforced by the Lutheran
tendency to insist that the secular realm, and our social ethical
activity within that realm, is wholly under law, specifically
the coercion of the political use of the law....

There is strong empirical evidence to support the position that
equates the "world," the Left Hand Kingdom with the realm of law

and coercion--is there not?   All of our common experience in this century bears witness that kindness and goodwill do not go very far in resolving our problems or in achieving justice. Slum landlords will not repair apartments unless they are threatened with heavy sentences, and wars are not halted until it becomes politically and militarily desirable to halt them. The evil in the secular realm is tenacious and malignant, and as long as it exists, it is unrealistic to speak of love and peace within the world. Surely, the rugged coercion of the law--conceived in its civil or political use--described admirably the realities of the realm of the "things of the earth"! Or does it? Does the experience of the twentieth century demonstrate that the secular realm is incapable of love, creativity, and even redemption? Or does it rather demonstrate that--no matter where humanity strives, whether in the secular realm or in the community of grace--evil is the inevitable companion of man, wherever he walks and whatever he plans?

I would suggest that the empirical presence of evil and injustice in the world does not necessarily imply that our social ethics--our efforts at achieving justice--are under the law and therefore carried out only in solemn obligation or in a spirit of negativity; rather it implies that evil is always inevitable and that therefore man stands in constant need of God's redemption. And if a social ethic could bring a glimpse of that redemption to the secular realm, it would actually be gospel and not law! And if our efforts in the Left Hand Kingdom are potentially of gospel significance, then a creativity and joyousness can be associated with them which has been lacking in our Lutheran tradition.

2. Along with this reservation about equating the secular realm with the first use of the law, a Christian today might well demur at the insistence--apparently endemic within our tradition-- that the secular realm is in some sense a lesser realm than the realm of faith, the Right Hand Kingdom. No Lutheran would really want--on theoretical grounds--to depreciate the "things of the earth," the secular realm. And yet, in our doctrinal position, the Left Hand Kingdom inevitably comes off second best, in some sense less dear to us than the Right Hand Kingdom. Even the current LWF study document on the lordship of Christ, despite, and even in the midst of, a concern to bring the two kingdoms together, insists that "the distinction between the secular and the spiritual kingdom of God corresponds to the biblical distinction between God's general government of the world and his specific eschatological acts of salvation." This distinction between the two kingdoms inevitably--

343

and even against our will--becomes an *invidious* distinction....

3. Even the emphasis on the Christian's responsibility to
serve his neighbor *(diakonia)* in the secular realm, to *meet his
needs* as it is generally put, must stand further scrutiny today.
Our theological tradition has thereby made activity in the world
functional--meeting the neighbor's physical and social needs. But
this is only half the story; secular activity is also *expressive*
of man's self-hood, and in this sense also participates in
redemption....

If social responsibility in this world is essential to human
destiny, then it aims at more than meeting the neighbor's needs
(although it does aim at that), just as it deserves to be designated
as something more than law and judgment. It must be understood
somehow as the vehicle of our redemption and sanctification. And
if this is so, then the secular realm in which social responsibility
is exercised--that is, *the world*--must be related to God in creative
and imaginative ways that are not best described as elements of
God's Left Hand Kingdom.

We can be passionate about the things of the earth because
we know that in our involvement in those things, our very redeemed
humanity, a gift from God the Creator, is being fulfilled. We
will not let the ardor of our passion be dampened by the insistence
of any theological tradition that our business in the world is
wholly functional. And to this affirmation, we bring also a massive
empirical evidence that what we are (namely, redeemed sons of God)
is inseparable from and realized in what we do (works in the secular
realm). We do our works in the world, not simply because we are
so sensitive to our neighbor, but because we are sensitive to what
is necessary to our humanity under God--and the two will ultimately
coincide--not in our will, but in God's plan.

223. Towards a Revolutionary Ethic*

The exceptional clause in the two-kingdom ethic which might
justify an *ad hoc* act of defiance of established authorities, even
when it reaches the stage of outright revolt, does not and can not
motivate a revolutionary transformation of the established order
of things--because the eschatological dynamic is missing. The aim
of a rebellion is to restore what has been lost; the aim of revolution
is to create something new. The vision of the radically new is what
links revolutionary action with eschatological hope. The problem
with the two-kingdom doctrine is that the revolutionary dynamic

---

*Carl Braaten, *The Future of God* (New York: Harper & Row,
1969), pp. 147-149.

discharged by the kingdom on the right hand did not set off any explosions in the kingdom on the left hand. There is manifestly a defective eschatology at work here. The dynamics of the coming kingdom of God have had profound effects upon the inner life of faith, reaching unequaled depths in the spirituality of a Kierkegaard. But it is the dynamics of quite another kingdom at work in the realm of social and political life. This means that the gospel may stir up a revolutionary storm only within the individual, never within society. The spiritual life of the Lutheran Christian is in a state of constant crisis; there the whole impact of the coming kingdom of God is experienced in judgment and forgiveness. The political and social characteristics of the biblical symbol of the kingdom of God have been suppressed in favor of the religious experience of the individual person.

The positive assets of the two-kingdom doctrine need not be lost in a reformulation of an eschatological ethic that points to the transformation of the world. The elements of truth in the two-kingdom doctrine are many, but here we point out only what is important for a revolutionary ethic. In distinguishing between two kingdoms, both of which are God's, it was possible for Lutherans to develop a theology of power which did not shrink from seeing it as the "strange work" of God's love. This is a revolutionary idea itself, for many an ethic of love has withered in the face of the show of power. How can power and love be united with each other? The two-kingdom ethic was an attempt to say that Christians are not to retreat from power situations in the secular realm, because that realm is God's and he is the source of all power. Christians may thus "occupy civil offices or serve as princes and judges, render decisions and pass sentence according to imperial and other existing laws, punish evil doers with the sword, engage in just wars, serve as soldiers, buy and sell, take required oaths, possess property, be married, etc." The Lutheran doctrine went on to condemn the position held by those sectarians who so zoomed off into the future of God's eschatological *shalom* that they withdrew from social and political responsibility. On the other hand, Lutheran doctrine taught Christians merely to *uphold* the secular orders, not to *change* them. The purpose of power is to serve as a dike against sin, to forestall chaos, to preserve law and order. The given situation as we know it must be defended against revolutionary change and radical progress. The two-kingdom doctrine has invariably engendered a conservative political ethic because the eschatological dynamic of the gospel is not released into the power situations which decide for or against the inner-historical transformation of society. Its theology of power, essential also in a revolutionary ethic, is made to serve the interests of the status quo. Its theology of power has been wedded to a static conception of the world. Hence, it has never been difficult to justify the use of power by a police force or a national army, for these use power to keep things as they are. Since revolutionary power always changes things and frequently threatens chaos and anarchy, one has assumed that God's will is on the side of change-lessness. To obey God's providential will is to resign oneself to the powers that be and to operate within the given system. This is a positivistic doctrine of God's providence.

The two-kingdom doctrine cannot support a revolutionary ethic as long as the realm of creation does not share the same eschatological future as the realm of redemption. Tillich, who broke with a static form of the two-kingdom doctrine in becoming a religious socialist, put it this way: "Its most obvious shortcoming is the fact that it contrasts the salvation of the individual with the transformation of the historical group and the universe, thus separating the one from the other." The church is then understood as the sphere in which individuals experience salvation and the outside world as somehow excluded from the future which Christ has pioneered. The kingdom of God toward which the church is pressing and for whose coming it prays in the Lord's Prayer is the goal also of the nations and kingdoms of this earth. The essential eschatological basis of the social and political dimensions of the church's message to the world is missing in the two-kingdom doctrine. The doctrines of creation and redemption are inadequately linked to the eschatological goal of both the church and the world in the future of God's coming kingdom. One could say that while there is an eschatology of redemption in this doctrine, there is no eschatology of creation.

346

CHAPTER 17

EMPIRICAL DATA

A. THE STEREOTYPE PERPETUATED

*224. Social Science Describes "The Lutheran Ethic"**

The Lutheran ethic emphasizes a particular image of man--
that man was without sin only prior to the temptation of Adam and
Eve. The Fall destroyed man's previously perfect nature, and he
became a totally depraved being. Because of man's inherently evil
nature, he is incapable of doing good by himself. The powerlessness
of man, stressed by Martin Luther, contrasts with the traditional
Roman Catholic belief that although man is born sinful, he may
overcome this state by good works. The *Book of Concord*, a summary
of the confessions and doctrines of Lutheranism, states that
"original sin in human nature is not only a total lack of good
in spiritual, divine things, but that at the same time it replaces
the lost image of God in man with a deep, wicked, abominable,
bottomless, inscrutable, and inexpressible corruption of his entire
nature in all its powers, especially of the highest and foremost
powers of the soul in mind, heart, and will.."...

Salvation, according to the Lutheran ethic, comes only as a free
gift of grace from God, through Jesus Christ, and is not affected by
the worldly deeds of men. Man is assured of salvation by grace alone
(*sola gratia*). His efforts do not pay for or add to his salvation.
Luther asserts: "For God wants to save us not by our own but by
extraneous (*fremde*)justice and wisdom, by a justice that does not come
from ourselves and does not originate in ourselves but comes to us from

---

*Lawrence Kersten, *The Lutheran Ethic* (Detroit: Wayne State
University Press, 1970), pp. 22-27.

somewhere else." Although both Catholicism and Lutheranism adhere to
doctrine of grace, Lutheranism deemphasizes the church hierarchy,
religious rituals, and works of merit that are regarded as
important steps in gaining grace for Catholics. Thus, for Lutherans
grace and salvation cannot be "obtained" through church authorities.
Faith and the possibility of salvation are more individual and
personal.

Although Lutheranism is usually considered to be a religion
stressing the grace of God rather than the Law of God, Old Testament
Law does make up an important segment of the Lutheran ethic. In
fact, Luther has been accused of using the Old Testament as if it
were a legal code. He quite naturally turned to the Bible in
seeking a system of ethics that could be used as an ideal standard
for all people. However, the specific purpose of the Law is to
act as a stimulus to repentance by pointing out man's sinful nature
and helplessness. The majority of Lutheran laymen today, in contrast
to their views of being saved by God's grace through faith and
trust, also say that they are saved by keeping the Ten Commandments
and living a good moral life. Luther's strong emphasis on the Law
of God thus exists today despite the contradictory evidence of
theology. A stress on moral conduct, based on Old Testament Law,
is almost as much a part of the thinking of the individual Lutheran
layman as is the concept of free grace....

The individual Lutheran's role in society is determined
primarily by Luther's concept of the calling. God calls an
individual to carry out certain duties, and all callings have the
same worth in the sight of God. The result is an earthly inequality,
and a spiritual equality which is "the objective historical order
of things in which the individual has been placed by God." Since
the social order is considered to be a direct manifestation of the
divine will, Lutherans should make no attempt to change it. The
role of the individual, according to the Lutheran ethic, is one of
quietism and passivity toward the secular world. The conservatism
concerning worldly matters results from the emphasis that Lutheranism
places on trust in God, on the distrust of man's motives, and on
the futility of his efforts. Since God's will is all that matters
and man is by nature a self-centered, sinful creature who cannot
be expected to solve worldly problems, it follows that patient
endurance of this world and anxious anticipation of the next become
the individual Lutheran's primary orientation.

Luther saw secular institutions as necessary to restrain
wickedness in a sinful and temporal world. He believed that such
institutions and the existing state of affairs were appointed and

ordained by divine providence. War, government, violence, law, and property were all viewed as part of God's plan. Whatever the existing situation of the social order, man can be assured that it has its good side, inasmuch as it is a product of God's will. All that remains for the individual Christian is obedience and humble submission to these institutions.

225. Critique of Kersten*

Kersten's study of Lutheran attitudes on questions of social involvement is sadly deficient on at least two counts. First, Kersten has obviously not read what contemporary Lutheran ethicists in the United States have said. Thus his conceptual framework rests completely on reading Luther through the eyes of Troeltsch and H. Richard Niebuhr. On this basis he simply assumes that one particular version (the nineteenth century's dualistic distortion) is the Lutheran ethic.

Secondly, at critical points Kersten misreads his own data, coming out with more conservative interpretations than the answers of his respondents warrant.

In spite of these objections, however, Kersten is probably right in claiming that he has found relationships between theological conservatism and a particular way of being politically conservative. He has also documented, perhaps unconsciously, that many characteristics of this theological conservatism cannot really be identified with the mainstream Lutheran tradition, as that tradition has been defined historically in terms of the distinction between Law and Gospel. Perhaps his very shortcomings will challenge us to get at some necessary tasks both in theological education and in ministry.

B. ANALYSIS OF THE CONTEMPORARY SITUATION

226. American Lutherans and the Two Kingdoms**

The task the editor of this volume has assigned to me is to review the series of recent sociological studies with data pertinent to the question of whether one can find evidences of the doctrine of the two kingdoms in contemporary American Lutheranism.[37]

There are two major recent studies of Lutherans in the United States, Kersten's (1970) study of pastors and laymen in Detroit and Strommen's (*et al.*, 1971) analysis of a nationwide sample of

---

*A summary of the review of Kersten in Karl H. Hertz, "Ethical Stances and Social Issues among American Lutherans: A Review Article," *Lutheran Quarterly*, 24 (1972), pp. 71-90.

**Samuel A. Mueller, "The Doctrine of the Two Kingdoms in Contemporary American Lutheranism: A Review of the Literature," January, 1975. Professor Mueller of the University of Akron prepared this manuscript especially for this book.

pastors and laymen. Both of these books provide abundant evidence
to the effect that Lutherans, especially the laity, tend to be
rather quietistic with respect to the involvement of the Church in
public affairs. Since the way the data are presented in the Strommen
volume makes it almost impossible to give an adequate summary for
readers unsophisticated in advanced statistical techniques, I here
rely on Kersten's data to give the reader a taste of this tendency.
Not presenting data from Strommen, *et al.* (1971) is not a great
loss, since the two sets of data agree very closely.

TABLE 1: Lay and Clergy Responses on Selected Questions Relating
to the Involvement of the Church in Public Affairs,
Detroit-Area Lutheran Laity, By Synod, Late 1960s

		Synod			
Question	Sample	LCA	ALC	LC-MS	WS
Denominations should issue policy statements on social and economic matters (% agreeing).	Lay	45	43	40	30
	Clergy	95	87	62	13
The church can best contribute to the solution of social problems by preaching the gospel and by winning individuals to salvation (% disagreeing).	Lay	10	10	4	5
	Clergy	48	30	22	0
Church bodies as a goup should take a public stand on political issues (% agreeing).	Lay	25	22	22	17
	Clergy	69	57	37	0
The most important thing is the salvation of mankind to eternal life rather than carrying on a social reform program here in this world (% disagreeing).	Lay	29	28	10	8
	Clergy	75	43	15	6
Approximate N's	Lay	242	192	223	229
	Clergy	54	54	117	16

Source: Kersten, 1970: 132, 237, 239.

The quietism of Lutheran laity is very evident from the data
in Table 1. In none of the four questions does the stance in favor
of involvement of the Church in public affairs receive a majority
vote from the laity of any of the four synods, and one can note a
consistent decline in support for such involvement as he moves
from the LCA on the left to the Wisconsin Synod on the right.
Support for social action is, however, more common among the clergy,
especially those of the LCA and, to a lesser extent, among those of
the ALC and the Missouri Synod. It is perhaps important to point
out that, for every one of the four questions presented in Table 1,
Wisconsin Synod laity are more likely than their pastors to endorse
the involvement of the Church in public affairs.

Another way of summarizing the data in Table 1 is to say that
synodical affiliation is related to one's attitude toward the

involvement of the Church in public affairs, but that this relationship is *much* stronger for the laity than for the clergy. This is
a familiar pattern, and it has been found in studies of many
different denominations (cf. Gibbs, *et al.*, 1973). Synodical
affiliation--and, more generally, one's position on an orthodoxy-
to-modernism continuum--is almost always more strongly related to
social activism among the clergy than among the laity. Gibbs,
et al. (1973) demonstrate that this pattern is a consequence of a
much higher degree of salience of religion among the clergy than
among the laity. When a lay sample is cut into salience "layers"
and the relationship between religious beliefs and social action
examined within each one, the very highest layer, perhaps the top
10 to 20 percent of the laity, show relationships similar to those
of the clergy. This fact has import for a local pastor--his most
deeply involved laity (those with the highest degree of salience)
are more likely to hold social action views similar to the pastor's
own than the less deeply involved laity, assuming that the theological
views of the pastor and his parishoners are in close agreement.

The higher salience of religion among the clergy also has
an important implication for this review. Since the correlations
between the orthodox-to-modernist continuum and social action
attitudes are quite low among the laity (Wuthnow, 1973), but much
higher among the clergy, the clergy studies will be stressed. If
any sort of evidence can be extracted from the studies available
concerning the two kingdoms doctrine today, that evidence should
be clearer among the clergy than among the laity.

Kersten (1970) and Strommen (*et al.*, 1971) serve to establish
an important relationship. Lutherans are not only quite quietistic;
both studies also present evidence to the effect that Lutherans
who are more "orthodox," i.e., those who give traditional responses
to survey questions based on simplistic interpretations of the
Apostle's Creed (cf. Glock and Stark, 1965:85-124; and Stark and
Glock, 1968) are more quietistic than those who give less orthodox
responses. This pattern holds among both clergy and laity, but
much more strongly among the clergy.

This relationship between theology and politics, however,
cannot be taken automatically to mean that Luther's doctrine of
the two kingdoms is at work. There are two reasons for this. First,
the measure of theology Kersten (1970) uses is a global one,
containing two questions on biblical liberalism, one on the
exclusivity of the Christian message, and another on original sin.
As Hertz (1970) has pointed out, none of these questions is specific
to any version of a specifically Lutheran theological heritage, nor

351

do any of them tap any aspect of the two kingdoms doctrine. Thus, a finding that those Lutherans who reject some or all of these statements call for the Church's involvement in public affairs more frequently than those Lutherans who accept all of them is hardly evidence in favor of the two kingdoms doctrine at work. The Strommen book contains a set of indices labeled "the heart of Lutheran piety." These indices probably come closer to measuring aspects of a specifically Lutheran theological heritage, but one can hardly extract support for the hypothesis that the two kingdoms doctrine is at work in the twentieth century from one of the major themes of the book--the notion that Lutherans who adulterate these historic aspects of Lutheran theology are the most likely to reject programs of social justice.

A recent monograph by King and Hunt (1972), based on two studies of Texas laity in four Protestant denominations, buttresses this conclusion. King and Hunt used a technique called factor analysis to sort a total of 118 questionnaire items on religion into a series of 10 "dimensions" of religiosity. The Lutherans were totally undistinguished in this analysis. No "two kingdoms" dimension appeared, not even when the Lutherans were examined separately, and on no single dimension was there a clustering of Lutherans at a single pole, a pattern that one might anticipate if these Lutheran laity shared a set of beliefs among themselves that they did not share with other Protestants.

The reference to other Protestant denominations in the King-Hunt study leads to a discussion of the other problem in assessing contemporary Lutheran emphasis on the two kingdoms doctrine from all-Lutheran studies like Kersten's and Strommen's. Such studies can be used to show that many (though not all) Lutherans are quietistic on attitude questions similar to those in Table 1, but *they cannot be used to demonstrate that this quietism is a consequence of the two kingdoms doctrine without comparisons to other denominations lacking such an historical theological heritage*. If the two kingdoms doctrine is operative in contemporary American Lutheranism, then we should expect patterns of relationships between theological beliefs and social action questions among Lutherans different from those in other denominations. To be ascribable to the two kingdoms doctrine, the distinctive Lutheran pattern would have to take either of two forms:

     a.   There should be no variation among Lutherans in terms of social action questions such as those in Table 1; i.e., *all* of the pastors and the laity would take a stance opposed to the involvement of the Church in public affairs; or

b. While there may be some variation within Lutheranism in terms of the responses to such questions, Lutherans should show lower amounts of support for social action than would be indicated on the basis of their other theological beliefs.

The preceding sections of this paper have thoroughly discredited the first of these two alternatives--there is a sharp (and systematic) variation within Lutheranism in terms of support for the involvement of the Church in public affairs. The second alternative remains to be evaluated.

The evaluation of this second alternative, of course, requires comparative data from a number of disparate denominations. Following the earlier idea that clergy studies should show sharper patterns than studies of the laity, I shall here depend on Jeffrey Hadden's *The Gathering Storm in the Churches* (1969) and Harold Quinley's *The Prophetic Clergy* (1974), along with an earlier treatment of Quinley's data by Stark, *et al.*, *Wayward Sheperds* (1971). These three books, together with works I shall mention in passing, are by far the most pertinent studies available on the topic.

The core argument of Hadden's (1969) book is that, while the clergy of major Protestant denominations typically endorse the involvement of the Church in public affairs, their laity do not and the Protestant churches of this country are therefore on a collision course with a laity backlash. The Lutheran studies I have reviewed so far provide no basis for believing that the lay-clergy cleavage does not exist within Lutheranism, but this is not really the main point to be gained from *The Gathering Storm* for the present purpose. What is more important in Hadden's book is his cross-tabulation of the ministers' theological self-ascription as being fundamentalist, conservative, neo-orthodox, or liberal[38] with their attitudes toward social issues.

Table 2 gives a sample of a consistent pattern that Hadden found. Within each of the six denominations for which he had data, Hadden found a strong association between a minister's theological self-ascription and his stance on social issues.[39] The most important aspect of Table 2 and others of a similar form in Hadden's book is that this pattern is consistent across a variety of denominations, some with radically different historical heritages with respect to the doctrine of the two kingdoms. On the basis of these data, it is impossible to find any support at all for the hypothesis that the two kingdoms doctrine is at work in American Lutheranism.

TABLE 2: Per Cent of Clergy Agreeing that "Most people who live in poverty could do something about their situation if they really wanted to," by Denomination and Theological Self-Ascription, National Sample, 1965

				Denomination					
Self-Ascription	Methodist	Episco-palian		Presby-terian	American Baptist		ALC		LC-MS
				% Agreeing					
Fundamentalist	61% (84)[a]	_[b]	(3)	53% (17)	52% (49)		51% (59)·	60%	(130)
Conservative	40 (734)	54%	(340)	26 (449)	39 (369)		37 (593)	36	(697)
Neo-orthodox	22 (799)	16	(382)	12 (493)	17 (101)		19 (213)	14	(44)
Liberal	19 (850)	16	(326)	11 (221)	14 (117)		23 (117)	_[b]	(12)
Gamma[c]	.50	.57		.58	.51		.38	.61	

[a]The number in parentheses following the percentage is the number of cases on which the percentage is based. Thus, the first cell of the table should be interpreted, "61% of the 84 Methodist ministers who described themselves as fundamentalists agreed with the question."

[b]The base for computations in these cells is too small to permit computation of meaningful percentages.

[c]Gamma is a measure of the degree of association between two variables. It is unity when the two variables (in this case, theological self-ascription and agreement or disagreement on the question) is perfect and zero when there is no relationship at all. Most survey analysts would regard a gamma of 0.4 as "very strong."

Source: Hadden, 1969:80.

If it were possible to find a clear denominational differentiation in Table 2 such that the two Lutheran bodies were sharply different from the other four, we would have support for that hypothesis. The important differences in Table 2, however, are by theological self-ascription, not by denomination. Lutherans are more conservative in the socio-political realm than other denominations, but only because larger proportions of Lutheran ministers regard themselves as fundamentalists or conservatives in the theological sense than is the case in the other bodies.

It is most unlikely, therefore, that any doctrine so denomination-specific as the two kingdoms doctrine has a major bearing on the socio-political views of clergymen, and, for the reasons noted above, it is even less likely that such a doctrine affects the views of the laity. The sharp differences on the socio-political items that exist among the clergy by theological self-ascription, however, raise an interesting question. If we assume that some aspect of theology produces these differences, we still have to search for the specific aspect of theology involved. This search will be guided by what we have already surmised--that adherence to the specific doctrine must vary much more by theological self-ascription than by denomination.

Stark and Glock (1969) discuss a number of potential theological candidates for this role. In a later work (Stark, *et al.*, 1971), they examine one prime candidate, other-worldliness, empirically on a sample of Protestant ministers in California. Using a theological scale derived from specific doctrinal questions rather than theological self-ascription, they found the familiar powerful relationship between theology and the minister's willingness to speak out on public affairs from his pulpit.

The next step in their analysis was the crucial one. Constructing a three-item scale of "other-worldliness," thay examined the data to see whether it was reasonable to conclude that other-worldliness "intervenes" between doctrinal orthodoxy and a clergyman's willingness to speak out on public affairs as the formal representative of the Church. Their conclusion is quite unequivocal:

> An important reason why clergymen do not address
> themselves to social issues in their sermons lies not
> merely in their commitment to traditional church doctrines,
> but that such doctrinal commitment leads them also to
> adopt an other-worldly, miraculous outloook, and this in
> turn makes preaching on such issues irrelevant. (Stark,
> *et al.*, 1971:104)

It will be noted that the indexes of social involvement used in this study were based on questions about whether the minister had actually *preached* (or had taken some other step *as a religious functionary*) on a specific socio-political issue. The three issues selected for analysis were Proposition 14 (an anti-fair housing referendum in California), the Delano-area grape strike lead by Caesar Chavez, and protests over U.S. military involvement in Viet Nam. Religious leaders were involved in all three issues, and in each of the three issues, the involvement of the Church in public affairs was controversial, both inside and outside of formal religious circles.

Quinley (1974) has provided an additional analysis of these data, and Table 3 is my own summary of his results. I have ranked the ministers of each of the nine sampled denominations in terms of their theological perspectives and in terms of their degrees of activism on each of the three issues. The ranking in each case is based on a composite of the ministers' responses to a series of individual questions.

TABLE 3: Rankings of Ministers in Nine Denominations in California
on Theology and Three Social Action Issues

	Issue			
Denomination	Theology[a]	Proposition 14[b]	Grape Strike[b]	Viet Nam[b]
United Church of Christ	1	4	1	2
Methodist	2	1	2	1
Presbyterian	3	2	5	3
Episcopalian	4	3	4	5
Lutheran Church in America	5	5	3	4
American Baptist	6	6	6	6
American Lutheran Church	7	7	7	7
Lutheran Church-Mo. Synod	8	8	8	8
Southern Baptist	9	9	9	9

Source: Derived from Quinley (1974:58, 114-15, 117-19).

[a] A rank of one means the most modernist; a rank of nine means the most
traditionalist.

[b] A rank of one means the most activist; a rank of nine means the least activist.

A quick glance at Table 3 reveals that the three social issue
rank orders are very similar to the theological rank order, the
largest exception being the relative quietism of United Church of
Christ clergy on Proposition 14. The other major exceptions in the
table, however, are very significant for our present purposes.
While both Missouri Synod and ALC clergy are "right where they should
be" (i.e., the Missouri Synod is ranked eighth in all four columns
and the ALC is ranked seventh in all four), LCA clergymen are *more*
activist on the grape strike (ranked third) and on Viet Nam protests
(ranked fourth) than the ranking of fifth on theology would indicate.
No conception of the two kingdoms doctrine would lead to such a
prediction, nor, I would add, to the pattern exhibited by the ALC
and the Missouri Synod. If the two kingdoms doctrine were operative,
we should expect Lutheran groups to be ranked *lower* on activism than
on theology. The hypothesis that other-worldliness is responsible
for the relative quietism of Lutherans in America fits this set of
data far better than any sort of two kingdoms hypothesis could do.

But this conclusion is not the entire story. The major theme
of Hadden's (1969) book is that ministers of every denomination are
more oriented toward activism than are the laity, despite the presence
of a substantial theology-activism relationship among the clergy and

356

its near-absence among the laity. This gulf is a large one in every denomination for which data are available in the works reviewed in this chapter, with the possible exception of the Wisconsin Synod clergy and laity in Kersten's (1970) study. It would be remiss not to discuss the reasons for this gap in an essay directed to clergy and seminarians.

There are, in general, two sorts of causal factors at work—social-psychological and social-structural. I have indicated a number of times that religion is more salient to the clergy than to the laity. Salience, in turn, is an aspect of what Allport (1966) would call "intrinsic" religiosity (King and Hunt, 1972; Gibbs, et al., 1973), a religious orientation which (Allport, 1966:455) "regards faith as a supreme value in its own right....A religious sentiment of this type floods the whole life with motivation and meaning. Religion is no longer limited to single segments of self-interest." There is a rather large literature (e.g., Allport and Ross, 1967) linking intrinsic religiosity to social ethics issues, independent of theological views or self-ascription.

One might argue that clergymen tend to become clergymen because their religiosity was more intrinsic to start with. There is undoubtedly some truth in this assertion, but the reader would do well to keep in mind a second reason for the pattern noted above. Ministers receive much of their personal social support from other ministers (Hadden, 1969; Quinley, 1974). To the extent that this occurs, the divergence of clerical views from those of the laity is deepened. The pattern, in fact, is even sharper than that. Several studies (Wood, 1970; Hadden, 1969; Hammond, 1966) agree on a basic point—the greater the degree to which a clergyman is "insulated" from the laity, the greater his involvement in social issues. Thus, denominational executives are more deeply involved than parish pastors; campus clergy are far more involved than other clergy; and ministers in relatively hierarchical denominations (in which the laity have little to say about the assignment of clergy to various posts) are more involved than those of more congregational denominations.

These two sources of activism, the social-psychological and the social-structural, undoubtedly interact with each other to compound the tendency toward activism in a situation in which salience of religion is high and in which the clergyman is relatively insulated from lay views. In closing, I would like to point out that in the case of the Lutheran clergy, both conditions seem to be met. The first condition is obvious. With respect to the second one, it may strike some readers as anomalous to say that Lutheran polity in the United States is "relatively hierarchical," but, when viewed from the perspective of the degree of insulation from the laity, the doctrine of the call, as it is practiced in all three of the major Lutheran bodies in this country, provides a great amount of insulation from the demands of the laity. Lutheran clergymen and seminarians would do well to remember that this combination of high salience and high insulation puts them into a religious world quite different from that of the laity, and while lay/clergy fissures over the involvement of the Church in public affairs have yet to become major in American Lutheranism, the conditions are ripe for such fissures to develop.

R E F E R E N C E S

Allport, Gordon W.
  1966   "The religious context of prejudice." *Journal for the Scientific Study of Religion* 5:447-57.

Allport, Gordon W., and J. Michael Ross
  1967   "Personal religious orientation and prejudice." *Journal of Personality and Social Psychology* 5:432-43.

Bornkamm, Heinrich
  1966   *Luther's Doctrine of the Two Kingdoms.* (Trans. Karl Hertz.) Philadelphia: Fortress Press.

Gibbs, David R., Samuel A. Mueller, and James R. Wood
  1973   "Doctrinal orthodoxy, salience, and the consequential dimension." *Journal for the Scientific Study of Religion* 12:33-52.

Glock, Charles Y., and Rodney M. Stark
  1965   *Religion and Society in Tension.* Chicago: Rand McNally.

Hadden, Jeffrey K.
  1969   *The Gathering Storm in the Churches.* Garden City, New York: Doubleday.

Hammond, Phillip E.
  1966   *The Campus Clergyman.* New York: Basic Books.

Hertz, Karl
  1972   "Ethical stances and social issues among American Lutherans." *The Lutheran Quarterly* 24:71-90.

Kersten, Lawrence L.
  1970   *The Lutheran Ethic.* Detroit: Wayne State University Press.

King, Morton B., and Richard A. Hunt
  1972   *Measuring Religious Dimensions.* Dallas: Southern Methodist University.

Quinley, Harold E.
1974   *The Prophetic Clergy*. New York: Wiley-Interscience.

Stark, Rodney, Bruce D. Foster, Charles Y. Glock, and Harold E. Quinley
1971   *Wayward Shepherds*. New York: Harper and Row.

Stark, Rodney, and Charles Y. Glock
1968   *American Piety*. Berkeley: University of California
        Press.

1969   "Prejudice and the churches." Pp. 70-95 in Charles Y.
        Glock and Ellen Siegelman (eds.), *Prejudice, U.S.A.*
        New York: Praeger.

Strommen, Merton P., Milo L. Brekke, Ralph C. Underwager, and
Arthur L. Johnson
1971   *A Study of Generations*. Minneapolis: Augsburg
        Publishing House.

Wood, James R.
1970   "Authority and controversial policy: the churches
        and civil rights." *American Sociological Review*
        35:1057-69.

Wuthnow, Robert
1973   "Religious commitment and conservatism: in quest of
        an elusive relationship." In Charles Y. Glock (ed.),
        Religion in Sociological Perspective. Belmont,
        California: Wadsworth.

359

PART VI

INTERNATIONAL LUTHERANISM

INTRODUCTION

The 1963 assembly of the Lutheran World Federation directed
its Commission on Theology to study "The Quest for True Humanity
and the Lordship of Christ." The outcome of the work carried on
in the various member churches includes not only the work of the
Study Committe of the German Democratic Republic but several
series of statements which the Commission itself developed. We
are reproducing here the first series of these statements.

CHAPTER 18

Bases For A Christian Ethic

227. Commission on Theology, LWF*

The Commission on Theology of the Lutheran World Federation
has gone into the problem in terms of the classical controversy.
Our starting point here has been the question of the source of
ethical knowledge. Is it derived from the reality of the world
around us or from faith? What is the relationship between these
two realities?

In an effort at clarification the following should be noted:

The Scope
of Christ's
Lordship
(1) No sphere of our life can be excluded from
Christ's lordship. The confession of Christ is
at the center of the New Testament kerygma; it
must, therefore, also be at the center of Christian
ethics. Christ is the church's Lord and the world's.
The reality of our life in its totality stands
under his lordship. No other power, institution,
or ideology has any such claim on our obedience.
We are his, "redeemed" and "purchased" by him, in
duty bound to serve him (Luther in the *Small
Catechism*). All our actions, whether public or
private, whether in the church or in society, must
be *based* on Christ's lordship.

But No
Ethical Code
(2) The thesis that Christ's lordship is the basis
of ethics needs qualification. To be based on the
lordship of Christ does not mean that ethics is to

---

*From Ivar Asheim, ed. *Christ and Humanity*, pp. 11-16

be derived from it. To imagine that the entire
content of ethics could be deduced from the concept
of the lordship of Christ could mean illegitimately
stretching this concept beyond proportion.

The Reality
of the
World

(3) To define the *content* of ethics we have to
turn to the reality of the world around us. In
the New Testament, the human relationships· and
social structures unquestionably presupposed, for
instance, in the so-called Tables of Duties, are
treated seriously and their particular importance
even stressed in the name of Christ. In and through
these relationships and structures Christians are
to perceive God's demands. ·But the claim of the
reality of the world upon Christians is not to be
seen as Christ's hidden presence within the various
human relationships and social structures. The
basis for this claim, rather, is the fact that in
the concrete reality of creation man as such is
confronted by his Creator.

But No
Direct Identi-
fication with
God's
Demand

(4) No direct identification may be made, of course,
between God's demand and the claims of social reality
at any given time. Christians are addressed as
free men, but precisely as free men they are set
within the structure already existing. This does
not mean, however, that they are unconditionally
bound to these structures; rather, they are to
prove what God's will is and not to become "slaves
of men" (1 Cor. 7:23). It is the Spirit of God
that the world does not possess who leads Christians
to this critical activity and enables them to reach
right decisions. Yet Christians will also have to
explain the position they take by rational arguments.
For what is involved is the need for rational
clarity consciously sustained by faith.

God's
Demand in
the Reality
of the
World

(5) Yet it must be pointed out that God's demand is
perceived *within* the reality of the world. Certainly
Scripture continues to be for Christians the ethical
norm, although it should be noted that it is not
via the church that God's law has to be brought into
the world. The law is not a derivative of the gospel.

God's demand already exists in the reality of the
world prior to our faith, addressing every man
via the concrete life situations in which he finds
himself by bringing home to him through these
situations the burdens and needs of his neighbor.

An Ethic of
Freedom

(6) One major concern in thus bracketing together
ethical demand and the reality of the world is
to ensure that we understand the evangelical ethic
as an ethic of freedom. If we were simply to
deduce from, or construct the entire content of
ethics on, the concept of the lordship of Christ,
we should be in danger of transforming Christian
freedom into obligatory obedience to instructions.
Christ our Redeemer would then appear as the
legislator for the world, and the gospel would be
turned into a demand for obedience or into an
ideal of human conduct and social order which it
would be our task today to copy. But Christian
discipleship is under the sign of the gospel, not
under that of law.

Freedom--
Liberation
and
Obligation

(7) Freedom in Christ means liberation from all
legalistic ideals as well as from all utopian
dreams of social order and personal conduct. It
thus enables us to accept the world for what it
really is. True, Christian freedom is freedom *from*
the world. But precisely because it is, it is also
at the same time freedom *for* the world. It does
not take us out of the world; it directs us into
the world as God's world. Christian freedom is
freedom to serve God the Creator. It makes it
possible for us to know the world as *God's* world,
his creation, to distinguish good and evil, and in
and through the reality of the world to perceive
God's will.

The Unity
of
Christian
Ethics

(8) Relating this to Christian doctrine, it means
that ethics must be firmly rooted in both the
first *and* the second articles of the Creed, in the
doctrine of creation and in the doctrine of Christ.
But this does not mean a two-track ethic or a
"double morality." We may distinguish between the

365

lordship of God and the lordship of Christ but we
cannot separate them; our life cannot be split up
into separate spheres (private and public) to be
apportioned respectively either to the lordship of
God or to that of Christ. In regard to all life's
relationships, "for us there is one God, the Father,
from whom are all things and for whom we exist, and
one Lord, Jesus Christ, through whom are all things
and through whom we exist" (1 Cor. 8:6). The
Christian ethos cannot be split up; its unity is
implicit in the unity of the triune God.

The Task
of
Achieving
Humanity

(9) These distinctions, which take the gospel as
the basis of the freedom of the Christian ethos
and find God's will expressed in the concrete
demand bound up with particular situations, enable
us to define ethical action as being laid upon us
in and with our existence as human beings. As
those who, on the one hand, act in faith we have
to demonstrate the freedom given us in Christ.
Ethical obligation means, on the other hand, that
we must take the humanity and condition of man
seriously. Both must be taken with equal seriousness.
The commandments of God set before us as normative
in Scripture have as their aim the maintenance of
humanity among men. The goal of ethics can therefore be defined as the *achievement of humanity*.

The
Necessity
for
Cooperation

(10) This has consequences for the relationship
between the specifically Christian and the universally
human. Since the task of ethics is given us in
and with our humanity, Christians and non-Christians
must, to a great extent, be able to act in ethical
agreement and to be ready to cooperate. The life
situation through which the ethical demand addresses
us is itself a bond. Across the barriers of
religious position there can be agreement about this
life situation. Even the New Testament does not
take the view that ethical knowledge is only
possible in faith. On the contrary, "what the
law requires" is seen as being engraved on the
heart of every man (Rom. 2:15).

366

(11) But this does not imply that the man who is
united to Christ by faith is now claimed by an
ethic having its source outside the Christian faith;
in his entire thought and action he is to remain
faithful to his Lord. Nevertheless, he is to aim
at what is good "not only in the Lord's sight but
also in the sight of men" (2 Cor. 8:21). The very
fact that he is committed to his faith means he
must be concerned to *communicate*, also with those
who do not share his faith, regarding the motives
of his action. Indeed, he is to reckon with the
possibility that these others may in certain
circumstances have gone further than he has both
in understanding the situation and in ethical
insight, and that he himself will therefore have
to learn from them. In this sense, the achievement
of humanity today is a task to be fulfilled in
solidarity with all men.

CONCLUSION

No one is more conscious of the shortcomings of this book than the editor himself. Many selections had to be omitted; almost all selections are excerpts from longer works; all too often the historical contexts could only be hinted at.

Yet several things seem clear. The first is, of course, that Luther himself presented no fully rounded doctrine nor completely elaborated political ethics. His primary interests lay elsewhere. His utterances on social and political questions grew out of concrete concerns to which he had to address himself.

Nor do the Lutheran Confessions contain a fully developed and explicit political ethic. In fact the Confessions demanded political decisions from their signers, but the contents of their affirmations centered on the chief articles of faith at issue in the Reformation.

Second, the ways in which Lutherans (and others) went about theological reflection tended to isolate theological propositions into deductive intellectual systems separated from other human undertakings. Seizing upon certain elements in Luther's thought in a socio-political climate in which church administrators found genuine independence from political control difficult, Lutheran theologians tended to move away from Luther's direct concern with social issues. Theology became in many ways an enterprise of the universities, elaborated as a separate academic discipline apart from fruitful relations with the intellectual activities of contemporary philosophers, scientists, and other creative thinkers.

Along with the increasing abstraction of theological thought

one found an accentuation of the inner life (a theme clearly present
in Luther) until the practice of the Christian faith virtually
disappeared within the spiritual borders of an invisible church.

Under these circumstances a corporate ethic became impossible.
The doors were open for the dualism which locked the civic life
and the spiritual life of Christians into two separate almost
impenetrable compartments. Only the cultivation of individual
personal piety remained as a viable option for the serious Lutheran
Christian. Thus dualism, inner spirituality, and individualism
went hand in hand in Lutheran history. The result was a segregation
of both ecclesiastical institutions and religious life for the rest
of society. At the same time as Pietism demonstrated, a serious
devotional life did not need to be strongly rooted in the institutional
life of the church.

The segregation that took place served the purposes of the
critics of the church as much as it apparently supported the status
quo. The Enlightenment writers, not unlike the pietists before
them, could attack both "dead orthodoxy" and a neutralized
institutional church, while claiming for themselves the honor of
defending freedom and faith in their pristine purity.

This development, I believe, prepared the way for the nineteenth
century ideological distortions of Luther, distortions in which
both conservatives and liberals shared. It is also this distortion
that was called into question in the twentieth century. The
challenge took two forms: it questioned whether the emphasis on
obedience did not reflect a partial view of what Luther had to say
about political questions; it brought together the various elements
in Luther's thought, elements which the Reformer had discussed
separately: the Christian's calling to live in the world; the
conceptions of "orders" or "hierarchies," which the theology of the
orders of creation had developed in a one-sided fashion; and the
ethical mandate to serve the needs of the neighbor. In addition,
the challengers to the dualistic view insisted that Luther himself
carried on his theological reflections in the context of particular
issues.

The arguments are by no means ended. For there are still
those who prefer to carry on theological work in the old way. They
prefer a religious institution that remains largely aloof from the
other structures of society.

The alternative to this approach is expressed by Luther, most
clearly in his famous debate with Erasmus. Against the scholarly
stance of the great humanist Luther simply insisted that there is
no neutral ground from which one can choose which way to go. It is

instead a question of knowing which side one is on.

The tragedy of many Lutherans in the 1930s was that they did not see the issue in these terms. They did not recognize that a time for clear confessional witness had arrived.

Choosing an alternative interpretation of Luther's doctrine does not guarantee that we in our generation will have a clearer vision. For an intellectual stance that insists on seeing theological propositions in their full historical contexts carries no warranty against failure. A political ethic that seeks to speak out on behalf of human freedom and concern for the welfare of all may still be mistaken in its decisions. Theologians and ethical systems stand under the judgment as much as all other human endeavors. Reflectively critical analysis that looks at one's own biases and at the same time listens carefully to its opponents is absolutely necessary, though not necessarily sufficient. We still live by faith.

Finally it is not accidental that our last selection comes out of the work of the Lutheran World Federation. For today, as especially the selections from Namibia so eloquently demonstrate, the Lutheran witness increasingly includes Lutheran theologians from all parts of the world. If the thrust of Luther's ethic, to play on the title of Ulrich Duchrow's *Christenheit und Weltverantwortung*, is indeed responsibility to the world, then Christians from all parts of the world will need to participate in discharging that responsibility.

NOTES

1. See Heinz-Horst Schrey, ed. *Reich Gottes und Welt. Die Lehre Luthers von den zwei Reichen,* "Wege der Forschung, Band CVII," (Darmstadt: Wissenschaftliche Buchgesellschaft, 1969), as well as the bibliography accompanying this volume for a partial selection of materials contributing to the debate.

2. This table is adapted from Ulrich Duchrow and Heiner Hoffmann, ed. *Die Vorstellung von zwei Reichen und Regimenten bis Luther* (Gütersloh: Gerd Mohn, 1972), p. 13.

3. All items in sections B, C, and D appear in Duchrow and Hoffmann.

4. Many editions of *The Republic* are available. An English text for the selection from Philo is found in P.H. Colson and G.H. Whitaker, trans. *Philo,* Loeb Classical Library, Vol. 5 (Cambridge: Harvard University Press, 1934.)

5. Cf. Wolfgang Huber, *Kirche und Oeffentlichkeit* (Stuttgart: Ernst Klett Verlag, 1973).

6. For an illuminating study of the shaping of a conservative mentality in Prussia see Robert M. Biger, *The Politics of German Protestantism: The Rise of the Protestant Church Elite in Prussia, 1815-1848* (Berkeley: University of California, 1972)

7. This opinion was still cited as "typical" in 1955 in an article in *O Mensageiro de Evangelho,* Vol. X, No. 8, p. 2, a paper of the Evangelical Union of Congregations of Santa Catarina.

8. Reinhard Köhne, "Karl von Koseritz und die Anfänge einer deutsch-brasioianischen Politik," (Dissertation, Münster, 1937), pp. 42ff.

9. This introduction to a large extent follows Ulrich Duchrow and Wolfgang Huber's introduction to the third volume of the German series.

10. In Ernst Wolf's 1932 essay (cf. no. 131 below) "two kingdoms" has not yet become a fixed technical term. The seminal work on the subject during the *Kirchenkampf* was Harald Diem, *Luthers Lehre von den zwei Reichen, untersucht von seinem Verständnis der Bergpredigt aus* (München: Kaiser Verlag, 1938.) This has recently been reprinted with an introduction by Gerhard Sauter in *Zur Zwei-Reiche-Lehre Luthers,* "Theologische Bücherei: Neudrucke und Berichte aus dem 20. Jahrhundert, Systematische Theologie," No. 49 (München: Kaiser Verlag, 1973.)

11. Again this introduction is in large part a translation of the introductory materials in the German reader, allowing for the omission of a number of selections in the English edition.

12. Cf. Huber, *Kirche und Oeffentlichkeit,* pp. 135ff.

13. Cf. Schrey, *Gottes Reich und Welt,* cited in note 1 above.

14. See note 11.

15. Hermann is referring to attacks which Ragaz and Barth had made upon the German theology of war. See Huber, *Kirche und Oeffentlichkeit*, p. 199ff.

16. In his note Holl insists that Troeltsch assumes this independence without providing any evidence for his position.

17. Again Holl accuses Troeltsch of depicting Luther in this fashion and of consequently coupling him with Machiavelli, an assertion for which Holl accuses Troeltsch of the same bad taste as the Roman biographer Denifle showed.

18. Barth's reply to Althaus is readily accessible in James M. Robinson, ed. *The Beginnings of Dialectical Theology*, Vol. I (Richmond: John Knox Press, 1968), pp. 47, 49-50, 52-53, 55-56. (Keith Crim is the translator.)

19. This passage shows clearly that at the time of Wolf's essay that "the doctrine of the two kingdoms" had not yet become terminologically fixed in theological discourse.

20. These theses were prepared at a conference of 10 clergymen and lay persons which the bishop of Köln-Aachen, Dr. Oberheid, a "chief of staff" and close collaborator of the Reichsbishop Müller called at Rengsdorf. The theses were sent to all evangelical pastors in the Rheinland.

21. The Erlangen theologians Paul Althaus and Werner Elert composed these proposals; six additional persons signed. The importance of their statement may be seen from the comment which Hermann Diem makes, "The theological foundations of the national-socialist state, as they were laid by Erlangen theologians in the Ansbach Proposals, were commonly held among conventional church-goers in Germany." From Sauter, *Zur Zwei-Reiche-Lehre Luthers*, p. 184.

22. Althaus and Elert use the distinction between law and gospel to derive the distinction between the two realms. See Huber, *Kirche und Oeffentlichkeit*, p. 441ff. Elert makes a sharp distinction between the two Words of God and relates these to the distinction between the order of grace and the order of creation. Althaus insisted very strongly on a primitive revelation (*Ur-Offenbarung*) and on a theology of the orders. Cf. his *Theologie der Ordnungen* (Gütersloh, 1934.)

23. This document was originally circulated anonymously and its author is not identified in the source. Peter Brunner has acknowledged his authorship in a letter of November 11, 1975, as well as indicating that he received considerable Gestapo harassment because of its tendencies to weaken the German will to fight. Professor James Luther Adams of Harvard Divinity School has also corroborated the circumstances surrounding Brunner's original public address in Wuppertal and the Gestapo reactions.

24. On the question of the refugees, see also Huber, *Kirche und Oeffentlichkeit*, p. 380ff.

25. Ulrich Duchrow is the author of the German original of this introduction.

26. Cf. No. 3 of the Barmen Theses.

27. Dr. Gyula Nagy wrote the introduction.

28. W. Kistner is the author of the introduction.

29. Klaus Eichholz is the author of the introduction.

30. H-J. Prien wrote the introduction.

31. From Paragraph 5 of the "Declaration of the Eighteen Representatives to the Congregations of the Evangelical Lutheran Church in Chile," Frutillar, November 3, 1974.

32. Quoted from Lukas de Vries, "Mission und Kolonialismus in Südwestafrika," (Dissertation, Brussels, 1971), as cited by Ulrich Duchrow in "Zweireichelehre als Ideologie," (Lecture, Helsinki University Theological Faculty, November 26, 1974.)

33. This expression is used, for example, by Gunars J. Ansons, "In einer Zeit des Umbruchs," *Lutherische Monatshefte*, XIV, 1 (1975), p. 31.

34. There is the added danger that the total structure of the regime is under-estimated and the problems are considered on too personal a level, even when it is always in place to enter into personal conversation with the President--as the church leadership of the IECLB did in 1970 on the basis of the Curitiba Declaration. See H-J. Prien, "Lateinamerika: Evolution oder Revolution?" *Estudos Teologicos*, XII (1972), 27-49. The initials IECLB represent the Portugese initials for "Evangelical Church of the Lutheran Confession in Brazil."

35. See Herman Brandt, "Die Evangelische Kirche Lutherischen Bekenntnisses in Brasilien und die Feiern zum 150. Jahrestag der Unabhängigkeit Brasiliens am 7. September 1972: Ein Beircht über die innerkirchliche Gesprächslage," *Zeitschrift für Evangelische Ethik*, XVII (1973), 43-49.

36. For context, see H-J. Prien, "Freiheit vom Absolutismus: Widerstand gegen die Repression in Brasilien," *Lutherische Monatshefte*, XIII, 1 (1974), 23-25 and 26-27, an excerpt from "Eu Ouvi Os Clamores Do Meu Povo," *Documento de Bispos E Superiores Do Nordeste* (Salvador, Brazil, 1973). The memorandum by the bishops from the Middle West has not been published in German, not even in the form of extracts.

37. In a volume like this one, it would be folly for a sociologist to attempt to define the doctrine of the two kingdoms. At the risk of oversimplification, I consider the doctrine to be a theological division of the world into two realms, the spiritual and the temporal, which, to use the words of a famous sociologist, may "touch but do not interpenetrate." I have been guided by Luther's essay "On Temporal Authority" and by Bornkamm (1966). The concern of this chapter is the contemporary American setting. For a treatment of American Lutheranism from a more historical perspective, see Hertz (1972).

38. Some researchers have used a self-ascription question such as this one, while others have formed scales by combining responses to a series of specific doctrinal questions. Hadden actually has both in his book, but he shows that the correlation between the two is very high. The use of the other method, therefore, would produce similar results.

39. Unfortunately, Hadden does not present data of the form of those in Table 2 for an item including the role of the Church in public affairs. A number of such items were included in his questionnaire and are discussed in other contexts in the book. The results appear to be absolutely consistent with the pattern in Table 2, and are, in any case, in very close agreement with those found by Stark, *et al.* (1971) and Quinley (1974), among others, using more direct questions concerning the role of the Church in public affairs. These studies are discussed below.

BIBLIOGRAPHY

Berggrav, Eivind. *Man and State*. Philadelphia, 1951.

Besse, H. *Marx-Weber-Troeltsch: Religionssoziologie und marxistische Ideologiekritik*. Munich, 1970.

Bigler, Robert M. *The Politics of German Protestantism: The Rise of the Protestant Church Elite in Prussia, 1815-1848*. Berkeley, 1972.

Bornkamm, Heinrich. *Luther's Doctrine of the Two Kingdoms in the Context of His Theology*. Tr. Karl H. Hertz. Philadelphia, 1966.

Boyens, A. *Kirchenkampf und Oekumene, 1933-1939*. Munich, 1969.

Brunner, Peter. "Luther and the World of the Twentieth Century," in *Luther in the Twentieth Century*, "Martin Luther Lectures, Volume V." Decorah, 1961.

Cochrane, A.C. *Christianity and Classical Culture*. New York, 1957.

Cochrane, A.C. *The Church's Confession Under Hitler*. Philadelphia, 1962.

Conway, J.S. *The Nazi Persecution of the Churches, 1933-1945*. New York, 1968.

Dahl, Nils A. "Is there a New Testament Basis for the Doctrine of the Two Kingdoms?" *Lutheran World*, XII (1965), 337-354.

Duchrow, Ulrich. *Christenheit und Weltverantwortung*. Stuttgart, 1970.

Duchrow, Ulrich and Heiner Hoffmann. *Die Vorstellung von Zwei Reichen und Regimenten bis Luther*, "Texte zur Kirchen- und Theologiegeschichte, edited by G. Ruhbach, No. 17," Gütersloh: Gerd Mohn, 1972

Duchrow, Ulrich, Wolfgang Huber, and Louis Reith, eds. *Umdeutungen der Zweireichelehre Luthers im 19. Jahrhundert*, "Texte zur Kirchen- und Theologiegeschichte, ed. G. Ruhbach, No. 21," Gütersloh: Gerd Mohn, 1975.

Duchrow, Ulrich and Wolfgang Huber, eds. *Die Ambivalenz der Zweireichelehre in den lutherischen Kirchen des 20. Jahrhunderts*, "Texte zur Kirchen- und Theologiegeschichte, ed. G. Ruhbach," Gütersloh: Gerd Mohn, 1976.

Elert, Werner. *The Structure of Lutheranism*. Tr. Walter A. Hansen. St. Louis, 1962. (This is volume I of *Die Morphologie des Luthertums*, Munich, 1931.)

Ferm, Vergilius. *The Crisis in American Lutheran Theology*. New York, 1927.

Forell, G.W. *Faith Active in Love*. Minneapolis, 1954.

Forell, G.W. "Luther and Politics." *Luther and Culture*, "Martin Luther Lectures, Volume IV." Decorah, 1960.

Hakamies, Ahti. *Eigengesetzlichkeit der natürlichen Ordnungen als Grundproblem der neueren Lutherdeutung. Studien zur Geschichte und Problematik der Zwei-Reiche-Lehre Luthers.* Witten, 1971.

Holl, Karl. *The Cultural Significance of the Reformation.* Tr. Karl and Barbara Hertz. New York, 1959.

Huber, Wolfgang. *Kirche und Oeffentlichkeit.* Stuttgart, 1973.

Jepsen, A. "What Can the Old Testament Contribute to the Discussion of the Two Kingdoms?" *Lutheran World,* XII (1965), 325-336.

Lau, Franz. "The Lutheran Doctrine of the Two Kingdoms." *Lutheran World,* XII (1965), 355-372.

Lazareth, William. *A Theology of Politics.* New York, 1960.

Letts, H.C.,ed. *The Lutheran Heritage.* Vol. 2 of "Christian Social Responsibility." Philadelphia, 1957.

Letts, H.C.,ed. *Life in Community.* Vol. 3 of "Christian Social Responsibility." Philadelphia, 1957.

Littell, F.H. and H.G. Locke, ed. *The German Church Struggle and the Holocaust.* Detroit, 1974.

Luebke, F.C. *Immigrants and Politics.* Lincoln, 1969.

Mauelshagen, C. *American Lutheranism Surrenders to the Forces of Conservatism.* Athens, Ga., 1936.

Meuser, F.W. *The Formation of the American Lutheran Church.* Columbus, 1958.

Morrison, Karl F. *The Two Kingdoms: Ecclesiology in Carolingian Political Thought.* Princeton, 1964.

Nelson, E. Clifford. *Lutheranism in North America, 1914-1970.* Minneapolis, 1972.

Niebuhr, H. Richard. *Christ and Culture.* New York, 1951.

Nygren, Anders. "Luther's Doctrine of the Two Kingdoms." *Ecumenical Review,* I (1949), 301-310.

Rohne, J.M. *Norwegian American Lutheranism up to 1872.* New York, 1926.

Rupp, Gordon. "Luther and Government." in H.G. Koenigsbergh, ed. *Luther a Profile.* New York, 1973.

Sauter, Gerhard. Intro. *Zur Zwei-Reiche-Lehre Luthers,* "Theologische Bucherei, Neudrucke und Berichte aus dem 20. Jahrhundert. Systematische Theologie. No. 49," Münich, 1973.

Schmid, Byron L., ed. *The Lutheran Churches Speak, 1960-1974.* New York, 1975.

Schrey, H.H.,ed. *Reich Gottes und Welt. Die Lehre von den zwei Reichen in der theologischen Diskussion der Gegenwart.* Darmstadt, 1969.

Sherman, F.H. "The Christian in Secular Society: Insights from the Reformation." *Una Sancta*, 25 (Pentecost, 1968), 96-106.

Spotts, F. *The Churches and Politics in Germany*. Middletown, Conn., 1973.

Stange, Douglas. *Radicalism for Humanity*. St. Louis, 1970.

Tappert, T.G.,ed. *Lutheran Confessional Theology in America, 1840-1880*. New York, 1973.

Tiefel, Hans. "Use and Misuse of Luther During the German Church Struggle." *Lutheran Quarterly*, 25 (1973), 395-411.

Tierney, B. *The Crisis of Church and State, 1050-1350*. Englewood Cliffs, 1964.

Tödt, H.E. "Ernst Troeltschs Bedeutung für die evangelische Socialethik." *Zeitschrift für evangelische Ethik*, 10 (1956), 227-236.

Tonkin, John. *The Church and the Secular Order in Reformation Thought*. New York, 1971.

Troeltsch, Ernst. *The Social Teaching of the Christian Churches*. Tr. Olive Wyon. New York, 1960.

Volkmar, Lloyd. *Luther's Response to Violence*. New York, 1974.

Walther, Chr. *Typen der Reich-Gottes-Verständnisses*. Munich, 1961.

Wentz, A.R. *A Basic History of Lutheranism in America*. Philadelphia, 1955.

Wentz, A.R. *Pioneer in Christian Unity: Samuel Simon Schmucker*. Philadelphia, 1967.

Ziemke, Donald. *Love for the Neighbor in Luther's Theology*. Minneapolis, 1961.

ACKNOWLEDGMENTS

Our thanks to Dr. Ulrich Duchrow and the Commission on Studies
of the Lutheran World Federation for the research that led to the
German edition of this work, and to the following publishers who
gave permission to quote excerpts from copyrighted material:

Concordia Publishing House and Fortress Press for The American
Edition of Luther's Works.

Concordia Publishing House for *The Church's Social Responsibilities*
by Martin Scharlemann.

Fortress Press for *Christ and Humanity* ed. by Ivar Asheim;
The Church and the Public Conscience by Edgar Carlson;
Life in Community, Vol. I, ed. by Harold C. Letts;
Christ Frees and Unites by Martin J. Heinecken;
and *The Scope of Grace* ed. by Phillip J. Hefner.

Harper & Row, Publishers, Inc. for *The Future of God* by Carl Braaten.
Copyright (c) 1969 by Carl E. Braaten.

Macmillan Publishing Co., Inc. for *The Rich Christian and Poor
Lazarus* by Helmut Gollwitzer, transl. by David Cairns.
Copyright (c) 1970 by St. Andrew's Press, Ltd.

Macmillan Publishing Co., Inc. and George Allen & Unwin, Ltd. for
The Social Teaching of the Christian Churches by
Ernst Troeltsch.

The Wayne State University Press, for *The Lutheran Ethic*
by Lawrence Kersten.

The Westminster Press for *Augustine: Earlier Writing*,
Vol. VI., The Library of Christian Classics. Edited by
John H.S. Burleigh. Published in the U.S.A. by The
Westminster Press, 1953.